75 PROSE PIECES

Second Edition

75 PROSE PIECES

Second Edition

RHETORICAL
PRINCIPLES
MODES
*FORM*S

ROBERT C. RATHBURN

MARTIN STEINMANN, JR.

EDITORS • UNIVERSITY OF MINNESOTA

CHARLES SCRIBNER'S SONS, NEW YORK

PREFACE

THIS REVISED EDITION of 75 Prose Pieces is, like the first edition, intended as an aid to writing, especially expository writing, in composition and communication courses; and this intention has guided both our choice and our arrangement of the pieces.

The student may, of course, read these pieces for their ideas and their information and thus be inspired to think and write on similar topics; for the range of topics is wide: literature and language, science and technology, history and philosophy, and social and educational policy. But we chose these pieces primarily either because they state or imply what seem to us good rhetorical principles or because they illustrate some rhetorical mode or device or some rhetorical form or genre. As rhetorical illustrations, they serve the student as models for imitation. Though most of the pieces are complete, some are excerpts, and intentionally so—to illustrate some mode of paragraph organization, for instance, or of classification, or such a mode as description, usually mixed with other modes. The shorter pieces, furthermore, because more nearly the length of much student writing, often serve the student very well as models for imitation. The pieces illustrate a wide range of rhetorical purposes and occasions, from those of workaday journalism to those of scientific writing and literary criticism. All serve such practical purposes as communicating information or expressing opinion, and many have literary merit as well. Pieces by Mark Twain, Edith Wharton, and Willa Cather, by Thomas Henry Huxley and Rachel Carson, by James, Yeats, Wells, Snow, Wolfe, and Hemingway appear in the company of anonymous ones. And, finally, though some of the pieces come from earlier writers, modern pieces are the rule because of their generally greater relevance as models for imitation.

The arrangement of the pieces—by rhetorical principles, modes, and forms—is to some extent, and necessarily, arbitrary. The pieces in Part I, "Principles," are there because they state or imply good rhetorical principles; but each has one or more modes of its own

and could appear in some section in Part II, in "Process Explanation" perhaps or in "Classification." The pieces in Part II,
"Modes," are there because they illustrate modes; but a given piece
may illustrate more than one mode—both process explanation and
comparison, for example—and it might well have been assigned to
another section of this part or, since the distinction between mode
and form is not hard and fast, to a section in Part III. The pieces
in Part III, "Forms," are there because they illustrate forms; but
they also, and inevitably, illustrate modes as well; the book review,
for example, is likely to illustrate most of the modes. Some forms,
moreover, are not illustrated in Part III but in one or both of the
other two parts: the news story and the philosophical essay, for
example.

In this revised edition, there are both some new pieces and
expanded headnotes. Our chief criterion for excluding pieces in the
first edition and substituting new ones has been timeliness. We
have regretfully put aside some pieces that dealt with then-current
events and substituted pieces that not only deal with now-current
events but are, we hope, equally useful rhetorically. The expanded headnotes describe and illustrate rhetorical principles,
modes, and forms more fully and analyze illustrative pieces more
fully.

In all but a few cases, we have kept spelling and punctuation of
pieces as they are in the original texts. We have supplied titles for
pieces originally untitled and given brief biographical sketches of
authors.

ROBERT C. RATHBURN
MARTIN STEINMANN, JR.

Minneapolis and St. Paul
September, 1965

Contents

PART I

Principles

THE PRINCIPLES of good writing are not so firmly established as those of, say, thermodynamics. For one thing, they are principles of psychology, not physics; and such principles are notoriously shaky, especially when they are products of intuition and introspection, not experiment. For another thing, they depend upon writers' goals and readers' tastes, and human goals and tastes are notoriously various. Clear communication is the goal of some writers, but not of all; simplicity suits the taste of some readers, but not of all.

The principles of good writing stated or implied in the following pieces have, nevertheless, considerable stability and breadth of acceptance. The writers that humanity has long managed to think well of have generally honored these principles, as have generations of cultivated readers. Biaggini and Thompson stress the desirability of being yourself. Being yourself does not, of course, imply saying the first thing that pops into your head. It implies saying what you believe or feel, not assuming beliefs or attitudes; it implies having something to say and saying it unaffectedly and unpretentiously. Maugham, the Fowlers, Quiller-Couch, Hemingway, and Mencken wittily state or imply principles of style, especially of diction or word choice: to prefer lucidity to obscurity, the familiar word to the far-fetched, consistency to elegant variation, the concrete word to the abstract, and the forthright word to the euphemism, for example. And Clark, Cowley, and Sullivan anatomize and evaluate three famous styles of our day: Timestyle, sociological style, and the style of sports reporting. (With Clark, compare " 'Tycoon,' " in "Definition.")

1

These writers' styles, as well as their advice, repay careful attention. Their practice of supporting generalizations with examples, for instance, implies a sound rhetorical principle. These pieces not only state or imply sound principles; they illustrate them.

E. G. BIAGGINI

AN EXERCISE IN DISCRIMINATION

E. G. Biaggini (1889-   ) was born in England and educated at London and Queensland universities. For many years, he has taught English in Australia; since 1929, at the University of Adelaide. He has written several textbooks other than The Reading and Writing of English *(1936) and several books about education, as well as a biography (1937) of George Sturt, whose essay "Keeping Christmas" appears later in this volume under his pseudonym, "George Bourne."*

SINCE the purpose of this book is to teach you to distinguish between the true and the false in what you read, and thus to develop within you the power to criticise and appreciate English literature, let us start our work with an exercise in discrimination. You should begin your attempt at evaluation by reading the following paper through in order to see what it is about; then decide provisionally which of the two contrasted passages you like the better; next try to make explicit to yourself on what grounds your decision is based; and finally examine the passages as closely as is necessary to confirm you in, or make you change, your first opinion. The exercise is quite easy and an intelligent adult reader will respond appropriately on a first reading. In fact the work should not be approached as if it were a task of difficulty; the best results will be obtained by treating the exercise as if it were something which had been encountered in your ordinary general reading.

EXERCISE I

Which of the following passages do you think the better? Give reasons for your choice.

A.   About horses I know very little and the only actual experience I have ever had with one showed that the beast knew more about me than I knew about him.

»»» From *The Reading and Writing of English.* By E. A. Biaggini, 1936. Reprinted by permission of the Hutchinson Publishing Group.

3

One English June, a friend and I set out on a fortnight's caravaning through the lanes of the New Forest and for the purpose had hired a horse and van from a man in Winchester. We had stipulated that the animal must be quiet and quiet it was! During fifteen whole days our united efforts could not persuade that horse to travel more than three miles an hour, and very seldom indeed did we travel more than ten miles a day. After a bit we concluded that the horse was infirm, and that it would be cruel to press it further, and accordingly one day as we had lunch by the roadside we took it out of the shafts so that it might graze on a neighbouring common. No sooner was the horse at liberty, however, than, with mane and tail flying, it set off at a good ten miles an hour in the direction of Winchester. Fortunately we had bicycles with us and before long were thoroughly enjoying an exciting chase. The animal was eventually overtaken and captured and led back in dejection to the scene of his escape, and during the rest of the trip we kept a sharp eye on him and allowed him no liberty. In spite of a certain hardening of our hearts, however, three miles an hour remained his pace and ten miles a day remained his limit.

At the end of the holiday the owner of the horse met us in Winchester from where we were to get the London train. 'Did you find him quiet?' he asked us and almost in chorus we replied yes. After settling up with the man we watched him mount the box and stir the horse into activity. To our amazement it broke into a brisk trot, and before we knew where we were the caravan was disappearing in a cloud of dust over the top of the hill which leads from the town. 'By Jove,' my friend said to me, 'that horse knows more about men than we know about horses.' I could not but agree and have felt since that had that horse the gift of speech his observations on his temporary masters would be exceedingly entertaining.

B. The horse is a noble animal and not the least of man's dumb friends. Without such a willing servant as the horse civilization would not have developed to the present stage.

The early pioneers of this country can bear witness to what has been said. When they first came here the prospect before them was a heart-breaking one indeed. There were no roads; in many places the country was rough and well-timbered; developmental material was hard to procure; and above all tractors, bush-devils, motor-cars, and other mechanical inventions had not come to the help of man. In these circumstances then the horse was invaluable, and without him Australia would certainly not have become the country it is. In spite of summer's heat and winter's cold; in spite of the dangers of drought, bush-fires, and flood; and in spite of the indescribable discomforts of life in a new country, man with the aid of the horse has won through and made the Australian wilderness smile.

A farmer friend of mine keeps one of his old horses in the best paddock and gives him no work whatever to do because once the faithful old creature had saved him from ruin. One night when everybody was asleep he came to the verandah of the homestead and whinnied until he woke the farmer. My friend, wondering what was wrong and how the horse had got out of the yard in which he had been locked up, hurried from his bed and immediately saw sparks and smoke going up from a post at the corner of the horse-yard. He rushed across and found that the horse had broken out and given him the alarm. The season was dry and the standing crops might easily have caught fire, but in a twinkling the farmer got the blaze under control. Naturally he was grateful to the horse and said it should work no more.

Such instances as these could be multiplied indefinitely; but enough has been said to show the goodness of this fine species. We should all be kind to animals in general and to horses in particular.

Now what has your response been, did you prefer A to B or B to A, and how strong were your feelings in the matter? To anticipate the many separate answers which may be given to this question is of course impossible, but a convenient way of beginning our discussion will be to sum up under two heads the arguments which will be advanced by those who favour A and B respectively.*

The defenders of A might say that the passage amused them, and that they read it with interest to the end and would like to read a whole book written in the same fashion, but that they could not stand many pages of B. They might add that A obviously tells them of an actual experience, and by implication

* The imaginary opinions now to be given are not really imaginary at all. Reference to Chapter I of my *English in Australia* (Oxford & Melbourne University Presses) will show that they are normal responses to the test.

at any rate something of the nature of the horse itself, while *B* only stimulates certain stock feelings they have had since they were small children in kindergarten classes, and really tells them nothing new and nothing real. And they might conclude that in *A* you are addressed as an equal (not as if you were still a child) in a natural unaffected manner; and that the tone of *B* is self-conscious and rather superior, and that you would not dare to read it aloud to interest your fellows in the playground, common-room, office, or shop.

The defenders of *B,* on the other hand, might say that it was a passage which dealt with a worthy subject in a dignified manner, and that *A* was written in an off-hand and conversational way. Further, they might say that, while *B* was carefully written, *A* contained such colloquial terms as 'after a bit' and 'By Jove', that it was ill-punctuated, and that in one place the word 'and' had been used four times in three lines. In conclusion, they might argue that passage *B* showed some love for one's country and an interest in its history; while *A* showed no reverence for, or interest in, anything.

Our problem, then, is to decide: Which of these views is the more just? As we do so we shall bring to light a number of important principles which should continually be borne in mind, and which will help you in later and more advanced stages of your work.

The first thing to notice in the imaginary representative opinions given above is that the arguments *against* passage *A* and the arguments *for* passage *B* are all concerned with secondary issues, while the arguments in *support* of *A* are based on first principles. This must be made clear.

It was said in favour of *A* that it was amusing and sufficiently interesting to lead the reader on to the end without undue effort; that it told him something convincing in a way which did not irritate him. This is good argument. Against *A* it was contended that it had technical faults, including colloquial expression, the excessive use of the word 'and', and imperfect punctuation. This is not such good argument; it is fault-finding rather than criticism.

Work should, of course, be properly performed and finished, but there is not a student in the land who would base his judgments on technical points if school-masters and others did not insist on their importance, and thus lead him to think that they matter more than they really do. Mistakes in construction and in grammar are serious not in themselves but because they prevent the clear and unimpeded expression of thought, and it is because they do this that such strenuous efforts are made to prevent and correct them. But in the excitement of our war against error we must not lose sight of the object of the war itself—the production of good work so that our thought may be better expressed. Now to express thought we must have thought, and if a writer have none there is no virtue in eloquence. If, then, it is argued in effect that the writer of A has something to say much has been said in his favour; and if B is to be preferred to it the writer of B must also have something to say; if he has not, the claim that he has written accurately and carefully carries but little weight.

In defence of B it was, of course, said that it dealt with a worthy subject. But this is really neither here nor there. The dictionary is full of worthy subjects, but it is not for that reason that you read it, and you certainly would not read a book on wireless, or ships, or dogs, or anything else, if it were palpably wrong and absurd. It will then not do to justify B on such grounds as these.

It will be agreed that passage A seems to be the record of an actual occurrence, and that it does by implication at any rate tell us something true about the nature of the horse. It might be said that we have heard the same story before in different forms and that consequently it is stale, but that cannot be helped. Different people in similar circumstances will have similar experiences, and so long as they describe those experiences in a natural and personal way their work will have freshness and carry conviction. In A the writer, for good or ill, is himself, and he describes the horse as it is and not almost as a lesser angel temporarily doing good work on earth. The passage, that is, can stand on its own legs, and there we can leave it.

About *B* more must be said. Our analysis can well begin with a question: Was the passage written seriously at all, or was its purpose to see how the simple and uncritical reader would respond to matter containing stock and conventional moral sentiment? The horse, you will notice, is spoken of as if he had been a conscious and willing agent in the development of a new country. Is this not completely ridiculous? The normal horse, like the normal man, is mostly concerned with a decently comfortable life and has not a passion for well-doing. Since he is referred to as a dumb animal we must not suppose that he can speak, but if he could talk to himself it seems far more likely that he would say: 'I have two greenhorns driving me to-day, so I will take things easy,' than that he would say: 'Here is a country which wants developing so I will co-operate willingly with my master in an attempt to open it up to civilisation.' You should, then, be able to see that *B* is twaddle. The horse is, of course, of untold use to the pioneer, but to speak of him in the sentimental fashion of passage *B* is almost as silly as thanking the hen for laying eggs or the sheep for growing wool.

The matter does not end here for the actual incident in the passage is as unsatisfactory as are the generalisations. How could an untrained horse be expected consciously and deliberately to give a fire alarm? It is true that in the presence of fire a horse might become restive and whinny, but this is not what is said. On the contrary the horse is pictured, as it were, as saying to itself: 'The post is alight, the season is dry, the crops may catch fire, so I will go and inform my master.' This is so unreasonable that we will spend no more time considering it, but instead take our stand on the conclusion that, so far as the matter goes, *A* is the better passage. Consequently the supposed opinion in its support was based on sound argument. But we have not yet finished our examination and have now to consider the passages from another point of view. To do this effectively will necessitate a slight digression.

Besides what is actually said in speech or writing, how it is said is an important matter. If your father dies of typhoid fever you could say so quite simply in plain terms, or you could say (it is to be hoped, however, that you won't) that your family has suffered a bereavement, or even that your father has kicked the bucket: which form you use of course matters very much. If you just say that your father has died of typhoid fever, everybody of sense and sensibility will know at once that this is a sad thing for you; if on the other hand you say that you have suffered a bereavement, you will be regarded by people of sense and sensibility as rather a foolish person who is deliberately trying to produce a certain attitude of sympathy towards himself; and if you merely say that your father has kicked the bucket, you will express rather graphically what has happened and as well show yourself to be a callous person. It can be seen then that besides what is said, how it is said is a matter of importance. Let us now examine how the writers of the two passages express themselves.

About the expression of A there is little to be said. Both those who may like it on account of its interest and humour, and those who may dislike it on account of its conversational tone and its (real or supposed) technical errors, will agree that its expression is normal and that the writer has made no unfair attempt to impress upon you the importance of himself or his subject. This, however, cannot be said about the other passage.

You should begin your examination of the expression of passage B by asking yourself the question: What is the significance of the use of the terms 'noble animal' and 'dumb friends' in the opening passage; or rather, what was the effect the possibly mischievous writer anticipated they would have on those who might take the passage seriously? He knew from experience, perhaps, as the skilful advertisement writer does, that they were expressions which would evoke a feeling of approval in uncritical people; they have now been doing this for two generations or more. In other words, he was possibly aware that he might play on people as a typist uses his machine, tapping certain keys to get certain results. In your attempt at literary appreciation and criticism, then, you will have to watch out that you are not treated as a typewriter. It is really not a flattering approach for a writer to make to you, and you should insist that those who write for your instruction or amusement should treat you as a person with a mind rather than as a machine with a keyboard. If your approval is sought it should be deserved; it certainly should not be given to a writer who by a mechanical device merely exploits your good will. How often this is done you will see as you continue the study of this book.

If you are not satisfied with this analysis you should ask yourself, what would your feelings be if you read a similar sentence about the ox, or the ass, or the mule, or the elephant, or the camel, written by a man from a country where those animals play a part similar to that played by the horse in Australia? Would you not feel it was a little extravagant and unusual? But you may say at any rate the horse *is* a fine animal to look at, he has a glossy coat, a fiery eye, an arched neck, a dignified gait, and in general a most impressive appearance. Very well! then call him a fine beast. On the racecourse and in state processions he indeed often looks that, but still it has to be added that the tough wiry horses which are usually found doing the rough work in the remote districts of new countries are esteemed for their utility rather than for their beauty. As a matter of fact the expressions 'noble animal' and 'dumb friend' were both vogue terms of an earlier generation, and are not used in a metaphorical sense by educated people to-day. The second term lives on in the Dumb Friends' League which still exists in England.

The remainder of the opening paragraph, and the whole of the second paragraph, are perhaps not quite so unsatisfactory as the opening sentence with its stock sentiment; but does not the expression (if it is to be taken seriously) remain unduly solemn to describe what after all is something quite ordinary and well-known to us? As we have seen, all that there is really to be said is that in pioneer life the horse is an extremely useful animal, but to say what is obvious with the air of one announcing a remarkable discovery, and to mix it up with a feeble moral dissertation in a self-important manner is to forfeit the regard of intelligent people.

The expression of the paragraph containing the story of the burning post is more satisfactory, so we shall not stop to examine it; but the conclusion of the passage is as weak as the opening sentence, and all that has been said about 'noble animal' and 'dumb friends' could with the necessary changes be said about 'the goodness of this fine species.' But if you have followed what has been said to this point you will be able to do that piece of examination for yourself. For our present purpose then we can conclude that (except as a joke) the expression of B is as unsatisfactory as its content, and that if only for negative reasons A is the better passage, and that the imaginary representative opinion in its favour which was used as a means of opening the discussion was a sound one.

You will now be interested to know the sources of the passages. Both A and B were written by the author of this book, but the moods in which they were written were very different: the first passage is an extract from a diary kept by him during a caravan holiday which he never expected anybody but his friends to read; the second was written with his tongue in his cheek in order to measure the ability of the ordinary man to detect insincere work. It is clear, then, that those who chose wrongly need be on their guard that on other occasions they are not imposed upon by specious writing. We shall not discuss here the difficult question of what constitutes good literature, but we can doubtless all agree that work which is not seriously intended should not be seriously regarded.

DENYS THOMPSON

from EMOTIVE USE OF WORDS

Denys Thompson (1907-   ) was born in England and educated at Cambridge University, where he took an M.A. with honors in classics and English. He has written several textbooks other than Reading and Discrimination *(one of them—*Culture and Environment *[1933]—with F. R. Leavis) and several books on advertising and the press; was closely associated with Leavis' famous literary quarterly,* Scrutiny; *and now edits the journal* The Use of English. *He has lectured widely on the teaching of English and is now headmaster of Yeovil School, in Somerset, England.*

WE START with newspapers, for they are universally read; and since publicity takes up so much space and provides the profits that a newspaper must make, we begin by examining the wording of an advertisement from a Sunday paper:

Away across the western ocean where Drake of Devon sailed, the *Italic* will carry you. You too will go adventuring after the treasure of the Indies. In golden hours, in glowing colours, in new fitness of body, and new delight of mind your treasure will be counted to you. No Galleon of Spain ever brought back home such great store of good things as you will bring back from your six weeks' luxurious cruise in this most modern motor vessel.

The professional copy writer of this is not arguing the merits of travel—the sense of what he says is unimportant—so much as playing upon the feelings of his reader, tired by a week's work in winter, to induce in him a comforted receptive frame of mind, in which he will be likely to act on the suggestion of a cruise. One notices immediately its literary pretensions—as if to say "this is a special occasion, no ordinary workaday affair"—and the fact that it employs the romantic feelings and vocabulary with which most of us have been familiar since we first learned history. The

»»» From *Reading and Discrimination.* Rev. ed. London: Chatto & Windus, 1953. Pp. 15-16. Reprinted by permission of Chatto & Windus and Denys Thompson.

dreamy rhythm of the first two sentences helps to lull the reader and causes him to suspend rational judgment, while he abandons himself to the illusion evoked by the associations of "Drake," "Devon," "adventure," "treasure," "galleons," and "Spain." There is also affectation in the pseudo-poetical order of the words, as in the opening sentence; the "personal touch"—"you too"—attempts to get on friendly terms with the reader.

W. SOMERSET MAUGHAM

THREE QUALITIES OF STYLE

W. Somerset Maugham (1874-1965) was an English writer whose career spanned more than six decades, from his first novel, Liza of Lambeth *(1897), to his last book of essays,* Points of View *(1959). In his last years he was considered the dean of English letters—"that sad, absurd and transitory eminence," as he himself once called it. A novelist and short-story writer, he was also a playwright and adapted his short stories for the films, notably in* Trio *(1950). Among his novels are* Of Human Bondage *(1915),* The Moon and Sixpence *(1919),* Cakes and Ale *(1930), and* The Razor's Edge *(1944). His plays include* Lady Frederick *(1912),* The Circle *(1921),* Our Betters *(1923), and* Sheppey *(1933). From his autobiography,* The Summing Up *(1938), come the following views on prose style.*

I KNEW that I should never write as well as I could wish, but I thought with pains I could arrive at writing as well as my natural defects allowed. On taking thought it seemed to me that I must aim at lucidity, simplicity and euphony. I have put these three qualities in the order of the importance I assigned to them.

XI

I have never had much patience with the writers who claim from the reader an effort to understand their meaning. You have only to go to the great philosophers to see that it is possible to express with lucidity the most subtle reflections. You may find it difficult to understand the thought of Hume, and if you have no philosophical training its implications will doubtless escape you; but no one with any education at all can fail to understand exactly what the meaning of each sentence is. Few people have written English with more grace than Berkeley. There are two sorts of obscurity that you find in writers. One is due to negligence and the other to wilfulness. People often write obscurely because they have never taken the trouble to learn to write clearly. This sort of obscurity you find too often in modern philosophers, in men of science, and even in literary critics. Here it is indeed strange. You would have thought that men who passed their lives in the study of the great masters of literature would be sufficiently sensitive to the beauty of language to write if not beautifully at least with perspicuity. Yet you will find in their works sentence after sentence that you must read twice to discover the sense. Often you can only guess at it, for the writers have evidently not said what they intended.

Another cause of obscurity is that the writer is himself not quite sure of his meaning. He has a vague impression of what he wants to say, but has not, either from lack of mental power or from laziness, exactly formulated it in his mind and it is natural enough that he should not find a precise expression for a confused idea. This is due largely to the fact that many writers think, not before, but as they write. The pen originates the thought. The disadvantage of this, and indeed it is a danger against which the author must be always on his guard, is that there is a sort of magic in the written word. The idea acquires substance by taking on a visible nature, and then stands in the way of its own clarification. But this sort of obscurity merges very easily into the wilful. Some writers who do not think clearly are inclined to suppose that their thoughts have a significance greater than at first sight appears. It is flattering to believe that they are too profound to be expressed so clearly that all who run may read, and very naturally it does not occur to such writers that the fault is with their own minds which have not the faculty of precise reflection. Here again the magic of the written word obtains. It is very easy to persuade oneself that a phrase that one does not quite understand may mean a great deal more than one realizes. From this there is only a little way to go to fall into the habit of setting down one's impressions in all their original vagueness. Fools can always be found to discover a hidden sense in them. There is another form of wilful obscurity that masquerades as aristocratic exclusiveness. The author wraps his meaning in mystery so that the vulgar shall not participate in it. His soul is a secret garden into which the elect may penetrate only after overcoming a number of perilous obstacles. But this kind of obscurity is not only pretentious; it is short-sighted. For time plays it an odd trick. If the sense is meagre time reduces it to a meaningless verbiage that no one thinks of reading. This is the fate that has befallen the lucubrations of those French writers who were seduced by the example of Guillaume Apollinaire. But occasionally it throws a sharp cold light on what had seemed profound and thus discloses the fact that these contortions of language disguised very commonplace notions. There are few of Mallarmé's poems now that are not clear; one cannot fail to notice that his thought singularly lacked originality. Some of his phrases were beautiful; the materials of his verse were the poetic platitudes of his day.

XII

Simplicity is not such an obvious merit as lucidity. I have aimed at it because I have no gift for richness. Within limits I admire richness in others, though I find it difficult to digest in quantity. I can read one page of Ruskin with delight, but twenty only with weariness. The rolling period, the stately epithet, the noun rich in poetic associations, the subordinate clauses that give the sentence weight and magnificence, the grandeur like that of wave following wave in the open sea; there is no doubt that in all this there is something inspiring. Words thus strung together fall on the ear like music. The appeal is sensuous rather than intellectual, and the beauty of the sound leads you easily to conclude that you need not bother about the meaning. But words are tyrannical things, they exist for their meanings, and if you will not pay attention to these, you cannot pay attention at all. Your mind wanders. This kind of writing demands a subject that will suit it. It is surely out of place to write in the grand style of inconsiderable things. No one wrote in this manner with greater success than Sir Thomas Browne, but even he did not always escape this pitfall. In the last chapter of *Hydriotaphia* the matter,

which is the destiny of man, wonderfully fits the baroque splendour of the language, and here the Norwich doctor produced a
piece of prose that has never been surpassed in our literature;
but when he describes the finding of his urns in the same splendid
manner the effect (at least to my taste) is less happy. When
a modern writer is grandiloquent to tell you whether or no a
little trollop shall hop into bed with a commonplace young man
you are right to be disgusted.

But if richness needs gifts with which everyone is not endowed,
simplicity by no means comes by nature. To achieve it needs
rigid discipline. So far as I know ours is the only language in
which it has been found necessary to give a name to the piece
of prose which is described as the purple patch; it would not
have been necessary to do so unless it were characteristic. English prose is elaborate rather than simple. It was not always so.
Nothing could be more racy, straightforward and alive than the
prose of Shakespeare; but it must be remembered that this was
dialogue written to be spoken. We do not know how he would
have written if like Corneille he had composed prefaces to his
plays. It may be that they would have been as euphuistic as
the letters of Queen Elizabeth. But earlier prose, the prose of
Sir Thomas More, for instance, is neither ponderous, flowery
nor oratorical. It smacks of the English soil. To my mind King
James's Bible has been a very harmful influence on English prose.
I am not so stupid as to deny its great beauty. It is majestical.
But the Bible is an oriental book. Its alien imagery has nothing
to do with us. Those hyperboles, those luscious metaphors, are
foreign to our genius. I cannot but think that not the least of
the misfortunes that the Secession from Rome brought upon the
spiritual life of our country is that this work for so long a period
became the daily, and with many the only, reading of our people.
Those rhythms, that powerful vocabulary, that grandiloquence,
became part and parcel of the national sensibility. The plain,
honest English speech was overwhelmed with ornament. Blunt
Englishmen twisted their tongues to speak like Hebrew prophets.
There was evidently something in the English temper to which

this was congenial, perhaps a native lack of precision in thought, perhaps a naïve delight in fine words for their own sake, an innate eccentricity and love of embroidery, I do not know; but the fact remains that ever since, English prose has had to struggle against the tendency to luxuriance. When from time to time the spirit of the language has reasserted itself, as it did with Dryden and the writers of Queen Anne, it was only to be submerged once more by the pomposities of Gibbon and Dr Johnson. When English prose recovered simplicity with Hazlitt, the Shelley of the letters and Charles Lamb at his best, it lost it again with De Quincey, Carlyle, Meredith and Walter Pater. It is obvious that the grand style is more striking than the plain. Indeed many people think that a style that does not attract notice is not style. They will admire Walter Pater's, but will read an essay by Matthew Arnold without giving a moment's attention to the elegance, distinction and sobriety with which he set down what he had to say.

The dictum that the style is the man is well known. It is one of those aphorisms that say too much to mean a great deal. Where is the man in Goethe, in his birdlike lyrics or in his clumsy prose? And Hazlitt? But I suppose that if a man has a confused mind he will write in a confused way, if his temper is capricious his prose will be fantastical, and if he has a quick, darting intelligence that is reminded by the matter in hand of a hundred things he will, unless he has great self-control, load his pages with metaphor and simile. There is a great difference between the magniloquence of the Jacobean writers, who were intoxicated with the new wealth that had lately been brought into the language, and the turgidity of Gibbon and Dr Johnson, who were the victims of bad theories. I can read every word that Dr Johnson wrote with delight, for he had good sense, charm and wit. No one could have written better if he had not wilfully set himself to write in the grand style. He knew good English when he saw it. No critic has praised Dryden's prose more aptly. He said of him that he appeared to have no art other than that of expressing with clearness what he thought with vigour. And

one of his Lives he finished with the words: 'Whoever wishes
to attain an English style, familiar but not coarse, and elegant
but not ostentatious, must give his days and nights to the volumes
of Addison.' But when he himself sat down to write it was with
a very different aim. He mistook the orotund for the dignified.
He had not the good breeding to see that simplicity and naturalness are the truest marks of distinction.

For to write good prose is an affair of good manners. It is,
unlike verse, a civil art. Poetry is baroque. Baroque is tragic,
massive and mystical. It is elemental. It demands depth and insight. I cannot but feel that the prose writers of the baroque
period, the authors of King James's Bible, Sir Thomas Browne,
Glanville, were poets who had lost their way. Prose is a rococo
art. It needs taste rather than power, decorum rather than inspiration and vigour rather than grandeur. Form for the poet
is the bit and the bridle without which (unless you are an
acrobat) you cannot ride your horse; but for the writer of prose
it is the chassis without which your car does not exist. It is not
an accident that the best prose was written when rococo with
its elegance and moderation, at its birth attained its greatest excellence. For rococo was evolved when baroque had become
declamatory and the world, tired of the stupendous, asked for
restraint. It was the natural expression of persons who valued
a civilized life. Humour, tolerance and horse sense made the
great tragic issues that had preoccupied the first half of the
seventeenth century seem excessive. The world was a more comfortable place to live in and perhaps for the first time in centuries
the cultivated classes could sit back and enjoy their leisure.
It has been said that good prose should resemble the conversation
of a well-bred man. Conversation is only possible when men's
minds are free from pressing anxieties. Their lives must be reasonably secure and they must have no grave concern about their
souls. They must attach importance to the refinements of civilization. They must value courtesy, they must pay attention to their
persons (and have we not also been told that good prose should
be like the clothes of a well-dressed man, appropriate but un-

obtrusive?), they must fear to bore, they must be neither flippant nor solemn, but always apt; and they must look upon 'enthusiasm' with a critical glance. This is a soil very suitable for prose. It is not to be wondered at that it gave a fitting opportunity for the appearance of the best writer of prose that our modern world has seen, Voltaire. The writers of English, perhaps owing to the poetic nature of the language, have seldom reached the excellence that seems to have come so naturally to him. It is in so far as they have approached the ease, sobriety and precision of the great French masters that they are admirable.

XIII

Whether you ascribe importance to euphony, the last of the three characteristics that I mentioned, must depend on the sensitiveness of your ear. A great many readers, and many admirable writers, are devoid of this quality. Poets as we know have always made a great use of alliteration. They are persuaded that the repetition of a sound gives an effect of beauty. I do not think it does so in prose. It seems to me that in prose alliteration should be used only for a special reason; when used by accident it falls on the ear very disagreeably. But its accidental use is so common that one can only suppose that the sound of it is not universally offensive. Many writers without distress will put two rhyming words together, join a monstrous long adjective to a monstrous long noun, or between the end of one word and the beginning of another have a conjunction of consonants that almost breaks your jaw. These are trivial and obvious instances. I mention them only to prove that if careful writers can do such things it is only because they have no ear. Words have weight, sound and appearance; it is only by considering these that you can write a sentence that is good to look at and good to listen to.

I have read many books on English prose, but have found it hard to profit by them; for the most part they are vague, unduly theoretical, and often scolding. But you cannot say this of Fowler's Dictionary of Modern English Usage. It is a valuable work. I do not think anyone writes so well that he cannot learn much from it. It is lively reading. Fowler liked simplicity, straight-forwardness and common sense. He had no patience with pre-tentiousness. He had a sound feeling that idiom was the backbone of a language and he was all for the racy phrase. He was no slavish admirer of logic and was willing enough to give usage right of way through the exact demesnes of grammar. English grammar is very difficult and few writers have avoided making mistakes in it. So heedful a writer as Henry James, for instance, on occasion wrote so ungrammatically that a school-master, finding such errors in a schoolboy's essay, would be justly indignant. It is necessary to know grammar, and it is better to write grammatically than not, but it is well to remember that grammar is common speech formulated. Usage is the only test. I would prefer a phrase that was easy and unaffected to a phrase that was grammatical. One of the differences between French and English is that in French you can be grammatical with com-plete naturalness, but in English not invariably. It is a difficulty in writing English that the sound of the living voice dominates the look of the printed word. I have given the matter of style a great deal of thought and have taken great pains. I have written few pages that I feel I could not improve and far too many that I have left with dissatisfaction because, try as I would, I could do no better. I cannot say of myself what Johnson said of Pope: 'He never passed a fault unamended by indifference, nor quitted it by despair.' I do not write as I want to; I write as I can.

But Fowler had no ear. He did not see that simplicity may sometimes make concessions to euphony. I do not think a far-fetched, an archaic or even an affected word is out of place when it sounds better than the blunt, obvious one or when it gives a sentence a better balance. But, I hasten to add, though I think you may without misgiving make this concession to pleasant sound, I think you should make none to what may obscure your meaning. Anything is better than not to write clearly. There is nothing to be said against lucidity, and against simplicity only the possibility of dryness. This is a risk that is well worth taking when you reflect how much better it is to be bald than to wear a curly wig. But there is in euphony a danger that must be considered. It is very likely to be monotonous. When George Moore began to write, his style was poor; it gave you the impression that he wrote on wrapping paper with a blunt pencil. But he developed gradually a very musical English. He learnt to write sentences that fall away on the ear with a misty languor and it delighted him so much that he could never have enough of it. He did not escape monotony. It is like the sound of water lapping a shingly beach, so soothing that you presently cease to be sensible of it. It is so mellifluous that you hanker for some harshness, for an abrupt dissonance, that will interrupt the silky concord. I do not know how one can guard against this. I suppose the best chance is to have a more lively faculty of boredom than one's readers so that one is wearied before they are. One must always be on the watch for mannerisms and when certain cadences come too easily to the pen ask oneself whether they have not become mechanical. It is very hard to discover the exact point where the idiom one has formed to express oneself has lost its tang. As Dr Johnson said: 'He that has once studiously formed a style, rarely writes afterwards with complete ease.' Admirably as I think Matthew Arnold's style was suited to his particular purposes, I must admit that his mannerisms are often irritating. His style was an instrument that he had forged once for all; it was not like the human hand capable of performing a variety of actions.

If you could write lucidly, simply, euphoniously and yet with liveliness you would write perfectly: you would write like Voltaire. And yet we know how fatal the pursuit of liveliness may be: it may result in the tiresome acrobatics of Meredith. Macaulay and Carlyle were in their different ways arresting; but at the heavy cost of naturalness. Their flashy effects distract the mind. They destroy their persuasiveness; you would not believe a man was very intent on ploughing a furrow if he carried a hoop with him and jumped through it at every other step. A good style should show no sign of effort. What is written should seem a happy accident. I think no one in France now writes more admirably than Colette, and such is the ease of her expression that you cannot bring yourself to believe that she takes any trouble over it. I am told that there are pianists who have a natural technique so that they can play in a manner that most executants can achieve only as the result of unremitting toil, and I am willing to believe that there are writers who are equally fortunate. Among them I was much inclined to place Colette. I asked her. I was exceedingly surprised to hear that she wrote everything over and over again. She told me that she would often spend a whole morning working upon a single page. But it does not matter how one gets the effect of ease. For my part, if I get it at all, it is only by strenuous effort. Nature seldom provides me with the word, the turn of phrase, that is appropriate without being far-fetched or commonplace.

H. W. FOWLER

AND F. G. FOWLER

GENERAL PRINCIPLES

H. W. Fowler (1858-1933) and his brother F. G. Fowler (1870-1918) were born in England; the former was educated at Rugby and Oxford, the latter at St. Paul's and Cambridge. Their fifteen years of fruitful collaboration produced an English translation (1904-1915) of the Roman poet Lucian and The Concise Oxford Dictionary (1911) as well as The King's English (1906). Their books on language, with H. W. Fowler's A Dictionary of Modern English Usage (1926), are the most famous and almost surely the best books of their kind.

ANY ONE who wishes to become a good writer should endeavour, before he allows himself to be tempted by the more showy qualities, to be direct, simple, brief, vigorous, and lucid.

This general principle may be translated into practical rules in the domain of vocabulary as follows:—

> Prefer the familiar word to the far-fetched.
> Prefer the concrete word to the abstract.
> Prefer the single word to the circumlocution.
> Prefer the short word to the long.
> Prefer the Saxon word to the Romance.[1]

These rules are given roughly in order of merit; the last is also the least. It is true that it is often given alone, as a sort of

---

[1] The Romance languages are those whose grammatical structure, as well as part at least of their vocabulary, is directly descended from Latin—as Italian, French, Spanish. Under Romance words we include all that English has borrowed from Latin either directly or through the Romance languages. And words borrowed from Greek in general use, ranging from *alms* to *metempsychosis*, may for the purposes of this chapter be considered as Romance. The vast number of purely scientific Greek words, as *oxygen*, *meningitis*, are on a different footing, since they are usually the only words for what they denote.

»»» From *The King's English*. 3rd ed. Oxford: The Clarendon Press, 1931. Pp. 11-17. Reprinted by permission of The Clarendon Press.

compendium of all the others. In some sense it is that: the writer whose percentage of Saxon words is high will generally be found to have fewer words that are out of the way, long, or abstract, and fewer periphrases, than another; and conversely. But if, instead of his Saxon percentage's being the natural and undesigned consequence of his brevity (and the rest), those other qualities have been attained by his consciously restricting himself to Saxon, his pains will have been worse than wasted; the taint of preciosity will be over all he has written. Observing that *translate* is derived from Latin, and learning that the Elizabethans had another word for it, he will pull us up by *englishing* his quotations; he will puzzle the general reader by introducing his book with a *foreword*. Such freaks should be left to the Germans, who have by this time succeeded in expelling as aliens a great many words that were good enough for Goethe. And they, indeed, are very likely right, because their language is a thoroughbred one; ours is not, and can now never be, anything but a hybrid; *foreword* is (or may be) Saxon; we can find out in the dictionary whether it is or not; but *preface* is English, dictionary or no dictionary; and we want to write English, not Saxon. Add to this that, even if the Saxon criterion were a safe one, more knowledge than most of us have is needed to apply it. Few who were not deep in philology would be prepared to state that no word in the following list (extracted from the preface to the *Oxford Dictionary*) is English:—*battle, beast, beauty, beef, bill, blue, bonnet, border, boss, bound, bowl, brace, brave, bribe, bruise, brush, butt, button.* Dr Murray observes that these 'are now no less "native", and no less important constituents of our vocabulary, than the Teutonic words'.

There are, moreover, innumerable pairs of synonyms about which the Saxon principle gives us no help. The first to hand are *ere* and *before* (both Saxon), *save* and *except* (both Romance), *anent* and *about* (both Saxon again). Here, if the 'Saxon' rule has nothing to say, the 'familiar' rule leaves no doubt. The intelligent reader whom our writer has to consider will possibly not know the linguistic facts; indeed he more likely than not takes *save* for a Saxon word. But he does know the reflections that the words, if he happens to be reading leisurely enough for reflection, excite in him. As he comes to *save*, he wonders, Why not *except*? At sight of *ere* he is irresistibly reminded of that sad spectacle, a mechanic wearing his Sunday clothes on a weekday. And *anent*, to continue the simile, is nothing less than a masquerade costume. The *Oxford Dictionary* says drily of the last word: 'Common in Scotch law phraseology, and affected by many English writers'; it might have gone further, and said ' "affected" in any English writer'; such things are antiquarian rubbish, Wardour-Street English. Why not (as our imagined intelligent reader asked)—why not *before, except*, and *about*? Bread is the staff of life, and words like these, which are common and are not vulgar, which are good enough for the highest and not too good for the lowest, are the staple of literature. The first thing a writer must learn is, that he is not to reject them unless he can show good cause. *Before* and *except*, it must be clearly understood, have such a prescriptive right that to use other words instead is not merely not to choose these, it is to reject them. It may be done in poetry, and in the sort of prose that is half poetry: to do it elsewhere is to insult *before*, to injure *ere* (which is a delicate flower that will lose its quality if much handled), and to make one's sentence both pretentious and frigid.

It is now perhaps clear that the Saxon oracle is not infallible; it will sometimes be dumb, and sometimes lie. Nevertheless, it is not without its uses as a test. The words to be chosen are those that the probable reader is sure to understand without waste of time and thought; a good proportion of them will in fact be Saxon, but mainly because it happens that most abstract words —which are by our second rule to be avoided—are Romance. The truth is that all five rules would be often found to give the same answer about the same word or set of words. Scores of illustrations might be produced; let one suffice: *In the contemplated eventuality* (a phrase no worse than what any one can pick for himself out of his paper's leading article for the day) is at once the far-fetched, the abstract, the periphrastic, the long, and the Romance, for *if so*. It does not very greatly matter by which of the five roads the natural is reached instead of the monstrosity, so long as it *is* reached. The five are indicated because (1) they differ in directness, and (2) in any given case only one of them may be possible.

We will now proceed to a few examples of how not to write, roughly classified under the five headings, though, after what has been said, it will cause no surprise that most of them might be placed differently. Some sort of correction is suggested for each, but the reader will indulgently remember that to correct a bad sentence satisfactorily is not always possible; it should never have existed, that is all that can be said. In particular, sentences overloaded with abstract words are, in the nature of things, not curable simply by substituting equivalent concrete words; there can be no such equivalents; the structure has to be more or less changed.

1. **Prefer the familiar word** to the far-fetched.

The old Imperial naval policy, which has failed conspicuously because it *antagonized the unalterable supremacy of Colonial nationalism.* —*Times.*
(stood in the way of that national ambition which must always be uppermost in the Colonial mind)

Buttercups made a sunlight of their own, and in the shelter of scattered coppices the pale *wind-flowers* still dreamed in whiteness.— E. F. BENSON.

We all know what an *anemone* is: whether we know what a *wind-flower* is, unless we happen to be Greek scholars, is quite doubtful.

The state of Poland, and the excesses committed by mobilized troops, have been of a far more serious nature than has been allowed to *transpire.*—*Times.* (come out)

Reform converses with possibilities, *perchance* with impossibilities; but here is sacred fact.—EMERSON. (perhaps)

Tanners and users are strongly of the opinion that there is no room for further enhancement, but on that point there is always room for doubt,

especially when the *export phase* is taken into consideration.—*Times.*
(state of the export trade)

Witchcraft has been put a stop to by Act of Parliament; but the mysterious relations which it *emblemed* still continue.—CARLYLE.
(symbolized)

It will only have itself to thank if future disaster rewards its *nescience* of the conditions of successful warfare.—*Outlook.* (ignorance)

Continual vigilance is imperative on the public to ensure . . .—
Times.
(We must be ever on the watch)

These manœuvres are by no means new, and *their recrudescence is hardly calculated to influence the development of events.—Times.*
(the present use of them is not likely to be effective)

'I have no particular business at L——', said he; 'I was merely going *thither* to pass a day or two.'—BORROW. (there)

2. Prefer the concrete word (or rather expression) to the abstract. It may be here remarked that abstract expression and the excessive use of nouns are almost the same thing. The cure consists very much, therefore, in the clearing away of noun rubbish.

The general poverty of explanation as to the diction of particular phrases seemed to point in the same direction.—Cambridge University Reporter.

(It was perhaps owing to this also that the diction of particular phrases was often so badly explained)

An elementary condition of a sound discussion is a frank recognition of the gulf severing two sets of facts.—Times.
(There can be no sound discussion where the gulf severing two sets of facts is not frankly recognised)

The signs of the times point to the necessity of the modification of the system of administration.—Times.
(It is becoming clear that the administrative system must be modified)

No year passes now without evidence of the truth of the statement that the work of government is becoming increasingly difficult.—
Spectator.
(Every year shows again how true it is that . . .)

The first private conference *relating to the question of the convocation of representatives of the nation* took place yesterday.—*Times.* (on national representation)

There seems to have been an absence of attempt at conciliation between rival sects.—*Daily Telegraph.* (The sects seem never even to have tried mutual conciliation)

Zeal, however, must not outrun discretion in changing abstract to concrete. *Officer* is concrete, and *office* abstract; but we do not *promote to officers,* as in the following quotation, but to *offices*—or, with more exactness in this context, to *commissions.*

Over 1,150 cadets of the Military Colleges were *promoted to officers* at the Palace of Tsarskoe Selo yesterday.—*Times.*

3. Prefer the single word to the circumlocution. As the word *case* seems to lend itself particularly to abuse, we start with more than one specimen of it.

Inaccuracies were *in many cases* due to cramped methods of writing.—*Cambridge University Reporter.* (often)

The handwriting was on the whole good, with a few examples of remarkably fine penmanship *in the case both of* boys and girls.— *Cambridge University Reporter.* (by both boys . . .)

Few candidates showed a thorough knowledge of the text of 1 Kings, and *in many cases the answers* lacked care.—*Ibid.* (many answers)

The matter will remain in abeyance until the Bishop has had time to become more fully acquainted with the diocese, and to ascertain which part of the city will be most desirable for *residential purposes.* —*Times.* (his residence)

M. Witte is *taking active measures for the prompt preparation of material for the study of the question of the execution of the Imperial Ukase dealing with reforms.*—*Times.* (actively collecting all information that may be needed before the Tsar's reform Ukase can be executed)

The Russian Government is at last face to face with the greatest crisis of the war, *in the shape of the fact that* the Siberian railway is no longer capable . . .—*Spectator.* (for) or (:)

Mr. J—— O—— has *been made the recipient of* a silver medal.— *Guernsey Advertiser.* (received)

4. Prefer the short word to the long.

One of the most important reforms mentioned in the rescript *is the unification of the organization of the judicial institutions and the guarantee for all the tribunals of the independence necessary for securing to all classes of the community equality before the law.—Times.*
(is that of the Courts, which need a uniform system, and the independence without which it is impossible for all men to be equal before the law)

I merely desired to point out *the principal reason which I believe exists for the great exaggeration which is occasionally to be observed in the estimate of the importance of the contradiction between current Religion and current Science put forward by thinkers of reputation.* —BALFOUR.
(why, in my opinion, some well-known thinkers make out the contradiction between current Religion and current Science to be so much more important than it is)

Sir,—Will you permit me to *homologate* all you say to-day regarding that selfish minority of motorists who . . .—*Times.* (agree with)

On the Berlin Bourse to-day the prospect of a general strike was cheerfully *envisaged.—Times.* (faced)

5. Prefer the Saxon word to the Romance.

Despite the unfavourable climatic conditions.—Guernsey Advertiser.
(Bad as the weather has been)

By way of general rules for the choice of words, so much must suffice. And these must be qualified by the remark that what is suitable for one sort of composition may be unsuitable for another. The broadest line of this kind is that between poetry and prose; but with that we are not concerned, poetry being quite out of our subject. There are other lines, however, between the scientific and the literary styles, the dignified and the familiar. Our rendering of the passage quoted from Mr Balfour, for instance, may be considered to fall below the dignity required of a philosophic essay. The same might, with less reason, be said of our simplified newspaper extracts; a great journal has a tone that must be kept up; if it had not been for that, we should have dealt with them more drastically. But a more candid plea for the journalist, and one not without weight, would be that he has not time to reduce what he wishes to say into a simple and concrete form. It is in fact as much easier for him to produce, as it is harder for his reader to understand, the slipshod abstract stuff that he does rest content with. But it may be suspected that he often thinks the length of his words and his capacity for dealing in the abstract to be signs of a superior mind. As long as that opinion prevails, improvement is out of the question. But if it could once be established that simplicity was the true ideal, many more writers would be found capable of coming near it than ever make any effort that way now. The fact remains, at any rate, that different kinds of composition require different treatment; but any attempt to go into details on the question would be too ambitious; the reader can only be warned that in this fact may be found good reasons for sometimes disregarding any or all of the preceding rules. Moreover, they must not be applied either so unintelligently as to sacrifice any really important shade of meaning, or so invariably as to leave an impression of monotonous and unrelieved emphasis.

ELEGANT VARIATION

Sir Arthur Quiller-Couch (1863-1944) was born in England and educated at Newton Abbot College, Clifton College, and Oxford. For a while he was a lecturer at Oxford; and, from 1912 until his death, he was King Edward VII Professor of English Literature at Cambridge and a Fellow of Jesus College there. He was not only professor and literary scholar, critic, and anthologist but also novelist, short-story writer, verse parodist, and (testimony to his versatility) yachtsman. He published more than fifty books in all.

LET US TURN to another trick of jargon; the trick of Elegant Variation, so rampant in the sporting press that there, without needing to attend these lectures [on the art of writing], the undergraduate detects it for laughter:—

Hayward and C. B. Fry now faced the bowling, which apparently had no terrors for the Surrey crack. The old Oxonian, however, took some time in settling to work. . . .

Yes, you all recognise it and laugh at it. But why do you practise it in your essays? An undergraduate brings me an essay on Byron. In an essay on Byron, Byron is (or ought to be) mentioned many times. I expect, nay exact, that Byron shall be mentioned again and again. But my undergraduate has a blushing sense that to call Byron Byron twice on one page is indelicate. So Byron, after starting bravely as Byron, in the second sentence turns into "that great but unequal poet" and thenceforward I have as much trouble with Byron as ever Telemachus with Proteus to hold and pin him back to his proper self. Halfway down the page he becomes "the gloomy master of Newstead"; overleaf he is reincarnated into "the meteoric darling of society"; and so proceeds through successive avatars—"this archrebel,"

»»» From "Interlude: On Jargon." From *On the Art of Writing.* New York: G. P. Putnam's Sons, 1916. Pp. 112-113. Reprinted by permission of G. P. Putnam's Sons.

"the author of *Childe Harold*," "the apostle of scorn," "the ex-Harrovian, proud, but abnormally sensitive of his club-foot," "the martyr of Missolonghi," "the pageant-monger of a bleeding heart." Now this again is jargon. It does not, as most jargon does, come of laziness; but it comes of timidity, which is worse. In literature as in life he makes himself felt who not only calls a spade a spade but has the pluck to double spades and redouble.

ERNEST HEMINGWAY

ABSTRACT AND CONCRETE WORDS

Ernest Hemingway (1899-1961) is the best-known and perhaps the best of 20th-century American novelists and short-story writers. Among his novels are The Sun Also Rises *(1926),* A Farewell to Arms *(1929),* For Whom the Bell Tolls *(1940), and* The Old Man and the Sea *(1952). His only play and his most famous short stories are in* The Fifth Column and the First Forty-Nine Stories *(1938). "Abstract and Concrete Words," an excerpt from* A Farewell to Arms, *expresses his distrust of abstract evaluative words and his admiration for concrete descriptive ones.*

I WAS ALWAYS embarrassed by the words sacred, glorious, and sacrifice and the expression in vain. We had heard them, sometimes standing in the rain almost out of earshot, so that only the shouted words came through, and had read them, on proclamations that were slapped up by billposters over other proclamations, now for a long time, and I had seen nothing sacred, and the things that were glorious had no glory and the sacrifices were like the stockyards at Chicago if nothing was done with the meat except to bury it. There were many words that you could not stand to hear and finally only the names of places had dignity. Certain numbers were the same way and certain dates and these with the names of the places were all you could say and have them mean anything. Abstract words such as glory, honor, courage, or hallow were obscene beside the concrete names of villages, the numbers of roads, the names of rivers, the numbers of regiments and the dates.

H. L. MENCKEN

from *EUPHEMISMS*

H. L. Mencken (1880-1956) was journalist, essayist, and scholar. At one time or another, he was the (or an) editor of the Baltimore Evening Herald, The Smart Set, The American Mercury, *and* The Nation. *His essays record, with both wit and invective, his disapproval of almost everything he saw: communism, fascism, and the New Deal; censorship, sentimentality, and Babbittry; chiropractors, undertakers, and schoolteachers. The liveliest of his essays are in the six series of* Prejudices (1919-1927). *His contempt for pretense, affectation, hypocrisy, genteelness, imbecility, and buncombe undoubtedly motivated, though it did not distort, his scholarship in his most enduring and best-selling work,* The American Language *(1st ed., 1919) and its two supplements (1945, 1948).*

THE AMERICAN, probably more than any other man, is prone to be apologetic about the trade he follows. He seldom believes that it is quite worthy of his virtues and talents; almost always he thinks that he would have adorned something far gaudier. Unfortunately, it is not always possible for him to escape, or even for him to dream plausibly of escaping, so he soothes himself by assuring himself that he belongs to a superior section of his craft, and very often he invents a sonorous name to set himself off from the herd. Here we glimpse the origin of a multitude of characteristic American euphemisms, *e.g., mortician* for *undertaker, realtor* for *real-estate agent, electragist* for *electrical contractor, aisle manager* for *floor-walker, beautician* for *hairdresser, exterminating engineer* for *rat-catcher,* and so on. *Realtor* was devised by a high-toned real-estate agent of Minneapolis, Charles N. Chadbourn by name. He thus describes its genesis:

It was in November, 1915, on my way to a meeting of the Minneapolis Real Estate Board, that I was annoyed by the strident peddling of a scandal sheet: "All About the Robbery of a Poor Widow by a

Real Estate Man." The "real estate man" thus exposed turned out to be an obscure hombre with desk-room in a back office in a rookery, but the incident set me to thinking. "Every member of our board," I thought, "is besmirched by this scandal article. Anyone, however unworthy or disreputable, may call himself a real estate man. Why do not the members of our board deserve a distinctive title? Each member is vouched for by the board, subscribes to its Code of Ethics, and must behave himself or get out." So the idea incubated for three or four weeks, and was then sprung on the local brethren.[1]

As to the etymology of the term, Mr. Chadbourn says:

Real estate originally meant a royal grant. It is so connected with land in the public mind that *realtor* is easily understood, even at a first hearing. The suffix *-or* means a doer, one who performs an act, as in *grantor, executor, sponsor, administrator.*

The Minneapolis brethren were so pleased with their new name that Mr. Chadbourn was moved to dedicate it to the whole profession. In March, 1916, he went to the convention of the National Association of Real Estate Boards at New Orleans, and made a formal offer of it. It was accepted gratefully, and is now defined by the association as follows:

A person engaged in the real estate business who is an active member of a member board of the National Association of Real Estate Boards, and as such, an affiliated member of the National Association, who is subject to its rules and regulations, who observes its standards of conduct, and is entitled to its benefits.[2]

In 1920 the Minneapolis Real Estate Board and the National Association of Real Estate Boards applied to Judge Joseph W. Molyneaux of Minneapolis for an injunction restraining the Northwestern Telephone Exchange Company from using *realtor* to designate some of its hirelings, and on September 10 the learned judge duly granted this relief. Since then the National Association has obtained similar injunctions in Virginia, Utah and other States. Its general counsel is heard from every time *realtor* is

---

[1] Private communication, Sept. 28, 1935.
[2] Realtor: Its Meaning and Use; Chicago (National Association of Real Estate Boards), 1925.

taken in vain, and when, in 1922, Sinclair Lewis applied it to George F. Babbitt, there was an uproar. But when Mr. Chadbourn was appealed to he decided that Babbitt was "fairly well described," for he was "a prominent member of the local board and of the State association," and one could scarcely look for anything better in "a book written in the ironic vein of the author of 'Main Street.'"[1] Mr. Chadbourn believes that *realtor* should be capitalized, "like *Methodist or American*,"[2] but so far it has not been generally done. In June, 1925, at a meeting of the National Association of Real Estate Boards in Detroit, the past presidents of the body presented him with a gold watch as a token of their gratitude for his contribution to the uplift of their profession. On May 30, 1934, the following letter from Nathan William MacChesney, general counsel of the National Association, appeared in the *New Republic*:

[*Realtor*] is not a word, but a trade right, coined and protected by law by the National Association of Real Estate Boards, and the term is a part of the trade-mark as registered in some forty-four States and Canada. Something over $200,000 has been spent in its protection by the National Association of Real Estate Boards in attempting to confine its use to those real estate men who are members of the National Association of Real Estate Boards, subject to its code for ethics and to its discipline for violation. It has been a factor in making the standards of the business generally during the past twenty years, and the exclusive right of the National Association of Real Estate Boards has been sustained in a series of court decisions, a large number of injunctions having been issued, restraining its improper use.

In 1924 the *Realtors' Bulletin* of Baltimore reported that certain enemies of realtric science were trying to show that *realtor* was derived from the English word *real* and the Spanish word *tor*, a bull, and to argue that it thus mean *real bull*. But this obscenity apparently did not go far; probably a hint from the alert general counsel was enough to stop it. During the same year I was in-

---

[1] Letter to W. A. Frisbie, editor of the Minneapolis *Daily News*. This was in 1922. The letter was subscribed "Yours *realtorially*." A copy was sent to Mr. Lewis, who preserves it in his archives.

[2] Private communication, Sept. 4, 1935.

formed by Herbert U. Nelson, executive secretary of the National Association, that "the real-estate men of London, through the Institute of Estate Agents and Auctioneers, after studying our experience in this respect, are planning to coin the word *estator* and to protect it by legal steps." This plan, I believe, came to fruition, but *estator* never caught on, and I can't find it in the Supplement to the Oxford Dictionary. *Realtor,* however, is there —and the first illustrative quotation is from "Babbitt"! In March, 1927, J. Foster Hagan, of Ballston, Va., reported to *American Speech* that he had encountered *realtress* on the window of a real-estate office there, but this charming derivative seems to have died a-bornin'. In 1925 or thereabout certain ambitious insurance solicitors, inflamed by *realtor,* began to call themselves *insurors,* but it, too, failed to make any progress.

Electragist, like *realtor,* seems to be the monopoly of the lofty technicians who affect it: "it is copyrighted by the Association of Electragists International, whose members alone may use it."[1] But *mortician* is in the public domain. It was proposed by a writer in the *Embalmers' Monthly* for February, 1895, but the undertakers, who were then *funeral-directors,* did not rise to it until twelve years later. On September 16, 1916, some of the more eminent of them met at Columbus, O., to form a national association, on the lines of the American College of Surgeons, the American Association of University Professors, and the Society of the Cincinnati, and a year later they decided upon National Selected *Morticians* as its designation.[2] To this day the association remains so exclusive that, of the 24,000 undertakers in the United States, only 200 belong to it. But any one of the remaining 23,800 is free to call himself a *mortician,* and to use all the other lovely words that the advance of human taxidermy has brought in. *Mortician,* of course, was suggested by *physician,* for undertakers naturally admire and like to pal with the resurrection

---

[1] Electragist, by Corneil Ridderhof, *American Speech,* Aug., 1927, p. 477. It means, according to Mr. Ridderhof, "a combined electrical dealer and contractor."

[2] I am indebted here to Mr. W. M. Krieger, executive secretary of the organization, the headquarters of which are in Chicago.

men, and there was a time when some of them called themselves *embalming surgeons.* A *mortician* never handles a *corpse;* he *prepares* a *body* or *patient.* This business is carried on in a *preparation-room* or *operating-room,* and when it is achieved the patient is put into a *casket*[1] and stored in the *reposing-room* or *slumber-room* of a *funeral-home.* On the day of the funeral he is moved to the *chapel* therein for the last exorcism, and then hauled to the cemetery in a *funeral-car* or *casket-coach.*[2] The old-time shroud is now a *négligé* or *slumber-shirt* or *slumber-robe,* the mortician's work-truck is an *ambulance,* and the cemetery is fast becoming a *memorial-park.* In the West cemeteries are being supplanted by public mausoleums, which sometimes go under the names of *cloisters, burial-abbeys,* etc.[3] To be laid away in one runs into money. The vehicle that morticians use for their expectant hauling of the ill is no longer an *ambulance,* but an *invalid-coach. Mortician* has been a favorite butt of the national wits, but they seem to have made no impression on it. In January, 1932, it was barred from the columns of the Chicago *Tribune.* "This decree goes forth," announced the *Tribune,* "not for lack of sympathy with the ambition of undertakers to be well regarded, but because of it. If they haven't the sense to save themselves from their own lexicographers, we shall not be guilty of abetting them in their folly."[4] But *mortician* not only continues to flourish; it also begets progeny, *e.g., beautician, cosmetician, radiotrician* and *bootician.*[5] The barbers, so far, have not devised

[1] *Casket* seems to have come in during the Civil War period. In 1863 Nathaniel Hawthorne denounced it in Our Old Home as "a vile modern phrase, which compels a person . . . to shrink . . . from the idea of being buried at all." At the start it had a rival in *case.* The latter was used in the Richmond *Examiner's* report of the funeral of Gen. J. E. B. Stuart, May 13, 1864. But the *Examiner,* in the same report, used *corpse* and *hearse.*

[2] Mortuary Nomenclature, *Hygeia,* Nov., 1925, p. 651.

[3] The *Mortician,* by Elmer Davis, *American Mercury,* May, 1927.

[4] *Editor and Publisher,* Jan. 30, 1932.

[5] I proposed the use of *bootician* to designate a high-toned big-city bootlegger in the *American Mercury,* April, 1925, p. 450. The term met a crying need, and had considerable success. In March, 1927, the San José *Mercury-Herald* said: "Our bootleggers are now calling themselves *booticians.* It

a name for themselves in *-ician,* but they may be trusted to do so anon. In my youth they were *tonsorial artists,* but in recent years some of them have been calling themselves *chirotonsors.*[1] Practically all American press-agents are now *public relations counsel, contact-managers* or *publicists,* all tree-trimmers are *tree-surgeons,* all milk-wagon and bakery-wagon drivers have become *salesmen,* nearly all janitors are *superintendents,* many gardeners have become *landscape-architects* (in England even the whales of the profession are simple *landscape-gardeners*), cobblers are beginning to call themselves *shoe-rebuilders,*[2] and the corn-doctors, after a generation as *chiropodists,* have burst forth as *podiatrists.* The American fondness for such sonorous appellations arrested the interest of W. L. George, the English novelist, when he visited the United States in 1920. He said:

> Business titles are given in America more readily than in England. I know one *president* whose staff consists of two typists. Many firms have four *vice-presidents.* In the magazines you seldom find merely an *editor;* the others need their share of honor, so they are *associate* (not *assistant*) *editors.* A dentist is called a *doctor.* I wandered into a university, knowing nobody, and casually asked for the *dean.* I was asked, "Which *dean?*" In that building there were enough deans to stock all the English cathedrals. The master of a secret society is *royal supreme knight commander.* Perhaps I reached the extreme at a theatre in Boston, when I wanted something, I forget what, and was told that I must apply to the *chief of the ushers.* He was a mild little man, who had something to do with people getting into their seats, rather a come-down from the pomp and circumstance of his title. Growing interested, I examined my programme, with the following result: It is not a large theatre, but it has a *press-representative,* a *treasurer* (box-office clerk), an *assistant treasurer* (box-office junior clerk), an *advertising-agent,* our old friend the *chief of the ushers,* a *stage-manager,*

---

seems that *bootlegger* has some trace of odium about it, while *bootician* has none." (Reprinted in the Baltimore *Evening Sun,* April 4, 1927.) On July 23, 1931, according to the Associated Press, a man arrested in Chicago, on being asked his profession, answered proudly that he was a *bootician.*

[1] In 1924 representatives of 3000 of them met in Chicago, and voted for *chirotonsor.* See the *Commonweal,* Nov. 26, 1924, p. 58.

[2] There is a *Shoe Rebuilders'* Association in Baltimore. See the Baltimore *Evening Sun,* Oct. 17, 1935.

a *head-electrician*, a *master of properties* (in England called *props*), a *leader of the orchestra* (pity this—why not *president?*), and a *matron* (occupation unknown).[1]

George might have unearthed some even stranger magnificoes in other playhouses. I once knew an ancient bill-sticker, attached to a Baltimore theatre, who boasted the sonorous title of *chief lithographer*. Today, in all probability, he would be called a *lithographic-engineer*. For a number of years the *Engineering News-Record*, the organ of the legitimate engineers, used to devote a column every week to just such uninvited invaders of the craft, and some of the species it unearthed were so fantastic that it was constrained to reproduce their business cards photographically in order to convince its readers that it was not spoofing. One of its favorite exhibits was a bedding manufacturer who first became a *mattress-engineer* and then promoted himself to the lofty dignity of *sleep-engineer*. No doubt he would have called himself a *morphician* if he had thought of it. Another exhilarating specimen was a tractor-driver who advertised for a job as a *caterpillar-engineer*. A third was a beautician who burst out as an *appearance-engineer*. In an Atlanta department-store the *News-Record* found an *engineer of good taste*—a young woman employed to advise newly-married couples patronizing the furniture department, and elsewhere it unearthed *display-engineers* who had been lowly window-dressers until some visionary among them made the great leap, *demolition-engineers* who were once content to be house-wreckers, and *sanitary-engineers* who had an earlier incarnation as garbage-men.

[1] Hail, Columbia!; New York, 1921, pp. 92-3.

JOHN W. CLARK

TIMESTYLE

John W. Clark (1907-   ) was educated at Harvard and at the University of Minnesota, where he is now professor of English and chairman of the department. Though he is a specialist in the language and the literature of the Old and Middle English periods, he takes a lively interest in modern British and American usage, as his collaboration with the English lexicographer Eric Partridge, British and American English Since 1900 *(1951), shows. His latest book is* Early English *(1957).*

A VERY SPECIAL case of journalese is the style of *Time* (or should one write "TIME"?), which began publication in 1923. By style here I mean language in a rather narrow sense as distinct from manner. The manner of *Time* combines oddly, even in a single sentence, the arch, the flip, and the hieratic. Of its style the leading features are the participial opening, inversion of subject and verb, descriptions used like titles ("World Historian Toynbee"), the omission of *the,* asyndeton (the omission of *and*), occasional preference of the possessive case to *of*-phrases ("at week's end") the ferreting out of a few impudently recherché words (for example, *tycoon*, about the only one that has caught on), and two kinds of blends—pronounceable but seldom pronounced (*cinemactress*) and unpronounceable (*GOPolitician*). Such "raciness" as it has is usually of the dismal *ersatz* variety; it is the very reverse of the colloquial. "If it were God's will," said Pantagruel of one of the more hideous of Panurge's incomprehensible gibberishes, "we would all speak so with our tailes." Happily, the only person who probably ever did speak so had to, and he was just reading aloud (presumably through the normal orifice)—the narrator for the radio and movie "March of Time." Some of these devices are not original with *Time,* but others of them are at

»»» From "American English." From *British and American English Since 1900.* By Eric Partridge and John W. Clark. London: Andrew Dakers Limited, 1951. Pp. 265-267. Reprinted by permission of Eric Partridge.

least mainly so, and are, alas, no longer peculiar to it, though fortunately even these are little imitated in writing except in (generally inferior) newspapers, and in speech hardly at all. That the style of *Time* (or *Time*style) has not been more widely and closely imitated than it has been is probably by no means ungratifying to its proprietors; its continued uniqueness is worth money to them. And I simply do not believe that any writer for *Time* writes that way either to his fiancée or to his milkman— or even to his boss.

Of all *Time's* mannerisms, I find habitual asyndeton uniquely irritating; have we, for God's sake, not enough time to write "and"? A close second is the omission of *the*. This is an altogether different thing from *The New Yorker's* omission of *a* at the beginning of such "Talk-of-the-Town" items as "Fellow we know came in yesterday." *Time's* ellipsis originates in the (or a) written language; *The New Yorker's* in the spoken, where the *a* is not consciously and deliberately omitted at all—it is thought but not uttered, because it gets thought before the breath reaches the larynx. The style of widely read periodicals does and should reflect and does and sometimes should modify ordinary speech; but there are writers on current American English who cannot tell the difference between *Time's* omitted *the* (which is completely uncolloquial in both origin and currency) and *The New Yorker's* omitted *a* (which is genuinely colloquial in both).

MALCOLM COWLEY

SOCIOLOGICAL HABIT PATTERNS IN
LINGUISTIC TRANSMOGRIFICATION

*Malcolm Cowley (1898-   ), educated at Harvard and Montpellier, is
historian and sociologist of literature, critic, editor, poet, and translator. He
is best-known, perhaps, as both representative and historian of those
American novelists, poets, and critics of the 1920's known as "the Lost
Generation," whom he describes in* Exile's Return *(1934; rev. ed., 1951).
His most recent major work is* The Literary Situation *(1954).*

I HAVE a friend who started as a poet and then decided to take
a postgraduate degree in sociology. For his doctoral dissertation
he combined his two interests by writing on the social psychology
of poets. He had visited poets by the dozen, asking each of them
a graded series of questions, and his conclusions from the interviews were modest and useful, though reported in what seemed
to me a barbarous jargon. After reading the dissertation I wrote
and scolded him. "You have such a fine sense of the poet's craft,"
I said, "that you shouldn't have allowed the sociologists to
seduce you into writing their professional slang—or at least
that's my judgmental response to your role selection."

My friend didn't write to defend himself; he waited until we
met again. Then dropping his voice, he said: "I knew my dissertation was badly written, but I had to get my degree. If I
had written it in English, Professor Blank"—he mentioned a
rather distinguished name—"would have rejected it. He would
have said it was merely belletristic."

From that time I began to study the verbal folkways of the
sociologists. I read what they call "the literature." A few sociologists write the best English they are capable of writing, and
I suspect that they are the best men in the field. There is no

»»» *The Reporter,* XV (September 20, 1956), 41-43. Copyright 1956 by
The Reporter. Reprinted by permission of *The Reporter* and Malcolm
Cowley.

mystery about them. If they go wrong, their mistakes can be seen and corrected. Others, however—and a vast majority— write in a language that has to be learned almost like Esperanto. It has a private vocabulary which, in addition to strictly socio- logical terms, includes new words for the commonest actions, feelings, and circumstances. It has the beginnings of a new grammar and syntax, much inferior to English grammar in force and precision. So far as it has an effect on standard English, the effect is largely pernicious.

Sometimes it misleads the sociologists themselves, by making them think they are profoundly scientific at points where they are merely being verbose. I can illustrate by trying a simple exercise in translation, that is, by expressing an idea first in English and then seeing what it looks like in the language of sociology.

An example that comes to hand is the central idea of an article by Norman E. Green, printed in the February, 1956, issue of the *American Sociological Review*. In English his argument might read as follows:

"Rich people live in big houses set farther apart than those of poor people. By looking at an aerial photograph of any Ameri- can city, we can distinguish the richer from the poorer neighbor- hoods."

I won't have to labor over a sociological expression of the same idea, because Mr. Green has saved me the trouble. Here is part of his contribution to comparative linguistics. "In effect, it was hypothesized," he says—a sociologist must never say "I assumed," much less "I guessed"—"that certain physical data categories including housing types and densities, land use characteristics, and ecological location"—not just "location," mind you, but "eco- logical location," which is almost equivalent to locational loca- tion—"constitute a scalable content area. This could be called a continuum of residential desirability. Likewise, it was hypothe- sized that several social data categories, describing the same census tracts, and referring generally to the social stratification system of the city, would also be scalable. This scale could be called a continuum of socio-economic status. Thirdly, it was hypothesized that there would be a high positive correlation between the scale types on each continuum."

Here, after ninety-four words, Mr. Green is stating, or concealing, an assumption with which most laymen would have started, that rich people live in good neighborhoods. He is now almost ready for his deduction, or snapper:

"This relationship would define certain linkages between the social and physical structure of the city. It would also provide a precise definition of the commonalities among several spatial distributions. By the same token, the correlation between the residential desirability scale and the continuum of socio-economic status would provide an estimate of the predictive value of aerial photographic data relative to the social ecology of the city."

Mr. Green has used 160 words—counting "socio-economic" as only one—to express an idea that a layman would have stated in thirty-three. As a matter of fact, he has used many more than 160 words, since the whole article is an elaboration of this one thesis. Whatever may be the virtues of the sociological style—or Socspeak, as George Orwell might have called it—it is not specifically designed to save ink and paper. Let us briefly examine some of its other characteristics.

FUZZING UP THE OBVIOUS

A layman's first impression of sociological prose, as compared with English prose, is that it contains a very large proportion of abstract words, most of them built on Greek or Latin roots. Often—as in the example just quoted—they are used to inflate or transmogrify a meaning that could be clearly expressed in shorter words surviving from King Alfred's time.

These Old English or Anglo-Saxon words are in number less than one-tenth of the entries in the largest dictionaries. But they are the names of everyday objects, attributes, and actions, and they are also the pronouns, the auxiliary verbs, and most of the prepositions and conjunctions, so that they form the grammatical structure of the language. The result is that most novelists use six Anglo-Saxon words for every one derived from French, Latin, or Greek, and that is probably close to the percentage that would be found in spoken English.

For comparison or contrast, I counted derivations in the passage quoted from the *American Sociological Review*, which is a typical example of "the literature." No less than forty-nine per cent of Mr. Green's prose consists of words from foreign or classical languages. By this standard of measurement, his article is more abstruse than most textbooks of advanced chemistry and higher mathematics, which are said to contain only forty per cent of such words.

In addition to being abstruse, the language of the sociologists is also rich in neologisms. Apparently they like nothing better than inventing a word, deforming a word, or using a technical word in a strange context. Among their favorite nouns are "ambit," "extensity" (for "extent"), "scapegoating," "socializee," "ethnicity," "directionality," "cathexis," "affect" (for "feeling"), "maturation" (for both "maturing" and "maturity"), and "commonalities" (for "points in common"). Among their favorite adjectives are "processual," "prestigeful," and "insightful"—which last is insightful to murder—and perhaps their favorite adverb is "minimally," which seems to mean "in some measure." Their maximal pleasure seems to lie in making new combinations of nouns and adjectives and nouns used as adjectives, until the reader feels that he is picking his way through a field of huge boulders, lost among "universalistic-specific achievement patterns" and "complementary role-expectation-sanction systems," as he struggles vainly toward "ego-integrative action orientation," guided only by "orientation to improvement of the gratification-deprivation balance of the actor"—which last is Professor Talcott Parsons's rather involved way of saying "the pleasure principle."

But Professor Parsons, head of the Sociology Department at Harvard, is not the only delinquent recidivist, convicted time and again of corrupting the language. Among sociologists in general there is a criminal fondness for using complicated terms when there are simple ones available. A child says "Do it again," a teacher says "Repeat the exercise," but the sociologist says "It was determined to replicate the investigation." Instead of saying two things are alike or similar, as a layman would do, the sociologist describes them as being either isomorphic or homologous. Instead of saying that they are different, he calls them allotropic. Every form of leadership or influence is called a hegemony.

A sociologist never cuts anything in half or divides it in two like a layman. Instead he dichotomizes it, bifurcates it, subjects it to a process of binary fission, or restructures it in a dyadic conformation—around polar foci.

THE NEW GRAMMAR

So far I have been dealing with the vocabulary of sociologists, but their private language has a grammar too, and one that should be the subject of intensive research by the staff of a very well-endowed foundation. I have space to mention only a few of its more striking features.

The first of these is the preponderance of nouns over all the other parts of speech. Nouns are used in hyphenated pairs or dyads, and sometimes in triads, tetrads, and pentads. Nouns are used as adjectives without change of form, and they are often used as verbs, with or without the suffix "ize." The sociological language is gritty with nouns, like sanded sugar.

On the other hand, it is poor in pronouns. The singular pronoun of the first person has entirely disappeared, except in case histories, for the sociologist never comes forward as "I." Sometimes he refers to himself as "the author" or "the investigator," or as "many sociologists," or even as "the best sociologists," when he is advancing a debatable opinion. On rare occasions he calls himself "we," like Queen Elizabeth speaking from the throne, but he usually avoids any personal form and writes as if he were a force of nature.

The second-personal pronoun has also disappeared, for the sociologist pretends to be speaking not to living persons but merely for the record. Masculine and feminine pronouns of the third person are used with parsimony, and most sociologists prefer to say "the subject," or "X——," or "the interviewee," where a layman would use the simple "he" or "she." As for the neuter pronoun of the third person, it survives chiefly as the impersonal subject of a passive verb. "It was hypothesized," we read, or "It was found to be the case." Found by *whom?*

The neglect and debasement of the verb is another striking feature of "the literature." The sociologist likes to reduce a transitive verb to an intransitive, so that he speaks of people's adapting, adjusting, transferring, relating, and identifying, with no more of a grammatical object than if they were coming or going. He seldom uses transitive verbs of action, like "break," "injure," "help," and "adore." Instead he uses verbs of relation, verbs which imply that one series of nouns and adjectives, used as the compound subject of a sentence, is larger or smaller than, dominant over, subordinate to, causative of, or resultant from another series of nouns and adjectives.

Considering this degradation of the verb, I have wondered how one of Julius Caesar's boasts could be translated into Socspeak. What Caesar wrote was *"Veni, vidi, vici"*—only three words, all of them verbs. The English translation is in six words: "I came, I saw, I conquered," and three of the words are first-personal pronouns, which the sociologist is taught to avoid. I suspect that he would have to write: "Upon the advent of the investigator, his hegemony became minimally coextensive with the areal unit rendered visible by his successive displacements in space."

The whole sad situation leads me to dream of a vast allegorical painting called "The Triumph of the Nouns." It would depict a chariot of victory drawn by the other conquered parts of speech —the adverbs and adjectives still robust, if yoked and harnessed; the prepositions bloated and pale; the conjunctions tortured; the pronouns reduced to sexless skeletons; the verbs dichotomized and feebly tottering—while behind them, arrogant, overfed, roseate, spilling over the triumphal car, would be the company of nouns in Roman togas and Greek chitons, adorned with laurel branches and flowering hegemonies.

FRANK SULLIVAN

THE CLICHÉ EXPERT TESTIFIES
ON BASEBALL

*Frank Sullivan (1892-   ), newspaperman and satirist, has almost made
a career of collecting and satirizing clichés. His interviews with Mr.
Arbuthnot, a mythical cliché expert, which have appeared in* The New
Yorker *off and on for years, are as perceptive as they are famous.*

Q—Mr. Arbuthnot, you state that your grandmother has passed
away and you would like to have the afternoon off to go to her
funeral.

A—That is correct.

Q—You are an expert in the clichés of baseball—right?

A—I pride myself on being well versed in the stereotypes of
our national pastime.

Q—Well, we'll test you. Who plays baseball?

A—Big-league baseball is customarily played by brilliant out-
fielders, veteran hurlers, powerful sluggers, knuckle-ball artists,
towering first basemen, key moundsmen, fleet base runners, ace
southpaws, scrappy little shortstops, sensational war vets, ex-
college stars, relief artists, rifle-armed twirlers, dependable main-
stays, doughty right-handers, streamlined backstops, power-
hitting batsmen, redoubtable infielders, erstwhile Dodgers, veteran sparkplugs, sterling moundsmen, aging twirlers, and rookie
sensations.

Q—What other names are rookie sensations known by?

A—They are also known as aspiring rookies, sensational new-
comers, promising freshmen, ex-sandlotters, highly touted strip-
lings, and youngsters who will bear watching.

Q—What's the manager of a baseball team called?

»»» *The New Yorker,* XXV (August 27, 1949), 22-25. Reprinted by permission of Frank Sullivan. Copyright © 1949 The New Yorker Magazine,
Inc.

A—A veteran pilot. Or youthful pilot. But he doesn't manage the team.

Q—No? What does he do?

A—He guides its destinies.

Q—How?

A—By the use of managerial strategy.

Q—Mr. Arbuthnot, please describe the average major-league-baseball athlete.

A—Well, he comes in three sizes, or types. The first type is tall, slim, lean, towering, rangy, huge, husky, big, strapping, sturdy, handsome, powerful, lanky, rawboned, and rugged.

Q—Quite a hunk of athlete.

A—Well, those are the adjectives usage requires for the description of the Type One, or Ted Williams, ballplayer.

Q—What is Type Two like?

A—He is chunky or stocky—that is to say, Yogi Berra.

Q—And the third?

A—The third type is elongated and does not walk. He is Ol' Satchmo, or Satchel Paige.

Q—What do you mean Satchmo doesn't walk?

A—Not in the sports pages, he doesn't. He ambles.

Q—You mentioned a hurler, Mr. Arbuthnot. What is a hurler?

A—A hurler is a twirler.

Q—Well, what is a twirler?

A—A twirler is a flinger, a tosser. He's a moundsman.

Q—Moundsman?

A—Yes. He officiates on the mound. When the veteran pilot tells a hurler he is to twirl on a given day, that is a mound assignment, and the hurler who has been told to twirl is the mound nominee for that game.

Q—You mean he pitches?

A—That is right. You have cut the Gordian knot.

Q—What's the pitcher for the other team called?

A—He is the mound adversary, or mound opponent, of the mound nominee. That makes them rival hurlers, or twirlers. They face each other and have a mound duel, or pitchers' battle.

Q—Who wins?

A—The mound victor wins, and as a result he is a mound ace, or ace moundsman. He excels on the mound, or stars on it. He and the other moundsmen on his team are the mound corps.

Q—What happens to the mound nominee who loses the mound duel?

A—He is driven off the mound.

Q—What do you mean by that?

A—He's yanked. He's knocked out of the box.

Q—What's the box?

A—The box is the mound.

Q—I see. Why does the losing moundsman lose?

A—Because he issues, grants, yields, allows, or permits too many hits or walks, or both.

Q—A bit on the freehanded side, eh? Where does the mound victor go if he pitches the entire game?

A—He goes all the way.

Q—And how does the mound adversary who has been knocked out of the box explain his being driven off the mound?

A—He says, "I had trouble with my control," or "My curve wasn't working," or "I just didn't have anything today."

Q—What happens if a mound ace issues, grants, yields, allows, or permits too many hits and walks?

A—In that case, sooner or later, rumors are rife. Either that or they are rampant.

Q—Rife where?

A—In the front office.

Q—What's that?

A—That's the place where baseball's biggies—also known as baseball moguls—do their asking.

Q—What do they ask for?

A—Waivers on erratic southpaw.

Q—What are these baseball biggies further known as?

A—They are known as the Shrewd Mahatma or as Horace Stoneham, but if they wear their shirt open at the neck, they are known as Bill Veeck.

Q—What do baseball biggies do when they are not asking for waivers?

A—They count the gate receipts, buy promising rookies, sell aging twirlers, and stand loyally by Manager Durocher.

Q—And what does Manager Durocher do?

A—He guides the destinies of the Giants and precipitates arguments with the men in blue.

Q—What men in blue?

A—The umpires, or arbiters.

Q—What kind of arguments does Durocher precipitate?

A—Heated arguments.

Q—And the men in blue do what to him and other players who precipitate heated arguments?

A—They send, relegate, banish, or thumb them to the showers.

Q—Mr. Arbuthnot, how do you, as a cliché expert, refer to first base?

A—First base is the initial sack.

Q—And second base?

A—The keystone sack.

Q—What's third base called?

A—The hot corner. The first inning is the initial frame, and an inning without runs is a scoreless stanza.

Q—What is one run known as?

A—A lone run, but four runs are known as a quartet of tallies.

Q—What is a baseball?

A—The pill, the horsehide, the old apple, or the sphere.

Q—And what's a bat?

A—The bat is the willow, or the wagon tongue, or the piece of lumber. In the hands of a mighty batsman, it is the mighty bludgeon.

Q—What does a mighty batsman do?

A—He amasses runs. He connects with the old apple. He raps 'em out and he pounds 'em out. He belts 'em and he clouts 'em.

Q—Clouts what?

A—Circuit clouts.

Q—What are they?

A—Home runs. Know what the mighty batsman does to the mighty bludgeon?

Q—No. What?

A—He wields it. Know what kind of orgies he fancies?

Q—What kind?

A—Batting orgies. Slugfests. That's why his team pins.

Q—Pins what?

A—All its hopes on him.

Q—Mr. Arbuthnot, what is a runner guilty of when he steals home?

A—A plate theft.

Q—And how many kinds of baseball games are there?

A—Five main classifications: scheduled tussles, crucial contests, pivotal games, drab frays, and arc-light tussles.

Q—And what does the team that wins—

A—Sir, a baseball team never wins. It scores a victory, or gains one, or chalks one up. Or it snatches.

Q—Snatches what?

A—Victory from the jaws of defeat.

Q—How?

A—By a ninth-inning rally.

Q—I see. Well, what do the teams that chalk up victories do to the teams that lose?

A—They nip, top, wallop, trounce, rout, down, subdue, smash, drub, paste, trip, crush, curb, whitewash, erase, bop, slam, batter, check, hammer, pop, wham, clout, and blank the visitors. Or they zero them.

Q—Gracious sakes! Now I know why ballplayers are old at thirty-five.

A—Oh, that isn't the half of it. They do other things to the visitors.

Q—Is it possible?

A—Certainly. They jolt them, or deal them a jolt. They also halt, sock, thump, larrup, vanquish, flatten, scalp, shellac, blast, slaughter, K.O., mow down, topple, whack, pound, rap, sink, baffle, thwart, foil, maul, and nick.

Q—Do the losers do anything at all to the victors?

A—Yes. They bow to the victors. And they taste.

Q—Taste what?

A—Defeat. They trail. They take a drubbing, pasting, or shel-lacking. They are in the cellar.

Q—What about the victors?

A—They loom as flag contenders. They're in the first division.

Q—Mr. Arbuthnot, what is the first sign of spring?

A—Well, a robin, of course.

Q—Yes, but I'm thinking of our subject here. How about when the ballplayers go south for spring training?

A—Ballplayers don't go south for spring training.

Q—Why, they do!

A—They do *not*. They wend their way southward.

Q—Oh, I see. Well, do all ballplayers wend their way south-ward?

A—No. One remains at home.

Q—Who is he?

A—The lone holdout.

Q—Why does the lone holdout remain at home?

A—He refuses to ink pact.

Q—What do you mean by that?

A—He won't affix his Hancock to his contract.

Q—Why not?

A—He demands a pay hike, or salary boost.

Q—From whom?

A—From baseball's biggies.

Q—And what do baseball's biggies do to the lone holdout?

A—They attempt to lure him back into the fold.

Q—How?

A—By offering him new contract.

Q—What does lone holdout do then?

A—He weighs offer. If he doesn't like it, he balks at terms. If he does like it, he inks pact and gets pay hike.

Q—How much pay hike?

A—An undisclosed amount in excess of.

Q—That makes him what?

A—One of the highest-paid baseball stars in the annals of the game, barring Ruth.

Q—What if baseball's biggies won't give lone holdout pay hike?

A—In that case, lone holdout takes pay cut, old salary, or job in filling station in home town.

Q—Now, when baseball players reach the spring training camp and put on their uniforms—

A—May I correct you again, sir? Baseball players do not put on uniforms. They don them.

Q—I see. What for?

A—For a practice session or strenuous workout.

Q—And why must they have a strenuous workout?

A—Because they must shed the winter's accumulation of excess avoirdupois.

Q—You mean they must lose weight?

A—You put it in a nutshell. They must be streamlined, so they plunge.

Q—Plunge into what?

A—Into serious training.

Q—Can't get into serious training except by plunging, eh?

A—No. Protocol requires that they plunge. Training season gets under way in Grapefruit and Citrus Leagues. Casey Stengel bars night life.

Q—Mr. Arbuthnot, what is the opening game of the season called?

A—Let me see-e-e. It's on the tip of my tongue. Isn't that aggravating? Ah, I have it—the opener! At the opener, fifty-two thousand two hundred and ninety-three fans watch Giants bow to Dodgers.

Q—What do those fifty-two thousand two hundred and ninety-three fans constitute?

A—They constitute fandom.

Q—And how do they get into the ballpark?

A—They click through the turnstiles.

Q—Now, then, Mr. Arbuthnot, the climax of the baseball season is the World Series, is it not?

A—That's right.

Q—And what is the World Series called?

A—It's the fall classic, or crucial contest, also known as the fray, the epic struggle, and the Homeric struggle. It is part of the American scene, like ham and eggs or pumpkin pie. It's a colorful event.

Q—What is it packed with?

A—Thrills. Drama.

Q—What kind of drama?

A—Sheer or tense.

Q—Why does it have to be packed with thrills and drama?

A—Because if it isn't, it becomes drab fray.

Q—Where does the fall classic take place?

A—In a vast municipal stadium or huge ballpark.

Q—And the city in which the fall classic is held is what?

A—The city is baseball mad.

Q—And the hotels?

A—The hotels are jammed. Rooms are at a premium.

Q—Tickets, also, I presume.

A—Tickets? If you mean the cards of admission to the fall classic, they are referred to as elusive Series ducats, and they *are* at a premium, though I would prefer to say that they are scarcer than the proverbial hen's teeth.

Q—Who attends the Series?

A—A milling throng, or great outpouring of fans.

Q—What does the great outpouring of fans do?

A—It storms the portals and, of course, clicks through the turnstiles.

Q—Causing what?

A—Causing attendance records to go by the board. Stands fill early.

Q—What else does the crowd do?

A—It yells itself hoarse. Pent-up emotions are released. It rides the men in blue.

Q—What makes a baseball biggie unhappy on the morning of a Series tussle?

A—Leaden skies.

Q—Who is to blame for leaden skies?

A—A character known to the scribes as Jupiter Pluvius, or Jupe.

Q—What does rain dampen?

A—The ardor of the fans.

Q—If the weather clears, who gets credit for that?

A—Another character, known as Old Sol.

Q—Now, the team that wins the Series—

A—Again, I'm sorry to correct you, sir. A team does not win a Series. It wraps it up. It clinches it.

Q—Well, then what?

A—Then the newly crowned champions repair to their locker room.

Q—What reigns in that locker room?

A—Pandemonium, bedlam, and joy.

Q—Expressed how?

A—By lifting youthful pilot, or his equivalent, to the shoulders of his teammates.

Q—In the locker room of the losers, what is as thick as a day in—I mean so thick you could cut it with a knife?

A—Gloom. The losers are devoid.

Q—Devoid of what?

A—Animation.

Q—Why?

A—Because they came apart at the seams in the pivotal tussle.

Q—What happens to the newly crowned champions later?

A—They are hailed, acclaimed, and fêted. They receive mighty ovations, boisterous demonstrations, and thunderous welcomes.

Q—And when those are over?

A—They split the Series purse and go hunting.

Q—Mr. Arbuthnot, if a powerful slugger or mighty batsman wields a mighty bludgeon to such effect that he piles up a record number of circuit clouts, what does that make him?

A—That is very apt to make him most valuable player of the year.

Q—And that?

A—That makes the kids of America look up to him as their hero.

Q—If most valuable player of the year continues the batting orgies that make the kids of America worship him, what then?

A—Then he becomes one of Baseball's Immortals. He is enshrined in Baseball's Hall of Fame.

Q—And after that?

A—Someday he retires and becomes veteran scout, or veteran coach, or veteran pilot. Or sports broadcaster.

Q—And then?

A—Well, eventually a memorial plaque is unveiled to him at the opener.

Q—Thank you, Mr. Arbuthnot. You have been most helpful. I won't detain you any longer, and I hope your grandmother's funeral this afternoon is a tense drama packed with thrills.

A—Thanks a lot. Goodbye now.

Q—Hold on a moment, Mr. Arbuthnot. Just for my own curiosity—couldn't you have said "thanks" and "goodbye" and let it go at that, without adding that "lot" and "now" malarkey?

A—I could have, but it would have cost me my title as a cliché expert.

PART II

Modes

RHETORICAL MODES, illustrated here in Part II, differ from rhetorical forms, illustrated in Part III, in that they are usually elements or aspects of works rather than works. A given work may well combine such modes as definition, analysis, classification, argumentation, and evaluation. The distinction between modes and forms is not hard and fast, however. For occasionally a mode is the only element of a work; this is frequently the case with analysis, for example, and with process explanation.

DESCRIPTION

DESCRIPTION consists of making particular statements about the physical properties of something or someone so that the reader may perceive the object described. The reader thus vicariously observes what the writer actually observed. The completeness of the reader's perception is governed by the amount and the precision of detail which the writer gives him. Such detail as the writer chooses to give depends upon his purpose; he may wish to be more or less complete in the description he gives the reader.

Accordingly, description of a person, place, or thing may consist of a few details or of so many that the description seems almost exhaustively complete. Whichever the case, details in a description always are selected details chosen to suit the purpose for which the object is described. For example, an ornithologist may describe a song bird by giving its precise measurements, shape, color, and markings so that the reader may have precise information about the bird's appearance. A poet may describe the same bird and use some of the same details, but his description is likely also to emphasize his evaluation of or emotional reaction to the bird. Either the ornithologist's technical description or the poet's impressionistic one will make the reader see— and sometimes, depending upon the details given, hear, taste, smell, or feel—the object. In addition, any description that includes more than technical details makes the reader not only perceive the object but also evaluate it or emotionally react to it. Of course, a different selection of details changes the evaluation or the reaction of the reader; for instance, from seeing the object as beautiful to seeing it as ugly, or from reacting to it pleasantly to reacting to it unpleasantly. Likewise, a technical description may vary in details; the description of the song bird, for instance, may stress habitat, nesting habits, and flight patterns and thus concentrate on the bird's actions more than its appearance. The writer in any case chooses those details that fit the purpose for which he describes the object; he omits other details not relevant to that purpose.

Impressionistic description needs technical details of size, shape, color, location, sound, and timing so that the reader may perceive as well as react to the object as the writer intended. Conversely, technical description may evoke an emotional reaction, albeit one beyond the writer's intention; for instance, the reader of the ornithologist's description may think the song bird pretty because he likes its blue color but not because the writer said the bird was pretty or confessed a liking for blue. Sometimes, of course, writers use technical description as a basis for evaluation of the object, as in the description of the Ford T by Clutton and Stanford.

The following pieces of description use many devices to obtain their effects. In his description of the food eaten by the Gant family, Wolfe adds up many sensory details to create the impression of good living. For example, he not only makes us see the row upon row of canned fruit but also makes us hear the shelves groan under such plenty. Additionally, he appeals to our tactile and kinetic senses when writing of "huge crinkled lettuces that wrenched cleanly from the loamy soil with small black clots stuck to their crisp stocks." We smell and taste the food as the Gants eat it; we hear the "heavy clangor" of the father's carving knife as he sharpens it. Such technically precise description as "fried apples seething in their gummed syrups" pictures the apples and reproduces their texture and the sound of their cooking; moreover, the precise phrasing of this passage, like other equally precise throughout the piece, builds up the emotion of joy and exemplifies the opening judgment that the Gants "fed stupendously." Clutton and Stanford's description of the Ford Model T is, of all the selections, closest to technical description in its presentation of exact measurements and other statistics; even so, the authors indulge in some evaluation, particularly in their nostalgic last paragraph mourning the passing of the Model T. Thus their rhetorical purpose is not merely technical description of the car but praise of it as a technological phenomenon. In the descriptions of places, Paton is more impersonally informative about Natal than is Brooks about Carmel. Although Paton finds his native place "exciting" and beautiful, he gives us much topographical, botanical, sociological, and economic detail so we too can see the excitement and beauty of its contrasts. Brooks approaches California more personally, writing of the people he knew at Carmel; however, his precise description of striking details of their appearance and their lives (and deaths) leads us to accept his judgments about the enervating effect of the place and its "lurking possibility of monstrous things." In contrast to Brooks' pointedly selective impressions, Mark Twain gives an exhaustive description of "the best house" in a river town with humorous asides such as "Piano—kettle in disguise" which make his piece an evaluation as well as an inventory of the house. As in all description, the details themselves—the titles of the music on the piano, the pictures of George Washington, for example—carry their own emotional charge so that just naming them produces a response in the reader at all familiar with the music or the pictures. By his chosen details and his reminiscent, humorous commentary, Mark Twain gives us an impression of the people who lived in such a house, shows their standards of beauty, and compares "The House Beautiful" to the greater beauty of Mississippi steamboats. In his reminiscent piece, George Bourne describes the occasion of Christmas as celebrated in his childhood so as to give his emotional reactions to it and thereby share those emotions with the reader. Additionally, as an adult he sees significance in details such as the "Chany Trow" song "older than the Reformation," significance which escaped him as a child. Thus his essay revalues the Christmas activities as well as describes them. Because he describes the actions of people—their Christmas customs—his piece seems nearer narration than the other descriptions in this section; but his piece is a description of typical Christmas activities, not a story about a single Christmas, and hence is descriptive more than narrative.

As a basic mode of discourse, description runs throughout the selections in other sections of this book. For example, descriptions of persons appear in Part III under "Autobiography and Biography" and "Character Sketches." In Part II under "Analogy, Comparison, Evaluation," Sir Geoffrey Crowther cannot compare English and American education without describing both kinds, nor can Anthony Trollope evaluate American hotels without describing them. Indeed, description is the handmaid of other rhetorical modes and forms, as is apparent in the following sections of this book.

THOMAS WOLFE

FOOD AT THE GANTS'

Thomas Wolfe (1900-1938) is an American novelist whose books depict his own struggle to become a writer. A North Carolinian, he was in the vanguard of the Southern literary renascence, now in full flower. Educated at the University of North Carolina and at Harvard, he taught English at New York University from 1924 to 1930 to support himself while working on his first novel, Look Homeward, Angel *(1929). A sequel,* Of Time and the River *(1935), and a book of short stories and essays,* From Death to Morning *(1935), were published in his lifetime. His posthumous novels include* The Web and the Rock *(1939) and* You Can't Go Home Again *(1940).*

THEY [the Gant family] fed stupendously. Eugene began to observe the food and the seasons. In the autumn, they barrelled huge frosty apples in the cellar. Gant bought whole hogs from the butcher, returning home early to salt them, wearing a long work-apron, and rolling his sleeves half up his lean hairy arms. Smoked bacons hung in the pantry, the great bins were full of flour, the dark recessed shelves groaned with preserved cherries, peaches, plums, quinces, apples, pears. All that he touched waxed in rich pungent life: his Spring gardens, wrought in the black wet earth below the fruit trees, flourished in huge crinkled lettuces that wrenched cleanly from the loamy soil with small black clots stuck to their crisp stocks; fat red radishes; heavy tomatoes. The rich plums lay bursted on the grass; his huge cherry trees oozed with heavy gum jewels; his apple trees bent with thick green clusters. The earth was spermy for him like a big woman.

Spring was full of cool dewy mornings, spurting winds, and storms of intoxicating blossoms, and in this enchantment Eugene first felt the mixed lonely ache and promise of the seasons.

In the morning they rose in a house pungent with breakfast cookery, and they sat at a smoking table loaded with brains and eggs, ham, hot biscuit, fried apples seething in their gummed syrups, honey, golden butter, fried steak, scalding coffee. Or there were stacked batter-cakes, rum-colored molasses, fragrant brown sausages, a bowl of wet cherries, plums, fat juicy bacon, jam. At the mid-day meal, they ate heavily: a huge hot roast of beef, fat buttered lima-beans, tender corn smoking on the cob, thick red slabs of sliced tomatoes, rough savory spinach, hot yellow corn-bread, flaky biscuits, a deep-dish peach and apple cobbler spiced with cinnamon, tender cabbage, deep glass dishes piled with preserved fruits—cherries, pears, peaches. At night they might eat fried steak, hot squares of grits fried in egg and butter, pork-chops, fish, young fried chicken.

For the Thanksgiving and Christmas feasts four heavy turkeys were bought and fattened for weeks: Eugene fed them with cans of shelled corn several times a day, but he could not bear to be present at their executions, because by that time their cheerful excited gobbles made echoes in his heart. Eliza baked for weeks in advance: the whole energy of the family focussed upon the great ritual of the feast. A day or two before, the auxiliary dainties arrived in piled grocer's boxes—the magic of strange foods and fruits was added to familiar fare: there were glossed sticky dates, cold rich figs, cramped belly to belly in small boxes, dusty raisins, mixed nuts—the almond, pecan, the meaty nigger-toe, the walnut, sacks of assorted candies, piles of yellow Florida oranges, tangerines, sharp, acrid, nostalgic odors.

Seated before a roast or a fowl, Gant began a heavy clangor on his steel and carving knife, distributing thereafter Gargantuan portions to each plate. Eugene feasted from a high chair by his father's side, filled his distending belly until it was drum-tight, and was permitted to stop eating by his watchful sire only when his stomach was impregnable to the heavy prod of Gant's big finger.

"There's a soft place there," he would roar, and he would cover the scoured plate of his infant son with another heavy slab of beef. That their machinery withstood this hammer-handed treatment was a tribute to their vitality and Eliza's cookery.

CECIL CLUTTON

AND JOHN STANFORD

FORD "T"

*Cecil Clutton (1909-   ) and John Stanford (1929-   ) are English
engineers. But both are authorities on and have written a good deal about
racing, sports, and antique motor cars. With Cyril Posthumus and Denis
Jenkinson, Clutton wrote* The Racing Car: Development and Design
(1956) and, with Paul Bird and Anthony Harding, compiled The Vintage
Motor Car Pocketbook *(1959). Stanford wrote* The Sports Car: Development and Design *(1957) and edits* The Bulletin of the Vintage Sports-Car
Club. *And Clutton and Stanford collaborated on* The Vintage Motor-Car
(1955).

HENRY FORD started making cars in 1891, and the world speed
record-breaking "999" was made in 1902; but the Ford Motor
Company, as it is known today, was not founded until 1903. Its
early products covered quite a wide range, from economy "run-
abouts" to the 2500-dollar, 6-litre, six-cylinder Model K introduced in 1906.

The model which first gives a noticeable foretaste of the "T"
is the 1906 Model N, while the "S" of the following year estab-
lishes the lines of the famous "T" brass radiator. Both of these
had the stroke smaller than the bore (3¾ in. × 3⅜ in.). In the
Ford catalogue of 1907 it is stated that: "The Model N was Mr.
Ford's conception of a runabout that was 'all automobile'—in
other words, all efficiency with none of the frills or fussings so
dear to the hearts of some motorists."

The Model T (62) was on sale towards the end of 1908 and
the catalogue is unequivocal in its claims: "There are excellent
features in other cars, but better features or as high-grade materials as are used in the Model T Ford cannot be found in any
other car at any price. A better car is not and cannot be made."

With such a highly individual car, it was perhaps risky to

»»» From *The Vintage Motor-Car*. New York: Charles Scribner's Sons,
1955. Pp. 133-135. Reprinted by permission of B. T. Batsford Ltd.

compare its merits with others; but as to the high-grade materials
there was no doubt, and this was one of the important reasons
for Ford's success as a manufacturer.

The outstanding importance of the "T" is that it was the first
car to be mass-produced in the fullest sense of the word. Others
had gone considerable distances in this direction, and Ford
himself claimed to have sold 25,000 cars before the "T", so that
he had gained all the experience necessary for this great venture.

The engine had a longer stroke than the "N" and "S", its
dimensions being 3¾ in.×4 in., which give a capacity of 2884 c.c.
It was designed for simplicity, strength, and flexibility. Very small
valves limited the crankshaft speed to about 1800 r.p.m. and the
power output to about the Treasury Rating of 22.4 h.p. Lubrica-
tion was by splash and maintenance was simplified by a detach-
able cylinder head, which was an unusual feature in 1908. A
trembler coil facilitated starting and for normal running there was
a magneto built into the flywheel. The limited power output en-
sured remarkable flexibility, and the lowest of the two speeds
was intended only for starting and excessively steep gradients.
Top-gear ratio was 3.64 to 1, which produced a top-gear range
of 3 to 45 m.p.h., while the overall weight of 13¾ cwt. facilitated
remarkably brisk acceleration. Petrol consumption was in the
neighbourhood of 30 m.p.g. Bottom gear, which was 10 to 1, had
an extreme maximum of 15 m.p.h. Reverse was even lower, and
could thus be used as an emergency low. In moments of acute
crisis it could even be used as an emergency brake, since the
gears were epicyclic, engaged by friction bands. The gearbox
was in unit with the engine, another unusual feature at this early
date. Although the gearbox gave extremely good service, it
exerted so much "drag" when the oil was cold that it was almost
impossible to turn the engine, and it became a matter of routine
to jack up one back wheel as a preliminary to starting on a cold
morning.

Control was effected as follows: the right-hand pedal controlled
a transmission brake; the central pedal operated reverse; the left-
hand pedal gave the two forward speeds and neutral—full depres-

sion produced low gear, neutral was half-way, and taking the foot off the pedal engaged top. The accelerator was hand-controlled only, by a long lever under the steering wheel, and a similar lever controlled the ignition advance and retard. The hand brake, when pulled on to the halfway position moved the left-hand pedal to its neutral position; further application operated the modest rear-wheel brakes.

Transverse springs were employed for both back and front axles.

Its simplicity, robustness, and very high ground clearance made the car ideal for the backwoodsman, and indeed it is extremely doubtful if the "T" has ever been improved upon for rough usage with minimum maintenance.

Over twenty styles of coachwork were available in the early years, but on colour Henry Ford was adamant—you could have any colour you liked as long as it was black.

In 1917 the Model T lost much of its attraction when its exterior appearance was drastically altered. The famous flat-sided brass radiator disappeared and the new style featured (in the words of the catalogue) "The stream-line hood, large radiator and enclosed fan, crown fenders, black finish and nickel trimmings" ("crown fenders" would be described in English as domed mudguards). Electric lighting and starting followed in 1919, and the model then continued with little alteration until 1927, when it was finally withdrawn. After a considerable pause it was replaced by the Model A, a very conventional machine with wire wheels, three-speed gearbox and four-wheel brakes (the "T" had never made this concession to progress and continued to the last with two minute brake drums on the back wheels only). While it was in preparation, others had taken the lead, and the "A" never replaced the immortal "T" in the public fancy. Indeed, the "Tin Lizzy" or "Flivver" had become almost a national characteristic, and at the end of its eighteen years in production the total number sold was fifteen million.

ALAN PATON

from NATAL

Alan Paton (1903-   ) was born in Natal, South Africa, which he describes in the following selection. A schoolmaster and prison official before turning to writing, he has become a spokesman on South African affairs, notably through his novels Cry, the Beloved Country *(1948) and* Too Late the Phalarope *(1953) and his social commentary* Hope for South Africa *(1959).*

NATAL is that part of South Africa that lies under the highest part of the Drakensberg escarpment. It is, in respect of its white inhabitants, the most British of the four provinces; however, the great majority of its people are Zulu-speaking. Durban is called the most English city, and so it is; but it is exciting because its streets are alive with the sights and sounds and voices of Europe and Africa and the East, all of this set in a scene of such natural luxuriance and colour as I do not remember to have seen surpassed by any other city of the world.

The coastal hills, once covered with low forest, are now largely given over to waving sugar-cane plantations. Tropical fruits grow in great abundance, pineapples, bananas, litchis, avocados, guavas, granadillas, mangos, and pawpaws. Flowering plants and shrubs and trees are equally abundant. In October and November, in Durban and Pietermaritzburg and many other towns, the jacarandas put out a wealth of mauve blossoms, which, fallen, carpet the streets below. In January in Durban the flat crowns of the flamboyants, noble trees in any season, are covered with scarlet flowers, while the spathodea, the African Flame, bears its large orange blooms almost the whole year round. The winter months are even more prodigal. While the interior plain burns brown and lifeless, here bougainvilleas cascade down from the houses, and the Golden Shower, bignonia venusta, covers roofs and walls in sheets of orange flame. The kaffirboom, erythrina caffra, puts forth its blood-red clusters and the poinsettias their scarlet bracts. Another striking bush is the acacia floribunda with its profusion of yellow flowers. A few miles inland from Durban, where the hills begin to rise sharply, the gardens in September and October are magnificent with flowering azaleas. Natal is justly called the Garden Province.

Durban is a city of more than a half-a-million people, of whom roughly one third are white, one third Zulu or Zulu-speaking, and one third Indians. It is one of the busiest ports of the whole continent, and is a thriving center of industry, possessing many splendid modern buildings.

Most of the white citizens of Durban live on the magnificent hill known as the Berea, which begins to rise a mile or two from the beaches, affording a cooler air and magnificent views of ocean and harbor. Its residential streets are planted with the flamboyant, jacaranda and spathodea; and these and many noble indigenous trees excite the admiration of almost every visitor.

Its main shopping thoroughfare is West Street, but one block to the north of this is the Indian city. When Indian laborers were brought to Natal, they were followed by traders, mostly Muslims, some of whom succeeded in establishing notable businesses. No visitor must neglect to visit this portion of the city. Here are shops displaying exquisite silks and Oriental jewellery, and others out of whose doors come the mingled fragrances of all the spices of the East. Here also are temples, mosques, and churches; and the Indian market, one of the sights of the city.

In the streets will be seen people of all races. Though young Indian girls usually wear European dress, when they are grown up they return to the sari, whose bright colors are to be seen on every hand. Many Muslim men wear the fez, and occasionally— but now a rare sight—may be seen some old humble man who wears the traditional clothes of the lowly laborer. Many Europeans will be seen also, mostly women out shopping. But the most striking sight will be Zulu women in tribal dress; they have probably come considerable distances to visit their husbands in Durban, and they cannot but attract attention when they walk unconcernedly through the streets of this twentieth-century city.

VAN WYCK BROOKS

CARMEL, CALIFORNIA

Van Wyck Brooks (1886-1963), essayist and critic, led 20th-century literary historians in their search into and revaluation of the American cultural past. From his America's Coming-of-Age *(1915) to his account of American writers and artists in Italy in* The Dream of Arcadia *(1958), he engaged in presenting and reinterpreting the artistic history of the United States. His most notable achievement is his literary history,* Makers and Finders, *consisting of* The Flowering of New England *(1936),* New England: Indian Summer *(1940),* The World of Washington Irving *(1944),* The Times of Melville and Whitman *(1947), and* The Confident Years *(1952). It is from* Scenes and Portraits *(1954), his "memories of childhood and youth," that the following view of Carmel comes.*

IN CARMEL I spent several months before the college term began and I undertook to teach at Leland Stanford, living in the alfresco fashion that everybody practised on this quite romantic peninsula of Monterey. The wild past was still present there with even the remains of an outlaw's camp, the hut of Joaquin Murieta in the San José canyon, where Easter lilies grew as daisies grow elsewhere; and there was the forest scenery that Robert Louis Stevenson, after his visit, pictured in *Treasure Island.* There were the white-washed Mexican shanties of John Steinbeck's *Tortilla Flat* and the old adobe house where John Steinbeck himself was living when I returned to the peninsula later, one of those dwellings with Castilian roses covering the red-tiled roofs that survived from the old Spanish Mexican colonial times. If, moreover, one no longer saw the caballeros of the eighteen-forties with strings of bells on their embroidered pantaloons, Jaime de Angulo, with his Arab horse and his red sash and El Greco beard, had all the look of a revenant from that earlier time. This was the Spanish ethnologist-doctor who had lived with the Indians in the Southwest, where he collected the Indian tales that he was to put into final form as a dying man forty years later on his mountain-top ranch. There was never a figure more fantastic than Jaime de Angulo came to be in those days when, living alone, looking out at the Pacific, a decayed Don Quixote, ragged and mad, he boxed with a pet stallion and carved his meat with a great knife that hung from his middle. But Carmel at all times abounded in every sort of anomalous type,—for one, the old newspaper-correspondent who conversed every night with the people of Mars and had twelve typewritten volumes of these conversations. George Sterling, the poet, who had precisely the aspect of Dante in hell, a suicide later, like his wife, haunted Point Lobos where the poetess Nora French had leaped from the cliff; while others who had come from the East to write novels in this paradise found themselves there becalmed and supine. They gave themselves over to day-dreams while their minds ran down like clocks, as if they had lost the keys to wind them up with, and they turned into beachcombers, listlessly reading books they had read ten times before and searching the rocks for abalones. For this Arcadia lay, one felt, outside the world in which thought evolves and which came to seem insubstantial in the bland sunny air.

I often felt in Carmel that I was immobilized, living as if in a fresco of Puvis de Chavannes, for there was something Theocritean, something Sicilian or Greek, in this afternoon land of olive trees, honey-bees and shepherds. There was also, down by the Big Sur, or, rather, beyond on the coastal trail, a no man's country as far as San Luis Obispo, a wilderness, sinister and dark, where, supposedly, robbers dwelt, another "Rogues' Harbour" like that of old Kentucky. One heard all manner of ominous tales of mysterious people hiding there, murderers who had escaped there, renegade whites and outcast Indians living in huts and caves, and the evil that seemed to brood over the region was all the stranger and more marked because of the splendid beauty of the mountainous coast. Even the lonely upland ranches that straggled by the road, northward from the Big Sur, overhanging the ocean, seemed somehow accursed or sad as one passed them on foot, as I did that first year on a three days' ramble, stopping at one ranch, for instance, where a tragic-looking woman was living quite alone with her steers and her sheep. At another ranch a burly bruiser with the look of a Mexican Brigham Young was riding with a troop of women, lashing his cattle. Long before Robinson Jeffers had published his poems about that coast one felt there a lurking possibility of monstrous things.

MARK TWAIN

THE HOUSE BEAUTIFUL

Mark Twain (pseudonym of Samuel Langhorne Clemens; 1835-1910) epito-
mizes American humor. Born in Florida, Missouri, and brought up in nearby
Hannibal on the Mississippi River, Clemens led a "various" youth and
young manhood as a journeyman printer, steamboat pilot, newspaper re-
porter, prospector in Nevada and California, and free-lance writer of travel
sketches before settling down to married respectability in Hartford, Connecti-
cut, as a novelist, an essayist, and a humorous lecturer. Through the persona
of Mark Twain, he came to be the national wit of his day. His travel books
include The Innocents Abroad *(1869),* Roughing It *(1872), and* A Tramp
Abroad *(1880). Two of his novels,* The Adventures of Tom Sawyer *(1876)*
and The Adventures of Huckleberry Finn *(1885) are—or used to be—part*
of the cultural experience of every American. From Life on the Mississippi
(1883) comes the following selection, which shows Mark Twain at his
humorous best, telling mainly the truth, but with some "stretchers."

WE TOOK PASSAGE in a Cincinnati boat for New Orleans; or on
a Cincinnati boat—either is correct; the former is the Eastern
form of putting it, the latter the Western.

Mr. Dickens declined to agree that the Mississippi steamboats
were "magnificent," or that they were "floating palaces"—terms
which had always been applied to them; terms which did not
overexpress the admiration with which the people viewed them.

Mr. Dickens's position was unassailable, possibly; the people's
position was certainly unassailable. If Mr. Dickens was comparing
these boats with the crown jewels; or with the Taj, or with the
Matterhorn; or with some other priceless or wonderful thing
which he had seen, they were not magnificent—he was right.
The people compared them with what *they* had seen; and, thus
measured, thus judged, the boats were magnificent—the term was
the correct one, it was not at all too strong. The people were
as right as was Mr. Dickens. The steamboats were finer than
anything on shore. Compared with superior dwelling-houses and

»»» "The House Beautiful," Ch. 38 of *Life on the Mississippi*, 1883, by Mark
Twain. Reprinted by permission of Harper & Row, Publishers.

first-class hotels in the valley, they were indubitably magnificent, they were "palaces." To a few people living in New Orleans and St. Louis they were not magnificent, perhaps; not palaces; but to the great majority of those populations, and to the entire populations spread over both banks between Baton Rouge and St. Louis, they were palaces; they tallied with the citizen's dream of what magnificence was, and satisfied it.

Every town and village along that vast stretch of double river-frontage had a best dwelling, finest dwelling, mansion— the home of its wealthiest and most conspicuous citizen. It is easy to describe it: large grassy yard, with paling fence painted white—in fair repair; brick walk from gate to door; big, square, two-story "frame" house, painted white and porticoed like a Grecian temple—with this difference, that the imposing fluted columns and Corinthian capitals were a pathetic sham, being made of white pine, and painted; iron knocker; brass door-knob —discolored, for lack of polishing. Within, an uncarpeted hall, of planed boards; opening out of it, a parlor, fifteen feet by fifteen—in some instances five or ten feet larger; ingrain carpet; mahogany center-table; lamp on it, with green-paper shade— standing on a gridiron, so to speak, made of high-colored yarns, by the young ladies of the house, and called a lamp-mat; several books, piled and disposed, with cast-iron exactness, according to an inherited and unchangeable plan; among them, Tupper, much penciled; also, *Friendship's Offering*, and *Affection's Wreath*, with their sappy inanities illustrated in die-away mezzo-tints; also, Ossian; *Alonzo and Melissa;* maybe *Ivanhoe;* also "Album," full of original "poetry" of the Thou-hast-wounded-the-spirit-that-loved-thee breed; two or three goody-goody works —*Shepherd of Salisbury Plain*, etc.; current number of the chaste and innocuous *Godey's Lady's Book*, with painted fashion-plate of wax-figure women with mouths all alike—lips and eyelids the same size—each five-foot woman with a two-inch wedge sticking from under her dress and letting on to be half of her foot. Polished air-tight stove (new and deadly invention), with pipe passing through a board which closes up the discarded good old fireplace. On each end of the wooden mantel, over the fireplace, a large basket of peaches and other fruits, natural size, all done in plaster, rudely, or in wax, and painted to resemble the originals—which they don't. Over middle of mantel, engraving—"Washington Crossing the Delaware"; on the wall by the door, copy of it done in thunder-and-lightning crewels by one of the young ladies—work of art which would have made Washington hesitate about crossing, if he could have foreseen what advantage was going to be taken of it. Piano—kettle in disguise— with music, bound and unbound, piled on it, and on a stand near by: "Battle of Prague"; "Bird Waltz"; "Arkansas Traveler"; "Rosin the Bow"; "Marseillaise Hymn"; "On a Lone Barren Isle" (St. Helena); "The Last Link Is Broken"; "She Wore a Wreath of Roses the Night When Last We Met"; "Go, Forget Me, Why Should Sorrow o'er That Brow a Shadow Fling"; "Hours That Were to Memory Dearer"; "Long, Long Ago"; "Days of Absence"; "A Life on the Ocean Wave, a Home on the Rolling Deep"; "Bird at Sea"; and spread open on the rack where the plaintive singer has left it, "*Ro*-holl on, silver *moo*-hoon, guide the *trav*-el-err on his *way*," etc. Tilted pensively against the piano, a guitar—guitar capable of playing the Spanish fandango by itself, if you give it a start. Frantic work of art on the wall—pious motto, done on the premises, sometimes in colored yarns, sometimes in faded grasses: progenitor of the "God Bless Our Home" of modern commerce. Framed in black moldings on the wall, other works of art, conceived and committed on the premises, by the young ladies; being grim black-and-white crayons; landscapes, mostly: lake, solitary sailboat, petrified clouds, pregeological trees on shore, anthracite precipice; name of criminal conspicuous in the corner. Lithograph, "Napoleon Crossing the Alps." Lithograph, "The Grave at St. Helena." Steel plates, Trumbull's "Battle of Bunker Hill," and the "Sally from Gibraltar." Copper plates, "Moses Smiting the Rock," and "Return of the Prodigal Son." In big gilt frame, slander of the family in oil: papa holding a book ("Constitution of the United States"); guitar leaning against mamma, blue ribbons fluttering from its neck; the young ladies, as children, in slippers and scalloped pantalettes, one embracing toy horse, the other beguiling kitten with ball of yarn, and both simpering up at mamma, who simpers back. These persons all fresh, raw, and red—apparently skinned. Opposite, in gilt frame, grandpa and grandma, at thirty and twenty-two, stiff, old-fashioned, high-collared, puff-sleeved, glaring pallidly out from a background of solid Egyptian night. Under a glass French clock dome, large bouquet of stiff flowers done in corpsy-white wax. Pyramidal what-not in the corner, the shelves occupied chiefly with bric-à-brac of the period, disposed with an eye to best effect: shell, with the Lord's Prayer carved on it; another shell—of the long-oval sort, narrow, straight orifice, three inches long, running from end to end—portrait of Washington carved on it; not well done; the shell had Washington's mouth, originally—artist should have built to that. These two are memorials of the long-ago bridal trip to New Orleans and the French Market. Other bric-à-brac: Californian "specimens"—quartz, with gold wart adhering; old Guinea-gold locket, with circlet of ancestral hair in it; Indian arrow-heads, of flint; pair of bead moccasins, from uncle who crossed the Plains; three "alum" baskets of various colors —being skeleton-frame of wire, clothed on with cubes of crystallized alum in the rock-candy style—works of art which were achieved by the young ladies; their doubles and duplicates to be found upon all what-nots in the land; convention of desiccated bugs and butterflies pinned to a card; painted toy dog, seated upon bellows attachment—drops its under-jaw and squeaks when pressed upon; sugar-candy rabbit—limbs and features merged together, not strongly defined; pewter presidential-campaign medal; miniature cardboard wood-sawyer, to be attached to the stovepipe and operated by the heat; small Napoleon, done in wax; spread-open daguerreo-types of dim children, parents, cousins, aunts, and friends, in all attitudes but customary ones; no templed portico at back, and manufactured landscape stretching away in the distance—that came in later, with the photograph; all these vague figures lavishly chained and ringed—metal indicated and secured from doubt by stripes and splashes of vivid gold bronze;

all of them too much combed, too much fixed up; and all of them
uncomfortable in inflexible Sunday clothes of a pattern which the
spectator cannot realize could ever have been in fashion; husband
and wife generally grouped together—husband sitting, wife standing, with hand on his shoulder—and both preserving, all these
fading years, some traceable effect of the daguerreotypist's brisk
"Now smile, if you please!" Bracketed over what-not—place of
special sacredness—an outrage in watercolor, done by the young
niece that came on a visit long ago, and died. Pity, too; for she
might have repented of this in time. Horsehair chairs, horsehair
sofa which keeps sliding from under you. Window-shades, of oil
stuff, with milkmaids and ruined castles stenciled on them in
fierce colors. Lambrequins dependent from gaudy boxings of
beaten tin, gilded. Bedrooms with rag carpets; bedsteads of the
"corded" sort, with a sag in the middle, the cords needing tighten-
ing; snuffy feather-bed—not aired often enough; cane-seat chairs,
splint-bottomed rocker; looking-glass on wall, school-slate size,
veneered frame; inherited bureau; wash-bowl and pitcher, possibly—but not certainly; brass candlestick, tallow candle, snuffers.
Nothing else in the room. Not a bathroom in the house; and no
visitor likely to come along who has ever seen one.

That was the residence of the principal citizen, all the way
from the suburbs of New Orleans to the edge of St. Louis. When
he stepped aboard a big fine steamboat, he entered a new and
marvelous world: chimney-tops cut to counterfeit a spraying
crown of plumes—and maybe painted red; pilot-house, hurricane-
deck, boiler-deck guards, all garnished with white wooden
filigree-work of fanciful patterns; gilt acorns topping the derricks;
gilt deer-horns over the big bell; gaudy symbolical picture on the
paddle-box, possibly; big roomy boiler-deck, painted blue, and
furnished with Windsor armchairs; inside, a far-receding snow-
white "cabin"; porcelain knob and oil-picture on every stateroom
door; curving patterns of filigree-work touched up with gilding,
stretching overhead all down the converging vista; big chandeliers
every little way, each an April shower of glittering glass-drops;
lovely rainbow-light falling everywhere from the colored glazing

of the skylights; the whole a long-drawn, resplendent tunnel, a bewildering and soul-satisfying spectacle! in the ladies' cabin a pink
and white Wilton carpet, as soft as mush, and glorified with a
ravishing pattern of gigantic flowers. Then the Bridal Chamber—
the animal that invented that idea was still alive and unhanged,
at that day—Bridal Chamber whose pretentious flummery was
necessarily overawing to the now tottering intellect of that hosan-
nahing citizen. Every stateroom had its couple of cozy clean
bunks, and perhaps a looking-glass and a snug closet; and sometimes there was even a wash-bowl and pitcher, and part of a
towel which could be told from mosquito-netting by an expert—
though generally these things were absent, and the shirt-sleeved
passengers cleansed themselves at a long row of stationary bowls
in the barber shop, where were also public towels, public combs,
and public soap.

Take the steamboat which I have just described, and you have
her in her highest and finest, and most pleasing, and comfortable,
and satisfactory estate. Now cake her over with a layer of ancient
and obdurate dirt, and you have the Cincinnati steamer awhile
ago referred to. Not all over—only inside; for she was ably
officered in all departments except the steward's.

But wash that boat and repaint her, and she would be about
the counterpart of the most complimented boat of the old flush
times: for the steamboat architecture of the West has undergone
no change; neither has steamboat furniture and ornamentation
undergone any.

GEORGE BOURNE

KEEPING CHRISTMAS

George Bourne (pseudonym of George Sturt; 1863-1927) wrote more than ten books about English country life. Though he had published six books before 1920, it was not until then that he gave up management of the family business, a wheelwright's shop in Farnham, England, his birthplace, and devoted himself entirely to writing. His best-known books are Change in the Village *(1912) and* The Wheelwright's Shop *(1923), both describing a way of life that was then passing and has now passed.*

GREEDINESS, not so much for food as for what I was to get in the shape of presents, seems to have dulled my memory too much in those yearly gatherings at the farm which it would be pleasant to recall now if the recollections were there to be recalled, and has left remembrance chiefly of my greed. For instance, I have not forgotten how defrauded I felt to receive a present of clothes, instead of a really desirable toy, or to get a "Church Service" (its covers brass-edged, and uneven enough to jag your skin) instead of a book worth studying—a really good book about animals, or Indians, or coral islands. I remember these disillusionments: the touches of old English life that must have come so plentifully with them and would be so good to think of now have left scarcely a trace. There is an "atmosphere"—that is all. And even that may have come to me afterwards, from reading books, seeing pictures, hearing Christmas carols. Carols, in fact, were not much heard at Street Farm. None the less, the sentiment—of "Good King Wenceslas" perhaps, or of "I saw three Ships"—seems to have pervaded the whole festivity.

Lasting over two or three days, this festivity—a yearly affair as I have said—must have meant more extra work than one cares to contemplate, to the Aunt in charge of the farm; but it may well have been a happy occasion to the Grandmother. A reunion of her

»»» Ch. 3 of *William Smith: Potter and Farmer, 1790-1858.* London: Chatto & Windus, 1919. Pp. 26-35.

family it was for her: the chief function of it being, probably, the Christmas dinner.

Twenty-one people at any rate, if not more, sat down to this meal, in the big kitchen. Sheets had been spread over the bacon flitches, to take chance contact with best coats or frocks. About half way down the room, with her back to the hearth, sat the Grandmother; her daughter Susan took the head of the table, to be handy for getting out to the copper and the cooking arrangements in the outbuildings at the back. There, at that end of the table, she carved the roast beef: while at the other end, back to window, a son-in-law carved the boiled—the "silverside," as I heard it called. Plenty of aunts and uncles and cousins filled the other places. But they were nothing to me. I was there myself—near the sitting-room door, so that was all right. It was "Christmas," and nothing else mattered. I don't even remember what there was to eat, besides the beef. I do surmise that a Christmas pudding with a sprig of holly in it was brought in at a later stage. Yet it isn't the pudding itself I recollect, so much as the Aunt's consternation one year, drowned in merriment from all her guests, at finding that pepper had been used instead of sugar in mixing the pudding. Other food—more noticeable though at suppertime—was mincepies, "scrap-pies," jam-tarts. These last were made as big as a dinner-plate, with fine crossbars of pastry atop, showing a good thick layer of jam. "Scraps"—very rich and tasty and indigestible—were fat slips and slithers of the inside of pig-meat, baked crisp and brown. When the Christmas dinner was over, all stood up and sang the verse that begins "Praise God from whom all blessings flow," by way of grace.

Good-tempered religiousness was never far away. The same company sometimes drew together in clusters in the sitting-room at night to sing hymns. Rather a waste of time, I always felt it, yet it didn't matter much, more pagan delights, with presents, being sure to come on the next day, and Christmas Day alone being frittered away with hymns. There was no instrumental music; the untutored singing was, almost certainly, an outrage from any artistic standpoint, yet in the retrospect it ranks with things as dear, as venerable, as, say, the little old churches and the ancient carols of England. The candlelight, or lamplight rather (I wish I could remember what the lamp looked like, or where it stood), was yellow, soft, and steady; the hymns were good to hear—at least so far as I remember—"Hark! the Herald Angels sing," and "Oh come, All ye Faithful."

If it didn't happen to be a Sunday, something more like a "sing-song" followed; and still a sentiment of earlier times prevailed, in the peaceful mellow lamplight. A purely sentimental gush applauded the Grandmother, when she could be induced to sing songs of her own girlhood. "Before the bright sun rises over the hill," was one of these ditties, sung to the tune of "My lodging's on the cold ground." Another was "Woodland Mary"—the tune of it very warbling and suggestive of the eighteenth century.

Here too I heard a song—"Oh, Happy Tawny Moor," besides one—"We'll give to the belly, boys, ale enough," which left me wondering who the belly boys could be. But the real delight was a couple of songs contributed by an uncle (Uncle Bill the Potter). He gave us an echo of Napoleon's war—"The Local Militia Lads," which went somehow like this:

"Your wicked plots are all found out, Bonay it will not do.
The Lo-o-cal Militia Lads will soon be after you."

"For the fifes and drums shall rattle and the bands shall sweetly play,
And the Lo-o-cal Militia Lads will boldly march away."

Better still was "Bright Phœbus hath mounted his Chariot of Day." I have sometimes suspected that a priggish laughter from the younger generation may have made the singer unwilling to do more: for some of us felt "superior"—good heavens!—and may have laughed too freely, at—what? I only know I laughed, though I never really saw any joke. Somebody had taught me it was "funny" that the Uncle had translated "chariot" into "char-yot." Many subsequent years have brought proof enough that it was a sort of privilege to hear the Wessex dialect and to see a Wessex countryman—broad-faced, twinkling-eyed—enjoying Christmas by the fireside of a genuine English farm.

It came rather as a shock to me to learn—not so many years ago—that the Christmas tree was an innovation at the farm, very little older than myself. I had always thought the evening given over to that delight a real survival of the most ancient folk-life. It was the one evening of the year; a spangled candle-lit greenery that beckoned across the seasons, with messages from far-off generations. I know better now: but so it truly seemed. Besides, the Christmas presents were brought down from the "birdy room" cupboard for that evening, making it, for me, an orgy of delight. It's unlikely that I thought anything about old times in the rapture of having new things.

Christmas trees are probably all much alike—though, in my own private mind, all others I ever heard of at the time were poor trumpery things, compared to this splendour in the kitchen at the old farm. There was, however, one feature most likely singular. On the floor all round the tree stood a ring of wax candles not much bigger than a pipe-stem, pushed each into a lump of clay for a candlestick. The lumps of clay—about as big as a hen's egg—were brought of course from Uncle Bill's pottery especially for this occasion. But the use of wet clay for an impromptu candlestick was no new thing. It was, rather, a piece of real English folk-life.

On another evening—it cannot have been the same as that of the Christmas-tree party—came the Mummers. You may read about this play in Hardy's "Return of the Native," but I saw it with my own eyes—not a revival by patronizing culture, but a true survival from the Middle Ages. I need not have hidden my sight in terror on my mother's knees. Yet how was I to know? When the street door opened upon the wintry night, and oddly dressed men came shambling into our lamp-lit kitchen out of the dark, how was I to guess that this clattering intrusion must have been all arranged beforehand? or that those figures in their gay ribbon and tinsel were only quiet villagers—Bill Russell, for instance, the farm lad? Bill Russell had been sitting by the kitchen fire—at the gloomier side, to be sure—only the evening before. And then that Mr. Ray. A joke arose about his name: for in answer to an uncle (by marriage), he called himself "Ray, sir."

Had he said "Racer" or "Razor"? There was a laugh about it, and to me it seemed witty beyond words. But this was when the show was over, and those fierce strangers had ceased to be terrible and begun to talk like safe, happy countryfolk again.

I didn't see all the show, then, yet plucked up courage to see that it had to do with a feud between a Turkish Knight and King George, with a Doctor and others intervening. I saw their dread wooden-sword play on the space cleared for them before the hearth; saw King George (I expect he was "Gearge") fall down with a flump, dead; saw the Doctor come forward then and bring him to life again, with a patent application. "Some calls it 'Okum-pocum,'" the Doctor said solemnly, as he bent over the body, "Some calls it 'Okum-pocum,' some calls it 'Inkum Pinkum'; but the right name is 'Elicompayne.'"

Yet what pleased most was Little Jumping Jack, because he was so screamingly humorous. As he said his piece:

> "Here comes I, little Jumping Jack,
>   With me wife and family at my back,"

he turned round; and there, sure enough, on his back was his wife and family—a row of Dutch dolls sewn on. Was such a funny thing ever heard of? Had it ever entered the wit of man to conceive so subtle a joke?

Wonders like these, it should be understood, were interruptions —joyous interruptions—to the prattle and games of children that were more or less continuous. For there were plenty of children— little boys and girls I have since learned to like, though I can hardly recover any impression of them from those old times. The games we had didn't often appeal to me strongly—they weren't romping enough; they were too formal, overdone with a singing ritual, too much of girls' games, in fact. What could a toddling boy do with "Tom Tiddler's Ground" or "Oranges and Lemons"? Silly stuff, I thought it. "Sheep, sheep, come home," wasn't so bad. It lent itself to real fun in scampering and wrestling.

Yet one game there was which, silly though I felt it then, suggests to me now one curious element that must have characterized all our play and prattle. We were little "countrified" children, carrying on our small doings with more or less of a dialect. The game went to the words,

"Chickamy, chickamy, Chany Trow."*

So at least we said. But long afterwards it dawned upon me that "Chaney Trow" was probably "China Trough," and that we had really been singing a broad Hampshire dialect, hundreds of years old.

Singing it; yes, and perhaps thinking its thoughts. At any rate one thing, older than the Reformation, remains from all that else forgotten chatter. For, while I am not sure that it was then I heard nice shuddering tales about Spring-heeled Jack (though I think it must have been then), I am quite sure it was on one of those Christmas nights I heard about the strange doings in the stable and the cowstalls. According to Corston, the carter, at midnight on Christmas Eve (or it may have been the night of Christmas Day) the horses in the stable and the cows in the stalls went down on their knees in worship of the newborn Christ.

Corston, it's true, was said to be an Irishman and a Roman Catholic. We didn't think that right. Yet still, who should know about the horses if he didn't, so fond of them as he was? So we told the legend with bated breath, renewing, in our own small persons, an emotion that may very well have been common all over England in the days of Queen Mary.

Compton's cab used to come early in the morning after the Christmas revels, to take me away, with my mother. This was soon after dawn, and we had breakfast by candlelight in the kitchen. At that dim grey hour the kitchen fire, newly built up with turfs, looked black and smoky; one had to sit pretty close to it to keep warm in the wintry air. Already, though, villagers were coming for milk served off the dresser under the window.

*"Chickamy, chickamy, Chany Trow,
  Follow me biddies wherever I go.
  Please Old Dame Blue Block,
  Tell me what it is o'clock.
  One—Come again at two;" etc.

NARRATION

NARRATION is the relation of a sequence of events, usually, although not always, in the order of their occurrence. Sometimes an anecdote or a story of a real or an imagined happening is told with a minimum of commentary because the story implies or demonstrates its own significance without explanation from the writer. In fact, sometimes comment spoils a story; for instance, the teller of a joke who must explain its point bores us by remarking upon what is obvious and blunts instead of enhances the effect of his story. The clever humorist usually avoids interpreting his story; so do many writers of modern fiction, as well as the newspaper reporter writing a straight news story. Except for description of setting and persons, these writers aim at almost pure narration; they arrange the order of events and record details of the action and the spoken words of the persons concerned in such a way that the stories carry their own points. That is, the experience seems funny or tragic or whatever on the face of its own details, with the reader, instead of the writer, supplying the reaction or interpretation, although the writer may engineer the reader's reaction by his manner of telling the story. It can be seen that even such attempts at pure narration cannot be wholly noninterpretative; interpretation creeps in via a descriptive word, a stress upon a certain detail of the action, and the very choice of quotations.

Most narration, however, is combined with description, analysis, comparison, and other expository modes of discourse. In expository narration the sequence of events is interrupted by non-narrative remarks about the significance of the happenings, and the narration may end with a summary statement about its significance or may begin with a statement forecasting the purpose for telling the story. The modern historian, for instance, or the writer of the interpretative news story wishes to make explicit the point of his narrative; therefore he adds expository comments to his account. He may evaluate the importance of the events or draw a comparison between the particular events in his story and events in other stories of other persons, times, or places. He may even compare his story of a happening with another's story of it so as to show that his account is more faithful to the facts or more sound in interpreting their significance. By combining analysis and comparison with narration, he emphasizes that he tells the story not merely for its intrinsic interest of novelty, humor, or excitement but for the general propositions about life that he supposes the story to illustrate.

As narration is served by description and exposition, so narration in turn serves the other modes of discourse. A narrative example may help a writer of an analysis or a comparison make more vivid and clear the general idea he is setting forth. For example, narration runs through Friedlander's and Grutzner's news stories in "Definition," and Darwin in analyzing the effects of the Chilean earthquake in "Analysis" must also tell of the events that occurred, since they are the raw material upon which his analysis is based. A process explanation is a special kind of narration that outlines the sequential actions by which a process may be or has been performed. The selections in "Autobiography and Biography" are examples of expository narration.

The pieces that follow are more narrative than descriptive or expository, though they necessarily contain bits of description and exposition. Fitzgerald's narrative, based on facts of his own life humorously interpreted, is closer than the other pieces to a story in which the point ("How did we spend all that money? Why didn't we save some?") is implied instead of stated. He narrates the events scenically, for the most part, with a good deal of dialogue; yet he also generalizes in an expository way when speaking of himself and his wife as members of the "newly rich" class. Furthermore, his title suggests a pseudoexpository purpose of writing a process explanation about "How to Live on $36,000 a Year." Marjorie Kinnan Rawlings also develops her story with scene and dialogue, but she is more frankly expository than Fitzgerald and sets forth the purpose of her story at the end of the first paragraph by defining the "comfort" of her title in terms of plumbing. In telling the story of her first novels, Willa Cather analyzes her motives for writing them as she did and compares their subjects and the readers' reception of them. In their stories of sea battles, Sir Walter Ralegh and John P. Marquand are reportorial; generally, they keep to the sequence of events, rarely stopping for an analytical comment. Ralegh is more straightforward in his progression from one major incident to the next, whereas Marquand is more impressionistic and circumstantial in the details of scene and scraps of conversation that he records. Aubrey Menen acts mainly as a reporter of scene and dialogue in his story, though he half-states, half-implies the point of his story in the final paragraph.

F. SCOTT FITZGERALD

HOW TO LIVE ON $36,000 A YEAR

F. Scott Fitzgerald (1896-1940) was a popular novelist and short-story writer of the decade following World War I whose work has been reprinted and has met with such critical favor among the postwar generation of World War II that some critics count him among the major novelists of the century. Born in St. Paul and educated at Princeton, he scored an instant hit with his first novel, This Side of Paradise *(1920), a story of undergraduate life at Princeton. His short stories in* The Saturday Evening Post, The Red Book, Scribner's, McCall's, *and other magazines added to his popularity and were collected in* Flappers and Philosophers *(1920),* Tales of the Jazz Age *(1922),* All the Sad Young Men *(1926), and* Taps at Reveille *(1935). His later novels include* The Beautiful and Damned *(1922),* The Great Gatsby *(1925), and* Tender Is the Night *(1934). The following article, first published in* The Saturday Evening Post *of April 5, 1924, recreates for today's readers the mood of the 'Twenties, as does most of Fitzgerald's work.*

"YOU OUGHT to start saving money," The Young Man With a Future assured me just the other day. "You think it's smart to live up to your income. Some day you'll land in the poorhouse."

I was bored, but I knew he was going to tell me anyhow, so I asked him what I'd better do.

"It's very simple," he answered impatiently; "only you establish a trust fund where you can't get your money if you try."

I had heard this before. It is System Number 999. I tried System Number 1 at the very beginning of my literary career four years ago. A month before I was married I went to a broker and asked his advice about investing some money.

"It's only a thousand," I admitted, "but I feel I ought to begin to save right now."

He considered.

"You don't want Liberty Bonds," he said. "They're too easy to turn into cash. You want a good, sound, conservative investment, but also you want it where you can't get at it every five minutes."

He finally selected a bond for me that paid 7 per cent and wasn't listed on the market. I turned over my thousand dollars, and my career of amassing capital began that day.

On that day, also, it ended.

THE HEIRLOOM NO ONE WOULD BUY

My wife and I were married in New York in the spring of 1920, when prices were higher than they had been within the memory of man. In the light of after events it seems fitting that our career should have started at that precise point in time. I had just received a large check from the movies and I felt a little patronizing toward the millionaires riding down Fifth Avenue in their limousines—because my income had a way of doubling every month. This was actually the case. It had done so for several months—I had made only thirty-five dollars the previous August, while here in April I was making three thousand—and it seemed as if it was going to do so forever. At the end of the year it must reach half a million. Of course with such a state of affairs, economy seemed a waste of time. So we went to live at the most expensive hotel in New York, intending to wait there until enough money accumulated for a trip abroad .

To make a long story short, after we had been married for three months I found one day to my horror that I didn't have a dollar in the world, and the weekly hotel bill for two hundred dollars would be due next day.

I remember the mixed feelings with which I issued from the bank on hearing the news.

"What's the matter?" demanded my wife anxiously, as I joined her on the sidewalk. "You look depressed."

"I'm not depressed," I answered cheerfully; "I'm just surprised. We haven't got any money."

"Haven't got any money," she repeated calmly, and we began to walk up the Avenue in a sort of trance. "Well, let's go to the movies," she suggested jovially.

It all seemed so tranquil that I was not a bit cast down. The cashier had not even scowled at me. I had walked in and said to him, "How much money have I got?" And he had looked in a big book and answered, "None."

That was all. There were no harsh words, no blows. And I knew that there was nothing to worry about. I was now a successful author, and when successful authors ran out of money all they had to do was to sign checks. I wasn't poor—they couldn't fool me. Poverty meant being depressed and living in a small remote room and eating at a *rôtisserie* on the corner, while I—why, it was impossible that I should be poor! I was living at the best hotel in New York!

My first step was to try to sell my only possession—my $1000 bond. It was the first of many times I made the attempt; in all financial crises I dig it out and with it go hopefully to the bank, supposing that, as it never fails to pay the proper interest, it has at last assumed a tangible value. But as I have never been able to sell it, it has gradually acquired the sacredness of a family heirloom. It is always referred to by my wife as "your bond," and it was once turned in at the Subway offices after I left it by accident on a car seat!

This particular crisis passed next morning when the discovery that publishers sometimes advance royalties sent me hurriedly to mine. So the only lesson I learned from it was that my money usually turns up somewhere in time of need, and that at the worst you can always borrow—a lesson that would make Benjamin Franklin turn over in his grave.

For the first three years of our marriage our income averaged a little more than $20,000 a year. We indulged in such luxuries as a baby and a trip to Europe, and always money seemed to come easier and easier with less and less effort, until we felt that with just a little more margin to come and go on, we could begin to save.

PLANS

We left the Middle West and moved East to a town about fifteen miles from New York, where we rented a house for $300 a month.

We hired a nurse for $90 a month; a man and his wife—they acted as butler, chauffeur, yard man, cook, parlor maid and chambermaid—for $160 a month; and a laundress, who came twice a week, for $36 a month. This year of 1923, we told each other, was to be our saving year. We were going to earn $24,000, and live on $18,000, thus giving us a surplus of $6,000 with which to buy safety and security for our old age. We were going to do better at last.

Now as everyone knows, when you want to do better you first buy a book and print your name in the front of it in capital letters. So my wife bought a book, and every bill that came to the house was carefully entered in it, so that we could watch living expenses and cut them away to almost nothing—or at least to $1,500 a month.

We had, however, reckoned without our town. It is one of those little towns springing up on all sides of New York which are built especially for those who have made money suddenly but have never had money before.

My wife and I are, of course, members of this newly rich class. That is to say, five years ago we had no money at all, and what we now do away with would have seemed like inestimable riches to us then. I have at times suspected that we are the only newly rich people in America, that in fact we are the very couple at whom all the articles about the newly rich were aimed.

Now when you say "newly rich" you picture a middle-aged and corpulent man who has a tendency to remove his collar at formal dinners and is in perpetual hot water with his ambitious wife and her titled friends. As a member of the newly rich class, I assure you that this picture is entirely libelous. I myself, for example, am a mild, slightly used young man of twenty-seven, and what corpulence I may have developed is for the present a strictly confidential matter between my tailor and me. We once dined with a bona fide nobleman, but we were both far too frightened to take off our collars or even to demand corned beef and cabbage. Nevertheless we live in a town prepared for keeping money in circulation.

When we came here, a year ago, there were, all together, seven merchants engaged in the purveyance of food—three grocers, three butchers and a fisherman. But when the word went around in food-purveying circles that the town was filling up with the recently enriched as fast as houses could be built for them, the rush of butchers, grocers, fishmen and delicatessen men became enormous. Trainloads of them arrived daily with signs and scales in hand to stake out a claim and sprinkle sawdust upon it. It was like the gold rush of '49, or a big bonanza of the 70's. Older and larger cities were denuded of their stores. Inside of a year eighteen food dealers had set up shop in our main street and might be seen any day waiting in their doorways with alluring and deceitful smiles.

Having long been somewhat overcharged by the seven previous food purveyors we all naturally rushed to the new men, who made it known by large numerical signs in their windows that they intended practically to give food away. But once we were snared, the prices began to rise alarmingly, until all of us scurried like frightened mice from one new man to another, seeking only justice, and seeking it in vain.

GREAT EXPECTATIONS

What had happened, of course, was that there were too many food purveyors for the population. It was absolutely impossible for eighteen of them to subsist on the town and at the same time charge moderate prices. So each was waiting for some of the others to give up and move away; meanwhile the only way the rest of them could carry their loans from the bank was by selling things at two or three times the prices in the city fifteen miles away. And that is how our town became the most expensive one in the world.

Now in magazine articles people always get together and found community stores, but none of us would consider such a step. It would absolutely ruin us with our neighbors, who would suspect that we actually cared about our money. When I suggested one day to a local lady of wealth—whose husband, by the way, is reputed to have made his money by vending illicit liquids —that I start a community store known as "F. Scott Fitzgerald— Fresh Meats," she was horrified. So the idea was abandoned.

But in spite of the groceries, we began the year in high hopes. My first play was to be presented in the autumn, and even if living in the East forced our expenses a little over $1,500 a month, the play would easily make up for the difference. We knew what colossal sums were earned on play royalties, and just to be sure, we asked several playwrights what was the maximum that could be earned on a year's run. I never allowed myself to be rash. I took a sum halfway between the maximum and the minimum, and put that down as what we could fairly count on its earning. I think my figures came to about $100,000.

It was a pleasant year; we always had this delightful event of the play to look forward to. When the play succeeded we could buy a house, and saving money would be so easy that we could do it blindfolded with both hands tied behind our backs.

As if in happy anticipation we had a small windfall in March from an unexpected source—a moving picture—and for almost the first time in our lives we had enough surplus to buy some bonds. Of course we had "my" bond, and every six months I clipped the little coupon and cashed it, but we were so used to it that we never counted it as money. It was simply a warning never to tie up cash where we couldn't get at it in time of need.

No, the thing to buy was Liberty Bonds, and we bought four of them. It was a very exciting business. I descended to a shining and impressive room downstairs, and under the chaperonage of a guard deposited my $4,000 in Liberty Bonds, together with "my" bond, in a little tin box to which I alone had the key.

LESS CASH THAN COMPANY

I left the bank, feeling decidedly solid. I had at last accumulated a capital. I hadn't exactly accumulated it, but there it was anyhow, and if I had died next day it would have yielded my wife $212 a year for life—or for just as long as she cared to live on that amount.

"That," I said to myself with some satisfaction, "is what is called providing for the wife and children. Now all I have to do is to deposit the $100,000 from my play and then we're through with worry forever."

I found that from this time on I had less tendency to worry about current expenses. What if we did spend a few hundred too much now and then? What if our grocery bills did vary mysteriously from $85 to $165 a month, according as to how closely we watched the kitchen? Didn't I have bonds in the bank? Trying to keep under $1,500 a month the way things were going was merely niggardly. We were going to save on a scale that would make such petty economies seem like counting pennies.

The coupons on "my" bond are always sent to an office on lower Broadway. Where Liberty Bond coupons are sent I never had a chance to find out, as I didn't have the pleasure of clipping any. Two of them I was unfortunately compelled to dispose of just one month after I first locked them up. I had begun a new novel, you see, and it occurred to me it would be much better business in the end to keep at the novel and live on the Liberty Bonds while I was writing it. Unfortunately the novel progressed slowly, while the Liberty Bonds went at an alarming rate of speed. The novel was interrupted whenever there was any sound above a whisper in the house, while the Liberty Bonds were never interrupted at all.

And the summer drifted too. It was an exquisite summer and it became a habit with many world-weary New Yorkers to pass their week-ends at the Fitzgerald house in the country. Along near the end of a balmy and insidious August I realized with a shock that only three chapters of my novel were done—and in the little tin safety-deposit vault, only "my" bond remained. There it lay—paying storage on itself and a few dollars more. But never mind; in a little while the box would be bursting with savings. I'd have to hire a twin box next door.

But the play was going into rehearsal in two months. To tide over the interval there were two courses open to me—I could sit down and write some short stories or I could continue to work on the novel and borrow the money to live on. Lulled into a sense of security by our sanguine anticipations I decided on the latter course, and my publishers lent me enough to pay our bills until the opening night.

So I went back to my novel, and the months and money melted away; but one morning in October I sat in the cold interior of a New York theater and heard the cast read through the first act of my play. It was magnificent; my estimate had been too low. I could almost hear the people scrambling for seats, hear the ghostly voices of the movie magnates as they bid against one another for the picture rights. The novel was now laid aside; my days were spent at the theater and my nights in revising and improving the two or three little weak spots in what was to be the success of the year.

The time approached and life became a breathless affair. The November bills came in, were glanced at, and punched onto a bill file on the bookcase. More important questions were in the air. A disgusted letter arrived from an editor telling me I had written only two short stories during the entire year. But what did that matter? The main thing was that our second comedian got the wrong intonation in his first-act exit line.

The play opened in Atlantic City in November. It was a colossal frost. People left their seats and walked out, people rustled their programs and talked audibly in bored impatient whispers. After the second act I wanted to stop the show and say it was all a mistake but the actors struggled heroically on.

There was a fruitless week of patching and revising, and then we gave up and came home. To my profound astonishment the year, the great year, was almost over. I was $5,000 in debt, and my one idea was to get in touch with a reliable poorhouse where we could hire a room and bath for nothing a week. But one satisfaction nobody could take from us. We had spent $36,000, and purchased for one year the right to be members of the newly rich class. What more can money buy?

TAKING ACCOUNT OF STOCK

The first move, of course, was to get out "my" bond, take it to the bank and offer it for sale. A very nice old man at a shining table was firm as to its value as security, but he promised that if I became overdrawn he would call me up on the phone and give me a chance to make good. No, he never went to lunch with depositors. He considered writers a shiftless class, he said, and assured me that the whole bank was absolutely burglarproof from cellar to roof.

Too discouraged even to put the bond back in the now yawning deposit box, I tucked it gloomily into my pocket and went home. There was no help for it—I must go to work. I had exhausted my resources and there was nothing else to do. In the train I listed all our possessions on which, if it came to that, we could possibly raise money. Here is the list:

1   Oil stove, damaged.
9   Electric lamps, all varieties.
2   Bookcases with books to match.
1   Cigarette humidor, made by a convict.
2   Framed crayon portraits of my wife and me.
1   Medium-priced automobile, 1921 model.
1   Bond, par value $1,000; actual value unknown.

"Let's cut down expenses right away," began my wife when I reached home. "There's a new grocery in town where you pay cash and everything costs only half what it does anywhere else. I can take the car every morning and—"

"Cash!" I began to laugh at this. "Cash!"

The one thing it was impossible for us to do now was to pay cash. It was too late to pay cash. We had no cash to pay. We should rather have gone down on our knees and thanked the butcher and grocer for letting us charge. An enormous economic fact became clear to me at that moment—the rarity of cash, the latitude of choice that cash allows.

"Well," she remarked thoughtfully, "that's too bad. But at least we don't need three servants. We'll get a Japanese to do general housework, and I'll be nurse for a while until you get us out of danger."

"Let them go?" I demanded incredulously. "But we can't let them go! We'd have to pay them an extra two weeks each. Why, to get them out of the house would cost us $125—in cash! Besides, it's nice to have the butler; if we have an awful smash we can send him up to New York to hold us a place in the bread line."

"Well, then, how can we economize?"

"We can't. We're too poor to economize. Economy is a luxury. We could have economized last summer—but now our only salvation is in extravagance."

"How about a smaller house?"

"Impossible! Moving is the most expensive thing in the world; and besides, I couldn't work during the confusion. No," I went on, "I'll just have to get out of this mess the only way I know how, by making more money. Then when we've got something in the bank we can decide what we'd better do."

Over our garage is a large bare room whither I now retired with pencil, paper and the oil stove, emerging the next afternoon at five o'clock with a 7,000-word story. That was something; it would pay the rent and last month's overdue bills. It took twelve hours a day for five weeks to rise from abject poverty back into the middle class, but within that time we had paid our debts, and the cause for immediate worry was over.

But I was far from satisfied with the whole affair. A young man can work at excessive speed with no ill effects, but youth is unfortunately not a permanent condition of life.

I wanted to find out where the $36,000 had gone. Thirty-six thousand is not very wealthy—not yacht-and-Palm-Beach wealthy—but it sounds to me as though it should buy a roomy house full of furniture, a trip to Europe once a year, and a bond or two besides. But our $36,000 had bought nothing at all.

So I dug up my miscellaneous account books, and my wife dug up her complete household record for the year 1923, and we made out the monthly average. Here it is:

HOUSEHOLD EXPENSES

	Apportioned per Month
Income tax	$ 198.00
Food	202.00
Rent	300.00
Coal, wood, ice, gas, light, phone and water	114.50
Servants	295.00
Golf clubs	105.50
Clothes—three people	158.00
Doctor and dentist	42.50
Drugs and cigarettes	32.50
Automobile	25.00
Books	14.50
All other household expenses	112.50
Total	$1,600.00

"Well, that's not bad," we thought when we had got thus far. "Some of the items are pretty high, especially food and servants. But there's about everything accounted for, and it's only a little more than half our income."

Then we worked out the average monthly expenditures that could be included under pleasure.

Hotel bills—this meant spending the night or charging meals in New York	$ 51.00
Trips—only two, but apportioned per month	43.00
Theater tickets	55.00
Barber and hairdresser	25.00
Charity and loans	15.00
Taxis	15.00
Gambling—this dark heading covers bridge, craps and football bets	33.00
Restaurant parties	70.00
Entertaining	70.00
Miscellaneous	23.00
Total	$400.00

Some of these items were pretty high. They will seem higher to a Westerner than to a New Yorker. Fifty-five dollars for theater tickets means between three and five shows a month, depending on the type of show and how long it's been running. Football games are also included in this, as well as ringside seats to the Dempsey-Firpo fight. As for the amount marked "restaurant parties"—$70 would perhaps take three couples to a popular after-theater cabaret—but it would be a close shave.

We added the items marked "pleasure" to the items marked "household expenses," and obtained a monthly total.

"Fine," I said. "Just $3,000. Now at least we'll know where to cut down, because we know where it goes."

She frowned; then a puzzled, awed expression passed over her face.

"What's the matter?" I demanded. "Isn't it all right? Are some of the items wrong?"

"It isn't the items," she said staggeringly; "it's the total. This only adds up to $2,000 a month."

I was incredulous, but she nodded.

"But listen," I protested; "my bank statements show that we've spent $3,000 a month. You don't mean to say that every month we lose $1,000 dollars?"

"This only adds up to $2,000," she protested, "so we must have."

"Give me the pencil."

For an hour I worked over the accounts in silence, but to no avail.

"Why, this is impossible!" I insisted. "People don't lose $12,000 in a year. It's just—it's just missing."

There was a ring at the doorbell and I walked over to answer it, still dazed by these figures. It was the Banklands, our neighbors from over the way.

"Good heavens!" I announced. "We've just lost $12,000!"

Bankland stepped back alertly.

"Burglars?" he inquired.

"Ghosts," answered my wife.

Mrs. Bankland looked nervously around.

"Really?"

We explained the situation, the mysterious third of our income that had vanished into thin air.

"Well, what we do," said Mrs. Bankland, "is, we have a budget."

"We have a budget," agreed Bankland, "and we stick absolutely to it. If the skies fall we don't go over any item of that budget. That's the only way to live sensibly and save money."

"That's what we ought to do," I agreed.

Mrs. Bankland nodded enthusiastically.

"It's a wonderful scheme," she went on. "We make a certain deposit every month, and all I save on it I can have for myself to do anything I want with."

I could see that my own wife was visibly excited.

"That's what I want to do," she broke out suddenly. "Have a budget. Everybody does it that has any sense."

"I pity anyone that doesn't use that system," said Bankland solemnly. "Think of the inducement to economy—the extra money my wife'll have for clothes."

"How much have you saved so far?" my wife inquired eagerly of Mrs. Bankland.

"So far?" repeated Mrs. Bankland. "Oh, I haven't had a chance so far. You see we only began the system yesterday."

"Yesterday!" we cried.

"Just yesterday," agreed Bankland darkly. "But I wish to heaven I'd started it a year ago. I've been working over our accounts all week, and do you know, Fitzgerald, every month there's $2,000 I can't account for to save my soul."

HEADED TOWARD EASY STREET

Our financial troubles are now over. We have permanently left the newly rich class and installed the budget system. It is simple and sensible, and I can explain it to you in a few words. You consider your income as an enormous pie all cut up into slices, each slice representing one class of expenses. Somebody has worked it all out; so you know just what proportion of your income you can spend on each slice. There is even a slice for founding universities, if you go in for that.

For instance, the amount you spend on the theater should be half your drug-store bill. This will enable us to see one play every five and a half months, or two and a half plays a year. We have already picked out the first one, but if it isn't running five and a half months from now we shall be that much ahead. Our allowance for newspapers should be only a quarter of what we spend on self-improvement, so we are considering whether to get the Sunday paper once a month or to subscribe for an almanac.

According to the budget we will be allowed only three-quarters of a servant, so we are on the lookout for a one-legged cook who can come six days a week. And apparently the author of the budget book lives in a town where you can still go to the movies for a nickel and get a shave for a dime. But we are going to give up the expenditure called "Foreign missions, etc.," and apply it to the life of crime instead. Altogether, outside of the fact that there is no slice allowed for "missing" it seems to be a very complete book, and according to the testimonials in the back, if we make $36,000 again this year, the chances are that we'll save at least $35,000.

"But we can't get any of that first $36,000 back," I complained around the house. "If we just had something to show for it I wouldn't feel so absurd."

My wife thought a long while.

"The only thing you can do," she said finally, "is to write a magazine article and call it How to Live on $36,000 a Year."

"What a silly suggestion!" I replied coldly.

MARJORIE KINNAN RAWLINGS

THE EVOLUTION OF COMFORT

Marjorie Kinnan Rawlings (1896-1953), born in Washington, D. C., was educated at the University of Wisconsin. Beginning her writing career in newspaper and magazine work, she turned to the writing of fiction in 1931. Her first novels, South Moon Under *(1933) and* Golden Apples *(1935), were followed by her Pulitzer Prize winner,* The Yearling *(1938). A collection of short stories,* When the Whippoorwill—, *appeared in 1940; her last novel,* The Sojourner, *in 1953. From her autobiographic account of the Florida back country,* Cross Creek *(1942), comes the following selection.*

WHEN I FIRST CAME to the Creek, I had for facilities one water faucet in the kitchen, a tin shower adjoining the Kohler shed and an outhouse. For the water faucet in the kitchen I was always grateful, for water pumps at the Creek are all placed in relation to the well and with little or no concern with distance from the house. When Martha lived in the Mackay house she had even no well, but must carry water from the Creek itself. My outside shower was acceptable enough in summer, though it meant going damply over the sand to the house afterward. In cold weather— and you may believe the Chamber of Commerce that we have none, or you may believe me that on occasion bird-baths have been frozen solid—in cold weather the outside shower was a fit device for masochistic monks. The icy spray that attacked the shoulders like splinters of fine glass was in the nature of a cross. I shall not forget the early Christmas afternoon, with six men gathered for dinner, the turkey savory in the oven, the pies cooling, the vegetables ready, the necessity if not the desire for the bath borne in on me, and the temperature at thirty-eight and dropping. I emerged shivering and snarled at the indifferent heavens, "The first time I get my hands on cash money, so help me, I shall have a bathroom."

Because of the cold shower, open at the front to a wandering world, an unfriendly shower, I took to watching for rain like a tree-toad. For when the soft sluiceways of the skies opened and the lichened shingle roof shed the waters in a surge down the northwest sheltered corner of the house, I could strip and accept the benediction. When the day was hot the rain was cool. When the day was cool the rain was many degrees warmer, and as bland as perfumed bath powder. The water faucet and the shower, then, could be endured. It seemed to me that I had done nothing in all my life to deserve the outhouse.

It had been years since I had come any closer to one than James Whitcomb Riley's verses on the subject. But I could look back on them almost with nostalgia, for those I had known had a certain coziness and a definite privacy. One of my fondest recollections is of an outhouse in Virginia. It stood under a locust, at the top of a little rise of ground. The terrain before one sloped down past a corner of the flower-bed, bright with balsam and phlox, to a valley where a cornfield was bordered by a line of willows. The blue hills of Virginia lifted in the distance. Three walls of the outhouse were gay with travel posters from Switzerland, the Rhine and Brittany. It was pleasant to follow pensively the depicted trails, highways and views. On the fourth wall hung a sonnet in French, a charming and vulgar and beautifully composed bit of comment on the circumstances in which the reader found himself at the moment. All was conducive to a sense of well-being.

The outhouse on Grandfather's farm was papered with perfectly beautiful colored pictures of reigning queens. Alexandra was magnificent. Wilhelmina was demure and very pretty in pale pink with a pearl and diamond crown. I cannot look today at the news pictures of the stout housewife in tweeds on a bicycle and believe that it is the same woman. The queen of Norway I recall as rather austere, the queen of Italy as blackly horselike. But all were queens, in full color, in décolleté and jewelled diadems. The building had a door with crescent windows and it stood discreetly behind a hickory tree and was reached by a high trim boardwalk bordered with marigolds.

The outhouse that I inherited at the Creek had no boardwalk, it had no queens, no marigolds, it had, amazingly, no door. It stood on a direct line with the dining room windows. One fortunate diner might sit with his back to it. The others could not lift their eyes from their plates without meeting the wooden stare of the unhappy and misplaced edifice. They were fortunate if they did not meet as well the eye of a belated occupant, assuring himself stonily that he could not be seen. For there was indeed a wire screen, and this screen had been, or so the instigator fatuously pretended, modernized with camouflage. Streaks of gray paint zigzagged across the screening. The effect was to make of a human being seated behind it a monster. The monster had gray bolts of lightning for arms and moss-gray tree-trunks for legs. Possibly the head of a human tall enough might have lifted to meet and be shielded by another streak of gray paint, or one short enough might have been veiled entirely, but I never peeked in fascination at any occupant of the infernal box whose face did not gaze recognizably out in a silent and steely torment.

The camouflage, cruelly, worked perfectly when approached from the path. The result was that it was impossible to tell, until too late, whether a living thing was trapped behind it. It seemed for a time that Uncle Fred had solved this problem. Two days after his arrival on a visit he asked in a low, strained voice, "Do you have an old piece of bright flannel I could cut up?" His manner prohibited questioning. I had been here too short a time to have acquired scraps of cloth, but I brought out a ragged quilt, flaming red in color. His face brightened. He went solemnly away and a little later a two-foot-square red flag stood in the middle of the path just outside the outhouse. The technique was obvious and simple. When one went in, one placed the flag in the path. When one came out, one put the flag back inside the outhouse. One went in and put the flag in the path. One returned to the house, forgetting to put the flag back again. The flag stood like a red light against traffic, for hours and hours and hours.

These were only the day hazards. Only a pillar of fire by night would have seemed sufficient comfort and guidance, and this was never provided except by the dubious assistance of lightning. There were provided instead, none the less appalling because harmless, spiders, lizards, toads and thin squeaking noises made by bats. Over all the dark hours hung the fear of snakes. I had arrived in Florida with the usual ignorant terror. If time proved that the sight of a snake was a rarity, there was no help then for the conviction that the next footstep would fall on a coiled rattler. An imaginary snake is so much more fearful than a real one, that I should rather handle a rattlesnake, as I have done since, than dream of one. I dreaded the sunset, thinking of the dark box of the outhouse. And once there, even on the blessed nights of moonlight, the small ominous thuds against floor and wall that by day were the attractive little green tree-toads, by night were the advance of nameless reptiles. I would not yield to the temptation of installing in the house the old-fashioned "conveniences," for that was an admission of defeat. I would stick it out and the first cash money should go into a bathroom.

The first cash money from the first orange crop, a good one, disappeared into mortgage and note payments, fertilizer and a Ford, for the seven-passenger Cadillac, a shabby behemoth from more affluent northern days, had literally torn its heavy heart out on the deep sand road to the Creek, and was sold for sixty dollars to a Negro undertaker. He must have towed it with the hearse, for it was past repairing. There was a year of low citrus prices and a year of freeze. Then my first Florida story, *Jacob's Ladder,* brought in the fantastic sum of seven hundred dollars.

The instant that I saw this wealth begin to dissolve as usual, I worked rapidly. I would not do anything so reckless as ordering a complete new bathroom outfit, but would shop around and pick up something second-hand. The boom was over, and in abandoned houses in unsold "scrub divisions" bathroom fittings were gathering rust and discoloration. Inquiry aroused fresh boom hope in various owners of the unwanted houses and a toilet without a seat immediately became worth its weight in gold.

My good friend carpenter Moe was at work on the building of the bathroom. The farmhouse had been built casually in three separate eras, and while the gap between the front and the back was now filled in with a porch, there was nothing but space between the main part of the house and the two large bedrooms with fireplaces that made up a wing. One stepped into the air from what, we decided, was not a French door but an Irish door. That vacuum was providential for a bathroom. It would link the two bedrooms to the house as cozily as though an architect had planned it; a careless architect, perhaps, for a difference in floor levels meant a step down from the first bedroom that has proved no friend to the aged, the absent-minded and the inebriated. Moe was pounding away while I lamented that I should have to go to Sears Roebuck after all. He laid down his hammer and sat back on his heels.

"Why, I know a feller's got a bathroom outfit," he said. "Hain't never been used. Brand new, and he's got no more use fer it than a dog. Feller right over in Citra. You come by for me this evenin' and we'll go make you a trade. Now I'm plumb proud I remembered that feller's new bathroom outfit, jest settin' there."

Moe and I drove to Citra that night. I had the fortunate feeling that time has taught me to mistrust more than nightmares and bad omens. We stopped at a shabby house on a side street and the owner of the bathroom set, presumably so irrelevant to his life, came to the door.

"I told this lady you had a bathroom set you got no use for," Moe said. "Don't say I ain't a friend to you. She'll take it off your hands and pay cash money for it if the price is right."

A small gloomy man scowled at me and did not answer.

Moe persisted, "Ain't you got a set the Baptist preacher give you afore he died?"

"Tain't a set. It's just the toilet. It's mine, all right, but I ain't exactly got it."

"Ain't it handy, where you can git it?"

The little man came to angry life.

He shouted, "It's in the smokehouse to the Baptist parsonage and I'll git it when I'm o' mind to! They don't want I should take it but they can't stop me. I've had nothin' but meanness from the Baptists all my life and I'll go off with that toilet when I'm ready."

Moe said with deliberate aggravation, "Mebbe you cain't prove it's yourn."

"I got no call to prove it. Everybody knows how it come to be mine. The Baptists was too mean to put in runnin' water for Preacher Wilson, so he give the toilet to me."

"Well, you got no more runnin' water than the Baptists. You want to sell it?"

The legatee pondered in the dusk.

"No," he said. "No, I don't. I tell you—I thought a heap o' Preacher Wilson. He give me that toilet—and it's all I got to remember him by."

Moe comforted me on the way home.

"Like as not it's a no-account thing," he said.

The toilet had to be ordered new after all, but passing over the catalogue lure of a green-pedestalled monument for washing one's hands and face, and a Venetian-style recessed tub—for in spite of the literary windfall, oranges were bringing twenty-five cents a box—I found a second-hand lavatory and a very good tub with crooked legs. The formal opening of the bathroom was a gala social event, with a tray of glasses across the lavatory, ice and soda in the bathtub, and a bouquet of roses with Uncle Fred's card in a prominent and appropriate position.

The royalties from my first book, *South Moon Under,* went mostly for old debts, but the second, *Golden Apples,* brought temporary prosperity again and I decided that nothing is more tangible for one's money than plumbing. New friends had found their way to the Creek and were old friends now, and when there was a week-end houseful, a second bathroom seemed the most hospitable gesture possible. I contracted again for Moe to add one beside my own bedroom. The oldest four of his boys were big enough by this time to give a hand with the carpentering and the small new room was filled with male Sykeses when we reached the point of measuring for the height of the shower. Moe was a realist.

"Git in the tub," he ordered me. "Stand up straight. We'll git this right the sure way."

I stepped in the tub and stood up straight.

"Now whereabouts you want this here stream o' water to hit you? 'Bout there?"

Four pairs of bright Sykes eyes helped us gauge the proper play of water on the bathing form, and I have never felt so undressed in my life. But the Sykeses rejoiced with me in the completed bathroom, and although the linoleum buckled for nearly a year, we all felt that we had achieved unparalleled elegance. If I give an impression of *nouveau riche* when I inform guests pointedly, "The *other* bathroom is beyond my room," I am not bragging, but only grateful. I go happily from one bathroom to the other, and when a flying squirrel thumps on the roof at night, the sound is pleasing, for I am safe inside, and I remember the old Scotch prayer:

> "From ghillies and ghosties,
> And long-legged beasties,
> And all things that go *boomp* in the night,
> Good Lord, deliver us."

WILLA CATHER

MY FIRST NOVELS

Willa Cather (1873-1947), born in Virginia, spent her youth in Nebraska. After graduating from the University of Nebraska, she became a journalist. In 1896, she was managing editor of The Home Monthly; *from 1898 to 1901, telegraph editor and drama critic of the Pittsburgh* Daily Leader; *from 1906 to 1908, after five years as a schoolteacher in Pittsburgh, a staff member of* McClure's Magazine, *in New York; and, from 1908 to 1912, managing editor. Her first book,* April Twilights (1903), *is verse. Her first novels are described in the following essay, published first in* The Colophon *in 1931. Her later novels include the Pulitzer Prize winner,* One of Ours (1922), The Professor's House (1925), Death Comes for the Archbishop (1927), Shadows on the Rock (1931), and Sapphira and the Slave Girl (1940).*

MY FIRST NOVEL, *Alexander's Bridge*, was very like what painters call a studio picture. It was the result of meeting some interesting people in London. Like most young writers, I thought a book should be made out of "interesting material," and at that time I found the new more exciting than the familiar. The impressions I tried to communicate on paper were genuine, but they were very shallow. I still find people who like that book because it follows the most conventional pattern, and because it is more or less laid in London. London is supposed to be more engaging than, let us say, Gopher Prairie; even if the writer knows Gopher Prairie very well and London very casually. Soon after the book was published I went for six months to Arizona and New Mexico. The longer I stayed in a country I really did care about, and among people who were a part of the country, the more unnecessary and superficial a book like *Alexander's Bridge* seemed to me. I did no writing down there, but I recovered from the conventional editorial point of view.

When I got back to Pittsburgh I began to write a book entirely

for myself; a story about some Scandinavians and Bohemians who
had been neighbours of ours when I lived on a ranch in Nebraska,
when I was eight or nine years old. I found it a much more absorb-
ing occupation than writing *Alexander's Bridge;* a different process altogether. Here there was no arranging or "inventing"; everything was spontaneous and took its own place, right or wrong.
This was like taking a ride through a familiar country on a horse
that knew the way, on a fine morning when you felt like riding.
The other was like riding in a park, with someone not altogether
congenial, to whom you had to be talking all the time. Since I
wrote this book for myself, I ignored all the situations and accents
that were then generally thought to be necessary. The "novel
of the soil" had not then come into fashion in this country. The
drawing-room was considered the proper setting for a novel, and
the only characters worth reading about were smart people or
clever people. "O. Henry" had made the short story go into the
world of the cheap boarding-house and the shop-girl and the
truck-driver. But Henry James and Mrs. Wharton were our most
interesting novelists, and most of the younger writers followed
their manner, without having their qualifications.

O Pioneers! interested me tremendously, because it had to do
with a kind of country I loved, because it was about old neighbours, once very dear, whom I had almost forgotten in the hurry
and excitement of growing up and finding out what the world was
like and trying to get on in it. But I did not in the least expect
that other people would see anything in a slow-moving story, without "action," without "humour," without a "hero"; a story concerned entirely with heavy farming people, with cornfields and
pasture lands and pig yards,—set in Nebraska, of all places! As
everyone knows, Nebraska is distinctly déclassé as a literary
background; its very name throws the delicately atuned critic
into a clammy shiver of embarrassment. Kansas is almost as unpromising. Colorado, on the contrary, is considered quite possible. Wyoming really has some class, of its own kind, like well-
cut riding breeches. But a New York critic voiced a very general

opinion when he said: "I simply don't care a damn what happens in Nebraska, no matter who writes about it."

O Pioneers! was not only about Nebraska farmers; the farmers were Swedes! At that time, 1912, the Swede had never appeared on the printed page in this country except in broadly humorous sketches; and the humour was based on two peculiarities: his physical strength, and his inability to pronounce the letter "j." I had certainly good reasons for supposing that the book I had written for myself would remain faithfully with me, and continue to be exclusively my property. I sent it to Mr. Ferris Greenslet, of Houghton Mifflin, who had published *Alexander's Bridge,* and was truly astonished when he wrote me they would publish it.

I was very much pleased when William Heinemann decided to publish it in England. I had met Mr. Heinemann in London several times, when I was on the editorial staff of *McClure's Magazine,* and I had the highest opinion of his taste and judgment. His personal taste was a thing quite apart from his business, and it was uncompromising. The fact that a second-rate book sold tremendously never made him hedge and insist that there must be something pretty good in it after all. Most publishers, like most writers, are ruined by their successes.

When my third book, *The Song of the Lark,* came along, Heinemann turned it down. I had never heard from him directly that he liked *O Pioneers!* but now I had a short hand-written letter from him, telling me that he admired it very much; that he was declining *The Song of the Lark* because he thought in that book I had taken the wrong road, and that the full-blooded method, which told everything about everybody, was not natural to me and was not the one in which I would ever take satisfaction. "As for myself," he wrote, "I always find the friendly, confidential tone of writing of this sort distressingly familiar, even when the subject matter is very fine."

At that time I did not altogether agree with Mr. Heinemann, nor with Randolph Bourne, in this country, who said in his review almost the same thing. One is always a little on the defensive about one's last book. But when the next book, *My Ántonia*, came along, quite of itself and with no direction from me, it took the road of *O Pioneers!*—not the road of *The Song of the Lark*. Too much detail is apt, like any other form of extravagance, to become slightly vulgar; and it quite destroys in a book a very satisfying element analogous to what painters call "composition."

SIR WALTER RALEGH

A SEA FIGHT OFF THE AZORES

Sir Walter Ralegh (1552?-1618) was, in a day when it was easier to be everything, an English historian, poet, courtier, scientist, soldier, navigator, explorer, and pirate. He was for a time a favorite of Queen Elizabeth. For her he explored much of the West Indies and of the eastern coast of North and South America and took part in many forays, some piratical, against the Spanish. In "A Sea Fight Off the Azores," he describes one of these. Upon the death of Elizabeth, in 1603, he was sent to the Tower of London upon a trumped-up charge of treason against James I. He was later released to search for gold along the Orinoco; but that expedition was ill-fated, and he was eventually beheaded on the original charge. While in the Tower, he made scientific experiments and wrote his History of the World *(1614).*

THE LORD THOMAS HOWARD, with six of her Majesty's ships, six victualers of London, the bark *Ralegh*, and two or three pinnaces, riding at anchor near unto Flores, one of the westerly islands of the Azores, the last of August in the afternoon, had intelligence by one Captain Middleton of the approach of the Spanish Armada. Which Middleton being in a very good sailer had kept them company three days before, of good purpose, both to discover their forces the more, as also to give advice to my Lord Thomas of their approach. He had no sooner delivered the news but the fleet was in sight.

Many of our ships' companies were on shore in the island, some providing ballast for their ships, others filling of water and refreshing themselves from the land with such things as they could either for money or by force recover. By reason whereof our ships being all pestered and roomaging, everything out of order, very light for want of ballast. And that which was most to our disadvantage, the one-half part of the men of every ship sick and utterly unserviceable. For in the *Revenge* there were

»»» From *A Report of the Truth of the Fight About the Isles of Azores This Last Summer Betwixt the Revenge, One of Her Majesty's Ships, and an Armada of the King of Spain.* London, 1592.

118

ninety diseased; in the *Bonaventure* not so many in health as
could handle her mainsail. For had not twenty men been taken
out of a bark of Sir George Cary's, his being commanded to be
sunk, and those appointed to her, she had hardly ever recovered
England. The rest for the most part were in little better state.
The names of her Majesty's ships were these as followeth: the
Defiance, which was admiral, the *Revenge,* vice-admiral, the
Bonaventure commanded by Captain Cross, the *Lion* by George
Fenner, the *Foresight* by Mr. Thomas Vavasour, and the *Crane*
by Duffield. The *Foresight* and the *Crane* being but small ships;
only the other were of the middle size; the rest, besides the bark
Ralegh commanded by Captain Thin, were victualers and of small
force or none.

The Spanish fleet having shrouded their approach by reason
of the island, were now so soon at hand as our ships had scarce
time to weigh their anchors, but some of them were driven to
let slip their cables and set sail. Sir Richard Grenville was the last
weighed, to recover the men that were upon the island, which
otherwise had been lost. The Lord Thomas with the rest very
hardly recovered the wind, which Sir Richard Grenville not being
able to do was persuaded by the master and others to cut his
mainsail and cast about, and to trust to the sailing of his ship;
for the squadron of Seville were on his weather bow. But Sir
Richard utterly refused to turn from the enemy, alleging that he
would rather choose to die than to dishonor himself, his country,
and her Majesty's ship, persuading his company that he would
pass through the two squadrons in despite of them, and enforce
those of Seville to give him way. Which he performed upon divers
of the foremost, who, as the mariners term it, sprang their luff,
and fell under the lee of the *Revenge.* But the other course had
been the better, and might right well have been answered in so
great an impossibility of prevailing. Notwithstanding, out of the
greatness of his mind he could not be persuaded.

In the meanwhile as he attended those which were nearest him,
the great *San Philip* being in the wind of him and coming towards
him becalmed his sails in such sort as the ship could neither make

way nor feel the helm, so huge and high cargoed was the Spanish
ship, being of a thousand and five hundred tons. Who after laid
the *Revenge* aboard. When he was thus bereft of his sails, the
ships that were under his lee, luffing up, also laid him aboard; of
which the next was the admiral of the Biscaines, a very mighty
and puissant ship commanded by Brittandona. The said *Philip* carried three tier of ordnance on a side, and eleven pieces in every
tier. She shot eight forthright out of her chase, besides those of
her stern ports.

After the *Revenge* was entangled with this *Philip,* four other
boarded her; two on her larboard and two on her starboard. The
fight thus beginning at three of the clock in the afternoon continued very terrible all that evening. But the great *San Philip* having
received the lower tier of the *Revenge,* discharged with crossbar-
shot, shifted herself with all diligence from her sides, utterly mis-
liking her first entertainment. Some say that the ship foundered,
but we cannot report it for truth unless we were assured.

The Spanish ships were filled with companies of soldiers, in
some two hundred besides the mariners, in some five, in others
eight hundred. In ours there were none at all, beside the mariners,
but the servants of the commanders and some few voluntary gentlemen only. After many interchanged volleys of great ordnance
and small shot, the Spaniards deliberated to enter the *Revenge,*
and made divers attempts, hoping to force her by the multitudes of
their armed soldiers and musketeers, but were still repulsed again
and again, and at all times beaten back into their own ships or
into the seas.

In the beginning of the fight the *George Noble* of London, having received some shot through her by the armadas, fell under the
lee of the *Revenge* and asked Sir Richard what he would command him, being but one of the victualers and of small force.
Sir Richard bid him save himself and leave him to his fortune.

After the fight had thus without intermission continued while
the day lasted and some hours of the night, many of our men
were slain and hurt, and one of the great galleons of the armada
and the admiral of the hulks both sunk, and in many other of the

Spanish ships great slaughter was made. Some write that Sir Richard was very dangerously hurt almost in the beginning of the fight and lay speechless for a time ere he recovered. But two of the *Revenge's* own company, brought home in a ship of line from the islands, examined by some of the lords and others, affirmed that he was never so wounded as that he forsook the upper deck, till an hour before midnight; and then being shot into the body with a musket, as he was a-dressing was again shot into the head, and withal his chirurgeon wounded to death. This agreeth also with an examination taken by Sir Francis Godolphin of four other mariners of the same ship being returned, which examination the said Sir Francis sent unto Master William Killigrew of her Majesty's privy chamber.

But to return to the fight, the Spanish ships which attempted to board the *Revenge,* as they were wounded and beaten off, so always others came in their places, she having never less than two mighty galleons by her sides and aboard her. So that ere the morning, from three of the clock the day before, there had fifteen several armadas assailed her; and all so ill approved their entertainment as they were by the break of day far more willing to hearken to a composition than hastily to make any more assaults or entries. But as the day increased, so our men decreased; and as the light grew more and more, by so much more grew our discomforts. For none appeared in sight but enemies, saving one small ship called the *Pilgrim,* commanded by Jacob Whiddon, who hovered all night to see the success, but in the morning bearing with the *Revenge,* was hunted like a hare amongst many ravenous hounds, but escaped.

All the powder of the *Revenge* to the last barrel was now spent, all her pikes broken, forty of her best men slain, and the most part of the rest hurt. In the beginning of the fight she had but one hundred free from sickness, and fourscore and ten sick, laid in hold upon the ballast. A small troop to man such a ship, and a weak garrison to resist so mighty an army. By those hundred all was sustained, the volleys, boardings, and enterings of fifteen ships of war, besides those which beat her at large. On the contrary, the Spanish were always supplied with soldiers brought from every squadron; all manner of arms and powder at will. Unto ours there remained no comfort at all, no hope, no supply either of ships, men, or weapons; the masts all beaten overboard, all her tackle cut asunder, her upper work altogether razed, and in effect evened she was with the water, but the very foundation or bottom of a ship, nothing being left overhead either for flight or defense.

Sir Richard, finding himself in this distress and unable any longer to make resistance, having endured in this fifteen hours' fight the assault of fifteen several armadas all by turns aboard him, and by estimation eight hundred shot of great artillery, besides many assaults and entries; and that himself and the ship must needs be possessed by the enemy, who were now all cast in a ring round about him, the *Revenge* not able to move one way or other but as she was moved with the waves and billow of the sea; commanded the master gunner, whom he knew to be a most resolute man, to split and sink the ship; that thereby nothing might remain of glory or victory to the Spaniards, seeing in so many hours' fight and with so great a navy they were not able to take her, having had fifteen hours' time, above ten thousand men, and fifty-and-three sail of men-of-war to perform it withal; and persuaded the company, or as many as he could induce, to yield themselves unto God and to the mercy of none else, but as they had like valiant resolute men repulsed so many enemies they should not now shorten the honor of their nation by prolonging their own lives for a few hours or a few days.

The master gunner readily condescended, and divers others; but the captain and the master were of another opinion, and besought Sir Richard to have care of them; alleging that the Spaniard would be as ready to entertain a composition as they were willing to offer the same; and that there being divers sufficient and valiant men yet living, and whose wounds were not mortal, they might do their country and prince acceptable service hereafter. And that whereas Sir Richard had alleged that the Spaniards should never glory to have taken one ship of her Majesty, seeing that they had so long and so notably defended themselves, they answered that the ship had six foot water in hold, three shot under water which were so weakly stopped as with the first working of the sea she must needs sink, and was besides so crushed and bruised as she could never be removed out of the place.

And as the matter was thus in dispute, and Sir Richard refusing to hearken to any of those reasons, the master of the *Revenge* (while the captain won unto him the greater party) was convoyed aboard the general, Don Alfonso Baçan. Who finding none over-hasty to enter the *Revenge* again, doubting lest Sir Richard would have blown them up and himself, and perceiving by the report of the master of the *Revenge* his dangerous disposition, yielded that all their lives should be saved, the company sent for England, and the better sort to pay such reasonable ransom as their estate would bear, and in the mean season to be free from galley or imprisonment. To this he so much the rather condescended as well, as I have said, for fear of further loss and mischief to themselves, as also for the desire he had to recover Sir Richard Grenville; whom for his notable valor he seemed greatly to honor and admire.

When this answer was returned, and that safety of life was promised, the common sort being now at the end of their peril, the most drew back from Sir Richard and the master gunner, being no hard matter to dissuade men from death to life. The master gunner, finding himself and Sir Richard thus prevented and mastered by the greater number, would have slain himself with a sword, had he not been by force withheld and locked into his cabin. Then the general sent many boats aboard the *Revenge*, and divers of our men fearing Sir Richard's disposition stole away aboard the general and other ships. Sir Richard, thus overmatched, was sent unto by Alfonso Baçan to remove out of the *Revenge*, the ship being marvelous unsavory, filled with blood and bodies of dead and wounded men like a slaughterhouse. Sir Richard answered that he might do with his body what he list, for he esteemed it not, and as he was carried out of the ship he swounded, and reviving again desired the company to pray for him. The general used Sir Richard with all humanity, and left nothing unattempted that tended to his recovery, highly commending his valor and worthiness, and greatly bewailing the danger wherein he was, being unto them a rare spectacle and a resolution seldom approved, to see one ship turn toward so many enemies, to endure the charge and boarding of so many huge armadas, and to resist and repel the assaults and entries of so many soldiers. All which and more is confirmed by a Spanish captain of the same armada, and a present actor in the fight, who being severed from the rest in a storm was by the *Lion* of London, a small ship, taken, and is now prisoner in London.

JOHN P. MARQUAND

IWO JIMA BEFORE H-HOUR

*John P. Marquand (1893-1960), American writer of popular magazine fiction,
found his métier in social satire with the Pulitzer Prize-winning novel* The
Late George Apley *(1937). He continued to discuss the problems of the man
with the New England conscience meeting the changing social standards of
20th-century Boston and New York in such novels as* H. M. Pulham, Esq.
(1941), So Little Time *(1943),* Point of No Return *(1949), and* Melville Goodwin, USA *(1951). The following article, first published in* Harper's Magazine
in 1945, shows Marquand's skill in reportage.

LIFE ON a battleship is largely conducted against a background
of disregarded words. For example, upon leaving Saipan, the
radio loudspeaker on the open bridge produced a continuous
program somewhat along the following lines:

"This is Peter Rabbit calling Audacity One—Peter Rabbit call-
ing Audacity One—over . . . Audacity One calling Peter Rabbit
. . . Come in, Peter Rabbit—over . . . Peter Rabbit to Audacity
One—Shackle. Charley. Able. Oboe. Noel Coward. Unshackle—
over . . . Audacity One to Peter Rabbit—continue as directed.
Over . . . Peter Rabbit to Audacity One—Roger. Over . . ."

Sometimes these guarded code conversations, all conducted
with flawless diction in clear unemotional tones, would reach a
degree of subtlety that bordered on the obvious.

"Tiger Two is now in a position to give the stepchildren a
drink. Will Audacity One please notify the stepchildren? . . .
Bulldog calling Turtle. A pilot is in the water, southeast of Hot
Rock. Pick him up. I repeat: in the water, southeast of Hot Rock.
Pick him up . . ."

There was never any way of telling whether or not the stepchildren received the drinks which Tiger was kind enough to
offer, or whether or not the pilot was rescued from the slightly
chilly waters off that unpleasant island of Iwo. Moreover, no one

seemed particularly to care. The admiral and the captain sat upon the bridge in comfortable high-chairs, not unlike those used by patrons in a billiard parlor. Their staff officers stood near them, and behind the staff officers stood the men with earphones and mouthpieces tethered by long insulated cords, and next came the marine orderlies with their .45 automatics. Occasionally a Filipino mess boy would appear from the small kitchenette below—doubtless called a galley—with sandwiches and coffee for the admiral and the captain. He would carry these on a tray, sparkling with bright silver, china, and napery, up two dark companion ladders to the open bridge. Once when the main battery of 14-inch guns was firing, some freak of concussion lifted him a good six inches off the deck. But guns or not, no one appeared to listen to the voices on that radio.

However, as hours merged into days during those vigils on the bridge, that constant flow of words could not help but appeal to the imagination of anyone whose experience on battleships and with naval affairs had been previously limited almost exclusively to an acquaintance with *Pinafore* and *Madame Butterfly*. Charley and Able and Peter Rabbit, who kept shackling and unshackling themselves, gradually became old friends. You began to wonder what was happening now to Audacity and Oboe. It would not have been tactful to ask, since each was a special ship, a unit of the task force, but once one of those characters revealed its identity. This was when Little Abner had words with Audacity off the beach of Iwo Jima on D day minus two.

"Little Abner calling Audacity," Little Abner said. "We've got three holes and so we're going back to the line."

"What line do you mean?" Audacity asked.

"What the hell line do you think?" Little Abner answered. "The firing line."

Little Abner was an LCI—Landing Craft Infantry, in case you do not understand naval initials. She was one of the LCI's equipped with rockets, assigned to strafe the beach, and the Jap batteries had taken her under fire at eight hundred yards.

In addition to the radio on the bridge, there was also entertainment down below. When the great ship withdrew from the area, and when General Quarters had changed to Condition Two, some unknown hands would place recordings of radio programs from home upon a loudspeaker that reached the crew's mess, the warrant officers' mess, and the wardroom. Thus, above the shuf- flings on the deck, the clatter of mess tins and dishes, would come blasts of music, roars of laughter and blatant comedy. There was no way of escaping it if you wanted to eat. Though you were seven-hundred-odd miles from Tokyo, you were back home again.

"And now Dr. Fisher's tablets for intestinal sluggishness present Willie Jones, and all the little Jones boys, and the Jones boys' orchestra." (Whistles, laughter, and applause from an unknown audience.) "But first a brief, friendly word from our sponsor. Folks, do you feel headachy and pepless in the morning? Just take one with a glass of warm water. But here he is, Willie Jones himself." (Whistles, applause, and cheers from that unknown audience.) "How are you tonight, Willie?"—"Well, frankly, Frank, I'm feeling kind of dumb." "You mean you're just your old self, then?" (Shrieks, whistles, and applause from the unknown audience.)

There was no way of turning the thing off, but no one seemed to mind. Perhaps after having been at sea almost continuously for thirty months, as had many members of that crew, these sounds gave a sort of reassurance that a past to which everyone was clinging still waited back at home. At the ship's service, days before the ship was cleared for action, you could buy all sorts of reminders of that past. The shaving creams and tooth- pastes were like old acquaintances. There was even Williams' Aqua Velva, though this line was finally discontinued when it was found that certain members of the crew were taking it internally. There was a selection of homely literature, such as *The Corpse in the Coppice* and *Murder Walks at Midnight* and *The Book of Riddles,* and there were fragile volumes of comics and nationally known brands of gum and candy. When men went to battle stations nearly all of them took a few of these things

along. When the ship was closed into hermetically sealed compartments and the ventilating system was cut off you could
see them reading by the ammunition hoist. You could see the
damage-control groups, with their gas masks, their tools and
telephones, reclining on the decks slowly devouring those pages
and chewing gum. They may not have enjoyed this literature for
itself but it must have given them about the only illusion of
privacy that there was in a life at sea, where privacy does
not exist.

"If you write this thing just the way you see it," an officer said,
"maybe it might mean something to people back home. They
might see what we're going through. They might understand—
they never understand back home."

That was what nearly everyone aboard said. They all had a
pathetic desire for people at home to know. Of course, if they
had thought about it, they would have realized that this was
impossible. There was too great a gap between civilian and naval
life. There were too few common values. The life aboard a ship
in enemy waters was even more complex and difficult of explanation than the life of troops ashore. There was a combination of
small personal comforts and of impending danger verging on
calamity that was ugly and incongruous. The living quarters of
the crew were overcrowded, but they had hot water and soap,
hot showers, and all sorts of things you would never get ashore.
There were clean clothes, and all the coffee you wanted day and
night, and red meat and other hot food, and butter and ice
cream. Yet, at the same time, the sense of danger was more intense. You could not run away from it as you could on land.
It might come at any minute of the day and night from tor-
pedoes, from the air, from a surface engagement. Almost any sort
of blow meant casualties and damage. Even a light shell on the
superstructure might cause complications incomparable to the
results of a similar blow on land.

II

There had been some hope that the task force of battleships, cruisers, and destroyers that was scheduled to bombard Iwo Jima for three days before the transports and the amphibious craft appeared might arrive there undetected, but the force was spotted by an enemy plane on the evening of February 15th. No one aboard saw that speck in the dark sky.

In the junior officers' wardroom there was a complete collection of all the intelligence which had been gathered regarding the island of Iwo. Nothing was a secret any longer. It was possible to scan the latest airplane photographs, which had been taken early in the month. There were maps showing the target areas assigned every unit, with batteries, pillboxes, and antiaircraft installations marked in red. There were reports on the soil of the island. The beach would be coal-black lava sand, and the land rose up from it quite sharply in terraces. Each terrace had been a former beach, since in the past few years the island had been rising from the sea. As one moved in from the water's edge the soil was a soft sand of volcanic ash, almost barren of vegetation and exceedingly difficult for any sort of vehicle to negotiate. Higher on the island were the cliffs of brown volcanic stone, suitable for construction of underground galleries. There were patches of coarse grass full of the mites that cause scrub typhus. There were hot springs, and there was the sulfur mine from which Iwo draws its name (Sulfur Island), and a small sugar plantation to the north near a single town called Moto-yama. There were believed to be fifteen thousand troops on the island. The defensive installations were all underground or carefully camouflaged. There was only one practical beach on which to land and there was no chance for tactical subtlety.

The most interesting unit of this informational material was a large relief map made out of soft, pliable rubber, that gave a bird's-eye view of the island we were approaching. Every contour of it was there in scale—the cliffs to the northward, the vegetation, the roads, the airstrips (two finished and one nearing completion), and Mount Suribachi, the low, brown volcanic cone on the southern tip.

There have already been a good many ingenious descriptions of the shape of Iwo Jima, including comparisons to a mutton chop and a gourd. The whole thing was about five miles long. Mount Suribachi, to the south, was a walled-in crater. Its northern slope was known to be studded with pillboxes and with artillery. Bushes and boulders on this slope ran down to the lowest and narrowest stretch on the island, which had beaches on the east and west. (The west beach, however, would not permit landing operations on account of the prevailing winds.) From here the land gradually rose upward, and the island broadened until it finally reached a width of two and one-half miles. The airstrips were on its central spine. The northern shores came down to the sea in cliffs. There were only eight square miles of this bleak, unpromising, and porous dry land.

Anyone could tell that the plans for the seizure of Iwo Jima must have been the main occupation of a large group of specialists for a long, long time. Heaps of secret orders showed the disposition at any given moment of every one of the hundreds of craft that would take part in the invasion. The thousands of pages made a scenario for an operation which might take place in an hour or a minute. Veterans of other invasions were not impressed by the infinite detail. They spoke of the plans for Normandy and the South of France, or they discussed the arrangements for Guam and Saipan.

"If you've seen one of them," they said, "you've seen them all."

No one spoke much on the bridge. It was chilly and rain was falling before daylight. We were a silent, blacked-out ship, moving slowly, and as far as one could tell, alone—except for voices on the bridge radio.

"Battleaxe One," the radio was saying, "Area Zebra. Shackle. Charley. Oswald. Henry. Able. Unshackle."

"We'll start firing at about ten thousand yards," someone said.

Then the first daylight began to stir across the water and we were among the shadows of other heavy ships, moving very slowly.

"Look," someone said, "there's the mountain."

There was a faint, pinkish glow on the rain clouds above the horizon and the first faint rays of an abortive sunrise struggling against the rain fell on a rocky mass some five miles dead ahead. It was the cone of Suribachi emerging from a misty haze of cloud, and cloud vapor covered the dark mass of the rest of Iwo Jima. After one glance at its first vague outlines, it would have been hard to have mistaken it for anything but a Japanese island, for it had the faint delicate colors of a painting on a scroll of silk.

Our spotting plane was warming up on the catapult aft and you could hear the roar of the motor clearly over the silent ship. Then there was a flat explosion as the plane shot over the water. When it circled for altitude and headed for the island, there was already light enough to see the faces on the bridge.

The captain dropped his binoculars and lighted a cigarette. The clouds were gradually lifting above the island. It was unexpectedly tedious waiting and wondering when we would begin to fire. The island lay there mute and watchful. A bell was ringing. "Stand by," someone said, and seconds later one of our 14-inch projectiles was on its way to Iwo Jima. The noise was not as bad as the concussion, for your chest seemed to be pushed by invisible hands when the big guns went off. There was a cloud of yellow smoke, not unlike the color of Mount Suribachi. Then everyone crowded forward to gaze at the island. It seemed a very long while before a cloud of smoke and gray sand rose up almost like water from land. Then another ship fired. The bombardment of Iwo Jima had begun and the island lay there in the dingy, choppy sea, taking its punishment stoically without a sound.

Even at a distance of five miles, which somehow does not seem as far at sea as it does on land, one had the inescapable impression that Iwo Jima was ready for it and accustomed to taking a beating. This was not strange, as we had bombed it from the air for successive dozens of days, and fleet units had already shelled it twice. Nevertheless, this lack of reaction was something that you did not expect, even though common sense told you that there would not possibly be any land fire until we closed the range.

Another aspect of that three-day bombardment before D day was even more unexpected, especially when one retained memories of the heavy and continuous fire by land batteries upon prepared positions in the last world war. The bombardment turned out to be a slow, careful probing for almost invisible targets, with long dull intervals between the firing. Occasionally one could see a cloud of drab smoke arise from another ship, and a long while afterward the sound of the explosion would come almost languidly across the water, and then there would be another plume of dust and rubble on another target area of Iwo Jima. Sometimes, when the breeze was light, the smoke from the big guns of another ship would rise in the air in a huge perfect ring. Of course common sense again gave the reason for this deliberate firing. The fleet had come too long a distance to waste its limited ammunition, and consequently the effect of every shot had to undergo careful professional analysis.

In the lulls between the firing there was always an atmosphere of unremitting watchfulness. While the crews of the antiaircraft batteries below us sat by their guns, smoking and talking, hundreds of eyes were examining the sky and land. There was air cover far above us. In the distance were underwater listeners on the destroyers and DE's that were screening us. Our own air watch, besides, was covering every sector of the sky—and you also knew that the enemy looked back at us from his hidden observation posts. That consciousness of eyestrain and listening never entirely vanished in those days at Iwo Jima, and because of it, not a moment on the bridge was restful.

The slow approach on Iwo Jima was somewhat like the weaving and feinting of a fighter watching for an opening early in the first round. To put it another way, our task force was like a group of big-game hunters surrounding a slightly wounded but dangerous animal. They were approaching him slowly and respectfully, endeavoring to gauge his strength and at the same time trying to tempt him into action. We moved all through the day, nearer and nearer to Iwo Jima. Planes from the carrier force came from beyond the horizon, peeling off through the clouds and diving toward the airstrip; but except for an occasional burst of automatic fire and a few black dots of flak, the enemy was very listless. Our minesweeps, small, chunky vessels, began operating very close to the island. There were a few splashes near them, but that was all. The Japanese commander was too good a soldier to show his hand.

As the day wore on, we crowded close and objects loomed very large ashore. You could see the coal-black strip of beach where our assault waves would land, and the sea broke on the rusting hulls of a few old wrecks. Above the beach were the gray terraces we had read about, mounting in gradual, uneven steps to the airstrip. Beside the airstrip there was a tangle of planes, smashed by our bombings and pushed carelessly aside, like rubbish on a city dump. To the north were the quarries which had been mentioned by the intelligence. You could see caves to the south on Mount Suribachi. We were very close for a battleship and we knew the enemy had 8-inch coast-defense guns.

We continued firing at pillboxes and at antiaircraft emplacements, but there was no return fire and no trace of life upon the island. We stayed there until the light grew dim, and then we turned to leave the area until next morning. Twelve hours of standing on the bridge and the concussion of the guns left everyone very tired. We must have done some damage but not enough to hurt.

III

It was different the next morning—D day minus two. When we returned to the dull work the island was waiting with the dawn. Today the sky was clearer and the sea was smoother, and the ships closed more confidently with the shore. The schedule showed that there was to be a diversion toward the middle of the morning, and the force was obviously moving into position.

"We're going to reconnoiter the beach with small craft," an officer explained. "And the LCI's will strafe the terraces with rockets."

It was hard to guess where the LCI's had come from, for they had not been with us yesterday—but there they were just behind us, on time and on order, like everything else in amphibious war. The sun had broken through the cloud ceiling and for once the sea was almost blue. The heavy ships had formed a line, firing methodically. Two destroyers edged their way past us and took positions nearer shore.

"Here come the LCI's," someone said. "You can see the small craft with them," and he gave the initials by which the small boats were identified. They were small open launches, manned by crews with kapok life jackets. They were twisting and turning nervously as they came to join the LCI's.

"Where are they going in those things?" I asked.

"They are going to see what there is along the beach," my friend answered. "Someone has to see." He spoke reprovingly, as though I should have known the routine that had been followed again and again in the Pacific.

Eight or ten LCI's—it was difficult to count them—were passing among the battleships, with their crews at their battle stations. They were small vessels that had never been designed for heavy combat. They had been built only to carry infantry ashore, but in the Pacific they were being put to all sorts of other uses—as messenger ships to do odd jobs for the fleet, as gunboats, and as rocket ships. Each had a round tower amidships where the commanding officer stood. Each had open platforms with light automatic guns, and now they were also fitted with brackets for the rockets. They were high and narrow, about a hundred feet overall, dabbed with orange and green paint in jungle camouflage. They were a long way from jungle shores, however, as they moved toward the beach of Iwo Jima.

Suddenly the scene took concrete shape. They would approach

within a quarter of a mile of shore under the cover of our guns. Without any further protection their crews stood motionless at their stations.

Afterward a gunner from one of the LCI's spoke about it.

"If we looked so still," he said, "it was because we were scared to death. But then everyone had told us there was nothing to be scared of. They told us the Japs never bothered to fire at LCI's."

They were wrong this time, probably because the small craft that followed gave the maneuver the appearance of a landing. For minutes the LCI's moved in and nothing happened. They had turned broadside to the beach, with small boats circling around them like water beetles, before the enemy tipped his hand and opened up his batteries. Then it became clear that nothing we had done so far had contributed materially to softening Iwo Jima. The LCI's were surrounded with spurts of water and spray and smoke. They twisted and backed to avoid the fire, but they could not get away. It all seemed only a few yards off, directly beneath our guns. Then splashes appeared off our own bows. The big ships themselves were under fire.

"The so-and-so has taken a hit," someone said. "There are casualties on the such-and-such." He was referring to the big ships, but at the moment it did not seem important. All you thought of were the LCI's just off the beach. We were inching into line with the destroyers.

It appeared later that when we had been ordered to withdraw we had disregarded the order, and thus all at once we were in a war of our own, slugging it out with the shore. There had been a great deal of talk about our gunnery and the training of our crews. There was no doubt that they knew their business when they began firing with everything that could bear. The 14-inch guns and the 5-inch batteries were firing as fast as they could load. The breeze from the shore blew the smoke up to the bridge in bilious clouds. The shore line of Iwo Jima became cloaked in white smoke as we threw in phosphorus. Even our 40-millimeters began to fire. It was hard to judge the lapse of time, but the LCI's must have let off their rockets according to the schedule while the Japanese were blinded by the smoke and counterfire. When the LCI's began to withdraw, we also moved off slowly. It was the first mistake the enemy had made, if it was a mistake—revealing those batteries, for the next day was mainly occupied in knocking them out.

The LCI's were limping back. One of them was listing and small boats were taking off her crew. Another was asking permission to come alongside. When she reached us the sun was beating on the shambles of her decks. There was blood on the main deck, making widening pools as she rolled on the sluggish sea. A dead man on a gun platform was covered by a blanket. The decks were littered with wounded. They were being strapped on wire stretchers and passed up to us over the side, since nothing as small as an LCI had facilities for wounded. The men who were unhurt were lighting cigarettes and talking quietly, but no one was smiling. The commanding officer was tall, bareheaded, and blond, and he looked very young. Occasionally he gave an order and then he, also, lighted a cigarette. When they began to hose off the blood on the deck, the crew must have asked for fresh water, because our men, gathered by the rail, began tossing down canteens. Then there was a call from our bridge.

"Can you proceed under your own power?"

The blond CO looked up. He evidently had not heard, because the question was repeated.

"Can you proceed under your own power?"

"We can't proceed anywhere for three days," the CO said.

They had passed up the wounded—seventeen of them—and then they passed up five stretchers with the dead—twenty-two out of a crew of about sixty.

"That officer ought to get a medal," I said to someone on the bridge.

"They don't give medals for things like that in the Navy," I was told.

It may be so, but I still hope he gets the medal.

That evening the Japanese reported that they had beaten off two landings on Iwo Jima and that they had sunk numerous craft, including a battleship and a destroyer. There was a certain basis of fact in this, since what had happened must have looked like a landing. One LCI was sinking, waiting for a demolition charge, as disregarded as a floating can.

After the reconnaissance of the beach had been accomplished, the pounding of Iwo Jima continued through the afternoon and through the whole next day. Planes drove in with bomb loads, while the ring of ships kept up their steady fire. At night the "cans," as the destroyers were called, continued a harassing fire. Incendiary bombs were dumped on the slopes of Suribachi. Rockets were thrown at it from the air. Fourteen-inch shells pounded into its batteries. The ship to starboard of us attacked the battery to the north on the lip of the quarry. The earth was blown away, exposing the naked concrete gun emplacements, but now that the novelty had worn off it was all a repetition of previous hours. The scene grew dull and very fatiguing, but the voices on the radio loudspeaker continued tirelessly.

"Dauntless reports a contact. . . . Bulldog is ready to give a drink to any of our pigeons that may need it. Audacity One to Tiger—I repeat: Did you get our message? Over . . . "

The island lay still, taking it. No visible life appeared until the last day, when an installation was blown up and a few men staggered out from it. Some of us on the bridge saw them and some did not. One Japanese ran a few steps and seemed to stop and stoop to pick up something. Then he was gone. We had probably seen him dying.

The Japanese commander was playing his cards close to his chest, revealing no more targets by opening fire. It was clear that he also had his plan, less complicated than ours, but rational. He might damage our heavy ships, but he could not sink them, or conceivably prevent the inevitable landing. He had clearly concluded to wait and take his punishment, to keep his men and weapons under cover, until our assault waves were on the beach. Then he would do his best to drive them off, and everyone at Iwo knows it was not such a bad plan, either. He did not come so far from doing it when he opened up his crossfire on the beach. Some pessimists even admit that he might have succeeded if it had not been for that coarse, light sand, which embedded the mortar shells as they struck, so that they only killed what was very near them.

IV

At the end of D day minus one our task force was still there, without many new additions, but it was different the next morning. At dawn on D day the waters of Iwo looked like New York harbor on a busy morning. The transports were there with three divisions of marines—a semicircle of gray shipping seven miles out. Inside that gray arc the sea, turned choppy by the unsettled weather, was dotted by an alphabet soup of ships.

There were fleets of LST's filled with amphibious tanks and alligators; there were LSM's; there were the smaller LCT's, and packs of LCI's gathering about the kill. The ring of warships was drawing tighter. Small boats were moving out bearing flags to mark the rallying points from which the landing waves would leave. It looked like a Hollywood production, except that it was a three-billion-, not a three-million-dollar extravaganza. There must have been as many as eight hundred ships clustered off Iwo Jima, not counting the small boats being lowered. The officers and crew faced it without surprise. Instead they pointed out small incidents and made critical remarks.

"See the LCVP's," someone said. He was pointing out the tiny dots around the transports where the landing craft were loading. "They'll be moving into position. Here come the planes." It was all working without a hitch, with H-hour not so far away. At nine o'clock exactly the first assault wave was due to hit the beach, but before that Iwo Jima was due to receive its final polishing. Its eight square miles were waiting to take everything we could pour into them, and they must have already received a heavier weight of fire than any navy in the world has previously concentrated upon so small an area.

Anyone who has been there can shut his eyes and see the place again. It never looked more aesthetically ugly than on

D-day morning, or more completely Japanese. Its silhouette was like a sea monster, with the little dead volcano for the head, and the beach area for the neck, and all the rest of it with its scrubby, brown cliffs for the body. It also had the minute, fussy compactness of those miniature Japanese gardens. Its stones and rocks were like those contorted, wind-scoured, water-worn boulders which the Japanese love to collect as landscape decorations. "I hope to God," a wounded marine said later, "that we don't get to go on any more of those screwy islands."

An hour before H-hour it shook and winced as it took what was being dished out to it. In fact, the whole surface of the island was in motion as its soil was churned by our shells and by the bombs from the carrier planes that were swooping down across its back. Every ship was firing with a rising tempo, salvo after salvo, with no more waiting for the shellburst to subside. Finally Iwo Jima was concealing itself in its own debris and dust. The haze of battle had become palpable, and the island was temporarily lost in a gray fog.

"The LST's are letting down their ramps," someone said.

There could not have been a better place to observe the whole spectacle than from the air-lookout station above the bridge, but there was too much to see. Only an observer familiar with the art and theory of amphibious warfare could possibly have unraveled all the threads, and an ordinary witness could only give as inaccurate an account as the innocent bystander gives to circumstances surrounding a killing on the street. There was no time any longer to ask questions or to digest kindly professional explanations. All the facts that one had learned from the secret documents were confused by the reality.

The LST's had let down their ramps and the amphibious vehicles which they had carried were splashing through the water, like machines from a production line. Watching them, I found myself speaking to a chief petty officer who was standing next to me.

"It's like all the cats in the world having kittens," I said, and the idea appeared to interest him.

The amphibious vehicles, churning up the sea into foaming circles, organized themselves in lines, each line following its leader. Then the leaders moved out to the floating flags, around which they gathered in circling groups, waiting for their signal to move ashore. The gray landing craft with the marines had left the transports some time before for their own fixed areas, and they also were circling, like runners testing their muscles before the race. The barrage which had been working over the beach area had lifted, and the beach, with the smoldering terraces above it, was visible again. It was time for the first wave to be starting.

It was hard to pick the first wave out in that sea of milling craft, but suddenly a group of the barges broke loose from its circle, following its leader in a dash toward shore. Close to land the leader turned parallel to the beach, and kept on until the whole line was parallel. Then the boats turned individually and made a dash for it. The Navy had landed the first wave on Iwo Jima—at nine o'clock on the dot—or, at least, not more than a few seconds after nine.

AUBREY MENEN

THE DEAD MAN IN THE SILVER MARKET

Aubrey Menen (1912-), an English novelist and essayist born of an Indian father and an Irish mother, has spent some of his life in India. There during World War II he organized publicity for the British government, after the war served the Indian government on a political mission, and later produced documentary and educational films for an advertising agency. Since 1947, he has given all his time to writing. Among his novels, mostly satirical, are The Prevalence of Witches *(1948),* The Backward Bride *(1950),* The Duke of Gallodoro *(1952), and* A Conspiracy of Women *(1965).* Dead Man in the Silver Market *(1953) contains thirteen autobiographical sketches.*

SOME YEARS LATER, in the middle of the Second World War, I was walking down the Silver Market of Old Delhi when I heard the sound of firing. Making my way towards it I turned a corner and came upon a small crowd defying an even smaller band of English soldiers. An elderly man of the poorest class, dressed only in a loin cloth, broke away from the crowd and ran towards the soldiers. One of these pointed an automatic weapon towards him, but the man did not stop. He was shouting in a confused and hysterical manner and it seemed to me that he was not in possession of his senses; no doubt as so often happens with Indians, the excitement and the previous shooting had loosened his grip upon his nerves. He ran on, full tilt towards the soldiers. The Englishman with the automatic weapon pressed the trigger and the Indian fell prone, jerking his legs in a fashion that was almost ludicrous and drumming with his fists on the ground. In a few moments he lay still, dead, with blood spouting from a series of wounds in his body. I noticed that the small of his back (for he died on his face) was torn in several places from the bullets which had passed through.

The crowd dispersed. They had been demanding that the English leave India. The man lay in the roadway in his blood,

until a street-cleaning cart, requisitioned for the purpose, bore
him away.

* * * * *

By a chance which was not remarkable I met one of the
soldiers who had been in the party that had done the shooting.
He was brought to my house by a friend who sought entertainment for English soldiers. He brought five or six, chosen from
a list with a pin and one of them was this young man.

He was square-faced, short, and agreeable in his manner,
though rough, in the style of the streets rather than the barracks.
He remembered the incident of the shooting well. It arose in
the conversation by accident and to his great amusement he
said that he had at last 'tumbled to where he had seen me before.'

It appeared that when the firing started I had taken refuge
in a small public latrine made of sheet iron and stakes. He had
observed this, and it had made him laugh.

I asked him where his home town was and he told me that
it was an industrial slum near Liverpool. He was much attached
to it. He described with nostalgia a road called 'The Gut' which
ran from the brass foundry to the railway bridge and had fourteen public houses. Here the boys would whistle at the girls or
buy them fried fish. He himself was something of a leader of his
generation. They had formed a gang that took its pleasure in
brushes with the police: they committed little crimes and ran
away, the police after them. Sometimes they were caught, but
not often. He had been bound over to keep the peace on one
occasion and, on another, let off by the magistrate with a warning. This leniency was allowed him because he was about to go
to war. He had been drafted to India. The shooting in the Silver
Market was the first action he had seen.

One of his soldier companions said:

"Well, I'm——glad I missed that——show. Poor bastards.
Some of them haven't got a rag to cover their arses."

At which the soldier from the slums squared his shoulders.

"I dunno so much," he said.

His companion said:

"What d'yer mean, 'You dunno so much?'"

"I mean," said the first soldier, "we've got t' keep Law an' Order."

I said:

"Those people you shot at in the Silver Market think they can keep law and order for themselves."

"They *think*," he said. "It takes more than thinkin'. They might, if we learned 'em 'ow to do it for an 'undred years or so. But then, I dunno." He pulled on his cigarette and disengaged some tobacco from his lower lip with a neat movement of his tongue. "Seems t'me, that sort of thing ain't learned. It's bred in yer bones."

The successor to the oligarchs, the heir to Lord Curzon, Clive and General Wellesley being a soldier in uniform, I changed the subject of the conversation by serving more whiskey.

LOGICAL ORGANIZATION

Unity and coherence are the two great rhetorical virtues, coherence presupposes unity, and the chief device for achieving coherence is logical organization. A piece of writing, whether a paragraph or a whole essay, has unity if everything in it is relevant to its subject. It has coherence if it has unity and if it makes that unity evident. And the chief device for making that unity evident is logical organization—organization achieved by classifying the various things in a piece of writing, putting like with like, and putting the resulting classes into an order that makes their relationships to one another evident. (See the headnotes to "Analysis" and "Classification.")

All three pieces here—examples of logical organization of a paragraph, of a section of an essay, and of an essay, respectively—have coherence (and, hence, unity); and all achieve that coherence chiefly by logical organization but also by other devices—notably, logical paragraph division, thesis and topic sentences, and transitional words and phrases. Santayana's paragraph, for example, has unity because everything in it is relevant to its subject, poets; it is about poets and nothing else. It has coherence because it has unity and because it makes that unity evident—by logical organization (classifying its statements about poets into two classes, statements about musicians and statements about psychologists, and putting the former first and the latter second), by a topic sentence ("Poets may be divided into two classes: the musicians and the psychologists"), and by transitional phrases ("The first," "on the other hand," and "not by . . . but by"). In Korg's piece, a section of an essay, the topic sentences for the later paragraphs are strictly forecast by the opening paragraph: its analytical, numbered list makes this piece the most formally obvious in organization of the three pieces. Faverty's short essay is a model of logical organization: between its opening, thesis paragraph and its closing paragraph, restating the thesis, are four paragraphs of details, each group organized by the topic sentence of its paragraph.

Use of logical organization and other devices for achieving coherence is characteristic of almost every other piece in this book as well as of these pieces presented here.

GEORGE SANTAYANA

TWO CLASSES OF POET

George Santayana (1863-1952), though born in Spain, spent most of his life elsewhere. He came to the United States as a boy; was educated at the Boston Latin School, Harvard, and Berlin; and from 1889 to 1912 taught philosophy at Harvard. From 1912 until his death, he lived in London, Paris, and Rome, writing philosophical essays, poetry, plays, literary criticism, and one novel. The most generally admired statement of his naturalistic philosophy is The Life of Reason *(5 vols.; 1905-1906). The best of his poetry and plays are in* The Poet's Testament *(1953); of his literary criticism, in* Essays in Literary Criticism *(1956). Perhaps general readers best like* Soliloquies in England *(1922); his autobiographical novel,* The Last Puritan *(1935), which, written after he was seventy, became a best-seller; and his three-part autobiography (1944, 1945, 1953).*

POETS MAY be divided into two classes: the musicians and the psychologists. The first are masters of significant language as harmony; they know what notes to sound together and in succession; they can produce, by the marshalling of sounds and images, by the fugue of passion and the snap of wit, a thousand brilliant effects out of old materials. The Ciceronian orator, the epigrammatic, lyric, and elegiac poets, give examples of this art. The psychologists, on the other hand, gain their effect not by the intrinsic mastery of language, but by the closer adaptation of it to things. The dramatic poets naturally furnish an illustration.

»»» Reprinted with the permission of Charles Scribner's Sons from *Essays in Literary Criticism* by George Santayana, edited by Irving Singer. (Published originally in *The Sense of Beauty*.)

JACOB KORG

MISCONCEPTIONS ABOUT POETRY

Jacob Korg (1922-   ), educated at the City College of New York and Columbia, has taught at Bard College and City College and is now professor of English at the University of Washington. He has written a biography, George Gissing *(1963), and essays on subjects ranging from the novels of Dickens to the poems of Hardy, Browning, and Dylan Thomas.*

KNOWLEDGE of the main characteristics of poetry enables us to correct three misconceptions about it that prevent many readers from understanding and enjoying it. These are:

1. The idea that poetry is an artificial and unnatural use of language.
2. The idea that it is an elaborate way of saying something that could be said more clearly in prose.
3. The idea that it always expresses exaggerated or sentimental emotions.

Poetry, far from being artificial or unnecessary, appears to be the oldest and most universal of the arts. In fact, the existence of well-developed poetic traditions among otherwise uncivilized peoples leads to the inference that what we call poetry may well have existed among prehistoric men before the form of communication called prose. The strongest expressive needs of primitive people are likely to be related to matters of feeling rather than to matters of fact, and their imaginations are likely to be far richer and more powerful than their intellects. The human race realized the value of accurate, objective description only comparatively late, as a part of the scientific attitude. Witches, goblins, and fairies came before molecules and light years, though both kinds of concepts serve the same purpose: they are ways by which man explains the realities of his universe

»»» From *An Introduction to Poetry.* New York: Holt, Rinehart and Winston, 1960. Pp. 4-5. Reprinted by permission of Holt, Rinehart and Winston, Inc.

147

to himself. The difference is that the former are imaginative, and the latter are intellectual. Primitive man does, of course, feel the need to describe the flash of lightning or the rumble of the earthquake, but in his description the factual element is likely to be submerged in the expression of the emotions he experiences. His account would be true to his feelings rather than to the objective reality. The result of expression under these conditions would be poetry. Thus, it is fairly obvious that poetry, whose primary concern is feeling, and whose primary instrument is the imagination, must have come earlier in human development than any but the most rudimentary prose. Prose, except for strictly utilitarian scraps of conversation, could not emerge until such a relatively advanced concept as an objective reality separate from the self could be developed. Poetry then, is not only older, but more primitive and more natural than prose.

We can also see, from our description of poetry, why it cannot be considered merely an elaborate and sententious way of saying things that could be expressed more directly. The subject-matter of poetry and prose is not the same, for poetry characteristically deals with subjects that cannot be adequately described in prose. It is a way of stretching the resources of language beyond their ordinary power, in order to communicate what language seems unable to communicate. In performing this minor miracle, poetry will often produce results that are difficult, and complicated enough to require close study. But to say, as some naive readers do, that the idea of a poem can be communicated just as well through the simpler and more direct resources of prose, is like saying that bread can be made of something less troublesome to procure than grain. The thought and feeling of a good poem depend upon the way in which they are expressed, and cannot exist apart from the language of the poem.

Probably the most widespread and most harmful misconception about poetry is the belief that it is always overemotional and sentimental. It is true that the romantic tradition, which specialized in intense emotions and the praise of nature has been dominant for many generations, and that it has been taken up by poets of little skill who write the sort of verse that is found in Sunday supplements and on Mother's Day cards. But popular verse of this kind has no more to do with real poetry than a hamburger prepared on a grill at a circus has to do with real cooking. Unfortunately the general public seems to form its idea of poetry on the evidence of these debased examples, and concludes, quite correctly, that this sort of thing is not worth bothering about.

FREDERIC E. FAVERTY

LEGENDS OF JOSEPH

Frederic E. Faverty (1902-   ) is the Morrison Professor of English at Northwestern University, where he has taught courses in world literature and English literature of the Victorian period. He is the editor of and a contributor to The Victorian Poets *(1956) and the author of* Matthew Arnold the Ethnologist *(1951). The following essay, like others in* Your Literary Heritage *(1959), first appeared in the Chicago* Tribune's *Sunday "Magazine of Books."*

IN ALL EARLY LITERATURES legend plays an important role. A striking example of the contribution which legends make to our literary heritage is to be found in one of the oldest of stories, yet a story that will never grow old—the Biblical narrative of Joseph and his brothers. Though the account in the Book of Genesis is a hurried one (how could it be otherwise, since in this one book the world is created and Adam, and the patriarchal succession is traced?), it is filled with folklore themes. For this reason it has caught the imagination of the world. It has had hundreds of adaptations and elaborations of which Thomas Mann's novel *Joseph and His Brothers* is only the most recent.

The story took firm root among the Jews and the Mohammedans. To the Jews Joseph was a popular hero and they were prolific in the creation of legends about him. The Mohammedans adopting a large body of this material, added legends of their own. The great Prophet himself in a revelation at Mecca received the "most excellent history" of Joseph from God, and, as scholars have since pointed out, from the Jews. At any rate, the twelfth and, some think, the most beautiful chapter of the Koran is devoted to the story. With a true instinct for the dramatic, the post-Koran writers in Arabia and Persia selected the most appealing of the many themes presented in Joseph's life—the unrequited love

»»» "Legends of Joseph" is from *Your Literary Heritage* by Frederic E. Faverty, published by J. B. Lippincott Company, 1959. Reprinted by permission of J. B. Lippincott Company.

of Potiphar's wife, or Zulaikha, as they renamed her—and made a romance of it.

According to Eastern legend, Joseph's feats were many and marvelous. One of the least of these was the gift of tongues: he spoke seventy-one languages. He founded the city of Memphis, and constructed a canal at Cairo for the discharge of the Nile's waters. The mighty pyramids were his handiwork, built as granaries for the storing of grain during the seven lean years. He was the Hermes of Egypt: to his ingenuity the world is indebted for the science of geometry, and for the first system of weights and measures. The use of papyrus for writing purposes was his discovery. He was one of the greatest of the interpreters of dreams. And finally, he was buried in the Nile so that his bones might bless its waters. Though these legends had their origin in the East, most of them found their way to Europe during the Middle Ages.

In the West from the early centuries of the Christian era until now Joseph has been regarded as the great prefiguration of Christ. The conception had its rise in the early allegorical interpretations of the Bible, the Old Testament being explained in the light of the New. Almost all Joseph's experiences could be shown to be foreshadowings of Christ's vicissitudes. Jacob was God the Father; Joseph, Christ. The wicked brothers were the Jews, whom Christ called brothers. Joseph's descent into the pit represented Christ's going down into the tomb. Both were robbed of their garments and were beaten. Joseph's cloak was Christ's body, left by him upon the cross. Both Joseph and Christ were sold for thirty pieces of silver. Both were sold by their own people and received by foreigners. Joseph encountered trouble in the house of Potiphar; Christ, in the synagogue—thus Potiphar's wife came to represent the synagogue, accustomed to commit adultery with strange gods. After privations, both rose to felicity—Joseph to the governorship of Egypt; Christ to the throne of God. Joseph saved Egypt; Christ, the world. The food which Joseph dispensed represents Christ's words, and the granaries of Egypt are the Scriptures in which Christ's teachings are stored. Even today

the Oberammergau Passion Play continues such allegorical interpretations.

Joseph is the hero of more than one hundred and fifty European
dramas, divided unequally among some thirteen languages. The
story has been treated also in the novel and in countless poems
and sermons. Of all the episodes in the story, that dealing with
Potiphar's wife has had the most appeal: the handsome but virtuous youth continently deaf to the importunings of a wicked lady.
Such extraordinary virtue lends itself, also, to satirical treatment.
Sheridan's Joseph Surface in *The School for Scandal*, unlike the
Egyptian Joseph, displays no inconvenient moral scruples, nor does
he betake himself in flight. A humorous and slightly cynical interpretation of Joseph's character is implied, also, in the application of his name, during the eighteenth century, to a long cloak
worn chiefly by women; it was buttoned all the way down the
front. Crabbe in *The Parish Register* records the custom:

> In the dear fashions of her youth she dress'd;
> A pea-green Joseph was her favorite vest.

His name is today applied in raillery to men who are overvirtuous.

Such is the story of our story. It was born in the East and there
had its most elaborate developments. It was carried to the West
and survived. Basically, its themes are the stuff of which folk tales
are made. And folk tales have a long life.

DEFINITION

A DEFINITION is a statement that a term (that is, a word or a phrase) has, has had, or shall have a certain meaning. Sometimes a definition has a form like " 'Carnivore' means the same thing as 'flesh-eating animal.' " More often, as in the following pieces, it has a form like "A carnivore is a flesh-eating animal" or "Carnivores are flesh-eating animals."

Three sorts of definition may be distinguished: (1) lexical, (2) stipulative, and (3) persuasive. A lexical definition simply records general usage, past or present, of a certain term; it is the sort of definition found in a good dictionary (or lexicon). The definition of "carnivore" above is lexical. A stipulative definition, on the other hand, records a certain writer's stipulation or resolution that a certain term in a certain context have a certain meaning. The definition of "student" in Instructions for Preparing Your Federal Income Tax Return for 1965 is stipulative: "The law defines a student as an individual who, during each of 5 calendar months during the year, is (a) a full-time student at an educational institution or (b) pursuing a full-time course of institutional on-farm training under the supervision of an accredited agent of an educational institution or of a State, or a political subdivision of a State" (p. 5). Thus, though a lexical definition is the outcome of an investigation, while a stipulative definition is the outcome of a decision, both sorts have the same purpose—namely, to clarify meaning for the reader. A persuasive definition, however, has (as its name suggests) a quite different purpose—namely, to persuade the reader to alter his attitude toward something. The following definitions of "communism" and "democracy," respectively, are persuasive: "True communism is governmental regulation of trade unions" and "True democracy is governmental regulation of trade unions." This definition of "communism" is a way of persuading the reader to think ill of governmental regulation of trade unions;

153

this definition of "democracy," a way of persuading him to think well of such regulation. For, in America, "communism" is a pejorative, a term with a negative emotional charge; "democracy," an honorific, a term with a positive emotional charge.

In a definition, the term to be defined ("carnivore," "student," "communism," "democracy") is called the definiendum; the term by which it is defined ("flesh-eating animal," "an individual who . . . ," "governmental regulation of trade unions"), the definiens. Notice that, in the definition of "student" above, "student" appears in both the definiendum and the definiens but that, in the latter, it apparently has its usual lexical sense ("a person enrolled in a course of study"), a fact that saves this definition from having the defect of circularity ("a student is a student").

Of the following definitions, those of "tycoon" (from a dictionary or lexicon) and "law" (Mill) are lexical; those of "sandwich" (Friedlander), "middle income" (Grutzner), "otherworldliness" (Lovejoy), and "plot" (Muir) are stipulative; and those of "responsible press" (Estabrook) and "good review" (Krutch) are persuasive. The pieces by Estabrook and Krutch might, indeed, have been included in "Argumentation and Persuasion" or, perhaps, in "Analogy, Comparison, Evaluation." Friedlander, Grutzner, and Mill show that definitions can be important. What "sandwich" or "middle income" or "law" means makes a difference; it's not just a matter of definition.

Definitions appear elsewhere in this book—in "Classification," for instance, in the pieces by Schwartz and Thiel and by Darton.

"TYCOON"

The following entry from A Dictionary of Americanisms *is reproduced in facsimile so that students may see what entries in a dictionary constructed "on historical principles" are and may compare this entry with entries in their abridged or desk dictionaries in which the historical evidence is summarized or omitted. In the entry framed below, the direction "[See note.]" refers to the note immediately following the direction and preceding the definitions.*

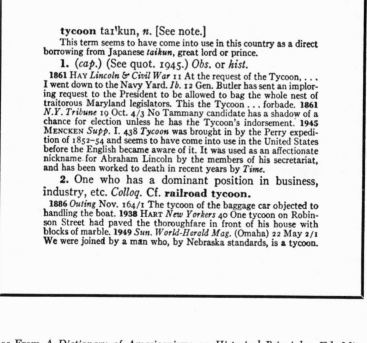

tycoon taɪˈkun, *n.* [See note.]
This term seems to have come into use in this country as a direct borrowing from Japanese *taikun*, great lord or prince.
1. (*cap.*) (See quot. 1945.) *Obs.* or *hist.*
1861 HAY *Lincoln & Civil War* 11 At the request of the Tycoon, . . . I went down to the Navy Yard. *Ib.* 12 Gen. Butler has sent an imploring request to the President to be allowed to bag the whole nest of traitorous Maryland legislators. This the Tycoon . . . forbade. **1861** *N.Y. Tribune* 19 Oct. 4/3 No Tammany candidate has a shadow of a chance for election unless he has the Tycoon's indorsement. **1945** MENCKEN *Supp.* I. 438 *Tycoon* was brought in by the Perry expedition of 1852–54 and seems to have come into use in the United States before the English became aware of it. It was used as an affectionate nickname for Abraham Lincoln by the members of his secretariat, and has been worked to death in recent years by *Time.*
2. One who has a dominant position in business, industry, etc. *Colloq.* Cf. **railroad tycoon.**
1886 *Outing* Nov. 164/1 The tycoon of the baggage car objected to handling the boat. **1938** HART *New Yorkers* 40 One tycoon on Robinson Street had paved the thoroughfare in front of his house with blocks of marble. **1949** *Sun. World-Herald Mag.* (Omaha) 22 May 2/1 We were joined by a man who, by Nebraska standards, is a tycoon.

»»» From *A Dictionary of Americanisms on Historical Principles.* Ed. Mitford M. Mathews. Chicago: University of Chicago Press, 1951. P. 1790. Copyright 1951 by the University of Chicago. Reprinted by permission of the University of Chicago Press.

PAUL J. C. FRIEDLANDER

SANDWICH SETTLEMENT

*Paul J. C. Friedlander (1910-   ) has been a newspaperman since 1932.
Since 1943, he has been on the New York* Times, *of which he is now travel
editor.*

THE BREACHES COMMITTEE of the International Air Transport
Association, solemnly assembled in London, last week handed
down its formal decision in the case of Pan American World Airways and Trans World Airways against four European carriers
in the matter of economy class sandwiches. With the wisdom
of a Solomon, the I. A. T. A. committee produced a new definition
of sandwiches so balanced that the plaintiffs and the defendants
—Air France, Scandinavian Airlines System, Swiss-air and K. L.
M. (Royal Dutch) Airlines—were satisfied that each had won
a moral victory. Although the defendants could have been fined
$25,000 each for each violation, the committee did not levy any
fines.

Biggest casualty of this trans-Atlantic operation was a few
cases of asparagus, stocked here by one of the airlines for use in
its sandwiches. The I. A. T. A. committee ruled that the airlines must not serve asparagus to its economy class passengers.
Also banned were smoked salmon, oysters, caviar, lobster, game
and pate de foie gras.

Since April 1, when the economy class service was started
across the North Atlantic, the airlines have struggled with their
consciences and their competitors over what kind of food they
should serve this least expensive of their services. Their guiding
light was the I. A. T. A. phrase "simple, inexpensive, cold sandwiches" but taking off from those three adjectives the foreign
carriers dreamed up some mighty pretty and good-tasting sand-

»»» The New York *Times,* April 27, 1958, pp. 1xx, 6xx. Reprinted by permission of the New York *Times.*

wiches, some open-face, some covered. The American-flag carriers clung to the traditional closed sandwich, and when the foreign lines spoke proudly of their food, the American lines filed charges and started the test case. And now I. A. T. A.'s commission has ruled that economy class meal service should be on the following lines:

A.—Meals to consist of sandwiches which may be of open or closed variety.

B.—Each sandwich to be a separate unit; the whole meal not to give the appearance of a cold plate.

C.—A substantial and visible part of each unit to consist of bread, roll or similar breadlike material.

D.—Each unit to be cold.

E.—Each unit to be simple, that is, not complicated; unadorned. This calls for a minimum of garnishing.

F.—Each unit to be inexpensive. This calls for the avoidance of materials normally regarded as expensive or luxurious such as (for example, but without limiting) smoked salmon, oysters, caviar, lobster, game, asparagus, pate de foie gras, and also for the avoidance of overgenerous or lavish helpings of permissible commodities such as meats, which affect the money value of the unit and destroy the necessary conditions of low cost and simplicity.

MUCH ADO

If this seems much ado about comparatively little, it is and was. Because it was so ludicrous—the picture of giant airlines taking time out from business to fight each other over what they should feed, or rather should not feed, their passengers—the controversy got a big play in the press in this country, in Canada and throughout Europe. A second reason for the interest was the big promotion given economy class by the airlines, the big sales pitch used to launch the third class, austerity service this month.

Potential passengers have seen advertised and merchandised extensively the advantages of flying economy class, saving money as well as time crossing the Atlantic in planes carrying as many as 100 passengers in fairly crowded seating arrangements, and with restricted service and amenities. The airlines claim that economy class is now $63 cheaper for a one-way New York-London ticket than the tourist rate, but this difference is between economy fare, $252, and the new tourist rate, $315. Before there was an economy service available, prior to April 1, tourist fare New York-London was $290. It was jumped $25 on April 1 to make a greater differential between economy and tourist classes. Thus, today's economy class ticket is $38 cheaper than tourist class was only thirty days ago.

LIMITED COMPETITION

Pan American Airways raised the cold sandwich issue in dead seriousness, arguing that since the airlines had agreed to serve cold, inexpensive sandwiches to economy passengers, they should live up to their agreement. Pan American warned that if not, economy service would go the way of tourist service, whose hot meals have been embellished in an effort to win patronage. Since the airlines do not compete as to price, their rates being identical with all I. A. T. A. members, and most of their planes are also identical, whatever competition there is must come in the kind of food and service they provide.

The argument that food competition could quickly destroy the basis for economy class—high-density seating at the lowest possible cost to the airline achieved by the least expensive food and cabin service to the customer—is a hard one to pin down. Most airline spokesmen run for cover when asked how much it costs them to put a meal on the passenger's tray. There have been reports that tourist hot meals cost the airlines about $4 a passenger. One European carrier whose reputation for good food aloft is worldwide, estimated that it was spending $2 to give each of its economy passengers a dinner, a breakfast and a snack in between. This seems like a not unreasonable expenditure out of a $252 fare.

The new I. A. T. A. ruling on what constitutes a sandwich left some airline officials here puzzled. One Scandinavian airline system spokesman predicted, "There will probably be another citation now over what constitutes a minimum of garnish." Another spokesman for the same airline was happy in the I. A. T. A.

announcement because "we have not been violating in the least the I. A. T. A. regulations. It leaves a wide range for imagination in sandwich-making and we intend to take advantage of it as we always have." This official estimated the cost of an economy class sandwich at about thirty-two cents; allowing eight sandwiches to a passenger on one crossing, the total food cost per passenger comes to $2.56, plus a few cents for coffee, milk or a cup of tea.

K. L. M. ESTIMATE

A spokesman for K. L. M. estimated the cost of all the food an economy passenger would eat across the Atlantic at about $2, including dinner, breakfast, in-between snacks and beverages. He said, "I don't think we have to make many changes as far as our sandwiches are concerned. I think we have used one or two of the restricted ingredients—asparagus was one, but our meals will not suffer from the few changes we might have to make.

"I think that with a little care and love and understanding, you can make a nice-looking sandwich with very inexpensive materials. You can also throw them together and have an ugly thing. We want to give a little care to our passengers."

While peace descends quietly over the international airline industry, passengers can expect the carriers to be hewing pretty close to the I. A. T. A. sandwich line for the next few weeks. Undoubtedly the carriers will be watching each other's meals like hawks, and this is one instance where one may, with not only impunity but with a kind of literary joy, use that cliché.

CHARLES GRUTZNER

HOUSING SNAGGED ON INCOME RANGE

Charles Grutzner (1903-   ) began his newspaper career in 1926, on the Brooklyn Times. *Since 1941, he has been on the New York* Times, *covering a variety of events, including the doings of special federal agencies, major trials, and the Korean War.*

THE MIDDLE INCOME family has become the most-talked-about group in housing circles, but there is no general agreement on what middle income is.

Legislators, housing experts, private builders, city planners and just about everyone else keep insisting that what America— and especially Manhattan—needs is much more middle income housing. They regret, in speeches and writing, the migration to the suburbs of middle-income families and see ways of luring them back across the city line.

But the family that fits one lawmaker's definition of middle income is viewed by some housing experts as low income. The family described by a private builder as middle income is marked off by a public housing official as high income.

A sampling has been made by The New York Times of the opinions of public officials and others concerned with the housing problem. The result is an amorphous sprawl that begins, according to some of the definitions, with an annual family income of $4,000 and reaches, in one developer's view, to $20,000 a year. The outer limits contract and swell with the individual views.

An effort was made in this year's state legislative session to prohibit the construction of any more middle-income housing by the New York City Housing Authority. The proposed ban, withdrawn by its Republican sponsors in a compromise on reorganization of the Housing Authority, failed to define middle-income housing.

»»» The New York *Times* April 7, 1958, pp. 1, 33. Reprinted by permission of the New York *Times.*

Similarly the sponsors of low-interest state and city loans, long-term amortization and tax abatement for private developers of limited-profit and cooperative housing did not write any definition of middle income into their successful bipartisan measures.

In New Jersey the State Legislature has up for final action a measure to permit local authorities to build middle-income housing. Public housing in New Jersey has been restricted up to now to low-income families. The permissive legislation offers no dollar definition of middle income—it leaves that to the local housing authorities.

Philip J. Cruise, chairman of the New York City Housing Authority, said his idea of a middle-income family was one whose total annual income was between $5,000 and $10,000. It would vary with the size of the family and would include the earnings of more than one member in some family units.

CITY LIMITS RAISED

The city raised income and rental limits recently in its no-cash-subsidy public housing program. These projects receive no public assistance beyond tax abatement. The newest one, which will accept its first tenants this spring, will have average monthly rentals of $23.56 a room. It will have maximum income limits for admission up to $7,490 a year for families of five or more persons.

Mr. Cruise expressed the view that public housing should not accept the upper half of the middle-income group—within his definition—if private builders were able to put up housing with the new state aids and Federal mortgage insurance to rent at $25 to $30 a room.

Joseph P. McMurray, State Housing Commissioner, said middle-income families—in terms of housing need—were those with incomes from $4,500 a year for a childless family to about $10,000 for a large family. Outside Manhattan, he said, the top limit might be $1,000 to $1,500 less.

Commissioner McMurray pointed out that Federally sub-sidized housing now provided low-rent apartments for families with incomes up to $4,700. He said the state's low-rent projects had an income limit for admission up to $5,900 for large families.

Mr. McMurray shared the opinion of Mr. Cruise that public subsidy should not be given at this time to housing for families above the $7,500-income level.

At present construction costs, said Mr. McMurray, completely unsubsidized private housing in Manhattan requires rents of at least $40 to $45 a room. With the markdown in land costs that is provided in Title I of the Federal Housing Act of 1949 and Federal mortgage insurance, rents could be brought down to $30 to $32 a room. But an average family with an income up to $7,500 should pay no more than $25 a room, according to Mr. McMurray.

For those families with incomes of $7,500 to $10,000 a year, Mr. McMurray suggested a tax abatement of less than the 40 per cent the city has granted to limited-dividend companies, along with low-interest loans. This plan, he said, would provide housing for the upper-middle-income families at various rent levels up to those of "completely unsubsidized housing."

Herman D. Hillman, regional director of the Public Housing Administration, said his agency was concerned only with housing for low-income families. Applying the Federal formula for low-income public housing, this would put the dividing line between low and middle income in New York City at $4,560 for a childless couple with a graduated rise to $7,440 for a family large enough to require four bedrooms. Anything below these figures the P. H. A. regards as low income in this city.

The Federal Government will subsidize low-rent housing up to a point where at least a 20 per cent gap exists between the top limit for income eligibility and the family income that would be needed to pay the lowest rents for private housing built without subsidy. Mr. Hillman said the New York City Housing Authority had failed to build Federally aided public housing up to the allowable 20 per cent gap, thereby falling short of serving adequately the upper range of this city's low-income group.

Robert C. Weaver, State Rent Administrator, said middle income, as a term used in housing, meant something quite different from what the words meant when applied to unrelated national statistics. On the basis of 1954-56 figures, one-third of all nonfarm families in the United States had annual incomes of less than $3,000; another third had from $3,000 to $5,500, and one-third had incomes of more than $5,500.

"Obviously," declared Mr. Weaver, "it would not be meaningful to define middle income in relation to housing as the group with incomes between $3,000 and $5,500."

On the basis of rents for private housing in this city and the availability of the so-called "aids to middle-income housing," Mr. Weaver defined middle income as between $4,500 and $7,000 for a childless couple and up to a range of $5,500 to $9,000 for a larger family.

SOME AID APPROVED

State Senator MacNeil Mitchell, Republican of Manhattan, and Assemblyman Alfred A. Lama, Democrat of Brooklyn, have sponsored successful measures making various forms of state and city aid—short of cash subsidy—available to private developers of middle-income housing. Senator Mitchell, who has not spelled out middle income in terms of dollars, said the Joint Legislative Committee on Housing, of which he is chairman, would make a study this year of income limitations.

The Joint Legislative Committee's 1956-57 report said private housing could be built here to rent from $19 to $23 a room if the Mitchell-Lama aids were used. With a smaller amount of tax exemption, such housing could rent for $25 a room. This, according to one of Senator Mitchell's aides, would put middle income between $4,500 and $8,000 for an average family, with a higher limit for large families.

Assemblyman Lama said an average middle-income family was one that could afford a monthly rent of $25 a room. For families with two or more children, this might require an income up to $10,000, and for smaller families, up to $7,500, he said.

Housing and living costs in Manhattan are such that a family with three children is in the middle-income group until the income goes above $20,000, according to Paul Tishman, who is building the Washington Square Village apartments.

"An income of $20,000 a year will buy about as much today as $10,000 did ten years ago," declared Mr. Tishman. "In another ten years we may have to consider the family with up to $30,000 as a high middle-income family."

Practically all new private housing built in Manhattan without tax abatement rents at $50 or more a room, except in Harlem, where a limited amount is available at $42 to $45 a room. Thus, said Mr. Tishman, a family requiring five and one-half rooms in Manhattan would need an income of $16,500 to $23,000—depending on whether it spent one-fifth or one-seventh of its income for rent—to justify living in new, unaided, private housing.

In Harlem and the boroughs beyond Manhattan, the top limit for the middle-income group might be $2,500 less, Mr. Tishman said.

A spokesman for Webb & Knapp, Inc., developer of the housing projects at Lincoln Square, Kips Bay, West Park and other Title I sites here and in other cities, said rents for middle-income housing in one city would be regarded as luxury rents in another.

In New York, he said, middle-income new housing rented at $30 to $45 a room. His estimate of what constituted middle income was $5,000 to $10,000 for a childless couple and $6,000 to $12,000 for families with children.

There has been some criticism of Title I housing that is clearly beyond the rental scale for middle-income families. Title I permits cities to acquire blighted areas and resell the properties at big discounts to private developers. The Federal Government makes good two-thirds the price difference and the city one-third.

JOHN STUART MILL

TWO SENSES OF "LAW"

John Stuart Mill (1806-1873), eldest son of the English philosopher James Mill, was himself an economist, a journalist, a logician, and a political and moral philosopher. At the age of seventeen, he published his first article in The Westminster Review. *A* System of Logic *(1843) and* Principles of Political Economy *(1848) preceded his essay* On Liberty *(1859), perhaps the most succinct statement of nineteenth-century Liberalism. Other important writings are his argument against* The Subjection of Women *(1869), his* Autobiography *(1873), and* Three Essays on Religion *(1874), in which the following selection appeared.*

No WORD is more commonly associated with the word Nature, than Law; and this last word has distinctly two meanings, in one of which it denotes some definite portion of what is, in the other, of what ought to be. We speak of the law of gravitation, the three laws of motion, the law of definite proportions in chemical combination, the vital laws of organized beings. All these are portions of what is. We also speak of the criminal law, the civil law, the law of honour, the law of veracity, the law of justice; all of which are portions of what ought to be, or of somebody's suppositions, feelings, or commands respecting what ought to be. The first kind of laws, such as the laws of motion, and of gravitation, are neither more nor less than the observed uniformities in the occurrence of phenomena: partly uniformities of antecedence and sequence, partly of concomitance. These are what, in science, and even in ordinary parlance, are meant by laws of Nature. Laws in the other sense are the laws of the land, the law of nations, or moral laws; among which, as already noticed, is dragged in, by jurists and publicists, something which they think proper to call the Law of Nature. Of the liability of these two meanings of the word to be confounded there can be no better example than the first chapter of

»»» From "Nature." From *Three Essays on Religion.* London, 1874.

Montesquieu; where he remarks, that the material world has its laws, the inferior animals have their laws, and man has his laws; and calls attention to the much greater strictness with which the first two sets of laws are observed, than the last; as if it were an inconsistency, and a paradox, that things always are what they are, but men not always what they ought to be. A similar confusion of ideas pervades the writings of Mr. George Combe, from whence it has overflowed into a large region of popular literature, and we are now continually reading injunctions to obey the physical laws of the universe, as being obligatory in the same sense and manner as the moral. The conception which the ethical use of the word Nature implies, of a close relation if not absolute identity between what is and what ought to be, certainly derives part of its hold on the mind from the custom of designating what is, by the expression 'laws of nature,' while the same word Law is also used, and even more familiarly and emphatically, to express what ought to be.

ARTHUR O. LOVEJOY

"OTHERWORLDLINESS"

Arthur O. Lovejoy (1873-1962)—born in Berlin but educated at the University of California, Harvard, and the University of Paris—was a philosopher and historian of ideas. The history of ideas is a discipline that he invented and pursued with great distinction, not only in such books as The Great Chain of Being *(1936) and* Essays in the History of Ideas *(1948), but in his editorship of the* Journal of the History of Ideas. *He taught and lectured at many universities here and abroad; at the time of his death he was professor emeritus of philosophy of Johns Hopkins University.*

. . . THERE ARE two conflicting major strains in Plato and in the Platonic tradition. With respect to the deepest and farthest-reaching cleavage separating philosophical or religious systems he stood on both sides; and his influence upon later generations worked in two opposite directions. The cleavage to which I refer is that between what I shall call otherworldliness and this-worldliness. By otherworldliness I do not mean a belief in and a preoccupation of the mind with a future life. To be concerned about what will happen to you after death, or to let your thought dwell much upon the joys which you hope will then await you, may obviously be the most extreme form of this-worldliness; and it is essentially such if that life is conceived, not as profoundly different in kind from this, but only as more of much the same sort of thing, a prolongation of the mode of being which we know in the world of change and sense and plurality and social fellowship, with merely the omission of the trivial or painful features of terrestrial existence, the heightening of its finer pleasures, the compensation of some of earth's frustrations. The two most familiar expressions by Victorian poets of the desire for a continuance of personal existence perfectly illustrate this. In nothing was Robert Browning's breezy gusto for the life that now is more manifest than in his hope to "fight on, fare ever, there as here." And when Tennyson's *meditatio mortis* ended with a prayer simply for "the wages of going on, and not to die" he, too, in his less robustious way, was declaring the sufficient worth of the general conditions of existence with which common experience has already acquainted us. Both writers were, indeed, giving utterance to a special form of this feeling which had been somewhat exceptional before the Romantic period—though our present historical survey will show us its earlier emergence—and was highly characteristic of their own age—an identification of the chief value of existence with process and struggle in time, an antipathy to satisfaction and finality, a sense of the "glory of the imperfect," in Professor Palmer's phrase. This is the complete negation of the otherworldliness of which I am speaking. For of that, even in its milder manifestations, a more or less sweeping *contemptus mundi* has been of the essence; it has had no necessary—though in most of its Occidental phases it has had an actual—connection with the craving for a separate personal immortality; and in its more thorough-going forms it has seen in that craving the last enemy to be overcome, the root of all the misery and vanity of existence.

By 'otherworldliness,' then—in the sense in which the term, I suggest, is an indispensable one for distinguishing the primary antithesis in philosophical or religious tendencies—I mean the belief that both the genuinely 'real' and the truly good are radically antithetic in their essential characteristics to anything to be found in man's natural life, in the ordinary course of human experience, however normal, however intelligent, and however fortunate. The world we now and here know—various, mutable, a perpetual flux of state and relations of things, or an ever-shifting phantasmagoria of thoughts and sensations, each of them lapsing into nonentity in the very moment of its birth—seems to the otherworldly mind to have no substance in it; the objects of sense and even of empirical scientific knowledge are unstable, contingent, forever breaking down logically into mere relations to other things which when scrutinized prove equally relative and elusive. Our judgments concerning them have seemed to many philosophers of many races and ages to lead us inevitably into mere quagmires of confusion and contradiction. And—the theme is of the tritest—the joys of the natural life are evanescent and delusive, as age if not youth discovers. But the human will, as conceived by the otherworldly philosophers, not only seeks but is capable of finding some final, fixed, immutable, intrinsic, perfectly satisfying good, as the human reason seeks, and can find, some stable, definitive, coherent, self-contained, and self-explanatory object or objects of contemplation. Not, however, in this world is either to be found, but only in a 'higher' realm of being differing in its essential nature, and not merely in degree and detail, from the lower. That other realm, though to those enmeshed in matter, occupied with things of sense, busy with plans of action, or absorbed in personal affections, it appears cold and tenuous and barren of interest and delight, is, to those who have been emancipated through reflection or emotional disillusionment, the final goal of the philosophic quest and the sole region in which either the intellect or the heart of man, ceasing, even in this present life, to pursue shadows, can find rest.

Such is the general creed of otherworldly philosophy; it is familiar enough, but we need to have it explicitly before us as the contrasting background for what is to follow.

EDWIN MUIR

"PLOT"

Edwin Muir (1887-1959) was a Scots poet, literary critic, and translator. His Collected Poems *(1953) show him to be a minor poet of great distinction. His* The Structure of the Novel *(1928), from which his definition of "plot" is taken, is a classic of modern critical theory. And the translations that he and his wife made from the German—of Hauptmann and Kafka, for example—are well-known for their excellence. From 1950 till his death, he was warden of Newbattle Abbey College, in Scotland.*

THE TERM "PLOT" stands outside these dangers [of question-begging terms]. It is a definite term, it is a literary term, and it is universally applicable. It can be used in the widest popular sense. It designates for everyone, not merely for the critic, the chain of events in a story and the principle which knits it together. It covers *Treasure Island* and *Tristram Shandy, Wuthering Heights* and *The Ambassadors, The Three Musketeers* and *Ulysses.* In all these novels a few things happen, and in a certain order, and in every novel things must happen and in a certain order. As they must needs happen, however, it is the order which distinguishes one kind of plot from another. Events move along one line in *Treasure Island,* along another in *Vanity Fair.* This volume [Muir's *The Structure of the Novel*] will be more specifically, then, a study of some of the lines along which events move in the novel; in other words, a survey of some of the main plots, each with its interior principle, which the novel has used. My concern will not be at all with what those plots "should be," but simply with what they are. The only thing which can tell us about the novel is the novel.

»»» From "Novels of Action and Character." Ch. 1 of *The Structure of the Novel.* London: The Hogarth Press, 1928. Pp. 16-17. Reprinted by permission of The Hogarth Press Ltd.

ROBERT H. ESTABROOK

"RESPONSIBLE PRESS"

Robert H. Estabrook (1918-   ) is associate editor of the Washington Post, *having previously served as editor of the* Post's *editorial page and as its London correspondent. He has been a reporter and an editorial writer for the Cedar Rapids (Iowa)* Gazette *and city editor of the Emmet County (Michigan)* Graphic. *He was a founder and has been chairman of the National Conference of Editorial Writers. In 1954 he won the Sigma Delta Chi award for best editorial.*

My own version of a responsible press as we complete the sixth decade of the Twentieth Century contains a number of elements which I have listed here, not necessarily in order of importance and with no attempt to be inclusive:

1. A responsible press will recognize the quintessential importance of full information, presented as completely, as fairly and as brightly as it knows how to do. It will recognize that the facts do not always speak for themselves, and that the apparent facts are not always the real facts. It will attempt to place the facts in perspective through interpretive stories, guarding at the same time against pandering to its editorial opinions in its news columns. It will acknowledge its mistakes candidly. It will constantly experiment with new techniques of presenting the news in more readable, comprehensive and intelligible form. It will recognize that responsibility and integrity are no barrier against wit, charm and graceful writing.

2. A responsible press will fulfill its opinion function by providing informed, provocative editorial comment. This is my particular end of the profession, and perhaps I may be pardoned a few digressions. James B. Reston of the New York *Times* said recently that only two voices have been heard above the singing commercials—Harry Golden of North Carolina and Harry Ash-

»»» From "What Is a Responsible Press?" Address delivered at the University of Michigan, Ann Arbor, December 16, 1959. Printed by permission of Robert H. Estabrook.

more of Little Rock. I should like to think that the literary lung capacity of the editorial page is a little stronger than that, and I think that it is. Nevertheless, there is something to what Mr. Reston says. Many of the country's editorial pages are so curtailed by inhibitions, prejudices, sacred cows, economic stereotypes, blind political partisanship and plain bad writing that they make up a pretty dismal chorus.

A good editorial page will have a credo of principles through which it speaks to its readers. It will give them an opportunity to talk back through letters to the editor. It will vary its tone, speaking neither in a sustained whisper or a sustained scream. It will guard against prefabricated, flannel-suited opinions that soon become flannel-mouthed opinions. It will be receptive to new ideas and will question old concepts. It will cherish its independence and will be wary of a narrow and automatic conformity. It will avoid becoming the mouthpiece only of particular segments of the society, and it will recognize the inconsistency between fair comment three years out of four and partisan atavism at election time. It will understand that this is a great and growing country which cannot be measured by old *status quo* yardsticks.

A good editorial page will always seek simplicity and readability, but it will shun the notion that it has to be flippant in order to be read. It will combine vigorous comment, when vigor is called for, with restraint and an explanation of its reasoning. It will deal in persuasion rather than in peremptives. It will retain a prudent doubt of its own omniscience, and it will not be dismayed when others share that doubt. It will recognize that as its readers become better educated and face more competing demands upon their time it will have to add something meaningful to their knowledge and understanding in order to justify itself and maintain their interest.

3. A responsible press will have a soul. It will understand and convey through its own behavior the abiding truth that newspapers are more than mere "businesses," even though they must be successful businesses in order to fulfill their broader ob-

ligations. It will scrutinize its own performance in the light of what William Allen White wrote 34 years ago about the late Frank Munsey:

Frank Munsey, the great publisher, is dead.
Frank Munsey contributed to the journalism of his day the talent of a meat packer, the morals of a money changer and the manners of an undertaker. He and his kind have about succeeded in transforming a once-noble profession into an eight per cent security.
May he rest in trust.

It will also take to heart, perhaps even while rejecting the generalization, the more recent criticism of the London *Economist*:

Most of the present generation of newspaper owners have not been newspapermen themselves and as a general rule take much less interest in the newsroom than in the advertising and accounting offices. The result is that editors and reporters are no longer fired by the traditional ambition to get all the news first and best or perish in the attempt. The profession has become safe, stodgy and standardized. Editors have apparently ceased thinking of themselves as the consciences of their communities and pride themselves instead on being businessmen.

4. A responsible press will do more than merely mirror the society as reflected in the daily news budget of tragedies, failures and accomplishments. It will recognize the aspirations of the society, seek to influence them for what it believes to be the public good and, by its own force as an educational medium, help to raise the level of culture.

5. A responsible press will be suspicious of power in all forms, public and private. It will respect dissent and it will avoid becoming identified with favorites. It will understand that a good newspaperman must be willing to see the misadventures of his best friend portrayed on the front page. It will demonstrate to readers through its own performance why freedom of the press is a public protection rather than a proprietary right. It will regard its relations with readers as a trust. It will welcome suggestions for improvement and encourage criticism of its shortcomings.

6. A responsible press will understand that in the competition with electronic journalism it must provide a depth of background that is not provided elsewhere. It must do, in the words of Barry Bingham of the Louisville *Courier-Journal,* "what television cannot or does not do." It will recognize that television is a superior entertainment medium, and it will aim at more than a repetition of the five-minute newscast. It will welcome innovation. It will adapt its search for more effective methods to the knowledge that some of the pressure of immediacy has been removed by other media which can get news flashes out faster. It will look carefully at techniques such as that developed by the *Wall Street Journal* for succinct treatment of run-of-the-mill news combined with exhaustive treatment of particular subjects of local, national or international importance. It will seek to encourage young new readers by making itself useful in the schools.

7. A responsible press will concentrate upon better training of its reporters and editors. It will insist upon more adequate background in the social and physical sciences and in languages. It will seek to buttress news skill and specialization with general awareness and understanding. It will recognize the need to attract more competent young people into newspaper careers through better pay, faster promotion and a less ritualistic employment structure.

8. A responsible press will remember the Eleventh Commandment: Thou shalt not take thyself too damned seriously.

JOSEPH WOOD KRUTCH

WHAT IS A GOOD REVIEW?

Joseph Wood Krutch (1893-   ), American literary critic and teacher, was educated at the University of Tennessee and at Columbia, where he took his Ph.D. degree and later taught both English and journalism. From 1943 to 1952 he was the Brander Mathews Professor of Dramatic Literature at Columbia. Among his many books are Comedy and Conscience after the Restoration *(1924),* The Modern Temper *(1929),* Samuel Johnson *(1944),* The Measure of Man *(winner of the National Book Award, 1954), and* Human Nature and the Human Condition *(1959). As drama critic and literary editor of* The Nation *from 1924 to 1952, he produced many reviews of the kind that he defines in the following essay.*

OF ALL LITERARY FORMS the book review is the one most widely cultivated and least often esteemed. To many the very phrase "literary form" may smack of pretense when applied to a kind of writing which is usually so casual; and formlessness may, indeed, be the only form of many commentaries on books. Book reviewing can, nevertheless, become an art in itself and would be such more often if the ambitious reviewer would only devote himself to the cultivation of its particular excellences instead of attempting, as he so often does, to demonstrate his capacities by producing something "more than a mere review." The best review is not the one which is trying to be something else. It is not an independent essay on the subject of the book in hand and not an aesthetic discourse upon one of the literary genres. The best book review is the best review of the book in question, and the better it is the closer it sticks to its ostensible subject.

To say this is not to say that a good review is easy to write; in certain technical respects it is, indeed, the most difficult of all forms of literary criticism for the simple reason that in no other is the writer called upon to do so many things in so short a space. The critical essay, no matter how extended it may be,

»»» *The Nation,* CXLIV (April 17, 1937), 438. Reprinted by permission of *The Nation.*

175

is not compelled to aim at any particular degree of completeness. It may—in fact it usually does—assume that the reader is sufficiently familiar with the work under discussion to make description unnecessary and it may also confine itself to whatever aspects of the subject the critic may choose.

But the book review as a literary form implies completeness; it has not really performed its function unless, to begin with, it puts the reader in possession of the facts upon which the criticism is based, and unless—no matter upon how small a scale—its consideration is complete. However penetrating a piece of writing may be, it is not a good review if it leaves the reader wondering what the book itself is like as a whole or if it is concerned with only some aspects of the book's quality.

I shall not pretend to say how large a proportion of the so-called reviews published in *The Nation* or anywhere else actually achieve the distinguishing characteristics of the book-review form, but a certain number of them do and the sense of satisfactoriness which they give can always be traced to the fact that, whatever other qualities they may have, they accomplish the three minimum tasks of the book reviewer. They describe the book, they communicate something of its quality, and they pass a judgment upon it.

Each of these things is quite different from the others, but only the last is usually considered as carefully as it ought to be by either reader or writer. Adequate description implies a simple account of the scope and contents of the book; its presence guarantees that the reader will not be left wondering what, in the simplest terms, the book is about. "Communication of quality" implies, on the other hand, a miniature specimen of what is commonly called "impressionistic criticism"; it means that the reviewer must somehow manage to recreate in the mind of the reader some approximation of the reaction produced in his own mind by the book itself. And in however low esteem this form of criticism may be held as a be-all and end-all (Mr. Eliot calls it the result of a weak creative instinct rather than of a critical impulse), it is indispensable in a book review if that review is to perform the function it is supposed to perform, and if it is to become what it is supposed to be—namely, not merely an account of a book on the one hand or an independent piece of criticism on the other, but a brief critical essay which includes within itself all that is necessary to make the criticism comprehensible and significant.

Your "reviewer" often envies the more lofty "critic" because the critic is supposed to be read for his own sake while the reviewer must assume that the reader is attracted more by his interest in the book discussed than by the reviewer himself. For that very reason he is likely either to treat reviewing as a casual affair or to seek for an opportunity to write something else under the guise of a review. He might be happier himself and make his readers happier also if he would, instead, take the trouble to ask what a review ought to be and if he would examine his own work in the light of his conclusions. It is not easy to do within the space of a thousand words or less the three things enumerated. It is less easy still to combine the description, the impression, and the judgment into a whole which seems to be, not three things at least, but one.

How many reviewers of novels, for instance, seem to know how much of a particular story has to be told in order to provide a solid basis for the impression they intend to convey? And if it is decided that some part of the story must be told, how many know, as a story-teller must, whether the incidents are striking enough to come first or must be introduced with some comment which creates the interest? Yet a first-rate review, despite its miniature scale, raises precisely the same problems as long narratives or expositions raise, and each must be solved as artfully if the review is to have such beauty of form as it is capable of. Doubtless the finest reviewer can hardly hope to have his art fully appreciated by the public. But there is every reason why he should respect it himself.

ANALYSIS

DEFINITION, analysis, and classification are results of distinct yet related processes. A definition, though a statement about a term, points to both a concept and a class of things, either of which can furnish the subject of a piece of writing. An analysis is the result of the division of either a concept or an individual member of a class into its constituent parts. A classification is the result of the sorting of all members of a class into groups or subclasses on a certain basis. For example, the definition of the term "carnivore" given in the introductory note to "Definition" points to both carnivority (a concept) and all carnivores (a class determined by that concept). An analysis of carnivority shows that this concept has two constituent parts: animality and flesh-eatingness. An analysis of an individual carnivore might show that it has cauliflower ears and pigeon toes. A classification of all carnivores on the basis of weight might show that they fall into two subclasses: fat carnivores and thin carnivores. Another example may serve as a further contrast between analysis and classification. If a piece of writing shows that the latest model of Cadillac convertible coupé has a V-8 engine of three-hundred horsepower, automatic transmission, and power steering, or if it shows that one individual coupé of this model has air conditioning and red-vinyl upholstery, then this piece of writing is an analysis. But, if it shows that, in respect of color, all such coupés fall into five subclasses—mist-blue coupés, dawn-gray coupés, and so on—then this piece of writing is a classification.

Of the seven following analyses, three are analyses of concepts: a law (Parkinson), a means of communication (Hall), and a sort of meaning and thinking (Aldrich); and four are analyses of individuals: a certain small college (Williams), a certain period of unemployment (Silberman), a certain earthquake (Darwin), and a certain ode (Tate). Parkinson's and Williams' analyses are sociological; Silberman's, economic; Darwin's, physical; Tate's, literary; Aldrich's, philosophical; and Hall's, anthropological.

Classifications appear in the next section of this book. Analysis and classification, however, often occur in the same piece of writing; both in combination and separately, they are well represented elsewhere in this book. See, for example, the two views of freshman English in "Argumentation and Persuasion."

C. NORTHCOTE PARKINSON

PARKINSON'S LAW

OR THE RISING PYRAMID

C. Northcote Parkinson (1909-   ), a British scholar specializing in Asian affairs, has written many books on historical and economic subjects, the latest being East and West (1963). Educated at Cambridge and the University of London, he has taught at several schools, was the Raffles Professor of History at the University of Malaya, and has been a visiting professor at American universities. As a major in the R. A. F., he was attached to the War Office during World War II. What he learned there of governmental administration inspired the article in The Economist upon which the following selection is based. When readers stopped laughing, they realized that his humor had a serious point, one pursued in The Law and the Profits (1960) and In-Laws and Outlaws (1962).

WORK EXPANDS so as to fill the time available for its completion. General recognition of this fact is shown in the proverbial phrase "It is the busiest man who has time to spare." Thus, an elderly lady of leisure can spend the entire day in writing and dispatching a postcard to her niece at Bognor Regis. An hour will be spent in finding the postcard, another in hunting for spectacles, half an hour in a search for the address, an hour and a quarter in composition, and twenty minutes in deciding whether or not to take an umbrella when going to the mailbox in the next street. The total effort that would occupy a busy man for three minutes all told may in this fashion leave another person prostrate after a day of doubt, anxiety, and toil.

Granted that work (and especially paperwork) is thus elastic in its demands on time, it is manifest that there need be little or no relationship between the work to be done and the size of the staff to which it may be assigned. A lack of real activity

»»» From Parkinson's Law and Other Studies in Administration. Boston: Houghton Mifflin Company, 1957. Pp. 2-13. Reprinted by permission of Houghton Mifflin Company.

180

does not, of necessity, result in leisure. A lack of occupation is not necessarily revealed by a manifest idleness. The thing to be done swells in importance and complexity in a direct ratio with the time to be spent. This fact is widely recognized, but less attention has been paid to its wider implications, more especially in the field of public administration. Politicians and taxpayers have assumed (with occasional phases of doubt) that a rising total in the number of civil servants must reflect a growing volume of work to be done. Cynics, in questioning this belief, have imagined that the multiplication of officials must have left some of them idle or all of them able to work for shorter hours. But this is a matter in which faith and doubt seem equally misplaced. The fact is that the number of the officials and the quantity of the work are not related to each other at all. The rise in the total of those employed is governed by Parkinson's Law and would be much the same whether the volume of the work were to increase, diminish, or even disappear. The importance of Parkinson's Law lies in the fact that it is a law of growth based upon an analysis of the factors by which that growth is controlled.

The validity of this recently discovered law must rest mainly on statistical proofs, which will follow. Of more interest to the general reader is the explanation of the factors underlying the general tendency to which this law gives definition. Omitting technicalities (which are numerous) we may distinguish at the outset two motive forces. They can be represented for the present purpose by two almost axiomatic statements, thus: (1) "An official wants to multiply subordinates, not rivals" and (2) "Officials make work for each other."

To comprehend Factor 1, we must picture a civil servant, called A, who finds himself overworked. Whether this overwork is real or imaginery is immaterial, but we should observe in passing, that A's sensation (or illusion) might easily result from his own decreasing energy: a normal symptom of middle age. For this real or imagined overwork there are, broadly speaking, three possible remedies. He may resign; he may ask

to halve the work with a colleague called B; he may demand
the assistance of two subordinates, to be called C and D. There
is probably no instance in history, however, of A choosing any
but the third alternative. By resignation he would lose his pen-
sion rights. By having B appointed, on his own level in the
hierarchy, he would merely bring in a rival for promotion to
W's vacancy when W (at long last) retires. So A would rather
have C and D, junior men, below him. They will add to his
consequence and, by dividing the work into two categories, as
between C and D, he will have the merit of being the only man
who comprehends them both. It is essential to realize at this
point that C and D are, as it were, inseparable. To appoint C
alone would have been impossible. Why? Because C, if by
himself, would divide the work with A and so assume almost
the equal status that has been refused in the first instance to
B; a status the more emphasized if C is A's only possible successor. Subordinates must thus number two or more, each being
thus kept in order by fear of the other's promotion. When C
complains in turn of being overworked (as he certainly will)
A will, with the concurrence of C, advise the appointment of
two assistants to help C. But he can then avert internal friction
only by advising the appointment of two more assistants to help
D, whose position is much the same. With this recruitment of
E, F, G, and H the promotion of A is now practically certain.

Seven officials are now doing what one did before. This is
where Factor 2 comes into operation. For these seven make so
much work for each other that all are fully occupied and A is
actually working harder than ever. An incoming document may
well come before each of them in turn. Official E decides that it
falls within the province of F, who places a draft reply before
C, who amends it drastically before consulting D, who asks G
to deal with it. But G goes on leave at this point, handing the
file over to H, who drafts a minute that is signed by D and
returned to C, who revises his draft accordingly and lays the
new version before A.

What does A do? He would have every excuse for signing

the thing unread, for he has many other matters on his mind. Knowing now that he is to succeed W next year, he has to decide whether C or D should succeed to his own office. He had to agree to G's going on leave even if not yet strictly entitled to it. He is worried whether H should not have gone instead, for reasons of health. He has looked pale recently—partly but not solely because of his domestic troubles. Then there is the business of F's special increment of salary for the period of the conference and E's application for transfer to the Ministry of Pensions. A has heard that D is in love with a married typist and that G and F are no longer on speaking terms—no one seems to know why. So A might be tempted to sign C's draft and have done with it. But A is a conscientious man. Beset as he is with problems created by his colleagues for themselves and for him—created by the mere fact of these officials' existence— he is not the man to shirk his duty. He reads through the draft with care, deletes the fussy paragraphs added by C and H, and restores the thing back to the form preferred in the first instance by the able (if quarrelsome) F. He corrects the English—none of these young men can write grammatically—and finally produces the same reply he would have written if officials C to H had never been born. Far more people have taken far longer to produce the same result. No one has been idle. All have done their best. And it is late in the evening before A finally quits his office and begins the return journey to Ealing. The last of the office lights are being turned off in the gathering dusk that marks the end of another day's adminstrative toil. Among the last to leave, A reflects with bowed shoulders and a wry smile that late hours, like gray hairs, are among the penalties of success.

From this description of the factors at work the student of political science will recognize that administrators are more or less bound to multiply. Nothing has yet been said, however, about the period of time likely to elapse between the date of A's appointment and the date from which we can calculate the pensionable service of H. Vast masses of statistical evidence have been collected and it is from a study of this data that Parkinson's Law has been deduced. Space will not allow of detailed analysis but the reader will be interested to know that research began in the British Navy Estimates. These were chosen because the Admiralty's responsibilities are more easily measurable than those of, say, the Board of Trade. The question is merely one of numbers and tonnage. Here are some typical figures. The strength of the Navy in 1914 could be shown as 146,000 officers and men, 3249 dockyard officials and clerks, and 57,000 dockyard workmen. By 1928 there were only 100,000 officers and men and only 62,439 workmen, but the dockyard officials and clerks by then numbered 4558. As for warships, the strength in 1928 was a mere fraction of what it had been in 1914—fewer than 20 capital ships in commission as compared with 62. Over the same period the Admiralty officials had increased in number from 2000 to 3569, providing (as was remarked) "a magnificent navy on land." These figures are more clearly set forth in tabular form.

ADMIRALTY STATISTICS

Year	Capital ships in commission	Officers and men in R.N.	Dockyard workers	Dockyard officials and clerks	Admiralty officials
1914	62	146,000	57,000	3249	2000
1928	20	100,000	62,439	4558	3569
Increase or Decrease	−67.74%	−31.5%	+9.54%	+40.28%	+78.45%

The criticism voiced at the time centered on the ratio between the numbers of those available for fighting and those available only for administration. But that comparison is not to the present purpose. What we have to note is that the 2000 officials of 1914 had become the 3569 of 1928; and that this growth was unrelated to any possible increase in their work. The Navy during that period had diminished, in point of fact, by a third in men and two-thirds in ships. Nor, from 1922 onward, was its strength even expected to increase; for its total of ships (unlike its total of officials) was limited by the Washington Naval Agreement of that year. Here we have then a 78 per cent increase over a period of fourteen years; an average of 5.6 per cent increase a year on the earlier total. In fact, as we shall see, the rate of increase was not as regular as that. All we have to consider, at this stage, is the percentage rise over a given period.

Can this rise in the total number of civil servants be accounted for except on the assumption that such a total must always rise by a law governing its growth? It might be urged at this point that the period under discussion was one of rapid development in naval technique. The use of the flying machine was no longer confined to the eccentric. Electrical devices were being multiplied and elaborated. Submarines were tolerated if not approved. Engineer officers were beginning to be regarded as almost human. In so revolutionary an age we might expect that store-keepers would have more elaborate inventories to compile. We might not wonder to see more draughtsmen on the payroll, more designers, more technicians and scientists. But these, the dock-yard officials, increased only by 40 per cent in number when the men of Whitehall increased their total by nearly 80 per cent. For every new foreman or electrical engineer at Portsmouth there had to be two more clerks at Charing Cross. From this we might be tempted to conclude, provisionally, that the rate of increase in administrative staff is likely to be double that of the technical staff at a time when the actually useful strength (in this case, of seamen) is being reduced by 31.5 per cent. It has been proved statistically, however, that this last percentage is irrelevant. The officials would have multiplied at the same rate had there been no actual seamen at all.

It would be interesting to follow the further progress by which the 8118 Admiralty staff of 1935 came to number 33,788 by 1954. But the staff of the Colonial Office affords a better field of study during a period of imperial decline. Admiralty statistics are complicated by factors (like the Fleet Air Arm) that make comparison difficult as between one year and the next. The Colonial Office growth is more significant in that it is more purely administrative. Here the relevant statistics are as follows:

1935	1939	1943	1947	1954
372	450	817	1139	1661

Before showing what the rate of increase is, we must observe that the extent of this department's responsibilities was far from constant during these twenty years. The colonial territories were not much altered in area or population between 1935 and 1939. They were considerably diminished by 1943, certain areas being in enemy hands. They were increased again in 1947, but have since then shrunk steadily from year to year as successive colonies achieve self-government. It would be rational to suppose that these changes in the scope of Empire would be reflected in the size of its central administration. But a glance at the figures is enough to convince us that the staff totals represent nothing but so many stages in an inevitable increase. And this increase, although related to that observed in other departments, has nothing to do with the size—or even the existence—of the Empire. What are the percentages of increase? We must ignore, for this purpose, the rapid increase in staff which accompanied the diminution of responsibility during World War II. We should note rather, the peacetime rates of increase: over 5.24 per cent between 1935 and 1939, and 6.55 per cent between 1947 and 1954. This gives an average increase of 5.89 per cent each year, a percentage markedly similar to that already found in the Admiralty staff increase between 1914 and 1928.

Further and detailed statistical analysis of departmental staffs would be inappropriate in such a work as this. It is hoped, however, to reach a tentative conclusion regarding the time likely to elapse between a given official's first appointment and the later appointment of his two or more assistants.

Dealing with the problem of pure staff accumulation, all our researches so far completed point to an average increase of 5.75 per cent per year. This fact established, it now becomes possible to state Parkinson's Law in mathematical form: In any public administrative department not actually at war, the staff increase may be expected to follow this formula—

$$x = \frac{2k^m + 1}{n}$$

k is the number of staff seeking promotion through the appointment of subordinates; l represents the difference between the ages of appointment and retirement; m is the number of man-hours devoted to answering minutes within the department; and n is the number of effective units being administered. x will be the number of new staff required each year. Mathematicians will realize, of course, that to find the percentage increase they must multiply x by 100 and divide by the total of the previous year, thus:

$$\frac{100\ (2k^m + 1)}{yn}\%$$

where y represents the total original staff. This figure will invariably prove to be between 5.17 per cent and 6.56 per cent, irrespective of any variation in the amount of work (if any) to be done.

The discovery of this formula and of the general principles upon which it is based has, of course, no political value. No attempt has been made to inquire whether departments *ought* to grow in size. Those who hold that this growth is essential to gain full employment are fully entitled to their opinion. Those who doubt the stability of an economy based upon reading each other's minutes are equally entitled to theirs. It would probably be premature to attempt at this stage any inquiry into the quantitative ratio that should exist between the administrators and the administered. Granted, however, that a maximum ratio exists, it should soon be possible to ascertain by formula how many years will elapse before that ratio, in any given community will be reached. The forecasting of such a result will again have no political value. Nor can it be sufficiently emphasized that Parkinson's Law is a purely scientific discovery, inapplicable except in theory to the politics of the day. It is not the business of the botanist to eradicate the weeds. Enough for him if he can tell us just how fast they grow.

LLOYD P. WILLIAMS

QUIESCENCE, TRADITION, AND DISORDER—CROSS-SECTION OF A SMALL COLLEGE

Lloyd P. Williams (1918-   ), a native of Dallas, received his bachelor's and master's degrees from North Texas State College and his doctor's degree from the University of Texas. A Ford post-doctoral fellow at Harvard in 1953-54, he taught at the University of Texas and the Ohio State University before going to the University of Oklahoma, where he is now professor of the history and philosophy of education. His many articles on education, including studies of Emerson as an educational thinker, show his concern for what he calls "the recovery of quality" in American education.

. . . It is inevitable that the facts described in history should not give an exact picture . . . ; they are transformed in the brain of the historian, they are moulded by his interests and coloured by his prejudices. ROUSSEAU.

CHEROKEE COLLEGE is the subject of this paper. Whereas the name is fictitious, the college is not. It is populated by real students, faculty members, administrators, and numerous auxiliary assistants. It is our purpose to analyze this small college, to note its most distinctive characteristics, to delineate its internal structure and dynamics, and to propose some realistic alternatives for the alleviation of the pathological conditions that beset it. It is hoped that this paper sheds some light, however modest, on the sociology of higher education.

Cherokee is collegiate, private, church-related, and coeducational. A romantic might say the natural environment of Cherokee, atop beautiful rolling hills, is the kind that a benevolent Provi-

»»» *American Association of University Professors Bulletin*, XLIII (Winter, 1957), 615-625. Reprinted by permission of the *AAUP Bulletin*.

dence must have created to induce men to quiet reflection. On the surface, here is an ideal college in an ideal community.

There is nothing particularly distinctive about the community. Small, semi-rural, middle-class, conservative, Republican, Protestant, and intellectually somnambulistic, it resembles hundreds of others. Of the motorists who pour through it on the main highway, many note, but few remember, the name of the hamlet. Some note, but few remember, the name of the local college. It has been here for more than a hundred years, and its life goes on much as collegiate life has gone on for decades. An overworked and underpaid staff performs all the ceremonials, and at graduation time, all the rituals associated with collegiate life. It acquiesces in the forms of democracy. And occasionally, when through the vicissitudes of fortune some fine mind finds itself in these surroundings, there is an outburst of intellectual vigor.

II

The administrative staff at Cherokee is large: a president, two vice-presidents, an academic dean, a registrar, a treasurer, a dean of students, a dean of men, a dean of women, an admissions director, an assistant admissions director, and a publicity director. The present president is a close relative of a former president, who, with zeal, self-sacrifice, and determination, nurtured the college through its uncertain years in the early twentieth century. His successor nurtured it through the hazardous years of the depression period. These successes, in conjunction with long-time control, have led the presidential family, unconsciously, to regard Cherokee as its personal property. The president himself is preoccupied with administrative trivia, and his interference in various offices throughout the college is frequent, unpredictable, and apparently compulsive. His approach to decision-making follows a triune principle—never make decisions unless it is absolutely necessary; postpone decision-making as long as possible; avoid making decisions in the presence of subordinates. The unconscious logic of the process seems to be —no decisions, no commitments; no commitments, no difficulties.

Vice-President "X" is a long-time personal friend of the president, and his intellectual and executive appendage. Only on rare occasions and in emergencies does he make decisions on his own. Nevertheless, he keeps tight control over all subordinates, encouraging a steady flow of clients in and out of his office. Meetings are called daily that demand the immediate attention of subordinates. Extensive discussions are held on matters of secondary importance or on questions about which only the president is in fact permitted to make decisions. Verbal commitments are made that somehow almost immediately call for another meeting to confirm or modify. This is a highly successful technique for maintaining control of subordinates, for after a sufficient lapse of time all parties concerned are confused as to what decisions were reached and what action, if any, should be taken. The result is another meeting for purposes of clarification. Status is important to Vice-President "X"; he wants his office to look attractive, and his secretaries to appear busy. Subordinates who show reluctance to go along with expedient administration are reminded by Vice-President "X" that "administration is a science."

Vice-President "Y" is a close relative of the president. He received his B.A. from Cherokee and was at one time, briefly, interim president. The business affairs of the college, for which he is responsible, are conducted on a basis of mystery. Neither the deans nor the faculty are consulted in financial matters; no budget committee exists; and the staff, including the dean, is only casually, perfunctorily, occasionally, and verbally informed of the financial status of the institution. The only individuals who may conceivably know what happens in the business office, other than Vice-President "Y" himself, are the president and Vice-President "X."

Vice-President "Y" came to the institution at the beginning of the great depression, imbued by his father with a zeal to thriftiness. The father was a powerful man—intellectually keen, driving, determined, dominant, scrupulously devout, unbending in opposition to alcohol and tobacco. Even though he is long dead, his influence remains heavy upon the institution; he is a potent father-figure to many of the small band of loyalists; he is spoken of with reverence; and he gave Vice-President "Y" a messianic fervor for keeping Cherokee solvent. The result: solvency takes precedence over all instructional considerations; no money is to be spent unless it is absolutely necessary; financial affairs must be kept under the immediate surveillance of his office; no alien must be permitted to lay a hand upon the treasury. There is a marked reluctance on the part of Vice-President "Y" and the president to spend money for anything intangible. Such things as secretarial services, teachers salaries, or guest artists run a poor second to the refurbishment of the football stadium or other improvements in the physical plant. The tangible is material, hence real; the intangible is immaterial, hence unreal.

III

The academic dean at Cherokee College occupies an extraordinary position in the administrative hierarchy—he is both an anomaly and an excrescence. By historical tradition, by definition, and by logic he should be the administrative head of the academic program. Not so at Cherokee. To the president, the dean appears to be a cross between a cheerleader for the faculty and a public relations counselor. He is supposed to make people feel good, and is expected deliberately to cultivate the alumni. He is supposed to get the college in the public eye. To Vice-President "X," the dean is a clerk and academic actuary. Both president and vice-president unconsciously use the dean as an agent for the discharge of frustration; both build ego, maintain status, and minimize anxiety by belittling any subordinate, including the dean, who, if he desires security, finds it in doing what he is told.

The dean has two clerical helpers. With the assistance of these two clerks, he is expected to (1) keep records on the academic progress of each student; (2) maintain daily attendance records; (3) organize and execute registration; (4) issue grades to students and to parents four times during each academic year; (5) handle the stenographic and mimeographic work for the entire faculty; (6) prepare the schedule of classes; (7) carry on the correspondence of the dean's office—volumes of which come from parents; and (8) periodically publish a bulletin of faculty news. These things are in addition to his manifest need to absorb the frustrations of an overworked and undervalued faculty and the necessity of conciliating the scores of patrons and petitioners who descend daily upon his office. Of course, the dean is expected to teach.

The president appoints the dean and then introduces him to the staff. In late years, the president has appointed the dean upon recommendation of Vice-President "X." The dean is thus in an ambivalent position between the need to express loyalty to his superiors, and a desire to serve the academic interests of the college by supporting, encouraging, and giving security to the teaching staff. The cumulative frustration inherent in this situation leads periodically to resignation: the turn-over of deans is rapid, the average tenure being two to three years.

Tradition and logic suggest that the function of a registrar is to register—specifically, to register the academic progress of the students and to maintain pertinent statistical records relative to it. Cherokee College is an exception, for the registrar performs such functions only casually and belatedly; other functions are considered more important. The registrar, by right of seniority, by right of custom, and by tacit higher echelon approval, rules the academic life of the college. Whereas some academic regulations are written down, many are not, and the registrar consistently and successfully resists any attempt by the dean or others to codify and publicize such regulations. The instruction committee of the college, nominally constituted to handle academic questions, is subverted by the registrar *via* the College *Bulletin*. The deletion, modification, or addition to the *Bulletin* of regulations is an annual occurrence, not predictable except for the fact that it will take place. Like Bolshevik history, the minutes of the instruction committee are rewritten as the registrar, who is also secretary of the committee, feels inclined. Less dramatic but equally effective techniques used by the registrar to control staff members, particularly new ones, and to maintain power over academic affairs, are those of ignoring a question or simulating crying. The net consequence of this lawlessness is to keep the junior executives and the registrar in a continuing imbroglio, that alternately simmers and seethes, but never terminates.

The dean of students, the dean of men, and the dean of women work in a sort of collective endeavor to house, feed, nurture, and counsel the students of Cherokee College—to counsel them in all aspects of their existence, leaving little to imagination or independent judgment. This paternalistic program enjoys the sanction and encouragement of the administration; but the more thoughtful members of the faculty note its increasing tendency to attract an uncritical type of student, lacking in initiative and imagination. Such a student is not likely to have a clear conception of what the higher learning is about, and rarely has he any clear notion of why he is in college or what he should study. Without any doubt, the personnel deans consider their counseling to be conducted in the most scientific spirit; some of the academic staff consider their efforts coddling.

Few features of Cherokee College are more striking than the absence of defined functions for the numerous administrative officers. There are no clear directives, written or verbal, defining the functions of any of these officers. The result is a state of administrative confusion. No one, student or faculty or junior administrator, knows for sure to whom to go for information, instruction, or definitive answers. Officers are not sure of their freedom; they are uncertain of the extent of their authority, and understandably hesitant to act. Directives countermand one another, attempts to exercise authority counterbalance one another, and senior administrators use their authority as a counterpoise to constrain subordinates, thus keeping the entire administrative hierarchy in a state of actionless equilibrium. Material waste is one consequence. More serious is the dissipation of psychic energy, the useless expenditure of precious time, and inevitable frustration that leads to an increase in anxiety and insecurity. Seriously concerned subordinates who attempt to attack this chaotic state of affairs are neutralized by such respectable administrative techniques as referring proposals to a committee, postponing consideration to a later date, or holding meetings with indecisive consequences.

IV

Offhand remarks sometimes reveal more than formal statements of value. In an unguarded moment, the president of Cherokee once remarked that the college had a good administration and the faculty was unimportant. Faculty members are easy to get, he affirmed confidently. The president, with the assistance of Vice-President "X," picks the faculty. Occasionally the academic dean is called in for consultation, but there is little evidence that his judgments carry any weight. The faculty is, of course, not seriously consulted in the selection of new staff members, although an occasional gesture is made in this direction.

Some forty full-time and some twenty part-time faculty members carry out the instructional responsibilities at Cherokee. A teaching load of sixteen hours is considered normal, with no allowance for heavy committee work or other college responsibilities. A few instructors have regularly taught more than twenty semester hours a term, and one instructor actually "taught" some forty hours in one term! Attempts to reduce the teaching load are skillfully parried by upper echelon authorities *via* the usual procrastination devices. Cherokee has four men and three women as full-time teachers in physical education, but is unable to maintain a full-time professor (or instructor) in sociology. Class sizes range from some sixty students in freshman social science to perhaps one or two in advanced Greek. However, publicity emphasizes the claim that Cherokee is a small college with small classes, where everybody gets individual attention. The salary scale ranges from $5800.00 for the highly talented football coach ($3800.00 for his principal assistant) to $3400.00 for a Harvard M.A. in social science.

There are no objective standards for the distribution of financial rewards within the college, nor are the published statements relative to promotions followed with any degree of diligence. Jungle conditions prevail in the relations between administration and faculty, for rank and salary are what one can get, and what one can get depends upon such variables and unpredictables as fate, accident, the professional market, and, some say, the president's digestion. Most of the staff is made up of kind, serious, and anxiety-ridden teachers, who serve Cherokee loyally in spite of continual provocation to rebellion. There is a small core of loyalists who stay with the college year after year, regardless of how unhappy internal conditions become. Paradoxically, this group does not necessarily comprise the prestige-privileged members of the faculty, nor does it necessarily comprise the highest-ranking and highest-paid. Length of service is no guarantee of tenure or preferential treatment. In fact, some long-service people are constantly overloaded and undercompensated. There appears to be no analyzable logic to the process by which one attains prestige status—some get it by accident, others by obsequiousness. Staff turnover at Cherokee is heavy. In one year, as many as eighteen new faculty members came to the college, including the academic dean, the dean of men, and the dean of women. Freshman social science appears to show the most frequent staff changes. Overload is the principal reason for such turnover. A one man department in economics shows four new staff members in four years. The lone psychologist is replaced about every two years.

The faculty at Cherokee College is an anxious one. It is quiescent, obsequious, diligent, conscientious, underpaid, overworked, and persevering. One professor, of some distinction in his field, has devoted forty years of his life to the college; but only a handful of the staff could wear ten-year pins. Few aspire to serious scholarship; virtually no one publishes. Politically, the staff is Republican; economically, it is convinced that free enterprise is the only sound principle upon which to base the nation's economic system. Outside of a small group, principally the social scientists, few seem seriously occupied with the issues of the day. Nevertheless, a few excellent scholars inhabit Cherokee. In Greek and in history are men who could hold good positions elsewhere, but prefer to stand by the college. There are able men in biology, philosophy, music, and world literature. Their loyalty is generally explained by undergraduate association with Cherokee, or family homes in close proximity, or denominational affiliation.

Only during the last three years have professors enjoyed the security of a yearly contract. Previously, there was no assurance of continued employment, even for a year. Contracts are now issued in the spring; previously the procedure was for the president to inform staff members during the summer whether or not their services would be needed during the coming academic year. A small chapter of the American Association of University Professors appears to be responsible for the introduction of written contracts into this phase of the business life of the college. The president is noticeably apprehensive about the Association, and since its leadership is in the hands of a few bright and well-educated young scholars, his apprehension is perhaps well-grounded. No other serious threat to family dominance has presented itself during this century, with the exception of the impersonal great depression.

V

The student body at Cherokee College is small—approximately eight hundred. It is equally divided between boys and girls at the beginning of each school year, but an imbalance rapidly appears, for a higher percentage of boys than girls drop out as the academic year progresses. This drop-out is predictable, as the office of admissions is required (for reasons of public relations, financial sagacity, and student morale) to admit as many boys as girls, even though the former frequently lack the educational background and intellectual ability to do college work that the girls generally possess. In anticipation of the drop-out, the College admits approximately ten per cent more boys than can be adequately housed or instructed. This situation not only places an additional burden upon the instructional staff; it also greatly increases the work of the admissions office, the dean's office, the treasurer's office and the personnel office, besides bringing anxious (or irate) parents to the campus to plead (or demand) special privilege and consideration. The dissipation of time and energy expended on counseling, salvaging, and ultimately separating this body of students from the college is both enormous and avoidable.

Intellectually, the student body shapes up into a reasonably balanced normal curve—skewed, perhaps, a bit toward the bottom. The girls are distinctly more able than the boys; more of them come with good high school records and high I Q's than do the boys. The elimination ratio of boys to girls is about five to one. Approximately one third of the student body is enrolled in the Department of Education, although the college deliberately advertises itself as a "Liberal Arts College." Home economics is popular; political science, on the other hand, rarely has over five or six declared majors. Political science, economics, and philosophy are not required for graduation. Each student must complete two courses in Bible. Political-mindedness is not a characteristic of the student body, nor is the faculty inclined to change this situation. That the student body should choose to hold a mock Republican convention in 1956 indicates the drift of sentiment. The orientation of the student body is overwhelmingly conservative, Republican, *laissez-faire,* and Protestant. *Laissez-faire* is uncritically equated with American business enterprise. Social activities consume quantities of time. Student government, abetted by the paternalistic philosophy of Cherokee, also fosters busyness, and a preoccupation with affairs distinctly outside of student competence; *e.g.,* academic and administrative problems. Apparently, top echelon administrative sanction for this frenetic activity and irrelevance is explained by the formula—vigorous activity, little study; little study, little inclination to serious questioning of the status quo; hence, intellectual quiescence and the assured support of the College by business and alumni.

VI

Cherokee College is church-related. The administrative staff belongs to the college church; many other staff members do also. However, there is no pressure on the faculty to belong to the college church, only the insistence that they participate in the activities of some evangelical Protestant denomination. The village has four Protestant churches, and no Roman Catholic church or mission. Very few Roman Catholics come to Cherokee. The presence of those that do come can be explained by geographical proximity, an amorous attachment, or the desire to gather academic credits in an environment that is not too strenuous.

Compulsory chapel is held three times a week, but contrary to the label, the programs may take any form—a religious lesson, an innocuous political address, eulogies of the football squad, or student government sessions. Each chapel is opened with a prayer and a hymn from the authorized hymnal. Staff members are expected to be seen in chapel frequently. Some students and a few staff members object to the indiscriminate mixing of religion, athletics, current events, and social announcements in chapel, and the chairman of Fine Arts desires particularly to enhance the aesthetic quality of chapel. However, the president, who maintains absolute control over chapel programming, and who presides whenever possible, resists any and all attempts at innovation. Aesthetically, chapel leaves much to be desired. Religiously, discussions center around the idea of salvation, redemption, and the "good news." Intellectually, discussions are uneven, varying from the trite to the profound; politically, they are orthodox, conventional, and stereotyped.

Religion in all its manifestations at Cherokee is formalistic, ceremonial, ritualistic, verbalistic, and innocuous. There is little serious attempt to ascertain what the Judaeo-Christian ethic means in daily life; what implications such an ethic has for the political or economic life of the nation; or what its meaning may be for daily human relations. Personal contacts between the administration and the staff are generally friendly, without being cordial. Even though alcohol and tobacco are proscribed, many people associated with Cherokee smoke surreptitiously on the campus, openly off the campus; some, including top administrative brass, take an occasional drink. To a serious critic, the atmosphere that seems to permeate the college runs along these lines: join the church (or a church), follow the forms, attend the ceremonies, publicly subscribe to the village *mores;* privately, do whatever you wish so long as you do it with discretion. Fighting on the side of truth and the angels is the minister of the college church. Able, intellectual, informed, sensitive, dedicated, enlightened—he preaches, Sunday after Sunday, unemotional and challenging sermons. But on occasion even he bows to community pressure, delivering a sermon in a more conventional vein. Reared on a soft and sentimental theology, many students neither understand him nor approve of him; one executive in the college—a pillar of the church—has actively sought the parson's resignation for failure to preach the gospel of salvation more vigorously.

The church with which Cherokee is affiliated contributes approximately $35,000.00 to an annual $800,000.00 budget. Such support seems skimpy to some staff members, hardly justifying denominational affiliation. An occasional dissenter will sometimes note that the better private institutions of the United States have broken or loosened their ties with denominational bodies. There is no evidence, however, that the dominant figures in the administrative hierarchy or the board of trustees, a predominant number of whom are clergymen of the denomination or prominent lay members, will likely entertain this heresy. Formally, the college provides an undergraduate training ground for young men who wish to attend the denominational seminary. Giving expression to a latent hostility and discontent, a few faculty members quietly and heretically counsel the better pre-theological students to attend divinity school at Harvard, Yale, Princeton, Chicago, or Oberlin.

VII

Scholarship and learning at Cherokee must necessarily take a subordinate place in the life of the institution, for preoccupation with power, status, and security dissipates both time and energy. A continuous power struggle goes on. New staff members rapidly become involved, both psychologically and actively. They come imbued with enthusiasm for the virtues of a small college. Their attempts actively to enter into the life of the institution are rebuffed with an intensity equal to their initial enthusiasm. Enthusiasm gives way to a determination not to kowtow, and this, finally, to pessimism, resignation and the recruitment of new staff members, some of whom repeat the same cycle.

Democracy receives considerable lip service in the college, but actually it is fictitious. The administration is generous in trivial matters; e.g., in permitting the staff to decide when to take a holiday in honour of the victorious varsity, or in giving crisp new five dollar bills to faculty children at Christmas. Rigid administrative control is maintained over faculty meetings. No one other than the president or Vice-President "X" presides, agenda are carefully restricted and are generally prepared without faculty advice. One technique used to control the staff, while at the same time creating the illusion of democracy and freedom, is reliance upon General Robert's *Rules of Order* at all types of meetings. Motions, amending motions, tabling motions, points of order, et cetera, fly so fast that serious items of business are lost, purposes are obscured, and legalism becomes an end in itself. A quiet attempt to achieve a meeting of minds is impossible. Both communist and noncommunist authoritarians have learned that mastery of parliamentary procedure is a tool well constituted to stifle democracy.

Psychologically, Cherokee is sick. The most noticeable consequences stemming from the present ethos and social structure of the College are frustration, emotional insecurity, anxiety, latent and manifest hostility, disguised and undisguised aggression, in conjunction with both self-effacing and self-depreciating tendencies on the part of many. Fear inhibits attention to scholarship; desire to maintain status obstructs concern with genuine academic endeavor; jealousy over trivial prerogative consumes energies that appropriately belong to the intellectual life of a healthy college. The lowering of morale both collectively and individually, that invariably results from internal discord, can have nothing but deleterious consequences for the study-teaching and research-writing functions of the staff. The habitual thwarting of normal aspirations and expectations of both teaching faculty and junior administrators is responsible for the extreme and continuing tension.

The cure for small college ineptness is not necessarily more money although this happy possibility has virtue not to be despised. The fundamental cure can be found only in a complete reorientation of the emotional-attitudinal life of the institution. Intellectual leadership based upon a quiet and continuing respect for scholarship must supplant leadership consumed with a public relations focus. The presumption that a beautiful campus is a substitute for scholarship, or that it guarantees an institution of higher learning, must be put to rest permanently. Administration by procrastination, deception, intimidation, and manipulation must be supplanted by administration that consistently gives encouragement and emotional security to scholars. Only a revolution in interpersonal relations, with sincerity and integrity at the core, will release the potential inherent in the scholars at Cherokee.

In many respects this College is probably not unlike scores of other colleges across the United States. It is this probability of typicalness that is especially disturbing, for it is a measure of the extent to which authoritarianism, anti-intellectualism, formalism, and irrelevance have captured American higher education. The college that has gone astray can return to its historic mission —the discovery and dissemination of Truth—only under the rigorous leadership of an administration and a staff habitually guided by a vision of freedom, scholarship, and intellectual greatness.

CHARLES E. SILBERMAN

WHAT HIT THE TEENAGERS

Charles E. Silberman (1925-   ), a native of Iowa, was educated at Columbia and later taught economics there. He joined the staff of Fortune *in 1953 and is now a member of its board of editors. His book* Crisis in Black and White *(1964) is an analysis of race relations.*

IN THE U.S., Eric Larrabee has remarked, childhood "is not only admired; it is looked upon as a national asset, somewhat on a par with the Declaration of Independence or the Mississippi River." But while childhood is regarded as a national asset, adolescence seems more and more to be regarded as a national problem, like traffic congestion, water pollution, or slums. Specifically, the current problem of teenagers is unemployment. Dr. James B. Conant, who helped direct national attention to the problem, has described it as "social dynamite"; President Kennedy called it "one of the most expensive and explosive social and economic problems now facing this country"; and Lyndon Johnson has given expansion of teenage employment top priority on the road to the Great Society. For teenagers, who represent just 8 percent of the labor force, account for 22 percent of total unemployment and about 35 percent of the *increase* in unemployment since the middle 1950's. All told, nearly 850,000 teenagers—14 percent of those in the labor force—are currently looking for work; another 300,000 teenage boys are, for various reasons, neither in school nor in the labor force. (Some are waiting to go into the Army, some are juvenile delinquents, some are unable to work, and some are just drifting.) And unemployed teenagers could very well increase this year, with a record number—500,000 or thereabouts—expected to pour into the labor force.

There is a certain irony, of course, in the fact that providing

more jobs for teenagers has become a major concern of states-
men and of social reformers; for during most of this century
and part of the last, reformers' zeal was devoted to the *elimination* of child labor. In 1904 the National Child Labor Committee
was organized to further that cause. In 1959, after voting down
several suggestions that the organization be dissolved, since its
original goal had long since been achieved, the trustees instead
established the National Committee on Employment of Youth. *Its*
objective is "to create greater job opportunities for America's
youth." At first, the new committee (technically, a division of the
old) felt the need to persuade people that a shortage of teenage
jobs really was a problem. "With all the headlines about delinquency," the committee's publicity director told the readers of
the New York *Times,* in a somewhat plaintive letter to the editor,
"it is important to remember that this is only one of many
juvenile problems . . . teenagers need help in planning for,
choosing, and getting suitable jobs . . ."

It didn't require a new organization, however, to bring teenage
unemployment to the forefront of public consciousness. The
recent increases in the number of teenagers wanting to work
have created a labor-market situation without precedent in the
last half-century. One would have to go back to around 1900
to find another peacetime period when the teenage labor force
was growing so rapidly. But the teenage labor market then was
an entirely different proposition. A third of the population was
living on the farm, only 15 percent of the high-school-age youngsters were actually attending school, and fewer than 10 percent
of them finished. The great majority went to work after the
sixth or eighth grade. In the cities, working-class families depended on the children's earnings to supplement the father's
meager wage; and farm families were even more dependent on
child labor.

But the growth of free and compulsory education signaled a
new trend—and the end of any large expansion of the teenage
labor force. Between 1910 and 1940 the proportion of fourteen-
to-seventeen-year-olds attending high school went up from 15

percent to more than 70 percent; the proportion graduating from high school went up from under 10 percent to over 50 percent. This change was accompanied (and to a considerable degree caused) by the enormous migration of Americans from the farm, where teenage labor was particularly valuable, to the city. In 1910 teenagers had been about 15 percent of the labor force; by 1940 they were 7.5 percent of it.

This long-run contraction of teenage employment was temporarily reversed during World War II, when every available hand was put to work. But it resumed as soon as the war ended; between 1947 and 1955 the number of teenagers in the labor force declined by 200,000 as the teenage "participation rate"— i.e., the proportion who were either at work or looking for work —continued to fall.

The participation rate is still declining, as the proportion of teenagers completing high school and attending college continues to rise. But the teenage population has been growing so rapidly that this declining percentage now represents a growing number. Between 1955 and 1960 the teenage labor force increased by 900,000, and it grew almost as much again between 1960 and 1964. It is now about six million. (For an explanation of how the figures in this article are derived, see page 228 [p. 221 here].)

A SEARCH FOR SOMETHING

Adolescence, as Professor Edgar Z. Friedenberg of the University of California has defined it, "is the period during which a young person learns who he is, and what he really feels." In the phrase of psychiatrist Erik H. Erikson, of Harvard, it is "the search for something and somebody to be true to." It is difficult for a youngster to learn who he is under the best of circumstances. It is even harder if he is unemployed, for unemployment can make the most secure man feel useless and unwanted. It is particularly hard for an unemployed adolescent to feel true to the society he lives in if he has an impoverished background. Indeed, the slum youngster's unemployment seems only to confirm his well-grounded suspicion that he can't "make it"—that decent jobs are not available to young people of his color, or his nationality, or his social class. The gates of life seem to clang shut when he is still at a remarkably early age.

Thus the concern now being expressed about teenage unemployment is amply justified. But the explanations of how the problem has come about, and what it portends, are inadequate. In the most common view, a high level of teenage unemployment is a symptom of far-reaching technological and economic changes. Technological change is said to be destroying unskilled jobs, most especially the traditional "entry jobs" through which teenagers used to make their way into the labor force—i.e., jobs that could be filled by youngsters with little education and no particular skill or training, but that might lead to more skilled and better-paying jobs later on. Eli E. Cohen, executive secretary of the National Committee on Employment of Youth, has estimated that some 250,000 "entry jobs" a year are disappearing as a result of technological change. Meanwhile—the argument continues—new technology is constantly increasing the educational requirements of jobs. "The machine," Secretary of Labor Willard Wirtz contends, "now has a high-school education in the sense that it can do most jobs that a high-school graduate can do, so machines will get the jobs because they work for less than a living wage. A person needs fourteen years of education to compete with machines."

In short, Wirtz, Cohen, and others see the teenage unemployment problem as rooted in the dwindling opportunities for the uneducated and untrained. In contrast to the 1920's or 1930's, they also believe, formal education and training have become young people's only reliable means of entry into the world of work. That is why Wirtz has proposed that an additional two years of school attendance be made compulsory. "Boys and girls simply have to be trained to fit into an economy which no longer includes the unskilled work they could get before. Anybody who drops out of school may very well be committing economic suicide." In a 1963 address Wirtz recalled that thirty years previously, when he taught high-school literature and grammar, very little of *Macbeth* or English syntax got through to the students. "But it didn't matter," he went on, for this was "a town where most of the boys were going into the boiler works, and if the girls didn't get married, they would probably get work at the glove factory." (The town, which Wirtz did not name, was Kewanee, Illinois.)

WHY CAN'T JOHNNY WORK?

Plausible as it sounds, this diagnosis both oversimplifies and overcomplicates the current situation, and contrasts it with a past that never was. In general, as *Fortune* demonstrated in the first two articles in this series, it is simply not true that new technology is eliminating the demand for relatively unskilled or poorly educated blue-collar workers; nor is technology raising the demand for people with a great deal of education and professional or technical training as rapidly as Wirtz suggests. (See "The Real News about Automation," January, 1965, and "The Comeback of the Blue-Collar Worker," February, 1965.) In particular, the much-discussed disappearance of "entry jobs" is a myth, based upon some fanciful reconstruction of the kinds of jobs teenagers used to get, and how they used to get them. Actually, those "entry jobs" that have been disappearing—e.g., bowling-alley pinboy, Western Union messenger, elevator operator—have typically been dead-end jobs, not jobs that led to something. And meanwhile a great many new jobs that teenagers can fill have been created, especially in trade and service industries.

Most important of all, the official diagnosis blurs the real problem about the dropouts. The problem is indeed a critical one for our society; but it is not, we shall see below, simply a matter of persuading potential dropouts to stay in school.

Why, then, *are* there so many unemployed teenagers? The answer, stripped to its essentials, is that the sudden expansion of the teenage population happened to coincide with a slowdown in the economy between 1957 and 1961. Teenagers had the bad luck to begin pouring into the labor force at a time when there was an oversupply of adult workers. Given a choice between experienced or, in any case, comparatively stable adults and inexperienced and relatively unstable teenagers, employers naturally hired the adults.

Typically, the adults in question were women; working wives often seek—and get—the kind of unskilled and part-time jobs that are most suitable for teenagers. To a degree that has not generally been appreciated, teenagers have been competing for jobs with their mothers. One of the major difficulties about finding jobs for teenagers has been the enormous, and completely unanticipated, increase in the proportion of married women who are in the labor force: from 20 percent in 1947 to 26 percent in 1953 and 34 percent in 1964. Had their participation rate stayed at the 1947 level, there would have been nearly six million fewer women working last year.

WHY THE STANDARDS ARE UP

Not surprisingly, the labor surplus has led to a stiffening of hiring standards all along the line. Thus adults without any previous work experience—for example, married women looking for part-time jobs while their children are in school—have also had difficulty finding jobs; when there is a choice, employers prefer an experienced to an inexperienced adult. *People seeking their first jobs constitute twice as large a proportion of the unemployed today as they did a decade ago.*

A distinction is in order at this point. Employers have raised the educational requirements for new employees—but not necessarily because the technical requirements of the jobs have changed. A great many employers have made a high-school diploma a prerequisite for employment simply as a screening device, to cut down the number of people who have to be interviewed or to ensure "a better class of workers." To some degree, publicity campaigns to persuade youngsters to stay in school, or to return if they've already dropped out, may make it harder for those who do drop out to find a job; if enough people are persuaded that dropouts are unemployable, they will insist on hiring only high-school graduates (or teenagers clearly determined to finish school) even for dead-end jobs.

Some companies are now discovering that they have overdone this upgrading. They are even learning that for some jobs the unambitious or not-too-bright dropout may be preferable to the high-school graduate. In staffing two plants, for example, Ford hired many young high-school graduates, expecting that this would raise productivity. Instead, the policy lowered productivity and increased absenteeism; the new workers tended to find the assembly line oppressive. In any case, Ford has substituted a literacy test administered by the U.S. Employment Service for formal credentials like high-school diplomas.

LIFE ON THE MARGIN

Teenage unemployment today is too high, not because the relatively unskilled and the poorly educated are unemployable, but because the aggregate demand for labor has been weak—which is to say, because the economy has not grown rapidly enough. Professor Stanley Lebergott of Wesleyan University, a profound academic student of the labor force, is one of the few who have argued persuasively against the notion that the unemployed are victims of under-education. This notion, he says, "misapprehends at least one fundamental characteristic of the unemployed"—the fact that they "are marginal in the existing state of offer and demand in the labor market. If all workers in the labor force had their education improved," Lebergott argues, "some would still be marginal," but "their marginality would then appear to be associated with some other simple single characteristic."

To be sure, the educational level of the entire labor force (i.e., including the unemployed) is rising rapidly; the median number of years of schooling went from 9.1 in 1940 to 11.1 in 1952 and 12.2 last year, and the proportion of workers aged eighteen to sixty-four with a high-school education or better has risen from 32 percent in 1940 and 44 percent in 1952 to 57 percent last year. But this change is the result of a great many things having nothing whatever to do with the amount of education people need for the job. The educational attainment of the labor force has risen because of the shift of population from rural to urban areas (a much larger proportion of youngsters finish high school in urban areas); the expansion of facilities for public education throughout the country; the rise in average income (which enables young people to stay in school longer); and a radical change in public attitudes toward education. Thus even the average laborer, household domestic, or service worker—as well as the craftsman, technician, or clerk—has more education than he had ten years ago.

In any case, there is no evidence of any decline in the number of "entry jobs." A detailed manpower survey by the New York State Department of Labor, for example, revealed that approximately two-thirds of all the jobs in existence in that state involve such simple skills that they can be—and are—learned in a few days, weeks, or at most months of on-the-job training. And the fact is that nearly half the Americans holding jobs today did not finish high school. Indeed, studies by Dr. A. J. Jaffe of Columbia University's Bureau of Applied Social Research indicate that even in industries experiencing the most rapid technological change and the highest rate of productivity growth half or more of the male production workers did not finish high school, i.e., they are "dropouts."

It is also a fact that in 1962, when output expanded by 6.3 percent, and again last year, when output increased by 4.6 percent, the economy was able to provide enough jobs to offset the entire increase in the teenage labor force. Indeed, teenagers accounted for 17 percent of the increase in employment last year and about the same in 1962. In 1963, on the other hand, when the growth rate slowed down to 3.4 percent, the number of jobs filled by teenagers actually declined.

THE TURN TO COMPETITION

At the same time, the structure of teenage employment has changed substantially in the last thirty years or so, as the chart

Net Change in Number of Teenage Workers 1930-60

The teenage unemployment crisis has not arisen only because there are more teenagers than ever. Actually, there are not many more in the labor force than there were in 1930. What *has* changed is that most are now in the competitive labor market, whereas in 1930 a large proportion were "unpaid family workers"— typically helping around the farm. The number of teenage farm workers declined by 900,000 between 1930 and 1960. Meanwhile, the number of nonfarm workers increased by 1,020,000 or one-third. The biggest increase, evenly divided between boys and girls, was in the form of 420,000 more "service workers," e.g., waiters and waitresses, hospital attendants.

on page 132 [p. 211 here] demonstrates. The chart is based on a detailed analysis of changes in teenage occupations between 1930 and 1960, and was developed for *Fortune* by industrial economist Alan Greenspan, president of Townsend-Greenspan & Co. (Only the decennial censuses provide the kind of detailed data necessary for such an analysis. Nineteen-thirty was chosen as the base year because it is about the closest that one can come to a "normal" pre-World War II year.) The most striking change, as the chart indicates, is the decline of 900,000 in the number of teenage agricultural workers. One-third of the teenage workers were on the farm in 1930, most of them classified as "unpaid family workers"—hence outside the operation of the competitive labor market; by 1960 the ratio was down to 10 percent. The change is even greater for teenage boys: 50 percent of the fourteen-to-seventeen-year-old boys, and 30 percent of the eighteen-to-nineteen-year-olds, were farm laborers in 1930. Most of the boys, in short, did not go directly into the boiler works when they abandoned *Macbeth;* only 27 percent of the teenage workers in 1930, in fact, were employed in manufacturing industries.

For all the talk about the disappearing "entry jobs," the number of unskilled and semiskilled teenage jobs outside of agriculture has increased twice as fast as the teenage population. Between 1930 and 1960 the number of teenage boys who were laborers and semiskilled blue-collar workers increased by 115,000, or 12 percent. It is true that teenage employment in manufacturing declined in these years; and Secretary Wirtz is right in suggesting that not many boys go into the boiler works nowadays. But plenty of them do go to work in the local supermarket, gas station, or parking lot. Or they become ushers, hospital attendants, busboys, and waiters; the number of such teenage "service workers" went up by 200,000, a threefold increase since 1930. The number of "sales workers" also increased by 200,000, but about three-quarters of that increase represents an expansion in the number of newspaper delivery boys.

Some traditional teenage jobs have virtually disappeared, of course, e.g., Western Union messenger, elevator operator, bowling-alley pinboy. But these jobs were never very important: there were just 5,000 to 6,000 male teenage elevator operators in 1930 (there are fewer than 2,000 now) and the number of teen-age Western Union messengers never exceeded 13,000, compared to 2,500 or thereabouts now. And despite the displacement of bowling-alley pinboys by automatic pin-setting machines, more teenage boys work in bowling alleys today than in 1930—e.g., as cashiers, porters, and "pin-chasers" (unjamming jammed automatic pinsetters).

Many of the jobs teenagers hold—perhaps even the majority—are essentially dead-end jobs. They *always* were; much of the current discussion about youth employment is based on nostalgia for a past that never existed—on what might be called "the sweatshops were fun" view of the case. Thus the U.S. Employ-ment Service officially laments the fact that "the time has passed when a young worker can begin an occupation with assurance that he has entered a lifetime vocation." Whenever that time was, it is not within the memory of anyone now alive.

Half or more of the teenagers in the labor market, moreover, have no particular desire to begin "a lifetime vocation"; they simply want a job that won't interfere too much with their studies. Some 3,200,000 teenagers—55 percent of those in the labor force—are also students, most of them holding or looking for jobs after school or during summer vacations. *All the increase in the teenage labor force in recent years—and all the increase in teenage unemployment—has occurred among teenagers attending school.* Since 1962 the number of students in the labor force has gone up by 450,000, or 17 percent. In the same period the num-ber of unemployed students has increased by 150,000, or 54 per-cent. More than half the unemployed teenage boys are now students.

The student workers represent an extraordinary new phe-nomenon. "This youthful work economy," the sociologist Reuel Denney of the University of Hawaii has written, "is not, by and large, vocationally directed, even though it may serve as a way of trying out possible occupations. It is rather a form of paid sociability combined with study, an existence in which the student-waiter brings some of the campus to the resort and uses the pool after hours."

The School-Age Population, 1964
(School-year averages, in thousands)

Age:	14-17	18-19	20-21	22-24
TOTAL	13,864	5,164	5,181	6,831
NOT IN SCHOOL:				
In labor force:	593	2,116	2,925	4,425
Employed	474	1,816	2,635	4,137
Unemployed	119	300	290	288
Not in labor force:	619	771	1,137	1,909
Total	1,212	2,887	4,062	6,334
IN SCHOOL:				
In labor force:	2,515	655	336	168
Employed	2,203	550	290	142
Unemployed	312	105	*	*
Not in labor force:	10,137	1,622	783	329
Total	12,652	2,277	1,119	497

* Less than 100,000.

It is natural to think of teenagers as being either in school or at work, but many are both. Among fourteen-to-seventeen-year-olds, for example, 91 percent, or 12,652,000, were in school; 2,203,000 of these were also working (mostly part time) and 312,000 were looking for work. Of the 1,212,000 out-of-school fourteen-to-seventeen-year-olds, 474,000 were working and 119,000 were unemployed. In the ages between twenty and twenty-four, almost a third of those in school were in the labor force. Those not in school or the labor force are predominantly girls. (Figures refer to the civilian population only.)

Not every student works as a waiter or a lifeguard in a summer resort, of course; many depend on year-round jobs to keep them in school. But for most, the earnings from a job are only one of several sources of income: parental support, private scholarships, public scholarships, and wages are all mingled together. For working after school or during vacations is no longer the mark of respectable poverty; on the contrary, students from middle-income families are more likely to be in the labor force than students from low-income families—perhaps because it is easier for the former to find jobs.

The real teenage employment problem involves the *out*-of-school youngsters. Contrary to the general impression, the out-of-school teenage labor force has not been growing in the last several years. The number of unemployed out-of-school teenage boys has actually declined slightly—from 243,000 in 1962 to 223,000 last year. It is these boys, three-fifths of them dropouts—plus another 300,000, 100,000 to 150,000 of whom could have been in the labor force but weren't—who constitute what Wirtz calls the "outlaw pack."* Many of them appear to be unemployable: they are—or seem to be—uninterested in working, unwilling or unable to adjust to the routine and discipline of a job, and generally apathetic, sullen, or hostile. Others seem willing enough to work, but have trouble following any task through to completion.

It is understandable that adults view these nonworking teenagers with deep misgivings, and are confounded by the story Wirtz tells, of asking an unemployed Harlem teenager whether he was looking for a job, and the youngster's replying, "Why?" To an adult, the answer seems obvious: men work because they have to. And thirty or forty years ago teenagers worked for the same reason—because of economic necessity, their own or their parents'. The children's earnings were depended upon to sup-

* Some economists define "the youth employment problem" as involving sixteen- to twenty-one-year-olds. In this age group there are 386,000 unemployed out-of-school males and 309,000 out of school and out of the labor force; perhaps 100,000 to 150,000 could be in the labor force.

plement the father's; the mother stayed home to raise the children. It was simply taken for granted that youngsters went to work when they left school; that was, in fact, why they left.

WHY WON'T JOHNNY WORK?

Today's teenagers, even those in slums, are in a quite different situation. If the family is intact, it is now the mother who is supplementing the father's wage. If the family is not intact the Welfare Department or the federal Aid to Dependent Children program provides the supplement.

Teenagers also lack the psychological pressures that make the great majority of adult men prefer work to idleness. In adult society, as Professor David Riesman has put it, "holding down a job is necessary to a sense of responsible and respectable adulthood." Not only do most working-class men believe that it is a man's duty to "bring home the bacon"; a sizable minority, Riesman argues, "believe that marriage is important because it provides a man with a family for whom he may work"—a paradoxical reversal of the comic-strip stereotype of male resentment at having been trapped by marriage into a life of servitude.

But these social and cultural pressures to work don't operate very effectively in teenage society; holding down a job is not necessarily a source of status, as in adult society, nor is unemployment a source of shame. On the contrary, in at least some city slums, teenage society displays a certain disdain for legitimate work. The kinds of menial jobs that are available are regarded as "slaving"; status and prestige attach, rather, to "the tough guy" who affects a show of bravado, or to "the hustler" who earns his living through petty criminality—e.g., as a runner for a numbers game.

And to the extent that work *is* a value to teenagers, the kind of work that is valued may not be the kind that is available —and certainly not the kind that leads to middle-class status. There is, in lower-class culture, a respect for manual or outdoor labor, especially labor having to do with *things*, and a corresponding disdain for many white-collar and service jobs; more precisely, there is a fear that holding such a job may diminish the teenager's virility. "We're outdoor types"; "we like to fiddle with engines," young men interviewed by *Fortune* remarked, in explaining why they were relucant to go back to school to qualify for white-collar jobs. "Only finks do I.B.M."

But if there is a disdain for white-collar work, so is there, quite often, a resentment of unskilled or semiskilled service jobs as too servile or degrading. Americans, and particularly young Americans, balk at accepting the role implied or required in such jobs as waiter, hospital attendant, household domestic; we do not have the British tradition of service without servility. Yet these jobs—not those for which a high-school diploma is really necessary—are the ones for which there is an unfilled and rapidly growing demand. (On the Labor Department's own calculations, the supply of high-school graduates over the next ten years will be "adequate to meet the demand for workers with this amount of education.")

The problem is compounded by the fact that service jobs tend to be badly paid, as well as low in status. The New Jersey Employment Service had great difficulty finding teenage applicants in Newark for a program to train hospital attendants. Applicants were assured a job if they finished the course. But the job, which was an hour-and-a-quarter bus ride away (weekly commutation: $5.20), paid $50 a week.

The problems, then, are considerable; and yet the teenage dropout is not a hopeless case. One striking characteristic of adolescence is its transiency: what the social workers' blandishments cannot accomplish, the process of aging can, and does. As the youngsters grow up, the same societal pressures that make the rest of us work begin to operate on them, too: they want to get married, have children, or at least move away from home into "pads" of their own. And so the youngsters who were delinquents at sixteen or seventeen turn into law-abiding citizens at twenty or twenty-one; those who seemed unemployable at seventeen or eighteen begin to settle down at nineteen or twenty and look for a steady job.

The process of finding one takes time; finding "the right job," in particular, can be a hit-or-miss affair, since employee and employer are usually brought together by word of mouth. (Only one-quarter of all hirings in the economy involve the use of a public or private employment service.) Hence eighteen- and nineteen-year-old boys change jobs more than twice as often as fourteen-to-seventeen-year-olds. Job changes reach a peak among the twenty-to-twenty-four-year-olds, but then drop abruptly, as family responsibilities and seniority rights stabilize employment. Indeed, among eighteen- and nineteen-year-old married men, the unemployment rate is 6.6 percent; for single men the same age it is 15.3 percent; and among twenty-to-twenty-four-year-olds the unemployment rate for the married men is only 4.3 percent, compared to 11.9 percent for single men.

None of this is intended to suggest that the aging process is a satisfactory solution to the teenage unemployment problem. Even among twenty- to twenty-one-year-old men, the unemployment rate for dropouts runs to 18 percent, compared to 9 percent for high-school graduates. More important, when the dropouts find work, as most ultimately do, they are likely to be restricted to mean, dirty, badly paid jobs.

THE POOR DROPOUTS

But persuading the dropouts to return to school, or requiring potential dropouts to stay in school until they're eighteen or twenty, won't solve anything; it could even make matters worse. In one sense, the dropouts show better judgment in dropping out than educators do in planning campaigns urging them to return. For the dropouts weren't learning anything when they were in school—nor, for the most part, were the schools terribly eager to keep them. In a group of dropouts studied by Professor S. M. Miller of Syracuse University, 90 percent of the boys were at least one grade behind the one they should have been in; nearly two-thirds were two or more grades behind. And a statewide study in Maryland indicated that nearly half the dropouts were reading at or below the sixth-grade level.

This academic failure, it should be emphasized, is not because the dropouts are unable to learn; at least two-thirds of them have I.Q.'s within the normal range. Since I.Q. tests substantially understate the native ability of youngsters coming from impoverished backgrounds, the proportion who should have been able to keep up is undoubtedly a good bit higher. And the dropouts *do* come predominantly from impoverished families. In the U.S. as a whole, 28 percent of the youngsters entering high school now drop out. (Another 5 percent leave *before* they enter high school.) But the high-school dropout rate runs as low as 8 percent in a settled middle- and upper-income, white-collar suburb like Pasadena, California, and as high as 38 percent in an industrial city like Detroit. More to the point, perhaps, the dropout rate in Detroit's slum neighborhoods—or in New York's, Chicago's, Philadelphia's, or any other large city's—runs as high as 60 to 70 percent.

"COLLEGE BOYS" AND "CORNER BOYS"

Some slum children do succeed in school. But their academic success is not based solely on intelligence; it involves, as well, an ability (and desire) to leave the slum psychologically at an early age. In his *Street Corner Society,* a now classic analysis of Italian teenage society of the 1930's, the sociologist William F. Whyte raised the question of why some of the children of Italian immigrants became successful lawyers or businessmen, while others stayed mired in the slums—in Whyte's phrase, remained "corner boys." "The most obvious explanation," he wrote, "is that . . . a college education is tremendously important for social and economic advancement." But that was "only a part of the story. Most of the college men were set apart from their fellows as early as the ninth grade. When they were still children, they fitted into a pattern of activity leading toward social mobility. College education was simply a part of that pattern.

"Both the college boy and the corner boy want to get ahead," Whyte explained. "The difference between them is that the college boy either does not tie himself to a group of close friends or else is willing to sacrifice his friendship with those who do not advance as fast as he does. The corner boy is tied to his group by a network of reciprocal obligations from which he is either unwilling or unable to break away."

The corollary is that the youngster who doesn't attune himself at an early age to middle-class values finds school a more and more hostile place. Indeed, to understand the dropouts' difficulties, particularly their sullen anger and aimless way of life, one must realize that the schools' failure is not just a failure to teach. It is more terrible; for the schools *do* teach these children something: namely, that they are incapable of learning. Or so it seems to the children. They begin this lesson in the first grade, when they have trouble learning to read. The curriculum is based on the assumption that youngsters come to school already equipped with a wide range of verbal skills and concepts that are necessary to learn to read—skills and concepts that middle-class children have imbibed with the air they breathe, but that most slum children have not yet acquired. This failure to learn to read becomes an increasing handicap as the youngsters go through school, for the amount of required reading increases at something like a geometric rate. It is not just their academic failure that oppresses, however. Edgar Friedenberg documents with devastating detail (in his new book, *Adolescence in a Mass Society*) the ways in which school organization itself seems calculated to show contempt for the students.

The result, as Robert Schrank of Mobilization for Youth has written, is that the life history of teenage slum dwellers has been "a continuum of failure." Lower-class dropouts, particularly Negroes and Puerto Ricans, "do not want to fail," Schrank argues, "and yet they know nothing else." This affects the youngsters' ability to perform on the job as well as in school. For the dropouts, as Schrank puts it, "have been conditioned to the idea that they are stupid." More important, they "have been conditioned to feel they are not capable of solving problems"; anything that smacks of problem-solving brings back what Schrank aptly terms "the reflex of failure." In sum, academic failure reinforces the slum youngster's sense of being trapped by an alien and hostile world, and persuades him that there is no way—certainly no legitimate way—for one of his background or his skin color to "make it" in the world at large.

ABOUT THE FIGURES

Some of the figures used in this article differ from those published by the Bureau of Labor Statistics. *Fortune's* figures, based on unpublished BLS data, are "school-year averages"; the published BLS statistics are annual averages. Since the teenage labor force runs 45 percent higher during the summer months than during the school year, an annual average overstates (by 650,000) the number of youngsters who are normally in the labor force.

More important, the annual averages substantially understate the number of teenagers who are students: during the summer months BLS classifies as students only those actually attending summer school. Thus students who go away to camp during the summer, or travel with their parents, or just loaf, are statistically indistinguishable from the "dropouts." In 1964, for example, the published figures (averaging all twelve months) show a rather frightening total of 1,045,000 teenage boys who were neither in school nor in the labor force. For the nine months of the school year, however, there were 70 percent fewer, i.e., 300,000.

The chart on page 132 [p. 211 here], showing changes in teenage occupations between 1930 and 1960, is based on data developed for *Fortune* by Alan Greenspan of Townsend-Greenspan & Co. from the decennial censuses for those years. The figures are necessarily imprecise because the Census Bureau used different definitions and different techniques of enumeration in the two years; however, the orders of magnitude may be considered reliable.

CHARLES DARWIN

A GREAT CHILEAN EARTHQUAKE

Charles Darwin (1809-1882), English naturalist, enunciated the theory of biological evolution in his Origin of Species *(1859) and* The Descent of Man *(1871). Although Alfred R. Wallace had arrived at the same conclusions independently, it was Darwin's* Origin *that aroused the controversy over the theory of natural selection and Darwin's name that became famous—and notorious—even though Darwin published Wallace's essay as well as his own findings. Darwin began his research as a naturalist attached to the surveying expedition of the* Beagle, *which explored the coasts of South America and Australasia from December, 1831, to October, 1836. From his journal of that voyage comes the following selection.*

FEBRUARY 20TH [1835].—This day has been memorable in the annals of Valdivia, for the most severe earthquake experienced by the oldest inhabitant. I happened to be on shore, and was lying down in the wood to rest myself. It came on suddenly, and lasted two minutes, but the time appeared much longer. The rocking of the ground was very sensible. The undulations appeared to my companion and myself to come from due east, whilst others thought they proceeded from south-west: this shows how difficult it sometimes is to perceive the direction of the vibrations. There was no difficulty in standing upright, but the motion made me almost giddy: it was something like the movement of a vessel in a little cross-ripple, or still more like that felt by a person skating over thin ice, which bends under the weight of his body.

A bad earthquake at once destroys our oldest associations: the earth, the very emblem of solidity, has moved beneath our feet like a thin crust over a fluid;—one second of time has created in the mind a strange idea of insecurity, which hours of reflection would not have produced. In the forest, as a breeze moved the trees, I felt only the earth tremble, but saw no other effect. Captain Fitz Roy and some officers were at the town during the

»»» From *The Voyage of the Beagle* (entries for February 20 and March 4, 1835). London, 1839.

shock, and there the scene was more striking; for although the houses, from being built of wood, did not fall, they were violently shaken, and the boards creaked and rattled together. The people rushed out of doors in the greatest alarm. It is these accompaniments that create that perfect horror of earthquakes, experienced by all who have thus seen, as well as felt, their effects. Within the forest it was a deeply interesting, but by no means an awe-inspiring phenomenon. The tides were very curiously affected. The great shock took place at the time of low water; and an old woman who was on the beach told me, that the water flowed very quickly, but not in great waves, to high-water mark, and then as quickly returned to its proper level; this was also evident by the line of wet sand. This same kind of quick but quiet movement in the tide, happened a few years since at Chiloe, during a slight earthquake, and created much causeless alarm. In the course of the evening there were many weaker shocks, which seemed to produce in the harbour the most complicated currents, and some of great strength.

March 4th.—We entered the harbour of Concepcion. While the ship was beating up to the anchorage, I landed on the island of Quiriquina. The mayor-domo of the estate quickly rode down to tell me the terrible news of the great earthquake of the 20th:—"That not a house in Concepcion or Talcahuano (the port) was standing; that seventy villages were destroyed; and that a great wave had almost washed away the ruins of Talcahuano." Of this latter statement I soon saw abundant proofs—the whole coast being strewed over with timber and furniture as if a thousand ships had been wrecked. Besides chairs, tables, book-shelves, etc., in great numbers, there were several roofs of cottages, which had been transported almost whole. The store-houses at Talcahuano had been burst open, and great bags of cotton, yerba, and other valuable merchandise were scattered on the shore. During my walk round the island, I observed that numerous fragments of rock, which, from the marine productions adhering to them, must recently have been lying in deep water, had been cast up high on the beach; one of these was six feet long, three broad, and two thick.

The island itself as plainly showed the overwhelming power of the earthquake, as the beach did that of the consequent great wave. The ground in many parts was fissured in north and south lines, perhaps caused by the yielding of the parallel and steep sides of this narrow island. Some of the fissures near the cliffs were a yard wide. Many enormous masses had already fallen on the beach; and the inhabitants thought that when the rains commenced far greater slips would happen. The effect of the vibration on the hard primary slate, which composes the foundation of the island, was still more curious: the superficial parts of some narrow ridges were as completely shivered as if they had been blasted by gunpowder. This effect, which was rendered conspicuous by the fresh fractures and displaced soil, must be confined to near the surface, for otherwise there would not exist a block of solid rock throughout Chile; nor is this improbable, as it is known that the surface of a vibrating body is affected differently from the central part. It is, perhaps, owing to this same reason, that earthquakes do not cause quite such terrific havoc within deep mines as would be expected. I believe this convulsion has been more effectual in lessening the size of the island of Quiriquina, than the ordinary wear-and-tear of the sea and weather during the course of a whole century.

The next day I landed at Talcahuano, and afterwards rode to Concepcion. Both towns presented the most awful yet interesting spectacle I ever beheld. To a person who had formerly known them, it possibly might have been still more impressive; for the ruins were so mingled together, and the whole scene possessed so little the air of a habitable place, that it was scarcely possible to imagine its former condition. The earthquake commenced at half-past eleven o'clock in the forenoon. If it had happened in the middle of the night, the greater number of the inhabitants (which in this one province amount to many thousands) must have perished, instead of less than a hundred: as it was, the invariable practice of running out of doors at the first trembling of the ground, alone saved them. In Concepcion each house, or row of houses, stood by itself, a heap or line of ruins; but in Talcahuano, owing to the great wave, little more than one layer of bricks, tiles, and timber, with here and there part of a wall left standing, could be distinguished. From this circumstance Concepcion, although not so completely desolated, was a more terrible, and, if I may so call it, picturesque sight. The first shock was very sudden. The mayor-domo at Quiriquina told me, that the first notice he received of it, was finding both the horse he rode and himself, rolling together on the ground. Rising up, he was again thrown down. He also told me that some cows which were standing on the steep side of the island were rolled into the sea. The great wave caused the destruction of many cattle; on one low island, near the head of the bay, seventy animals were washed off and drowned. It is generally thought that this has been the worst earthquake ever recorded in Chile; but as the very severe ones occur only after long intervals, this cannot easily be known; nor indeed would a much worse shock have made any great difference, for the ruin was now complete. Innumerable small tremblings followed the great earthquake, and within the first twelve days no less than three hundred were counted.

After viewing Concepcion, I cannot understand how the greater number of inhabitants escaped unhurt. The houses in many parts fell outwards; thus forming in the middle of the streets little hillocks of brickwork and rubbish. Mr. Rouse, the English consul, told us that he was at breakfast when the first movement warned him to run out. He had scarcely reached the middle of the courtyard, when one side of his house came thundering down. He retained presence of mind to remember, that if he once got on the top of that part which had already fallen, he would be safe. Not being able from the motion of the ground to stand, he crawled up on his hands and knees; and no sooner had he ascended this little eminence, than the other side of the house fell in, the great beams sweeping close in front of his head. With his eyes blinded, and his mouth choked with the cloud of dust which darkened the sky, at last he gained the street.

As shock succeeded shock, at the interval of a few minutes, no one dared approach the shattered ruins; and no one knew whether his dearest friends and relations were not perishing from want of help. Those who had saved any property were obliged to keep a constant watch, for thieves prowled about, and at each little trembling of the ground, with one hand they beat their breasts and cried "Misericordia!" and then with the other filched what they could from the ruins. The thatched roofs fell over the fires, and flames burst forth in all parts. Hundreds knew themselves ruined, and few had the means of providing food for the day.

Earthquakes alone are sufficient to destroy the prosperity of any country. If beneath England the now inert subterranean forces should exert those powers, which most assuredly in former geological ages they have exerted, how completely would the entire condition of the country be changed! What would become of the lofty houses, thickly packed cities, great manufactories, the beautiful public and private edifices? If the new period of disturbance were first to commence by some great earthquake in the dead of night, how terrific would be the carnage! England would at once be bankrupt; all papers, records, and accounts would from that moment be lost. Government being unable to collect the taxes, and failing to maintain its authority, the hand of violence and rapine would remain uncontrolled. In every large town famine would go forth, pestilence and death following in its train.

Shortly after the shock, a great wave was seen from the distance of three or four miles, approaching in the middle of the bay with a smooth outline; but along the shore it tore up cottages and trees, as it swept onwards with irresistible force. At the head of the bay it broke in a fearful line of white breakers, which rushed up to a height of 23 vertical feet above the highest spring-tides. Their force must have been prodigious; for at the Fort a cannon with its carriage, estimated at four tons in weight, was moved 15 feet inwards. A schooner was left in the midst of the ruins, 200 yards from the beach. The first wave was followed by two others, which in their retreat carried away a vast wreck of floating objects. In one part of the bay, a ship was pitched high and dry on shore, was carried off, again driven on shore, and again carried off. In another part, two large vessels anchored near together were whirled about, and their cables were thrice wound round each other: though anchored at a depth of 36 feet, they were for some minutes aground. The great wave must have travelled slowly, for the inhabitants of Talcahuano had time to run up the hills behind the town; and some sailors pulled out seaward, trusting successfully to their boat riding securely over the swell, if they could reach it before it broke. One old woman with a little boy, four or five years old, ran into a boat, but there was nobody to row it out: the boat was consequently dashed against an anchor and cut in twain; the old woman was drowned, but the child was picked up some hours afterwards clinging to the wreck. Pools of salt-water were still standing amidst the ruins of the houses, and children, making boats with old tables and chairs, appeared as happy as their parents were miserable. It was, however, exceedingly interesting to observe, how much more active and cheerful all appeared than could have been expected. It was remarked with much truth, that from the destruction being universal, no one individual was humbled more than another, or could suspect his friends of coldness—that most grievous result of the loss of wealth. Mr. Rouse, and a large party whom he kindly took under his protection, lived for the first week in a garden beneath some apple-trees. At first they were as merry as if it had been a picnic; but soon afterwards heavy rain caused much discomfort, for they were absolutely without shelter.

In Captain Fitz Roy's excellent account of the earthquake, it is said that two explosions, one like a column of smoke and another like the blowing of a great whale, were seen in the bay. The water also appeared everywhere to be boiling; and it "became black, and exhaled a most disagreeable sulphureous smell." These latter circumstances were observed in the Bay of Valparaiso during the earthquake of 1822; they may, I think, be accounted for, by the disturbance of the mud at the bottom of the sea containing organic matter in decay. In the Bay of Callao, during a calm day, I noticed, that as the ship dragged her cable over the bottom, its course was marked by a line of bubbles. The lower orders in Talcahuano thought that the earthquake was caused by some old Indian women, who two years ago being offended stopped the volcano of Antuco. This silly belief is curious, because it shows that experience has taught them to observe, that there exists a relation between the suppressed action of the volcanoes, and the trembling of the ground. It was necessary to apply the witchcraft to the point where their perception of cause and effect failed; and this was the closing of the volcanic vent. This belief is the more singular in this particular instance, because, according to Captain Fitz Roy, there is reason to believe that Antuco was noways affected.

The town of Concepcion was built in the usual Spanish fashion, with all the streets running at right angles to each other; one set ranging S.W. by W., and the other set N.W. by N. The walls in the former direction certainly stood better than those in the latter: the greater number of the masses of brickwork were thrown down towards the N.E. Both these circumstances perfectly agree with the general idea, of the undulations having come from the S.W.; in which quarter subterranean noises were also heard: for it is evident that the walls running S.W. and N.E. which presented their ends to the point whence the undulations came, would be much less likely to fall than those walls which, running N.W. and S.E., must in their whole lengths have been at the same instant thrown out of the perpendicular; for the undulations, coming from the S.W., must have extended in N.W. and S.E. waves, as they passed under the foundations. This may be illustrated by placing books edgeways on a carpet, and then, after the manner suggested by Michell, imitating the undulations of an earthquake: it will be found that they fall with more or less readiness, according as their direction more or less nearly coincides with the line of the waves. The fissures in the ground generally, though not uniformly, extended in a S.E. and N.W.

direction; and therefore corresponded to the lines of undulation or of principal flexure. Bearing in mind all these circumstances, which so clearly point to the S.W. as the chief focus of disturbance, it is a very interesting fact that the island of S. Maria, situated in that quarter, was, during the general uplifting of the land, raised to nearly three times the height of any other part of the coast.

The different resistance offered by the walls, according to their direction, was well exemplified in the case of the Cathedral. The side which fronted the N.E. presented a grand pile of ruins, in the midst of which door-cases and masses of timber stood up, as if floating in a stream. Some of the angular blocks of brickwork were of great dimensions; and they were rolled to a distance on the level plaza, like fragments of rock at the base of some high mountain. The side walls (running S.W. and N.E.), though exceedingly fractured, yet remained standing; but the vast buttresses (at right angles to them, and therefore parallel to the walls that fell) were in many cases cut clean off, as if by a chisel, and hurled to the ground. Some square ornaments on the coping of these same walls, were moved by the earthquake into a diagonal position. A similar circumstance was observed after an earthquake at Valparaiso, Calabria, and other places, including some of the ancient Greek temples. This twisting displacement, at first appears to indicate a vorticose movement beneath each point thus affected; but this is highly improbable. May it not be caused by a tendency in each stone to arrange itself in some particular position, with respect to the lines of vibration,—in a manner somewhat similar to pins on a sheet of paper when shaken? Generally speaking, arched doorways or windows stood much better than any other part of the buildings. Nevertheless, a poor lame old man, who had been in the habit, during trifling shocks, of crawling to a certain doorway, was this time crushed to pieces.

I have not attempted to give any detailed description of the appearance of Concepcion, for I feel that it is quite impossible to convey the mingled feelings which I experienced. Several of the officers visited it before me, but their strongest language failed to give a just idea of the scene of desolation. It is a bitter and humiliating thing to see works, which have cost man so much time and labour, overthrown in one minute; yet compassion for the inhabitants was almost instantly banished, by the surprise in seeing a state of things produced in a moment of time, which one was accustomed to attribute to a succession of ages. In my opinion, we have scarcely beheld, since leaving England, any sight so deeply interesting.

In almost every severe earthquake, the neighbouring waters of the sea are said to have been greatly agitated. The disturbance seems generally, as in the case of Concepcion, to have been of two kinds: first, at the instant of the shock, the water swells high up on the beach with a gentle motion, and then as quietly retreats; secondly, some time afterwards, the whole body of the sea retires from the coast, and then returns in waves of overwhelming force. The first movement seems to be an immediate consequence of the earthquake affecting differently a fluid and a solid, so that their respective levels are slightly deranged: but the second case is a far more important phenomenon. During most earthquakes, and especially during those on the west coast of America, it is certain that the first great movement of the waters has been a retirement. Some authors have attempted to explain this, by supposing that the water retains its level, whilst the land oscillates upwards; but surely the water close to the land, even on a rather steep coast, would partake of the motion of the bottom: moreover, as urged by Mr. Lyell, similar movements of the sea have occurred at islands far distant from the chief line of disturbance, as was the case with Juan Fernandez during this earthquake, and with Madeira during the famous Lisbon shock. I suspect (but the subject is a very obscure one) that a wave, however produced, first draws the water from the shore, on which it is advancing to break: I have observed that this happens with the little waves from the paddles of a steam-boat. It is remarkable that whilst Talcahuano and Callao (near Lima), both situated at the head of large shallow bays, have suffered during every severe earthquake from great waves, Valparaiso, seated close to the edge of profoundly deep water, has never been overwhelmed, though so often shaken by the severest shocks. From the great wave not immediately following the earthquake, but sometimes after the interval of even half an hour, and from distant islands being affected similarly with the coasts near the focus of the disturbance, it appears that the wave first rises in the offing; and as this is of general occurrence, the cause must be general: I suspect we must look to the line, where the less disturbed waters of the deep ocean join the water nearer the coast, which has partaken of the movements of the land, as the place where the great wave is first generated; it would also appear that the wave is larger or smaller, according to the extent of shoal water which has been agitated together with the bottom on which it rested.

The most remarkable effect of this earthquake was the permanent elevation of the land; it would probably be far more correct to speak of it as the cause. There can be no doubt that the land round the Bay of Concepcion was upraised two or three feet; but it deserves notice, that owing to the wave having obliterated the old lines of tidal action on the sloping sandy shores, I could discover no evidence of this fact, except in the united testimony of the inhabitants, that one little rocky shoal, now exposed, was formerly covered with water. At the island of S. Maria (about thirty miles distant) the elevation was greater; on one part, Captain Fitz Roy found beds of putrid mussel-shells *still adhering to the rocks,* ten feet above high-water mark: the inhabitants had formerly dived at lower-water spring-tides for these shells. The elevation of this province is particularly interesting, from its having been the theatre of several other violent earthquakes, and from the vast numbers of sea-shells scattered over the land, up to a height of certainly 600, and I believe, of 1000 feet. At Valparaiso, as I have remarked, similar shells are found at the height of 1300 feet: it is hardly possible to doubt that this great elevation has been effected by successive small uprisings, such as that which accompanied or caused the earthquake of this year, and likewise by an insensibly slow rise, which is certainly in progress on some parts of this coast.

The island of Juan Fernandez, 360 miles to the N.E., was, at the time of the great shock of the 20th, violently shaken, so that the trees beat against each other, and a volcano burst forth under water close to the shore: these facts are remarkable because this island, during the earthquake of 1751, was then also affected more violently than other places at an equal distance from Concepcion, and this seems to show some subterranean connexion between these two points. Chiloe, about 340 miles southward of Concepcion, appears to have been shaken more strongly than the intermediate district of Valdivia, where the volcano of Villarica was noways affected, whilst in the Cordillera in front of Chiloe, two of the volcanoes burst forth at the same instant in violent action. These two volcanoes, and some neighbouring ones, continued for a long time in eruption, and ten months afterwards were again influenced by an earthquake at Concepcion. Some men, cutting wood near the base of one of these volcanoes, did not perceive the shock of the 20th, although the whole surrounding Province was then trembling; here we have an eruption relieving and taking the place of an earthquake, as would have happened at Concepcion, according to the belief of the lower orders, if the volcano of Antuco had not been closed by witchcraft. Two years and three quarters afterwards, Valdivia and Chiloe were again shaken, more violently than on the 20th, and an island in the Chonos Archipelago was permanently elevated more than eight feet. It will give a better idea of the scale of these phenomena, if (as in the case of the glaciers) we suppose them to have taken place at corresponding distances in Europe:—then would the land from the North Sea to the Mediterranean have been violently shaken, and at the same instant of time a large tract of the eastern coast of England would have been permanently elevated, together with some outlying islands—a train of volcanoes on the coast of Holland would have burst forth in action, and an eruption taken place at the bottom of the sea, near the northern extremity of Ireland

—and lastly, the ancient vents of Auvergne, Cantal, and Mont d'Or would each have sent up to the sky a dark column of smoke, and have long remained in fierce action. Two years and three quarters afterwards, France, from its centre to the English Channel, would have been again desolated by an earthquake, and an island permanently upraised in the Mediterranean.

The space, from under which volcanic matter on the 20th was actually erupted, is 720 miles in one line, and 400 miles in another line at right angles to the first: hence, in all probability, a subterranean lake of lava is here stretched out, of nearly double the area of the Black Sea. From the intimate and complicated manner in which the elevatory and eruptive forces were shown to be connected during this train of phenomena, we may confidently come to the conclusion, that the forces which slowly and by little starts uplift continents, and those which at successive periods pour forth volcanic matter from open orifices, are identical. From many reasons, I believe that the frequent quakings of the earth on this line of coast, are caused by the rending of the strata, necessarily consequent on the tension of the land when upraised, and their injection by fluidified rock. This rending and injection would, if repeated often enough (and we know that earthquakes repeatedly affect the same areas in the same manner), form a chain of hills;—and the linear island of St. Mary, which was upraised thrice the height of the neighbouring country, seems to be undergoing this process. I believe that the solid axis of a mountain differs in its manner of formation from a volcanic hill, only in the molten stone having been repeatedly injected, instead of having been repeatedly ejected. Moreover, I believe that it is impossible to explain the structure of great mountain-chains, such as that of the Cordillera, where the strata, capping the injected axis of plutonic rock, have been thrown on their edges along several parallel and neighbouring lines of elevation, except on this view of the rock of the axis having been repeatedly injected, after intervals sufficiently long to allow the upper parts or wedges to cool and become solid;—for if the strata had been thrown into their present highly-inclined, vertical, and even inverted positions, by a single blow, the very bowels of the earth would have gushed out; and instead of beholding abrupt mountain-axes of rock solidified under great pressure, deluges of lava would have flowed out at innumerable points on every line of elevation.

JOHN KEATS

ODE ON A GRECIAN URN

John Keats (1795-1821) is among the most famous of the poets of the English Romantic movement. One of his most distinguished poems, the "Ode on a Grecian Urn" (written, 1819; published, 1820), is reproduced here to accompany the following criticism of it by Allen Tate.

I

THOU STILL unravish'd bride of quietness,
 Thou foster-child of silence and slow time,
Sylvan historian, who canst thus express
 A flowery tale more sweetly than our rhyme:
What leaf-fring'd legend haunts about thy shape
 Of deities or mortals, or of both,
  In Tempe or the dales of Arcady?
What men or gods are these? What maidens loth?
 What mad pursuit? What struggle to escape?
  What pipes and timbrels? What wild ecstasy? 10

II

Heard melodies are sweet, but those unheard
 Are sweeter; therefore, ye soft pipes, play on;
Not to the sensual ear, but, more endear'd,
 Pipe to the spirit ditties of no tone:
Fair youth, beneath the trees, thou canst not leave
 Thy song, nor ever can those trees be bare;
  Bold Lover, never, never canst thou kiss,
Though winning near the goal—yet, do not grieve;
 She cannot fade, though thou hast not thy bliss,
  For ever wilt thou love, and she be fair! 20

III

Ah, happy, happy boughs! that cannot shed
  Your leaves, nor ever bid the Spring adieu;
And, happy melodist, unwearied,
  For ever piping songs for ever new;
More happy love! more happy, happy love!
  For ever warm and still to be enjoy'd,
    For ever panting, and for ever young;
All breathing human passion far above,
  That leaves a heart high-sorrowful and cloy'd,
    A burning forehead, and a parching tongue.   30

IV

Who are these coming to the sacrifice?
  To what green altar, O mysterious priest,
Lead'st thou that heifer lowing at the skies,
  And all her silken flanks with garlands drest?
What little town by river or sea shore,
  Or mountain-built with peaceful citadel,
    Is emptied of this folk, this pious morn?
And, little town, thy streets for evermore
  Will silent be; and not a soul to tell
    Why thou art desolate, can e'er return.   40

V

O Attic shape! Fair attitude! with brede
  Of marble men and maidens overwrought,
With forest branches and the trodden weed;
  Thou, silent form, dost tease us out of thought
As doth eternity: Cold Pastoral!
  When old age shall this generation waste,
    Thou shalt remain, in midst of other woe
Than ours, a friend to man, to whom thou say'st,
  Beauty is truth, truth beauty,—that is all
    Ye know on earth, and all ye need to know.   50

ALLEN TATE

from A READING OF KEATS

*Allen Tate (1899-)—poet, novelist, biographer, and literary critic—
bears something of the relationship to mid-twentieth-century America that
Dr. Samuel Johnson bore to mid-eighteenth-century England. He is, and
has been for almost thirty years, not only one of the most distinguished of
American writers but also one of the most influential. He was a leader of the
southern agrarian movement in literature and politics and one of the founders of the famous literary magazine* The Fugitive; *and recently he has been
closely associated with the New Criticism. He was an editor of* Hound
and Horn *and* The Kenyon Review *and the editor of* The Sewanee Review,
*perhaps three of the most important American literary quarterlies of the
century. Since 1951, he has been professor of English at the University of
Minnesota and senior fellow of the Indiana School of Letters. The best of
his poetry is collected in* Poems, 1922-1947 (1948); *of his criticism, in* On
the Limits of Poetry (1948).

IF WE glance at "Ode on a Grecian Urn," we shall see Keats
trying to unify his pictorial effects by means of direct philosophical statement. "Do I wake or sleep?" at the end of the Nightingale ode asks the question: Which is reality, the symbolic
nightingale or the common world? The famous Truth-Beauty
synthesis at the end of the "Grecian Urn" contains the same
question, but this time it is answered. As Mr. Kenneth Burke
sees it, Truth is the practical scientific world and Beauty is the
ideal world above change. The "frozen" figures on the urn, being
both dead and alive, constitute a scene which is at once per-
ceptible and fixed. "This transcendent scene," says Mr. Burke,
"is the level at which the earthly laws of contradiction no longer
prevail."[5] The one and the many, the eternal and the passing,
the sculpturesque and the dramatic, become synthesized in a
higher truth. Much of the little that I know about this poem I

[5] Kenneth Burke, "Symbolic Action in a Poem by Keats," *Accent,* vol. 4,
No. 1 (Autumn, 1943), p. 42.

»»» Reprinted from *Collected Essays* by Allen Tate by permission of the
publisher, Alan Swallow. Copyright 1948, 1960, by Allen Tate.

have learned from Mr. Burke and Mr. Cleanth Brooks, who have studied it more closely than any other critics; and what I am about to say will sound ungrateful. I suspect that the dialectical solution is Mr. Burke's rather than Keats's, and that Mr. Brooks's "irony" and "dramatic propriety" are likewise largely his own.[6] Mr. Brooks rests his case for the Truth-Beauty paradox on an argument for its "dramatic propriety"; but this is just what I am not convinced of. I find myself agreeing with Mr. Middleton Murry (whom Mr. Brooks quotes), who admits that the statement is out of place "in the context of the poem itself." I would point to a particular feature, in the last six lines of stanza four, which I feel that neither Mr. Burke nor Mr. Brooks has taken into a certain important kind of consideration. Here Keats tells us that in the background of this world of eternal youth there is another, from which it came, and that this second world has thus been emptied and is indeed a dead world:

> What little town by river or sea-shore
> Or mountain-built with peaceful citadel,
>   Is emptied of this folk, this pious morn?
> And, little town, thy streets for evermore
> Will silent be; and not a soul to tell
>   Why thou art desolate, can e'er return.

Mr. Burke quite rightly sees in this passage the key to the symbolism of the entire poem. It is properly the "constatation" of the tensions of the imagery. What is the meaning of this perpetual youth on the urn? One of its meanings is that it is perpetually anti-youth and anti-life; it is in fact dead, and "can never return." Are we not faced again with the same paradox we had in the Nightingale ode, that the intensest life is achieved in death? Mr. Burke brings out with great skill the erotic equivalents of the life-death symbols; and for his analysis of the developing imagery throughout we owe him a great debt. Yet I feel that Mr. Burke's own dialectical skill leads him to consider the poem, when he is through with it, a philosophical discourse; but it is, if it is anything (and it is a great deal), what is ordinarily known

[6] *The Well Wrought Urn* (New York, 1947), pp. 139-152.

as a work of art. Mr. Burke's elucidation of the Truth-Beauty proposition in the last stanza is the most convincing dialectically that I have seen; but Keats did not write Mr. Burke's elucidation; and I feel that the entire last stanza, except the phrase "Cold Pastoral" (which probably ought to be somewhere else in the poem) is an illicit commentary added by the poet to a "meaning" which was symbolically complete at the end of the preceding stanza, number four. Or perhaps it may be said that Keats did to some extent write Mr. Burke's elucidation; that is why I feel that the final stanza (though magnificently written) is redundant and out of form.

To the degree that I am guilty with Mr. Burke of a prepossession which may blind me to the whole value of this poem (as his seems to limit his perception of possible defects) I am not qualified to criticize it. Here, towards the end of this essay, I glance back at the confession, which I made earlier, of the distance and detachment of my warmest admiration for Keats. It is now time that I tried to state the reasons for this a little more summarily, in a brief comparison of the two fine odes that we have been considering.

Both odes are constructed pictorially in spatial blocks, for the eye to take in serially. Though to my mind this method is better suited to the subject of the Grecian Urn, which is itself a plastic object, than to the Nightingale ode, I take the latter, in spite of the blemishes of detail (only some of which we have looked at), to be the finer poem. If there is not so much in it as in the Grecian Urn for the elucidation of verbal complexity, there is nowhere the radical violation of its set limits that one finds in the last stanza of the Grecian Urn:

> Thou shalt remain, in midst of other woe
> Than ours, a friend to man, to whom thou say'st,
> Beauty is truth, truth beauty,—that is all
> Ye know on earth, and all ye need to know.

It is here that the poem gets out of form, that the break in "point of view" occurs; and if it is a return to Samuel Johnson's dislike of "Lycidas" (I don't think it is) to ask how an urn can say anything, I shall have to suffer the consequences of that view. It is Keats himself, of course, who says it; but "Keats" is here not implicit in the structure of the poem, as he is in "Ode to a Nightingale"; what he says is what the mathematicians call an extrapolation, an intrusion of matter from another field of discourse, so that even if it be "true" philosophically it is not a visible function of what the poem says. With the "dead" mountain citadel in mind, could we not phrase the message of the urn equally well as follows: Truth is *not* beauty, since even art itself cannot do more with death than preserve it, and the beauty frozen on the urn is also dead, since it cannot move. This "pessimism" may be found as easily in the poem as Keats's comforting paradox. So I should return to the Nightingale ode for its superior *dramatic* credibility, even though the death-life antinomy is not more satisfactorily resolved than in the Grecian Urn. The fall of the "I" of "Ode to a Nightingale" into the trance-like meditation in the first stanza and the shocked coming to at the end *ground* the poem in imaginable action, so that the dialectics of the nightingale symbol do not press for resolution. So I confess a reserved agreement with Brooks and Warren.

EDWARD T. HALL

THE VOICES OF TIME

Edward T. Hall (1914-   ), American anthropologist, was educated at Pomona College, the University of Denver, the University of Arizona, and Columbia University. He has done anthropological field work in the Southwestern United States, Micronesia, and Europe and has taught at Denver, Bennington, and Illinois Institute of Technology, where he is professor of anthropology. He also has served the U. S. State Department as director of the Point IV training program in the Foreign Service Institute.

TIME TALKS. It speaks more plainly than words. The message it conveys comes through loud and clear. Because it is manipulated less consciously, it is subject to less distortion than the spoken language. It can shout the truth where words lie.

I was once a member of a mayor's committee on human relations in a large city. My assignment was to estimate what the chances were of non-discriminatory practices being adopted by the different city departments. The first step in this project was to interview the department heads, two of whom were themselves members of minority groups. If one were to believe the words of these officials, it seemed that all of them were more than willing to adopt non-discriminatory labor practices. Yet I felt that, despite what they said, in only one case was there much chance for a change. Why? The answer lay in how they used the silent language of time and space.

Special attention had been given to arranging each interview. Department heads were asked to be prepared to spend an hour or more discussing their thoughts with me. Nevertheless, appointments were forgotten; long waits in outer offices (fifteen to forty-five minutes) were common, and the length of the interview was often cut down to ten or fifteen minutes. I was usually kept at an impersonal distance during the interview. In only one case did the department head come from behind his desk. These men had a position and they were literally and figuratively sticking to it!

The implication of this experience (one which public-opinion pollsters might well heed) is quite obvious. What people do is frequently more important than what they say. In this case the way these municipal potentates handled time was eloquent testimony to what they inwardly believed, for the structure and meaning of time systems, as well as the time intervals, are easy to identify. In regard to being late there are: "mumble something" periods, slight apology periods, mildly insulting periods requiring full apology, rude periods, and downright insulting periods. The psychoanalyst has long been aware of the significance of communication on this level. He can point to the way his patients handle time as evidence of "resistances" and "transference."

Different parts of the day, for example, are highly significant in certain contexts. Time may indicate the importance of the occasion as well as on what level an interaction between persons is to take place. In the United States if you telephone someone very early in the morning, while he is shaving or having breakfast, the time of the call usually signals a matter of utmost importance and extreme urgency. The same applies for calls after 11:00 P.M. A call received during sleeping hours is apt to be taken as a matter of life and death, hence the rude joke value of these calls among the young. Our realization that time talks is even reflected in such common expressions as, "What time does the clock *say?*"

An example of how thoroughly these things are taken for granted was reported to me by John Useem, an American social anthropologist, in an illuminating case from the South Pacific. The natives of one of the islands had been having a difficult time getting their white supervisors to hire them in a way consistent with their traditional status system. Through ignorance the supervisors had hired too many of one group and by so doing had disrupted the existing balance of power among the natives. The entire population of the island was seething because of this error. Since the Americans continued in their ignorance and refused to hire according to local practice, the head men of the two factions met one night to discuss an acceptable reallocation of jobs. When they finally arrived at a solution, they went en masse to see the plant manager and woke him up to tell him what had been decided. Unfortunately it was then between two and three o'clock in the morning. They did not know that it is a sign of extreme urgency to wake up Americans at this hour. As one might expect, the American plant manager, who understood neither the local language nor the culture nor what the hulla-baloo was all about, thought he had a riot on his hands and called out the Marines. It simply never occurred to him that the parts of the day have a different meaning for these people than they have for us.

On the other hand, plant managers in the United States are fully aware of the significance of a communication made during the middle of the morning or afternoon that takes everyone away from his work. Whenever they want to make an important an-nouncement they will ask: "When shall we let them know?" In the social world a girl feels insulted when she is asked for a date at the last minute by someone whom she doesn't know very well, and the person who extends an invitation to a dinner party with only three or four days' notice has to apologize. How different from the people of the Middle East with whom it is pointless to make an appointment too far in advance, because the informal structure of their time system places everything beyond a week into a single category of "future," in which plans tend to "slip off their minds."

Advance notice is often referred to in America as "lead time," an expression which is significant in a culture where schedules are important. While it is learned informally, most of us are fa-miliar with how it works in our own culture, even though we cannot state the rules technically. The rules for lead time in other cultures, however, have rarely been analyzed. At the most they are known by experience to those who lived abroad for some time. Yet think how important it is to know how much time is required to prepare people, or for them to prepare themselves, for things to come. Sometimes lead time would seem to be very extended. At other times, in the Middle East, any period longer than a week may be too long.

How troublesome differing ways of handling time can be is well illustrated by the case of an American agriculturalist assigned to duty as an attaché of our embassy in a Latin country. After what seemed to him a suitable period he let it be known that he would like to call on the minister who was his counterpart. For various reasons, the suggested time was not suitable; all sorts of cues came back to the effect that the time was not yet ripe to visit the minister. Our friend, however, persisted and forced an appointment which was reluctantly granted. Arriving a little before the hour (the American respect pattern), he waited. The hour came and passed; five minutes—ten minutes—fifteen minutes. At this point he suggested to the secretary that perhaps the minister did not know he was waiting in the outer office. This gave him the feeling he had done something concrete and also helped to overcome the great anxiety that was stirring inside him. Twenty minutes—twenty-five minutes—thirty minutes—forty-five minutes (the insult period)!

He jumped up and told the secretary that he had been "cooling his heels" in an outer office for forty-five minutes and he was "damned sick and tired" of this type of treatment. This message was relayed to the minister, who said, in effect, "Let him cool his heels." The attaché's stay in the country was not a happy one.

The principal source of misunderstanding lay in the fact that in the country in question the five-minute-delay interval was not significant. Forty-five minutes, on the other hand, instead of being at the tail end of the waiting scale, was just barely at the beginning. To suggest to an American's secretary that perhaps her boss didn't know you were there after waiting sixty seconds would seem absurd, as would raising a storm about "cooling your heels" for five minutes. Yet this is precisely the way the

minister registered the protestations of the American in his outer
office! He felt, as usual, that Americans were being totally
unreasonable.

Throughout this unfortunate episode the attaché was acting
according to the way he had been brought up. At home in the
United States his responses would have been normal ones and
his behavior legitimate. Yet even if he had been told before he
left home that this sort of thing would happen, he would have
had difficulty not *feeling* insulted after he had been kept waiting
forty-five minutes. If, on the other hand, he had been taught the
details of the local time system just as he should have been
taught the local spoken language, it would have been possible
for him to adjust himself accordingly.

What bothers people in situations of this sort is that they don't
realize they are being subjected to another form of communication, one that works part of the time with language and part of
the time independently of it. The fact that the message conveyed
is couched in no formal vocabulary makes things doubly difficult, because neither party can get very explicit about what is
actually taking place. Each can only say what he thinks is happening and how he feels about it. The thought of what is being
communicated is what hurts.

AMERICAN TIME

People of the Western world, particularly Americans, tend to
think of time as something fixed in nature, something around us
and from which we cannot escape; an ever-present part of the
environment, just like the air we breathe. That it might be
experienced in any other way seems unnatural and strange, a
feeling which is rarely modified even when we begin to discover
how really differently it is handled by some other people. Within
the West itself certain cultures rank time much lower in over-all
importance than we do. In Latin America, for example, where
time is treated rather cavalierly, one commonly hears the expression, "Our time or your time?" "*Hora americana, hora mejicana?*"

As a rule, Americans think of time as a road or a ribbon

stretching into the future, along which one progresses. The road has segments or compartments which are to be kept discrete ("one thing at a time"). People who cannot schedule time are looked down upon as impractical. In at least some parts of Latin America, the North American (their term for us) finds himself annoyed when he has made an appointment with somebody, only to find a lot of other things going on at the same time. An old friend of mine of Spanish cultural heritage used to run his business according to the "Latino" system. This meant that up to fifteen people were in his office at one time. Business which might have been finished in a quarter of an hour sometimes took a whole day. He realized, of course, that the Anglo-Americans were disturbed by this and used to make some allowance for them, a dispensation which meant that they spent only an hour or so in his office when they had planned on a few minutes. The American concept of the discreteness of time and the necessity for scheduling was at variance with this amiable and seemingly confusing Latin system. However, if my friend had adhered to the American system he would have destroyed a vital part of his prosperity. People who came to do business with him also came to find out things and to visit each other. The ten to fifteen Spanish-Americans and Indians who used to sit around the office (among whom I later found myself after I had learned to relax a little) played their own part in a particular type of communications network.

Not only do we Americans segment and schedule time, but we look ahead and are oriented almost entirely toward the future. We like new things and are preoccupied with change. We want to know how to overcome resistance to change. In fact, scientific theories and even some pseudoscientific ones, which incorporate a striking theory of change, are often given special attention.

Time with us is handled much like a material; we earn it, spend it, save it, waste it. To us it is somewhat immoral to have two things going on at the same time. In Latin America it is not uncommon for one man to have a number of simultaneous jobs which he either carries on from one desk or which he moves between, spending a small amount of time on each.

While we look to the future, our view of it is limited. The future to us is the foreseeable future, not the future of the South Asian that may involve centuries. Indeed, our perspective is so short as to inhibit the operation of a good many practical projects, such as sixty- and one-hundred-year conservation works requiring public support and public funds. Anyone who has worked in industry or in the government of the United States has heard the following: "Gentlemen, this is for the long term! Five or ten years."

For us a "long time" can be almost anything—ten or twenty years, two or three months, a few weeks, or even a couple of days. The South Asian, however, feels that it is perfectly realistic to think of a "long time" in terms of thousands of years or even an endless period. A colleague once described their conceptualization of time as follows: "Time is like a museum with endless corridors and alcoves. You, the viewer, are walking through the museum in the dark, holding a light to each scene as you pass it. God is the curator of the museum, and only He knows all that is in it. One lifetime represents one alcove."

The American's view of the future is linked to a view of the past, for tradition plays an equally limited part in American culture. As a whole, we push it aside or leave it to a few souls who are interested in the past for very special reasons. There are, of course, a few pockets, such as New England and the South, where tradition is emphasized. But in the realm of business, which is the dominant model of United States life, tradition is equated with *experience,* and experience is thought of as being very close to if not synonymous with know-how. Know-how is one of our prized possessions, so that when we look backward it is rarely to take pleasure in the past itself but usually to calculate the know-how, to assess the prognosis for success in the future.

Promptness is also valued highly in American life. If people are not prompt, it is often taken either as an insult or as an indication that they are not quite responsible. There are those, of a psychological bent, who would say that we are obsessed with time. They can point to individuals in American culture who are literally time-ridden. And even the rest of us feel very strongly about time because we have been taught to take it so seriously. We have stressed this aspect of culture and developed it to a point unequaled anywhere in the world, except, perhaps, in Switzerland and north Germany. Many people criticize our obsessional handling of time. They attribute ulcers and hypertension to the pressure engendered by such a system. Perhaps they are right.

SOME OTHER CONCEPTS OF TIME

Even within the very borders of the United States there are people who handle time in a way which is almost incomprehensible to those who have not made a major effort to understand it. The Pueblo Indians, for example, who live in the Southwest, have a sense of time which is at complete variance with the clock-bound habits of the ordinary American citizen. For the Pueblos events begin when the time is ripe and no sooner.

I can still remember a Christmas dance I attended some twenty-five years ago at one of the pueblos near the Rio Grande. I had to travel over bumpy roads for forty-five miles to get there. At seven thousand feet the ordeal of winter cold at one o'clock in the morning is almost unbearable. Shivering in the still darkness of the pueblo, I kept searching for a clue as to when the dance would begin.

Outside everything was impenetrably quiet. Occasionally there was the muffled beat of a deep pueblo drum, the opening of a door, or the piercing of the night's darkness with a shaft of light. In the church where the dance was to take place a few white townsfolk were huddled together on a balcony, groping for some clue which would suggest how much longer they were going to suffer. "Last year I heard they started at ten o'clock." "They can't start until the priest comes." "There is no way of telling when they will start." All this punctuated by chattering teeth and the stamping of feet to keep up circulation.

Suddenly an Indian opened the door, entered, and poked up the fire in the stove. Everyone nudged his neighbor: "Maybe they are going to begin now." Another hour passed. Another Indian came in from outside, walked across the nave of the church, and disappeared through another door. "Certainly now they will begin. After all, it's almost two o'clock." Someone guessed that they were just being ornery in the hope that the white men would go away. Another had a friend in the pueblo and went to his house to ask when the dance would begin. Nobody knew. Suddenly, when the whites were almost exhausted, there burst upon the night the deep sounds of the drums, rattles, and low male voices singing. Without warning the dance had begun.

After years of performances such as this, no white man in his right mind will hazard a guess as to when one of these ceremonial dances will begin. Those of us who have learned now know that the dance doesn't start at a particular time. It is geared to no schedule. It starts when "things" are ready!

As I pointed out, the white civilized Westerner has a shallow view of the future compared to the Oriental. Yet set beside the Navajo Indians of northern Arizona, he seems a model of long-term patience. The Navajo and the European-American have been trying to adjust their concepts of time for almost a hundred years. So far they have not done too well. To the old-time Navajo time is like space—only the here and now is quite real. The future has little reality to it.

An old friend of mine reared with the Navajo expressed it this way: "You know how the Navajo love horses and how much they love to gamble and bet on horse races. Well, if you were to say to a Navajo, 'My friend, you know my quarter horse that won all the races at Flagstaff last Fourth of July?' that Navajo would eagerly say 'yes, yes,' he knew the horse; and if you were to say, 'In the fall I am going to give you that horse,' the Navajo's face would fall and he would turn around and walk away. On the other hand, if you were to say to him, 'Do you see that old bag of bones I just rode up on? That old hay-bellied mare with the knock-knees and pigeon toes, with the bridle that's falling apart and the saddle that's worn out? You can have that horse, my friend, it's yours. Take it, ride it away now.' Then the Navajo would beam and shake your hand and jump on his new horse and ride away. Of the two, only the immediate gift has reality; a promise of future benefits is not even worth thinking about."

In the early days of the range control and soil conservation programs it was almost impossible to convince the Navajo that there was anything to be gained from giving up their beloved sheep for benefits which could be enjoyed ten or twenty years in the future. Once I was engaged in the supervision of the construction of small earth dams and like everyone else had little success at first in convincing Navajo workmen that they should work hard and build the dam quickly, so that there would be more dams and more water for the sheep. The argument that they could have one dam or ten, depending on how hard they worked, conveyed nothing. It wasn't until I learned to translate our behavior into their terms that they produced as we knew they could.

The solution came about in this way. I had been discussing the problem with a friend, Lorenzo Hubbell, who had lived on the reservation all of his life. When there were difficulties I used to find it helpful to unburden myself to him. Somewhere in his remarks there was always a key to the underlying patterns of Navajo life. As we talked I learned that the Navajo understood and respected a bargain. I had some inkling of this when I noticed how unsettled the Indians became when they were permitted to fall down on the job they had agreed to do. In particular they seemed to be apprehensive lest they be asked to repay an unfulfilled obligation at some future time. I decided to sit down with the Navajo crew and talk to them about the work. It was quite useless to argue about the future advantages which would accrue from working hard; linear reasoning and logic were meaningless. They did respond, however, when I indicated that the government was giving them money to get out of debt, providing jobs near their families, and giving them water for their sheep. I stressed the fact that in exchange for this, they must work eight hours every day. This was presented as a bargain. Following my clarification the work progressed satisfactorily.

One of my Indian workmen inadvertently provided another

example of the cultural conflict centering around time. His name was "Little Sunday." He was small, wiry, and winning. Since it is not polite to ask the Navajo about their names or even to ask them what their name is, it was necessary to inquire of others how he came to be named "Little Sunday." The explanation was a revealing one.

In the early days of the white traders the Indians had considerable difficulty getting used to the fact that we Europeans divided time into strange and unnatural periods instead of having a "natural" succession of days which began with the new moon and ended with the old. They were particularly perplexed by the notion of the week introduced by the traders and the missionaries. Imagine a Navajo Indian living some forty or fifty miles from a trading store that is a hundred miles north of the railroad deciding that he needs flour and maybe a little lard for bread. He thinks about the flour and the lard, and he thinks about his friends and the fun he will have trading, or maybe he wonders if the trader will give him credit or how much money he can get for the hide he has. After riding horseback for a day and a half to two days he reaches the store all ready to trade. The store is locked up tight. There are a couple of other Navajo Indians camped in the hogan built by the trader. They say the trader is inside but he won't trade because it's Sunday. They bang on his door and he tells them, "Go away, it's Sunday," and the Navajo says, "But I came from way up on Black Mesa, and I am hungry. I need some food." What can the trader do? Soon he opens the store and then all the Navajo pour in. One of the most frequent and insistent Sunday visitors was a man who earned for himself the sobriquet "Big Sunday." "Little Sunday," it turns out, ran a close second.

The Sioux Indians provide us with another interesting example of the differing views toward time. Not so long ago a man who was introduced as the superintendent of the Sioux came to my office. I learned that he had been born on the reservation and was a product of both Indian and white cultures, having earned his A.B. at one of the Ivy League colleges.

During a long and fascinating account of the many problems which his tribe was having in adjusting to our way of life, he suddenly remarked: "What would you think of a people who had no word for time? My people have no word for 'late' or for 'waiting,' for that matter. They don't know what it is to wait or to be late." He then continued, "I decided that until they could tell time and knew what time was they could never adjust themselves to white culture. So I set about to teach them time. There wasn't a clock that was running in any of the reservation classrooms. So I first bought some decent clocks. Then I made the school buses start on time, and if an Indian was two minutes late that was just too bad. The bus started at eight forty-two and he had to be there."

He was right, of course. The Sioux could not adjust to European ways until they had learned the meaning of time. The superintendent's methods may have sounded a bit extreme, but they were about the only ones that would work. The idea of starting the buses off and making the drivers hold to a rigid schedule was a stroke of genius; much kinder to the Indian, who could better afford to miss a bus on the reservation than lose a job in town because he was late.

There is, in fact, no other way to teach time to people who handle it as differently from us as the Sioux. The quickest way is to get very technical about it and to make it mean something. Later on these people can learn the informal variations, but until they have experienced and then mastered our type of time they will never adjust to our culture.

Thousands of miles away from the reservations of the American Indian we come to another way of handling time which is apt to be completely unsettling to the unprepared visitor. The inhabitants of the atoll of Truk in the Southwest Pacific treat time in a fashion that has complicated life for themselves as well as for others, since it poses special problems not only for their civil and military governors and the anthropologists recording their life but for their own chiefs as well.

Time does not heal on Truk! Past events stack up, placing an ever-increasing burden on the Trukese and weighing heavily on the present. They are, in fact, treated as though they had just occurred. This was borne out by something which happened shortly after the American occupation of the atoll at the end of World War II.

A villager arrived all out of breath at the military government headquarters. He said that a murder had been committed in the village and that the murderer was running around loose. Quite naturally the military government officer became alarmed. He was about to dispatch M.P.s to arrest the culprit when he remembered that someone had warned him about acting precipitously when dealing with "natives." A little inquiry turned up the fact that the victim had been "fooling around" with the murderer's wife. Still more inquiry of a routine type, designed to establish the place and date of the crime, revealed that the murder had not occurred a few hours or even days ago, as one might expect, but seventeen years before. The murderer had been running around loose in the village all this time.

A further example of how time does not heal on Truk is that of a land dispute that started with the German occupation in the 1890s, was carried on down through the Japanese occupation, and was still current and acrimonious when the Americans arrived in 1946.

Prior to Missionary Moses' arrival on Uman in 1867 life on Truk was characterized by violent and bloody warfare. Villages, instead of being built on the shore where life was a little easier, were placed on the sides of mountains where they could be better protected. Attacks would come without notice and often without apparent provocation. Or a fight might start if a man stole a coconut from a tree that was not his or waylaid a woman and took advantage of her. Years later someone would start thinking about the wrong and decide that it still had not been righted. A village would be attacked again in the middle of the night.

When charges were brought against a chief for things he had done to his people, every little slight, every minor graft would be listed; nothing would be forgotten. Damages would be asked for everything. It seemed preposterous to us Americans, particularly when we looked at the lists of charges. "How could a chief be so corrupt?" "How could the people remember so much?"

Though the Truk islanders carry the accumulated burden of time past on their shoulders, they show an almost total inability to grasp the notion that two events can take place at the same time when they are any distance apart. When the Japanese occupied Truk at the end of World War I they took Artie Moses, chief of the island of Uman, to Tokyo. Artie was made to send a wireless message back to his people as a demonstration of the wizardry of Japanese technology. His family refused to believe that he had sent it, that he had said anything at all, though they knew he was in Tokyo. Places at a distance are very real to them, but people who are away are very much away, and any interaction with them is unthinkable.

An entirely different handling of time is reported by the anthropologist Paul Bohannan for the Tiv, a primitive people who live in Nigeria. Like the Navajo, they point to the sun to indicate a general time of day, and they also observe the movement of the moon as it waxes and wanes. What is different is the way they use and experience time. For the Tiv, time is like a capsule. There is a time for visiting, for cooking, or for working; and when one is in one of these times, one does not shift to another.

The Tiv equivalent of the week lasts five to seven days. It is not tied into periodic natural events, such as the phases of the moon. The day of the week is named after the things which are being sold in the nearest "market." If we had the equivalent, Monday would be "automobiles" in Washington, D.C., "furniture" in Baltimore, and "yard goods" in New York. Each of these might be followed by the days for appliances, liquor, and diamonds in the respective cities. This would mean that as you traveled about the day of the week would keep changing, depending on where you were.

A requisite of our own temporal system is that the components must add up: Sixty seconds have to equal one minute, sixty minutes one hour. The American is perplexed by people who do not do this. The African specialist Henri Alexandre Junod, reporting on the Thonga, tells of a medicine man who had memorized a seventy-year chronology and could detail the events of each and every year in sequence. Yet this same man spoke of the period he had memorized as an "era" which he computed at "four months and eight hundred years' duration." The usual reaction to this story and others like it is that the man was primitive, like a child, and did not understand what he was saying, because how could seventy years possibly be the same as eight hundred? As students of culture we can no longer dismiss other conceptualizations of reality by saying that they are childlike. We must go much deeper. In the case of the Thonga it seems that a "chronology" is one thing and an "era" something else quite different, and there is no relation between the two in operational terms.

If these distinctions between European-American time and other conceptions of time seem to draw too heavily on primitive peoples, let me mention two other examples—from cultures which are as civilized, if not as industrialized, as our own. In comparing the United States with Iran and Afghanistan very great differences in the handling of time appear. The American attitude toward appointments is an example. Once while in Tehran I had an opportunity to observe some young Iranians making plans for a party. After plans were made to pick up everyone at appointed times and places everything began to fall apart. People would leave messages that they were unable to take so-and-so or were going somewhere else, knowing full well that the person who had been given the message couldn't possibly deliver it. One girl was left stranded on a street corner, and no one seemed to be concerned about it. One of my informants explained that he himself had had many similar experiences. Once he had made eleven appointments to meet a friend. Each time one of them failed to show up. The twelfth time they swore they would both be there, that nothing would interfere. The friend failed to arrive. After waiting for forty-five minutes my informant phoned his friend and found him still at home. The following conversation is an approximation of what took place:

"Is that you, Abdul?" "Yes." "Why aren't you here? I thought we were to meet for sure." "Oh, but it was raining," said Abdul with a sort of whining intonation that is very common in Parsi.

If present appointments are treated rather cavalierly, the past in Iran takes on a very great importance. People look back on what they feel are the wonders of the past and the great ages of Persian culture. Yet the future seems to have little reality or certainty to it. Businessmen have been known to invest hundreds of thousands of dollars in factories of various sorts without making the slightest plan as to how to use them. A complete woolen mill was bought and shipped to Tehran before the buyer had raised enough money to erect it, to buy supplies, or even to train personnel. When American teams of technicians came to help Iran's economy they constantly had to cope with what seemed to them an almost total lack of planning.

Moving east from Iran to Afghanistan, one gets farther afield from American time concepts. A few years ago in Kabul a man appeared, looking for his brother. He asked all the merchants of the market place if they had seen his brother and told them where he was staying in case his brother arrived and wanted to find him. The next year he was back and repeated the performance. By this time one of the members of the American embassy had heard about his inquiries and asked if he had found his brother. The man answered that he and his brother had agreed to meet in Kabul, but neither of them had said what year.

Strange as some of these stories about the ways in which people handle time may seem, they become understandable when they are correctly analyzed. To do this adequately requires an adequate theory of culture. Before we return to the subject of time again—in a much later chapter of this book—I hope that I will have provided just such a theory. It will not only shed light on the way time is meshed with many other aspects of society but will provide a key to unlock some of the secrets of the eloquent language of culture which speaks in so many different ways.

VIRGIL C. ALDRICH

PICTORIAL MEANING
AND PICTURE THINKING

Virgil C. Aldrich (1903-   ) was born in India but educated at Ohio Wesleyan, Oxford, the Sorbonne, and the University of California. He is both a philosopher and a teacher. He has published widely in philosophical journals. "Pictorial Meaning and Picture Thinking" is a fruit of one of his special interests and studies, analysis of various sorts of meaning. Since 1946, he has been professor of philosophy at Kenyon College.

PROFESSOR CHARLES W. MORRIS, in his essay "Empiricism, Religion, and Democracy," writes:

Imagine a community of men living on a cell in the blood stream of one of us, but so small that we have no evidence, direct or indirect, of their existence. Imagine further that they themselves are provided with scientific instruments of the type we use, and possess a method of science and a body of scientific knowledge comparable to ours. One of the bolder of these thinkers proposes that the universe they inhabit is a Great Man. Is this hypothesis admissible on scientific grounds or is it to be laughed down by the Minute Empiricists on the ground that it is "metaphysical"? We Macroscopic Empiricists would at least seem to have to favor the hypothesis! But then why at our own level cannot a similar hypothesis be raised: namely, that *we* are parts of a Great Man, the whole of our known universe being perhaps but a portion of the Great Blood Stream? . . . The liberal empiricist I have championed would side with the Minute Empiricists in asserting that the hypothesis is empirically meaningful since the properties ascribed to the Great Man would be properties drawn from objects that had been observed; he would merely say that in terms of evidence available to them this hypothesis was too poorly confirmed to have a place in their system of scientific knowledge.[1]

I have quoted Morris at length, because the excerpt highlights the point to the examination of which this essay is given, namely,

[1] *Conference on Science, Philosophy and Religion*, New York, p. 219.

»»» *Kenyon Review*, V (Summer, 1943), 403-412. Reprinted by permission of Virgil C. Aldrich.

the concept of "empirically significant possibilities" and a way of treating it which persists despite recent refinements in the general theory of meaning—a way I take to be inadequate. If as competent a specialist in the theory of signs as Morris (and C. I. Lewis) can go wrong on this count, it is little wonder that the mistake is such a common one among those who have given the matter less systematic attention. The matter concerns a kind of meaning, or a way of using language, that has not been isolated with sufficient rigor from other kinds, the result being a tendency to accommodate it under the general category of cognitive sense, to the detriment of both kinds, as we shall see. The ill-advised mixture converts both into renegades that frequently lead inquiry and discussion into an impasse.

Another illustration—and yet others later—will help us to detect, isolate, and tag the new kind of sense.

Suppose someone—whom we shall call Typical Tom—says there is a little blue devil in his watch. We open it and find nothing but the usual mechanism. Tom says the little devil disappears into thin air the moment the watch is opened. We then weigh the watch, when it is open and again when it is closed, noticing no difference in weight. Tom says the little blue imp, like any genuine spirit, is an immaterial and therefore imponderable substance. Then we observe that the watch keeps time accurately, which would be unlikely with a blue devil inside, getting its tail and legs caught in the gears and hairspring. Well, we can guess what Tom says to that. And so on.

To such a position as Tom's there are four usual reactions. The first, and least cautious, is the assertion that Tom's blue-devil utterance is patently false. But a plainly false expression is, by definition, one that can be disproved; and there is *no* way to disprove, there is *no* evidence against, what Tom says. The second reaction to it is the more cautious objection that he's talking nonsense—making "pure nonsense," which explains our inability to prove the falsity of his utterance. But even little children could clearly understand—and be delighted by—Tom's remark, and would clamor for its expansion into a story about the little blue devil. So evidently Tom has made himself intelligible in some sense. A third reaction might be the suggestion that Tom's utterance is indeed significant but only with motivational or emotive meaning. (In Morris' own terminology, one might say Tom's expression contains "motivators" or "expressors," but no "referors.") But Tom correctly points out that, for him, the blue-devil utterance did not express a mood or feeling, neither was it aimed at getting somebody to do something.

Suppose now we ask Tom how he *knows* that a little blue devil haunts his watch, pointing out that one can *imagine* the presence or absence of anything in it. He then concedes that his original statement, "It is *true* that there is a little blue devil in my watch," is too strong, and weakens it to read, "It is just *possible* that there is . . . etc."

This, I take it, is the position that Morris would assume, adding of course, as he did in the Blood Stream case, that the blue-devil hypothesis is "too poorly confirmed to have a place in the system of scientific knowledge." Moreover, this conclusion seems in general so harmless from any point of view—that of the scientist, artist, speculative cosmologist, theologian, moralist—that it is the one most commonly arrived at. It has, in addition, the air of being "liberal," in as much as it seems to give the speculative imagination the important place it apparently has even in the field of scientific inquiry. Such difficulties as the position has appear only after analysis of meaning has been pressed beyond the province of specific interests. For general methodology, pressing the analysis further is crucial and shows the way out of verbal predicaments even on the level of common discourse—predicaments that are simply battered down out of the way (instead of being solved) by disputants who don't understand them. So let us try to formulate—here necessarily in a rough and popular way—certain distinctions.

The main point we are going to make is that Tom's utterance, "It is possible that there is a little blue devil in the watch," is comparable to the expression, "It is possible that please go away." As the expression "please go away" does not make cognitive sense— it is neither true nor false—but motivational, so the expression

"There is a little blue devil in the watch" does not make cognitive sense but (what we shall call) *pictorial* sense. Our task now is to so define pictorial meaning as to disengage it from the cognitive with which it is so readily confused, and to explain why the confusion is so prevalent. With this task we now come to grips.

Discourse frequently takes a turn that makes argument concerning its subject-matter irrelevant. But this happens in at least two quite different ways. That there is a grain of sand in the watch is arguable. That there is a neutrino in the watch is also appropriately argued. But people would naturally refuse even to argue the proposition that the mechanism of the watch consists of nothing but thirteen hydrogen atoms, because the proposition is too plainly false. They would be annoyed with anyone who would continue elaborating such a position. This is *one* way in which argument becomes irrelevant. But suppose it were said that the watch is the cosy habitat of an army of a million little archers, each armored in mother-of-pearl and bearing a bow made of a splinter of diamond, all too small ever to be observed; and when the watch is closed it is filled with a soft, iridescent radiance— the light of their world; each tick of the match marks off a day in their lives and an hour a life-span; they are unerring marksmen, capable in that twilight of knocking the spinning electrons out of their orbits with their golden arrows . . . .

Now in this case also we would find argument irrelevant, but is it because the utterance is too plainly false, or, in Morris' words, "too poorly confirmed"? This would be an inadequate estimate, since there is *no* possible evidence against the utterance, and it may be "poorly confirmed" in the sense that "please go away" is poorly confirmed, neither expression being the sort with respect to which the demand for evidence is relevant.

But the important point is that in this case of the archer, far from being annoyed at the elaboration of such a position, we *want more*. It is as if the sense that is now being made lies in a different dimension of meaning, or differs in kind, from that of the expressions concerning the grain of sand, the neutrino, and the thirteen hydrogen atoms. We have shifted gears into a different form of discourse, which in its own way may be highly intelligible and even important (if charged also with emotive and motivational significance) without formulating an empirically significant "possibility" awaiting confirmation. We shall call such meaning "pictorial" and we call its formulation "picture thinking."

One is tempted to object that all four of the above expressions formulate empirically significant possibilities, the only difference being that the archer possibility is so much more picturesque than the others (sand, neutrino, etc.) that we naturally incline to contemplate and enjoy it for its own sake, thus ignoring the question —which nevertheless remains relevant—of its truth or falsity. In short, it formulates an empirically significant possibility.

The answer to this hinges mostly on a terminological issue: people who say that a sentence formulates an "empirically possible" state of affairs usually mean that it is true or false and that some day it *might* be confirmed or infirmed. (This, I take it, is what Morris means; it is true or false that there are little men on a blood cell in one of us, and if we had fine enough instruments and if there *are* little men on blood cells, we would detect their existence, etc.) But the archer-situation has been so couched (or could be) as not only to make proof or disproof impossible but to make the demand for either irrelevant, while retaining a very clear-cut intelligibility of the pictorial sort. We conclude, therefore, that language can be used with the primary intention of expressing or evoking pictures (imagery), and in a way that differs from the sign usage that formulates empirically significant possibilities.

So far, our illustrations have involved cases where the pictorial intent is so salient as to be fairly readily distinguished from the cognitive or empirical. We don't ordinarily argue the blue devil or archer utterances because we "get," by a kind of linguistic instinct or habitual propriety, what the speaker primarily means by them. His primary intention is obvious, namely, to tease and entertain us (and himself) with pictures that, as verbally treated by him, have nothing to do even with *possibilities* for matters of fact.

2.

But pictorial sense can be made of practically anything, and *this may be the only kind of sense that is being made even where the aim is to make statements about matters of fact.* It is in such cases that disputants reach an impasse, which blocks them until a distinction is made between the pictorial and the cognitive content of the expression in question. Instances of such predicaments are common. Let us examine some.

We are looking at a scarf and "observe" that, in a certain light, it is "red." Typical Tom says that maybe it isn't "really" red. We call in others to take a look, or ourselves look more closely, or even make measurements of wave-frequency, etc., getting a confirmation of our judgment. But Tom says that what he means by "red" is a visual sensation in each one of our minds and, for all we will ever know, no two of these sensations are alike. Yours may actually be blue while mine is green, though both of us have been taught to say "red" when we are aware of these color patches as data in our minds.

Now it would be a mistake to say wholesale that Tom is talking nonsense. He evidently "means" something by these remarks and, moreover, most of us "get" something at the receiver's end of the communication. What is evoked in most of us by the utterance is a set of pictures, such as two non-overlapping, translucent spheres ("minds") inside one of which we imagine a tiny blue patch and a green patch in the other, as effects of streams of light radiation reaching the spheres from a common external source. Then, if we imagine each of these spheres as hovering near the head of a human organism which says "red" when the color patch appears in its sphere, the picture is complete, and we have understood what Tom said. But his primary intention in this case is to say something that might be true of matters of fact, something that is "just possible." Has he succeeded in this? The fact that he has not said anything demonstrably *false* must not, it should be remembered, be taken by itself as a sign of his having formulated an empirically significant possibility, for reasons noted above. An examination of what Tom put across by his utterance shows that he has made himself intelligible in the dimension of pictorial meaning. But that he has made sense of any other than the blue devil kind is doubtful. And if, objecting to the picturesque turn we have given his expression, he attempts a "literal" interpretation, he will, in this quest for its empirical (cognitive) meaning, find himself looking in a dark room for a black cat that isn't there. ("Attempting a literal interpretation" means, of course, trying to get the expression coordinated with some matters of fact that serve as evidence for or against it; but it has been so worded as to preclude this possibility.) It is the function of the philosophical analyst to show Tom that, with respect to cognitive significance, he has failed to understand himself, since, in that dimension of meaning, he has either said nothing, or something so ill-defined as to be unintelligible without preliminary (and perhaps strange) linguistic conventions. But this, of course, does not militate against the intelligibility of the expression in its dimension of pictorial significance.

Current discussion of the dimensions of space provide us with another illustration of how one may make pictorial sense only, while intending to say something true about matters of fact. People say they "observe" up to three dimensions, but can't even "imagine" a fourth. Typical Tom, associating the "possible" with the "imaginable," concludes from this that the hyperspace theorists don't know what they are talking about. (Even Poincaré suggests that someday we may be able, after strenuous exercise, to "imagine a fourth dimension," whereupon non-Euclidean geometry will possibly become more "convenient" than the Euclidean.) But this is to make the mistake of supposing that when we say, "Space has n dimensions," the pictures evoked by the expression define its cognitive meaning. Strictly speaking, the cognitive sense even of the expression, "Space has three dimensions," is left untouched by what one can or can't imagine: what this expression means empirically, through operational definitions, is as "unimaginable" as the one about four or more dimensions. Or, putting it yet another way, the sense in which three dimensions *can* be "observed" or "imagined" is precisely the sense in which the fourth dimension can be observed or imagined; in both cases, something is to be observed that proves or disproves the propositions about space, and in the same general way.

The writings of Jeans and Eddington are a fertile source of illustrations of our point about pictorial meaning. "There is a mysterious world outside us to which our minds can never penetrate"; an "inscrutable absolute behind appearances," etc. The analysis of such expressions in the light of the distinction made above is obvious, so we shall not here give them special attention. Our moral is that one should be on guard against the little blue devil, since he can assume many shapes and, if undetected, bedevil discourse in a very tantalizing way.

But special attention should be given something that so far we have dealt with only implicitly. From an inspection of linguistic properties or grammatical form alone, one cannot safely tell what the primary intention of the speaker is. Typical Tom, upon looking into the watch or into a Mexican jumping bean and seeing no little blue devils might well have admitted at once that he was wrong. This would show that he not only intended to make empirical (factual) sense, but actually did. He was construing "blue devil" in a factually significant way. On the other hand, blue-devil sense (pictorial) might readily be made even of the expression about the grain of sand in the watch. Tom might teasingly say, upon not observing one inside, that there is one there anyway, only of a peculiar invisible sort, etc. This is what we meant by saying that practically anything can be construed pictorially, in a way that does not limit or define even a *possible* state of affairs for matters of fact. Thus, pictorial sense can be made even of objects in the field of sense-perception, and the artist makes a profession of this. Morris' mistake was the initial one of supposing that his little-men hypothesis about an object of perception, namely a blood cell, formulated an empirically significant possibility. From this mistaken assumption he argued the cognitive significance of the hypothesis of our being caught in a Cosmic Blood Stream or parts of a Great Man.

Traditionally, "theory" and "cognition" (knowledge) have meant something involving contemplation and spectacle—"vision," with emphasis on picture-thinking and pictorial meaning. This essay would be properly doomed to the limbo of all dogmatisms if its thesis were either that the words "theory" and "knowledge" and "cognitive significance" *cannot* mean these things, or that pictorially significant sign-usage is unimportant. Its thesis is, rather, that since even the traditional theorists tended to argue what they called "theories," and since pictorial meaning is intrinsically non-arguable, as we have seen after isolating it from another sort that is arguable, we had better let "theory" and "cognitive meaning" involve this latter kind of sense and preclude the former. There is nothing anti-liberal in such a proposal. Indeed, it is aimed at liberating both the intellect and the imagination each for its special task. It explains, moreover, the sense one has of "understanding" an expression before it is in any way cognitively coordinated with matters of fact—such understanding being a grasp of pictorial significance.

The popular (and half true) notion that even the task of the scientist is implemented by a lively imagination here calls for comment. It has been noted that we have not, existentially speaking, drawn a line between a "field (or realm) of imagination" and a "field of sense-perception," confining the scientist to the latter. In fact, we flout the distinction by saying that, given *any* item, whether perceived or imagined, then either pictorial or cognitive sense can be made of it, according to the way in which it is construed and articulated. That is why much of the experimental work of the great scientist can be (and usually is) of the armchair variety. Not that he is, in such moments, doing what the poet or artist does, but rather that he is articulating imagined states of affairs in empirically (factually) significant propositions. This is the crucial difference. The notion that the great theorist is necessarily half-poet is mistaken and misleading. Of course, he may also be a poet, but not with respect to theoretic acumen. Much of the published work of theorists such as Eddington, Montague, Santayana, and others, great though it is as a provocative for thought and imagination, is marred by the failure to distinguish theorizing from picture thinking.

CLASSIFICATION

CLASSIFICATION—the result of the sorting of all members of a class into groups or subclasses on a certain basis—is best described, as it is described in the headnote to "Analysis," in the context of definition and analysis. But to this description must be added the three rules of classification and a few words about the purpose of classification. That a classification should be (1) complete, (2) discrete, and (3) consistent sums up these rules. A classification is complete only if it assigns every member of the class to one of the subclasses; it is discrete only if it assigns no member of the class to more than one subclass; and it is consistent only if it assigns members of the class to subclasses on only one basis. Of these three rules, the third is the most fundamental. For, if a classification follows the third rule, it also follows the other two rules; and, conversely, if it breaks the third rule, it also breaks the other two. If, for example, a classification of all people begins on the basis of hair color but (breaking the third rule) shifts to other bases (weight, religion, occupation, and eating habits, say), then it might end up with these subclasses—blonds, fat people, Protestants, plumbers, and vegetarians—and consequently (breaking the second rule) with some people in two or more subclasses (a blond, fat, Protestant plumber who is a vegetarian would be in all five subclasses) and (breaking the first rule) with some people in no subclass (a brunet, skinny, Catholic undertaker who is a carnivore would be in none). The six classifications in the following pieces observe this third rule and, hence, the other two rules, though most of them do not state the basis of classification.

The purpose of classification might seem to be simply exercise of the classifier's logical faculties; but, though classification does exercise them, this is not its purpose. In practice, it always has a practical purpose. Teachers could classify their pupils on the basis of hair color, length of toenails, height of metatarsal arch, or tastes in pizza; but they don't, for classification of them on such bases would serve no purpose. Instead, they classify them on the basis of performance in the work, or knowledge of the work, of the course.

In the classifications that follow, Hawthorne classifies works of narrative fiction on the basis of the relation of the work to reality; Schwartz and Thiel, rocks on the basis of manner of formation; "Search for Bestsellers," publishers on the basis of size; Darton, children's books on the basis of subject; and Snow, educated persons on the basis of culture. Bates discusses the difficulty of using race as a basis for classification of human beings (that is, the difficulty of assigning a precise meaning to "race").

NATHANIEL HAWTHORNE

TWO MODES OF NARRATIVE FICTION

Nathaniel Hawthorne (1804-1864), who depicted his native New England in his novels and stories, was born in Salem, Massachusetts, and was educated at Bowdoin College. His most famous novels are The Scarlet Letter *(1850) and* The House of the Seven Gables *(1851); his better-known stories come from* Twice-Told Tales *(1st series, 1837; 2nd series, 1842).*

WHEN A WRITER calls his work a romance, it need hardly be observed that he wishes to claim a certain latitude, both as to its fashion and material, which he would not have felt himself entitled to assume had he professed to be writing a novel. The latter form of composition is presumed to aim at a very minute fidelity, not merely to the possible, but to the probable and ordinary course of man's experience. The former—while, as a work of art, it must rigidly subject itself to laws, and while it sins unpardonably so far as it may swerve aside from the truth of the human heart— has fairly a right to present that truth under circumstances, to a great extent, of the writer's own choosing or creation. If he thinks fit, also, he may so manage his atmospherical medium as to bring out or mellow the lights, and deepen and enrich the shadows, of the picture. He will be wise, no doubt, to make a very moderate use of the privileges here stated, and, especially, to mingle the marvellous rather as a slight, delicate, and evanescent flavor, than as any portion of the actual substance of the dish offered to the public. He can hardly be said, however, to commit a literary crime, even if he disregard this caution.

»»» From Preface to *The House of the Seven Gables.* New York, 1851.

GEORGE M. SCHWARTZ

AND GEORGE A. THIEL

THE CLASSES OF ROCKS

*George M. Schwartz (1892-   ) and George A. Thiel (1892-   ) took
their Ph.D. degrees at the University of Minnesota in 1923 and taught geology
there for forty years until their retirement as professors emeriti. Professor
Schwartz has worked for the Wisconsin and the Minnesota State Geological
Surveys as well as for the U.S. Geological Survey. Professor Thiel has been
a civilian member of the Atomic Energy Commission and has been associated
with the Office of Scientific Research and Development. Authors of many
technical papers on the geology of the Lake Superior and Upper Mississippi
River regions, they are co-authors, with Peggy Harding Love, of* Minnesota's
Rocks and Waters *(1954), a geological story for the general reader.*

A ROCK is defined broadly as any material that forms an essential
part of the earth's crust. Most rocks can be defined somewhat
more definitely as aggregates of one or more minerals or organic
remains. Some rocks consist almost entirely of one mineral; the
St. Peter sandstone, for example, at places consists of 99 per cent
quartz. Most rocks, however, contain several minerals.

All rocks are subdivided into three major groups:

1. *Igneous rocks,* formed by solidification of molten material.

2. *Sedimentary rocks,* formed at the surface of the earth by
deposition of material transported by water, wind, and ice, and
by organisms.

3. *Metamorphic rocks,* formed from pre-existing rocks by the
action of heat, pressure, and chemical solutions at some depth in
the earth's crust.

»»» From "Minerals and Rocks." Ch. 3 of *Minnesota's Rocks and Waters.*
Minneapolis: University of Minnesota Press, copyright 1954, by the University of Minnesota. Pp. 69-70. Reprinted by permission of the University
of Minnesota Press.

269

SEARCH FOR BESTSELLERS

ANYONE CAN be a publisher. In the course of any normal year the book lists will record, as publishers of at least one new book, approximately a thousand names. From year to year it is never precisely the same thousand, for it includes (besides institutions and societies and firms whose publishing activities are adjuncts to other quite different operations) a number of private individuals who, having realized that the only essentials needed are to have something to be printed and an accommodating printer, have satisfied what seems to be a fairly common urge, and are not to be tempted again.

By comparison, the number of book publishers generally recognized as such is not large. All told, there are hardly more than 350 houses to provide us with all our books of whatever kind. Some are specialist firms, producing only educational books, or religious books, or technical works. There are firms which serve particular professions, such as medicine or the law, and never go outside their rigidly limited orbits; there are other firms whose complete catalogues, substantial volumes in themselves, cover ranges of learning that would daunt the doughtiest. Then to close this list abruptly, there are the firms which publish the general literature that the average person would expect to find in any good bookshop—the child's picture book, the inexpensive classic, the latest novel and the most important biography of the day. The distinguishing marks separating one kind of publisher from another are blurred. There are specialist publishers who are also in the front rank on the general side.

THREE CATEGORIES

Some of these publishers are very big, some are very small. In terms of size publishers have always defied easy classification.

»»» *The Times* (London), February 1, 1958, p. 7. Reprinted by permission of *The Times*.

The trade itself is usually content with three categories, Large, Medium, and Small. There are half a dozen firms whose annual sales amount to more—in two or three cases much more—than £1m. a year. They, manifestly, are Large. Small is less than £200,000. Firms which occupy the ample space between these two figures are Medium. But, of the 350 publishers, 25 per cent. are responsible for at least 75 per cent. of the total business.

Total sales by publishers in 1956 amounted to over £56,-500,000; in 1939 the figure was £10m. When every allowance has been made for increase in price—and reckoned over the whole range of books the price has hardly more than doubled—it is clear that a great many more books are being bought now than before the war, and that the bulk of the vastly increased sales revenue is now rejoicing the hearts of the dominant 25 per cent.

Not that publishers, any more than farmers, ever rejoice in public. Both sow hopefully, conscious that elements beyond their control may make or mar their harvest. A promising crop may ripen too early or lose its value in a glut. Both can be harmed by wind and weather. This is by no means only a metaphor so far as the book trade is concerned. A prolonged heat wave can kill 50 books stone dead, and fog and sleet can do irreparable harm to the vital Christmas trade. Still, the fact remains that, when all is said, the established publishers are more prosperous to-day than at any time since that golden age that ended in 1914. To quote the cautious opening sentence of last year's annual report of the Publishers' Association: "In spite of continuing signs of monetary inflation—or perhaps because of them—the publishing trade continued in 1956 to wear an air of prosperity."

THE BIG MACHINE

In an expanding economy, fortune seems always willing to favour the already fortunate. Big firms tend to become bigger, and with increasing sales they must develop their sales organization and become bigger still. To-day, for better or for worse, and many people fear it is for worse, is the day of the big machine. Against it the small publisher may, with flair and luck, still bring off his occasional resounding success, but, other things being equal, he is at a disadvantage in any sustained competition.

The big machine, when it moves into top gear, can achieve spectacular results, often for books of quite indifferent quality, a fact which no one but the operator of the machine can view with pleasure. When, furthermore, it attracts for such books all the enormous perquisites which to-day are the supplementary rewards of successful book publication—film, book club, digest, serial, translation, and all the other rights—the effect on the observer is lowering. Fortunately, it is satisfactory to be able to record that the machine has been known to fail.

A story is told of an occasion, two or three years ago, when this machine went into action on behalf of a book for which the managing director had ordered what his staff termed "the full treatment." The advance Press publicity developed to its crescendo, there were the usual Sunday newspaper serialization, the successive announcements of sales of every kind of subsidiary right, and on publication day the pyramids of copies in the bookshop windows. A week later the pyramids had mysteriously melted away. Later, the publisher, his warehouse filled with returned copies, held the inevitable inquest to find out what had gone wrong. "Nothing went wrong," the sales manager assured him. "It was only that nobody would buy it."

AMALGAMATION

What seems to be generally regarded as the most conspicuous and significant development during recent years has been the amalgamations and working associations between groups of firms. Amalgamation between publishers, of course, is an old story. The genealogies of some of the nineteenth century publishing houses are as tortuous as those of the Hapsburgs. But these were amalgamations pure and simple. One party absorbed, or was absorbed by, the other. The arrangement whereby Secker & Warburg Ltd. and Rupert Hart-Davis Ltd. have recently become members of what is called the Heinemann Group is wholly different. Both these firms, which carried the stamp of individuality on all the books that bore their imprint, retain that individuality, under the same publishing direction as before, unimpaired. What they have acquired is the benefit of a sales organization, at home and oversea, more powerful than anything a small publisher could hope to acquire. Here is an instance of the big machine working beneficently and well.

Individualism is the glory of British publishing, but it is coming increasingly to be realized that individualism has definite limits. In his relation with his authors, his printers and binders, the publisher is quite rightly an individualist. The fact that the ordinary book-buyer will enter a bookshop and demand one particular book by one particular author is a justification of individualism on the part of everybody concerned. But when that end has been reached, many thoughtful people in the book trade consider, further individualism serves no useful purpose.

WASTEFUL

They feel that it is wasteful of time and money for 300 different little groups of clerks to be sending out 300 different little lots of invoices for books dispatched from 300 different little warehouses to the same bookshops. Doubtless the day when this work will be done, more efficiently and more cheaply, by a central organization, is inevitable though distant. In the meantime a number of smaller publishers are joining forces in their distributive arrangements.

Down the years, English literature has owed much to the small independent publisher who has risked his slender resources on sponsoring and cherishing an author whose quality bigger and wealthier publishers have failed to perceive. It is a commonplace of bibliography to find that writers' names that have become renowned appeared first over imprints that are now only a memory. "The desert is strewn with the bones and wreckage of our caravans," wrote Mr. John Lehmann, before he gave up book publishing, "and yet our merchandise was far from worthless: it is remarkable how much of it can be discovered piled on the camels of those greater caravans that passed us by."

Nevertheless, for the small man there are compensations, not the least of which is that he can personally remain a publisher at a time when the head of a large house or group of companies must be preoccupied with administration; and, if the small publisher is fortunate enough to find authors who are loyal to him as well as successful, he can relish his status as a David among Goliaths.

F. J. HARVEY DARTON

CHILDREN'S BOOKS

F. J. Harvey Darton (1867-1936) was an English publisher who collected and was an authority on children's books. He contributed articles on them to the Encyclopædia Britannica *(10th ed.) and the* Cambridge History of English Literature. *His* Children's Books in England *(1932) is still the standard work on its subject and an outstanding contribution to social history.*

§ 1

By "CHILDREN'S BOOKS" I mean printed works produced ostensibly to give children spontaneous pleasure, and not primarily to teach them, nor solely to make them good, nor to keep them *profitably* quiet. I shall therefore exclude from this history, as a general rule, all schoolbooks, all purely moral or didactic treatises, all reflective or adult-minded descriptions of child-life, and almost all alphabets, primers, and spelling-books; though some works in each category will be mentioned because they purposely gave much latitude to amusement, or because they contained elements which have passed into a less austere legacy. The definition is given as a broad principle liable to perpetual exception.

Roughly speaking, under its terms, there were no children's books in England before the seventeenth century, and very few even then. There were plenty of schoolbooks and guides to conduct, but none which would openly allow a child to enjoy himself with no thought of duty nor fear of wrong. Children's books did not stand out by themselves as a clear but subordinate branch of English literature until the middle of the eighteenth century. To-day, in the statistics of printed matter, they are second only to works of fiction. To put it commercially, it is less than two centuries since they became a definite object of the activities of the book-trade; that is to say, since authors first

»»» From "An Introductory Survey." Ch. 1 of *Children's Books in England: Five Centuries of Social Life.* Cambridge, England: University Press, 1932. Pp. 1-9. Reprinted by permission of the Cambridge University Press.

wrote them, and merchants first produced them, *habitually,* in quantities and with a frequency which implied that they were meant for a known, considerable, permanent class of readers ready to receive them. Because an arbitrary date is a convenience, and for no other reason, I will say that that commencement took place in 1744, when John Newbery, the most authentic founder of this traffic in minor literature, published his first children's book.

It is worth while to quote some particulars of this engaging work. It is by way of being a "key" publication. It was called *A Little Pretty Pocket Book.* The frontispiece shows a mother or a governess teaching a boy and girl. Underneath is the inscription "Delectando monemus. Instruction with Delight". The expanded title states that the *Pocket Book* was

intended for the Instruction and Amusement of Little Master Tommy and Pretty Miss Polly, with an agreeable Letter to read from Jack the Giant Killer, as also a Ball and a Pincushion, the use of which will infallibly make Tommy a good Boy, and Polly a good Girl. . . . Price of the Book alone, 6*d.*, with a Ball or Pincushion, 8*d.*

It was published at the sign of the *Bible and Crown,* near Devereux Court, London, close to the Grecian Coffee House, one of Oliver Goldsmith's haunts. John Newbery in 1744 had just come to London from Reading, where he had been an assistant and partner of William Carnan, printer and bookseller. He had also had business connections with Collins, the Salisbury bookseller. In London, besides the *Bible and Crown,* he set up an establishment at the *Golden Ball,* close to the Royal Exchange, probably for the sake of the sea-borne and Eastern Counties trade, which came by road through Whitechapel and by river up to London Bridge. In 1745, however, he transferred the whole of his business to the more famous address, "the *Bible and Sun,* near the Chapter House, in St. Paul's Churchyard". Here his successors remained as publishers till the reign of George V.

These facts have some importance in a small historical way. More to the immediate purpose are a few further details of the *Pocket Book's* contents. The most significant point is that Newbery deliberately set out to provide amusement, and was not afraid to say so. Fifty years before he might not have ventured to such lengths, and he would hardly have said anything about the good looks of Miss Polly, whatever her excellence. He certainly puts instruction before amusement; but his ideas of both instruction and amusement differed greatly from those exhibited by his few and intermittent predecessors in this style of publishing, which he was to make peculiarly his own. In fact, after some preliminary remarks meant for parents, instruction is dragged in only by the scruff. Most of the book is taken up with pictures of children playing games, and little rhymes not very securely relevant to them.[1] The pedagogue is mollified by the heading of each pastime, which is, with no relevance at all, a letter of the alphabet—"The Great A Play", "The Great B Play", and so on. There are also "Little a [b, etc.] Games", with rhymes not more congruous. For instance, "The Little s Game" stands at the head of

> Here's great K and L,
> Pray Dame can you tell,
> Who put the Pig-Hog
> Down into the Well?

and "the Little t Game" is

> So great O, and P,
> Pray what do you see?
> *A naughty Boy whipt;*
> But that is not me.

[1] It may be of interest to mention the games. They are Chuck-Farthing: Kite-Flying: Maypole Dancing: Taw (marbles): Hoop and Hide (Hide and Seek): Thread the Needle (a chase-game): Fishing: Blindman's Buff: Shuttle-Cock: King [of the Castle] I am: Peg Farthing (driving a coin out of a circle with a pegtop): Knock-out and Span (marbles): Hop, Step, and Jump: "Boys and Girls come out to Play": "I sent a Letter to my Love": Pitch and Hussel: Cricket (with two stumps and a curved-club bat): Stool-Ball (here a sort of rounders): Swimming: Base Ball (rounders as now played): Trap-Ball: Tip-Cat: Fives: Leap-Frog: Birds'-Nesting (reprobated): Train-Banding: "All the Birds in the Air" (a mimicry game): Hop-Hat: Shooting: Hop-Scotch: "Who will play at my Squares"? (cards!): and Riding.

These are accompanied by small blocks, respectively, of a well and of a boy being birched upon an extensive bare rump. Such blocks had done duty in more than one *abecedarium* of a generation earlier.

It might have been expected that with such careless treatment of instruction itself Newbery would have indulged his fancy over Jack the Giant Killer. But the moralists of the preceding ages had banished Jack from the nursery (a feat often attempted), and they had also been very suspicious of any recommendation to play at ball. Newbery compromised ingeniously with their point of view. The "letter" from Jack was simply an instruction in the proper use of the ball and pincushion. Each object had one side red, the other black. Every good deed done by Tommy and Polly was to be marked by sticking a pin into the red half, every ill deed by one in the black. And Jack had another function. Towards the end of the *Pocket Book* four fables are given, and he is introduced as the author of the rhymed morals attached to them. Thus all trace of the brutal and licentious giganticide is whitewashed, though his familiar name is used as an attraction. He is turned into an agent of conscious virtue.

But it was not enough to offer a giant as a bait. Two other "letters" appear in the volume. They display the earthly reward of eminence in book-learning. The well-schooled, satisfactory boy is shown as eventually riding in a coach and six, the good girl as being given a fine gold watch.

There is some probability that Newbery wrote the *Pocket Book* himself. It is of a piece with the known character of the man, "Jack Whirler" of Johnson's *Idler* (No. 19). He was a kind of business bumble-bee, though a worker too. In the *Pocket Book's* address to parents he shows admiration of Locke on Education, but almost in the same breath gives advice which is pure Rousseau: and one of his most characteristic productions, *The Twelfth-Day Gift* (1767), has a frontispiece which might almost serve as his coat-of-arms. It shows two men carrying, on a sort of stretcher, a monstrous fine cake. Underneath is the motto "Trade and Plumb-cake for ever, Huzza!"

It is no good pretending that John Newbery was consistent, or had any reasoned theory of infant psychology, or was an apostle of this or that school of educational thought. He was simply an active and benevolent tradesman, who was the first to see that, in his line of business, children's books deserved special attention and development. He produced almost nothing original that has passed into the nursery library to live for ever. Even his most famous juvenile publication, *Goody Two-Shoes,* is utterly dead. His personality and his friendships—what he was and what he did, in fact—have endured longer than any of his wares. He prospered, and his books proved by success that they met a want.

They will come up for closer examination in due course. Here I would only dwell on the features just selected from the *Little Pretty Pocket Book:* the claim to provide amusement with instruction, the use of the alphabet both as a form of amusement and, by its mere presence, as an instrument of education, the bold introduction of the unedifying name of the Giant Killer, the inclusion of fables, and the various small commercial touches which made it clear, as indeed the very form of the stout little book does, that the producer had a social rather than a scholastic or religious market quite plainly in view. Those little details all suggest various things that must have been in some sort of existence already. What was the social—or the mercantile—inheritance of which Newbery, not a real creator nor a daring innovator, was able to take advantage immediately he set out to make his fortune as a London bookseller? What was the nature of any children's books which existed before his time, why at that particular time was their development brought, as if by an abrupt miracle, into touch with that of "adult" English literature —in fact, why and how, such as they were, were they themselves ever composed and published at all?

Most of the answer lies in the Newbery slogan, as it might be called to-day—"Trade and Plumb-cake for ever". That would not have been a natural war-cry for a middle-class commercial man in England before about the reign of George II. It was natural for at least a century afterwards. And children's books, written as such, have been in England almost entirely a product of the large domesticated middle-class, which began to exist, free of civil war, not wildly excited about religion nor very heedful of political arts, but increasingly conscious and desirous of freedom, under the Hanoverian dynasty. There lies nearly all the rest of the answer. The reading habit had come into middling social life, and the English novel was born. The microcosm of children was to receive the reflection of this slow great change in the English character. Internal peace, increasing trade at home and abroad, wider literacy in all but the lowest classes, made such an opportunity for a quick brain as had not existed hitherto; and Newbery possessed the business intuition and the vague idealism to seize it.

§ II

But what were the precise materials which, in that fortunate conjunction, Newbery combined and used? It is clear that he found already in his lumber room or property store several things that are still known in nurseries: the *Pocket Book*, even in its own period, is evidently both ancient and modern. Consider the features already outlined. How many of them legitimately belong to "children's books", in a long view, and to what extent need their historical nature be examined here? They can be regarded for the moment as separate abstractions.

(a) *The Fable* was explicitly present in Newbery's compilation. In one form or another, it is still in every nursery library, and, however you define a children's book, no one will seriously deny Aesop the right of entry. In England anyone who could read and get hold of a book was likely to meet him, as soon as Caxton had put him into the best English. Fables, likewise, have always been the oral possession of the illiterate. They have, moreover, been a common vehicle of education, and have assumed other forms also. It is obvious that their development into a "children's book" in the more restricted sense ought to be scrutinized. On the other hand, the study of the fable as such, and of the book or person called Aesop in particular, is a special branch of learning, and would be entirely out of place here.

(b) *Romance*, in a semi-literary sense, is present only by implication. Jack the Giant-Killer was said to have been in the employ of King Arthur, of whom other publications show that Newbery was aware. Jack, however, is really a figure of folk-lore. Newbery did not know the then uninvented word "folk-lore". Moreover, he seems not to have touched the chief subjects of the Middle Age Romances. Nevertheless, children read versions of them in his day, as other evidence proves. Jack may therefore be taken, in this connection, as a sign-post to a subject which, since children certainly read those Romances now also, it is necessary to explore slightly. But the only question is how the tales of Bevis, St George and the rest became children's books, before or after Newbery's time; not who first wrote them, nor when, nor why.

(c) *Conduct and Education* are inherent in the *Pocket Book* from the title-page onwards. The words cover aspects of juvenile life which are separable only in logic, not completely in practice. In fact, the confusion between "instruction" and "amusement", and the struggle about them in the minds of purveyors of both (in Newbery's, for instance), are to no small extent the real subject of this book. But treatises on the way to behave, and schoolbooks, are only relevant here if and when they influenced more genuine children's books, or contained border-line material for them, like the genial alphabet in the *Pocket Book* itself, or made references to them, usually of a derogatory nature, but useful as evidence of what was really read.

These three elements in Newbery's first juvenile publication, then, will have to be exhibited, with some notice of the condition in which he found them, and how they came to be available to him and to children. They were all in print at least two centuries before 1744. A fourth element, by far the most important, was actually much later than they in reaching type. This is the *Fairy-*

Tale, for which Jack's person may be said to stand here, rather clumsily. Whether as literature or folk-lore, the Fairy-Tale appeared but scrappily between the covers of printed books before 1744, and for a long while afterwards. In Newbery's day it was not high in the favour of the judicious. That very fact must be investigated, because, with the kindred Nursery Rhyme, the Cabinet of the Fairies is both the corner- and the coping-stone of any child's library. But nothing whatever need be said here about anthropology or the distribution of folk-lore. It does not concern us to know whether or not Cinderella was a native of Borrioboola-Gha, on the left bank of the Niger. It is much more to the point to discover why the contemporaries of Mrs Jellyby encouraged such an alien in England, and what, even earlier, Newbery knew about glass slippers and fairy godmothers.

Two further considerations arise out of the *Pocket Book.* Newbery was at pains to placate a public opinion which demanded a "moral": why? The reason is to be discovered in the Puritans' concern for children seventy years or more before he went to Devereux Court. Their attempts to write for children, whether one calls the result "children's books" or not, had a lasting influence on those books both in England and in America. They are usually displayed as examples of exactly what should not be offered to young minds. But justice demands rather closer inquiry into both motives and products; and Bunyan cannot be ignored, even if *The Pilgrim's Progress* was not meant for children.

The other significant phenomenon is the cheap price of this well-printed, compact little volume, and the apparent ease with which a young man from Berkshire became important in the multifarious book-trade of England. Though newspapers were increasing in number, and even spreading "literary intelligence", the distribution of popular booklets was not by any means automatic: at least, not very clearly so. The machinery which lay to Newbery's hand is very well worth close inspection. Children's books, of sorts—not the fully developed sort—were in circulation before ever he made a business of them.

§ III

What this amounts to is not a contradiction of the statement that children's books began to be published in 1744. It merely means that 1744 is a date comparable to the 1066 of the older histories. There is written history and even a kind of archaeology about the period before Newbery the Conqueror. It is summarized in the next few chapters. Its value is precisely the value of pre-Norman adult history. It is the chronicle of the English people in their capacity of parents, guardians and educators of children; with this reservation, that in these pages the child at leisure is to be considered as their preoccupation, and their care for its routine of intellectual discipline very largely (though not entirely) set aside. It is in their human aspect that I wish to see those who wrote children's books; as kind people inspired more by love and happiness than by purpose, though happiness was often enough seen as duty and duty uncompromisingly said to be happiness.

It is, in fact, just by reason of his human personality that Newbery stands out. There were woven into the experience of his time all those earlier strands which can be classified and picked out separately in a retrospect. But they too were always part of the fabric of everyday life rather than neat categories of evolution. I do not want to forget that, nor to label past things "quaint" because we have forgotten their ordinary touch and feel, and even their faint fragrance. If 1744 is as it were a line drawn, it is only an imaginary one, though the air is clearer this side of it. Another, as will be seen, could be drawn as truthfully and usefully at the year 1865. But people still living to-day were children in 1865, and never saw the line and are unaware of it now. There will be plenty of evidence of continuity before and after Little Master Tommy and Pretty Miss Polly had their agreeable letter from Jack the Giant Killer.

§ IV

So much for preconceptions which it is hoped to avoid and by-ways which it would be tiresome and needless to enter. There is one other notable thing in that eighteenth-century emergence of the children's book-trade, and that is that the three most famous wares in its market, as well as in our market to-day, were not children's books at all: *The Pilgrim's Progress, Gulliver's Travels* and *Robinson Crusoe*. It would be stupid to let any definition crowd them out, especially as editions of them have always been prepared specially for children. But the fact remains that they, and a few lesser works, were created for adults and simply annexed by children—and by young children at that.

There is room for endless discussion on that subject; but not here. It raises the question, what *constitutes* a children's book— not whether this or that volume is a book written for children and read by them, but what qualities such a book does possess if it is read and should possess if it is purposely written. That is a matter for psychologists, empirical and theoretical alike: not for the historian of books which have existed and of the people who wrote them.

With that, it is time to consider the juvenile literature of days when there were not so many things to think about even as in 1744.

C. P. SNOW

THE TWO CULTURES

C. P. Snow (1905-   ) has had a distinguished career in science, education, government, and letters. Educated at the University of Leicester and Cambridge University, he was a fellow of Christ's College at Cambridge from 1930 to 1950. Entering government service, he was a Civil Service commissioner from 1945 to 1960; in 1964 he was named Parliamentary secretary to the Ministry of Technology. As a novelist, he is known especially for his Strangers and Brothers *series, the first volume of which appeared under that title in 1940 and the latest,* Corridors of Power, *in 1964. Two novels of the series,* The Masters *(1951) and* The New Men *(1954), jointly were awarded the James Tait Black Memorial Prize in 1954. He gave the Rede Lecture at Cambridge entitled* The Two Cultures and the Scientific Revolution *(1959), a further exploration of the topic he first raised in the following essay. He was invited to Harvard in 1960 to give the Godkin Lectures, later published as* Science and Government *(1961). He was knighted in 1957 and created Baron Snow in 1964.*

"IT'S RATHER ODD," said G. H. Hardy, one afternoon in the early Thirties, "but when we hear about 'intellectuals' nowadays, it doesn't include people like me and J. J. Thomson and Rutherford." Hardy was the first mathematician of his generation, J. J. Thomson the first physicist of his; as for Rutherford, he was one of the greatest scientists who have ever lived. Some bright young literary person (I forget the exact context) putting them outside the enclosure reserved for intellectuals seemed to Hardy the best joke for some time. It does not seem quite such a good joke now. The separation between the two cultures has been getting deeper under our eyes; there is now precious little communication between them, little but different kinds of incomprehension and dislike.

The traditional culture, which is, of course, mainly literary, is behaving like a state whose power is rapidly declining—standing on its precarious dignity, spending far too much energy on Alex-

»»» *New Statesman and Nation,* LII (October 6, 1956), 413-414. Reprinted by permission of the *New Statesman* and C. P. Snow.

andrian intricacies, occasionally letting fly in fits of aggressive pique quite beyond its means, too much on the defensive to show any generous imagination to the forces which must inevitably reshape it. Whereas the scientific culture is expansive, not restrictive, confident at the roots, the more confident after its bout of Oppenheimerian self-criticism, certain that history is on its side, impatient, intolerant, creative rather than critical, good-natured and brash. Neither culture knows the virtues of the other; often it seems they deliberately do not want to know. The resentment which the traditional culture feels for the scientific is shaded with fear; from the other side, the resentment is not shaded so much as brimming with irritation. When scientists are faced with an expression of the traditional culture, it tends (to borrow Mr. William Cooper's eloquent phrase) to make their feet ache.

It does not need saying that generalisations of this kind are bound to look silly at the edges. There are a good many scientists indistinguishable from literary persons, and vice versa. Even the stereotype generalisations about scientists are misleading without some sort of detail—e.g., the generalisation that scientists as a group stand on the political Left. This is only partly true. A very high proportion of engineers is almost as conservative as doctors; of pure scientists, the same would apply to chemists. It is only among physicists and biologists that one finds the Left in strength. If one compared the whole body of scientists with their opposite numbers of the traditional culture (writers, academics, and so on), the total result might be a few per cent. more towards the Left wing, but not more than that. Nevertheless, as a first approximation, the scientific culture is real enough, and so is its difference from the traditional. For anyone like myself, by education a scientist, by calling a writer, at one time moving between groups of scientists and writers in the same evening, the difference has seemed dramatic.

The first thing, impossible to miss, is that scientists are on the up and up; they have the strength of a social force behind them. If they are English, they share the experience common to us all—

of being in a country sliding economically downhill—but in addition (and to many of them it seems psychologically more important) they belong to something more than a profession, to something more like a directing class of a new society. In a sense oddly divorced from politics, they are the new men. Even the staidest and most politically conservative of scientific veterans, lurking in dignity in their colleges, have some kind of link with the world to come. They do not hate it as their colleagues do; part of their mind is open to it; almost against their will, there is a residual glimmer of kinship there. The young English scientists may and do curse their luck; increasingly they fret about the rigidities of their universities, about the ossification of the traditional culture which, to the scientists, makes the universities cold and dead; they violently envy their Russian counterparts who have money and equipment without discernible limit, who have the whole field wide open. But still they stay pretty resilient: they are swept on by the same social force. Harwell and Winscale have just as much spirit as Los Alamos and Chalk River: the neat petty bourgeois houses, the tough and clever young, the crowds of children: they are symbols, frontier towns.

There is a touch of the frontier qualities, in fact, about the whole scientific culture. Its tone is, for example, steadily heterosexual. The difference in social manners between Harwell and Hampstead, or as far as that goes between Los Alamos and Greenwich Village, would make an anthropologist blink. About the whole scientific culture, there is an absence—surprising to outsiders—of the feline and oblique. Sometimes it seems that scientists relish speaking the truth, especially when it is unpleasant. The climate of personal relations is singularly bracing, not to say harsh: it strikes bleakly on those unused to it, who suddenly find that the scientists' way of deciding on action is by a full-dress argument, with no regard for sensibilities and no holds barred. No body of people ever believed more in dialectic as the primary method of attaining sense; and if you want a picture of scientists in their off-moments it could be just one of a knock-about argument. Under the argument there glitter egotisms as rapacious as any of ours: but, unlike ours, the egotisms are driven by a common purpose.

How much of the traditional culture gets through to them? The answer is not simple. A good many scientists, including some of the most gifted, have the tastes of literary persons, read the same things, and read as much. Broadly, though, the infiltration is much less. History gets across to a certain extent, in particular social history: the sheer mechanics of living, how men ate, built, travelled, worked, touches a good many scientific imaginations, and so they have fastened on such works as Trevelyan's *Social History,* and Professor Gordon Childe's books. Philosophy, the scientific culture views with indifference, especially metaphysics. As Rutherford said cheerfully to Samuel Alexander: "When you think of all the years you've been talking about those things, Alexander, and what does it all add up to? *Hot air,* nothing but *hot air.*" A bit less exuberantly, that is what contemporary scientists would say. They regard it as a major intellectual virtue, to know what not to think about. They might touch their hats to linguistic analysis, as a relatively honourable way of wasting time; not so to existentialism.

The arts? The only one which is cultivated among scientists is music. It goes both wide and deep; there may possibly be a greater density of musical appreciation than in the traditional culture. In comparison, the graphic arts (except architecture) score little, and poetry not at all. Some novels work their way through, but not as a rule the novels which literary persons set most value on. The two cultures have so few points of contact that the diffusion of novels shows the same sort of delay, and exhibits the same oddities, as though they were getting into translation in a foreign country. It is only fairly recently, for instance, that Graham Greene and Evelyn Waugh have become more than names. And, just as it is rather startling to find that in Italy Bruce Marshall is by a long shot the best-known British novelist, so it jolts one to hear scientists talking with attention of the works of Nevil Shute. In fact, there is a good reason for that: Mr. Shute was himself a high-class engineer, and a book like *No Highway* is packed with technical stuff that is not only accurate but often original. Incidentally, there are benefits to be gained from listening to intelligent men, utterly removed from the literary scene and unconcerned as to who's in and who's out. One can pick up such a comment as a scientist once made, that it looked to him as though the current preoccupations of the New Criticism, the extreme concentration on a tiny passage, had made us curiously insensitive to the total flavour of a work, to its cumulative effects, to the epic qualities in literature. But, on the other side of the coin, one is just as likely to listen to three of the most massive intellects in Europe happily discussing the merits of *The Wallet of Kai-Lung*.

When you meet the younger rank-and-file of scientists, it often seems that they do not read at all. The prestige of the traditional culture is high enough for some of them to make a gallant shot at it. Oddly enough, the novelist whose name to them has become a token of esoteric literary excellence is that difficult high-brow Dickens. They approach him in a grim and dutiful spirit as though tackling *Finnegans Wake,* and feel a sense of achievement if they manage to read a book through. But most young technicians do not fly so high. When you ask them what they read—"As a married man," one says, "I prefer the garden." Another says: "I always like just to use my books as tools." (Difficult to resist speculating what kind of tool a book would make. A sort of hammer? A crude digging instrument?)

That, or something like it, is a measure of the incommunicability of the two cultures. On their side the scientists are losing a great deal. Some of that loss is inevitable: it must and would happen in any society at our technical level. But in this country we make it quite unnecessarily worse by our educational patterns. On the other side, how much does the traditional culture lose by the separation?

I am inclined to think, even more. Not only practically—we are familiar with those arguments by now—but also intellectually and morally. The intellectual loss is a little difficult to appraise. Most scientists would claim that you cannot comprehend the world unless you know the structure of science, in particular of physical science. In a sense, and a perfectly genuine sense, that is true. Not to have read *War and Peace* and *La Cousine Bette* and *La Chartreuse de Parme* is not to be educated; but so is not to have a glimmer of the Second Law of Thermodynamics. Yet that case ought not to be pressed too far. It is more justifiable to say that those without any scientific understanding miss a whole body of experience: they are rather like the tone deaf, from whom all musical experience is cut off and who have to get on without it. The intellectual invasions of science are, however, penetrating deeper. Psycho-analysis once looked like a deep invasion, but that was a false alarm; cybernetics may turn out to be the real thing, driving down into the problems of will and cause and motive. If so, those who do not understand the method will not understand the depths of their own cultures.

But the greatest enrichment the scientific culture could give us is—though it does not originate like that—a moral one. Among scientists, deep-natured men know, as starkly as any men have known, that the individual human condition is tragic; for all its triumphs and joys, the essence of it is loneliness and the end death. But what they will not admit is that, because the individual condition is tragic, therefore the social condition must be tragic, too. Because a man must die, that is no excuse for his dying before his time and after a servile life. The impulse behind the scientists drives them to limit the area of tragedy, to take nothing as tragic that can conceivably lie within men's will. They have nothing but contempt for those representatives of the traditional culture who use a deep insight into man's fate to obscure the social truth—or to do something pettier than obscure the truth, just to hang on to a few perks. Dostoevski sucking up to the Chancellor Pobedonostsev, who thought the only thing wrong with slavery was that there was not enough of it; the political decadence of the *avant garde* of 1914, with Ezra Pound finishing up broadcasting for the Fascists; Claudel agreeing sanctimoniously with the Marshal about the virtue in others' suffering; Faulkner giving sentimental reasons for treating Negroes as a

different species. They are all symptoms of the deepest temptation of the clerks—which is to say: "Because man's condition is
tragic, everyone ought to stay in their place, with mine as it happens somewhere near the top." From that particular temptation,
made up of defeat, self-indulgence, and moral vanity, the scientific culture is almost totally immune. It is that kind of moral
health of the scientists which, in the last few years, the rest of us
have needed most; and of which, because the two cultures
scarcely touch, we have been most deprived.

MARSTON BATES

from THE KINDS OF MAN

Marston Bates (1906-   ), American naturalist, was educated at the University of Florida and at Harvard. He has done research for many organizations, among them the Museum of Comparative Zoology and the international health division of the Rockefeller Foundation. Since 1952 he has been a professor of zoology at the University of Michigan. His books include The Natural History of Mosquitoes *(1949),* The Nature of Natural History *(1950),* Where Winter Never Comes *(1952),* Coral Island *(1958), and* Animal Worlds *(1963), as well as* The Prevalence of People *(1955), from which the following selection comes.*

No TWO of the two and a half billion living men are alike. Identical twins come closest—coming from a single egg that split in two after fertilization, identical twins have identical genetic constitutions. They are also generally treated almost alike after birth, so that they tend to have similar experiences; but the experiences are never completely identical; and close friends, at least, can recognize differences in the resulting personalities.

With the exception of these identical twins, it seems likely that no two humans who ever lived have had the same genetic constitution. The possible combinations of human genes run to many millions of millions, and the few thousands of millions of men who have so far come into existence represent only a small fraction of these possibilities. When we combine the biological variability with the cultural variability, the diversity becomes staggering.

Yet there is a certain order in the diversity. No two people are alike, but some people are more alike than others; and they may be alike in various sorts of ways—in appearance, personality, age, ability, or what-have-you. In order to study this variability, we have to attack the problem of classifying it, of finding an expression for whatever orderly relationships may exist.

It would be interesting to try to make a survey of all of the different ways in which men have been classified; but this would be an immense undertaking. Some of the classifications have been simple—Greeks and barbarians, Christians and heathen, freemen and slaves. Other classifications, however, have been both complex and subtle. Our interest here is in classifications that have been used in studying populations—but the subject is diverse enough even with this limitation. Studies of population rarely deal with mankind as a whole; they deal with Frenchmen, coal miners, Arabs, farmers, Negroes, New Yorkers, school children, criminals, or some other category in some kind of a classificatory system. Any such list obviously contains quite different sorts of categories, some based on nationality, others on race, or religion, or occupation, or age.

Let's look at race first. So much has been written about this that it seems criminal to add to the verbiage. I'll at least try to be brief. The trouble, of course, is that the description and classification of human physical types has got almost hopelessly blurred by emotional considerations. We are hardly able to distinguish between this race and that without getting involved with questions as to whether this race is "better" than that—brighter, more advanced, or nearer to the angels.

Some people would like to abandon the word "race" altogether and substitute a more neutral term like "ethnic group." But this flight from words is a losing game because the objectionable connotations catch up so rapidly. We can see this with the history of words for excretory products and places to deposit them. We invent a nice expression, but as soon as it gets generally established, the niceness starts to wear off and we have to invent a new expression. I had rather avoid the whole process, keep away from rest rooms and powder rooms and go back to Anglo-Saxon—but my wife objects. At least, I can cling to "race."

It still may be difficult to give race any precise meaning: but this perhaps is part of the problem, that we mistakenly try to use a general and vague term specifically and with precision. We are trying, with race, to describe the geographical variability of human physical traits. Now this geographical variability is a real thing, not only with man, but with a great many other organisms, particularly with land mammals. Populations that are partly or wholly isolated by geographical barriers of one sort or another—including mere distance—tend to follow divergent evolutionary paths and thus, with the passage of time, to become more and more different. The tendency to become different may be counterbalanced in varying degree by mixture among the populations, which makes an opposite tendency toward uniformity. No surviving populations of men have been sufficiently isolated for a long enough time to have evolved into recognizably distinct species; but many populations have been isolated enough to allow the development of considerable differences.

There is rather general agreement about the main stocks—Negroid, Mongoloid and Caucasian—and these show a general geographical pattern with the Negroid centering in Africa; the Caucasian in Europe, the Near East and India; and the Mongoloid in the Far East and America. Endless subdivisions can be made within each of these basic divisions. Carleton Coon, for instance, in his detailed study of the *Races of Europe,* finds ten main racial types among European Caucasians, each with various subtypes. All of these, of course, are abstractions, but they are made in an effort to describe a diversity that is real.

The main racial stocks all blend into one another completely, so that no arbitrary line can be drawn between any two of them. And then there are various populations that don't fit any of the main types—especially some of the dark-skinned peoples of the Pacific. The Australian blackfellows, too, are different enough perhaps to be listed as a fourth main type, though they may be classed as "Negroid" on skin color alone, or as a "primitive White type" if attention is paid to other traits, such as hair.

The trouble is that man has been in a state of flux for a long time, with races emerging or disappearing or blending as populations remained stationary and isolated or got involved with migratory shifts. We can see the process of race formation now in Hawaii. A new but recognizable type (the "Neo-Hawaiian") seems to be emerging there from the mixture of Mongoloid and European peoples with the local Polynesians. The Polynesians in turn probably emerged as a recognizable type from a mixture of antecedent types somewhere in southeast Asia a few thousand years ago. And the process can thus be projected back in time as an alternation of mixing and isolating, hybridizing and segregating, pressures. The problem of dealing with race is the problem of dealing with a dynamic process, of describing particular cross sections in time and space through a system in flux.

One of the curious things about this race business is that while a considerable variety of physical types can be fairly well described and defined, attempts to show differences in behavior and physiology that correspond to these physical types have been generally unsuccessful. Because of this, race is not a very meaningful term in population study.

There are, to be sure, broad correlations between population behavior and race, such as the great multiplication and spread of the Caucasian type during the last three hundred years, the relative stability of the African Negro populations, and the trend toward extinction of many racial types such as the Australian and the Polynesian. But these trends are all understandable, not in terms of race but in terms of culture; and race and culture behave generally as independent variables.

It is true that Western civilization, which has been the aggressive and dominant culture of the last three hundred years, is primarily the culture of the Caucasian people of Western Europe. Attempts to explain this culture in terms of racial characteristics of these peoples, however, have not been very convincing. At least they fail to explain why European Caucasians remained in a barbarian stage while other racial types were building dominant and aggressive civilizations. They fail to explain the ease with which in some cases other races, such as the Mongoloids represented by the Japanese, have picked up and used Western cultural elements. The whole situation is much more understandable in terms of geographical distribution of resources, and the interplay of historical, cultural and economic factors; and neither racial mentality nor racial physiology need be brought into the explanation at all.

The use of the racial terms "White" and "Negro" in the United States is interesting in this regard. The population of the United States clearly has three quite different geographical (and racial) origins: the local American Indians, and the immigrants from Europe and tropical Africa. Cultural forces in the United States have tended to maintain the distinctness of these groups, so that the mixing has not been as thorough as in other countries (like Brazil and Honduras) where somewhat different cultural forces have been in operation. But even so there has been a great deal of mixing, so that it is difficult to be sure that any individual is of purely African, Indian or European descent. (Who can keep track of all of his ancestors for, say, ten generations? And remember that Prince Henry of Portugal started raiding the African coast back in 1441, and sold the captured slaves all over Europe.)

"White" and "Negro" are commonly used categories in population studies in the United States, but I can't see that this usage has much to do with race. All sorts of statistical differences can be found between the two groups, but the differences seem to reflect economic rather than racial characteristics. Individuals listed as "Negro" may have more Europeans than Africans in their immediate ancestry, which doesn't make sense to me. If we were really interested in race, surely the way to make the separation would be between people with a preponderance of Europeans in their immediate ancestry and people with a preponderance of Africans—though how one would determine this, I don't know.

I agree with the people who maintain that race is a meaningless term as it is currently used in the United States—but this is not saying that it is a meaningless term under all circumstances. It is most useful as a biological concept. But the determining factors of group differences in human behavior—including population behavior—seem to be cultural rather than biological.

Actually, the most meaningful units in population analysis

are political—nations, empires and colonies. The statistics, of course, are gathered according to political units by the various governments, which might tend to give a spurious sort of reality to the units surveyed. But the influence of the national state has become so pervasive in the modern world that we cannot doubt its reality. Only with great difficulty can we generalize about population trends among different races because the trends are the product, not of racial characters, but of cultural forces that find expression within political units. Our most important classification, then, is not into whites and blacks, but into English, French, Japanese, Chinese, Americans (in the restricted sense), Mexicans, and so forth.

The more you think about this, the more curious it seems. The national state, historically, is a recent invention. The whole idea is sometimes blamed on the French Revolution and subsequent Napoleonic adventures. "Italy" and "Germany" did not appear on the scene as nations until 1870. To be sure, many nations, like France and England, have had long histories of national sovereignty over areas closely similar to their present boundaries, but this seems not so much a "natural" phenomenon as a result of a series of geographical and historical accidents.

No national state corresponds to a racial grouping. Israel may be attempting to unite the two, but no anthropologist can distinguish Jews in any racial sense. Some nations are fairly homogeneous racially, but they represent at most a piece of that particular racial stock, with the rest scattered among other nationalities.

"National character" has lately become a perfectly respectable subject for anthropological study. The concept of the Englishman, the American or the German seems to be just as real as the concept of some racial type, or some tribal culture. We tend to think of the American melting pot as a rather special phenomenon; and it is, since the other national characters are rarely smelted from such a diversity of materials. But the other national characters are thus, perhaps, all the more easily shaped.

The political frontier, as every traveler knows, is a very real element of geography. Often it is much more difficult to cross than a river, a mountain range, or a desert. These frontiers thus bound population isolates—define populations more sharply than most "natural" boundaries. Where the frontiers are drawn right across populations that were previously united, as has happened in Europe, governments have sometimes managed large population transfers to speed up and consolidate the isolating effect of the frontier. That, I suppose, is the answer to the reality of national character—the omnipotence and reality of governments, with the power to direct and control many of the forces that shape a culture. Though, of course, there is the opposite theory, that the government is the product of the culture, of the national character.

At any rate, population studies generally deal with national units and their political appendages; and these differ enough from one another to make it clear that the political units are something more than statistical conveniences. Countries with similar cultural and economic developments tend to show similar population trends, so that we can often generalize about Western Europe, Latin America, Southeast Asia, and the like. National differences within such groupings may still be considerable, however, as with France, England, Ireland, the Netherlands and Italy.

PROCESS EXPLANATION

PROCESS explanation is a special form of narration. It recounts the step-by-step procedure by which some action is done or has been done. In addition to being narrative, a process explanation may be analytical and descriptive. Often a process is general and repeatable and may be performed by anyone possessing the requisite ability, equipment, and need to do it. Process writing involves the matter of point of view or, put more simply, the question of who writes to whom for what purpose. A process explanation may be either directive or informative, depending upon whether the author writes to instruct a reader wishing to perform the process himself or to inform a reader wishing merely to learn how an interesting process is or was done. The simplest form of process writing uses the recipe style of a cookbook; there the point of view is second person and the mood imperative—the reader is told, "Do this, do that—beat the eggs, sift the flour." Obviously the reader is being directed, not merely informed. In less streamlined form, the recipe style is modified to "you do this, you do that"; the assumption remains, however, that the reader wishes to do the action. Sometimes, but not so often as formerly, directive explanations are written with a third-person agent performing the action —"the cook does this, she does that." The informative explanation usually employs the third-person point of view—"the miner does this, he does that"—under the assumption that the reader may want to learn how a miner works without taking out a union card and going to work in the mines himself. Sometimes the informative explanation tells how something was done; then, of course, the writer narrates in the past tense and either from the third-person point of view (if the process was done by others) or from the first-person point of view (if the process was done by himself).

Of the process explanations which follow, the first is primarily directive and the second primarily informative. "How to Buy a

Dog" is addressed to the reader, "you," who is interested in buying a dog and wants to know the best way to go about doing so.
The article takes the reader step-by-step through the process:
timing of the purchase, questions of choice about the size, sex,
breed, and disposition of the dog, its health, and so forth. The
article thus enables the reader to make a thoughtful purchase
instead of an impulsive one. The explanation is informative to a
reader mildly interested in dogs, but that is not its main intent;
its cautious advice shows that it is addressed to the reader interested in canny purchasing. Nancy Hale, on the other hand, writes
an autobiographic account of her struggle as a fiction writer to
turn to a different kind of writing job, the collection and editing
of an anthology. Her first-person narrative chiefly informs the
reader of the difficulties she found the process beset with and of
how she overcame them. Her chronological organization lets the
reader live through the process with her; yet her concentration
upon details of the process and her generalizations about the
methods of a fiction writer and of a literary historian make the
narrative expository. Indeed, she utilizes comparison often in her
account of her discovery of how to satisfy her fiction-writer's
intent to make her anthology "a work of art." Although her purpose is primarily to inform the reader about how she did something, another anthologist certainly can find Miss Hale's process
explanation instructive and pick up hints for improving his own
method of going about a similar task.

Processes are explained in other pieces in this book. In "Letters," Maxwell Perkins in a third-person explanation informs Scott
Fitzgerald about the process of marketing books. In "Argumentation and Persuasion," the writers frequently explain what has been
done as prelude to arguing what ought to be done; in arguing a
policy that they think should be pursued, the writers use the
conditional mood and the future tense and sometimes address the
reader as "you" or include him as "we" (as do Rice and Kitzhaber, for instance). Finally, process explanation, both informative and directive, runs throughout Part I, which discusses ways
to write.

HOW TO BUY A DOG

IF YOU are planning to buy your family a dog for Christmas, CU's [Consumers Union's] first suggestion to you is: "Don't!" Not only is there a good chance that the price will be lower after the holiday season, but by then your household will have had a chance to settle down and to prepare to receive the new puppy properly. All of you will have more time to make him feel at home, to house-break him, and to give him whatever other care and attention he needs.

HOW BIG A DOG

The size of the dog you buy should be determined, at least in part, by the size of your home and its location. A big dog needs a lot of space just to walk around in. Generally, he also needs more exercise. If he cannot get his exercise unescorted, and if you are a conscientious dog owner, you will have to exercise along with him. However good this might be for you, you may find that it's more exercise than you want. A large dog, too, will need more food, and the difference in cost may be noticeable in the household budget. (An average-size dog eats about $10 worth of dog food a month.)

A smaller dog is likely to be better for an apartment or a small house, as well as easier to travel with or to ship.

Most authorities advise against taking a puppy away from its mother until it is at least eight weeks old and has been weaned. But they also add, one should not wait much longer than that.

At eight weeks, most puppies still are too young for house training and usually need more shots, further worming, and perhaps other special care. Most experts maintain, however, that through this period it is best that the dog receive the individual care and attention he can get only in your home.

»»» *Consumer Reports,* XXIV (November, 1959), 578-580. Reprinted by permission of Consumers Union of U.S., Inc.

On the other hand, an adult dog—one a year or more old—usually will prove satisfactory if he has a good disposition and is used to being around a house. But if the dog's owner is getting rid of him because of some undesirable trait, the new owner should be prepared to take the time and trouble to try to "train out" the trait—or to pay an expert trainer to do the job for him. He should be prepared, too, for the possibility that the dog simply is untrainable.

Some experts prefer male dogs, others are staunch feminists. Actually, CU's consultants agree, insofar as temperament is concerned, a dog's sex does not guarantee its acceptability as a pet. However, if you want to buy a female to raise puppies, you must be willing to put up with the horde of male dogs which will lay siege to your house for two or three weeks twice a year when your pet is in heat or to board her out at a kennel during these periods. On the other hand, there's no need to rule out a female if you do not want puppies; spaying, a routine operation, will eliminate the whole problem.

LONG- OR SHORT-HAIRED?

A long-haired dog who is allowed to roam the woods and fields will come home with more burrs and knots in his fur than a short-haired dog will and under any circumstances is likely to need more combing and brushing. He will be a little harder to wash, too, and will take longer to dry. A few breeds, such as the poodle, need clipping every two to three months and, at $10 to $25 per clipping, this can be a factor to reckon with.

Long-haired dogs generally shed more than short-hairs do in the spring and fall, but thorough and frequent brushing or combing will avoid excess fallout in the home. Most of the short-haired breeds will shed also—all year 'round if they are confined to the house a good part of the time.

PUREBRED OR MIXED-BREED?

If you want a dog simply as a household pet (i.e., for companionship and fun), you are likely to be just as well satisfied with a carefully chosen mixed-breed as with a purebred—and at a considerable saving in money.

While you probably can acquire a suitable mixed-breed pup at nominal cost (see section titled "Where to Buy Him") or without charge from a neighbor or friend who suddenly has been blessed with a larger dog family than he needs, you are likely to have to pay a substantial sum for a purebred. Note, however, that the owner of a registered purebred dog may be able to recover the price of the dog—and possibly turn a nice profit besides—through stud fees or the sale of pups.

Purebred prices range greatly, not only from breed to breed, but within a given breed. Variations are largely the result of the shifting demand in different areas and of the varying quality, training and condition of the puppies themselves. A purebred with a minor defect which bars him as a show dog but which would make no difference in a pet often can be had at a price little, if any, higher than that for a good mixed-breed. The simplest way to get an idea of prices in your own part of the country is to consult the classified ads in your local newspapers or to check with some local kennels or pet shops.

If you want a dog primarily for breeding, show, or prestige purposes, obviously you will choose a purebred. Purebreds offer other advantages as well, but these may or may not be of interest to you. When you buy a mixed-breed puppy, you are likely to be, in large measure, buying a pig in a poke. Unless the pup's mother and father are very similar in such characteristics as size, hair type and length, coloring, and disposition, probably even an expert could not predict reliably how the pup will turn out or what he will look like when he grows up.

THE QUESTION OF DISPOSITION

A purebred pup, on the other hand, is almost sure to grow into a near-duplicate of his parents in appearance. As for disposition, this is hard to predict in either a purebred or mixed-breed. In either case, it will depend to some extent on the way you yourself treat and train the puppy, especially during the first few months after you bring him home.

Many a mutt, either naturally or after training, has turned out to be a fine hunting or working dog, but if you are buying a pup mainly for hunting, herding, or some other special use, your chances of satisfaction probably will be greater with a pure-bred of a breed which has been painstakingly developed over the years for that particular purpose.

If you have youngsters, the answer to the question "Will he be good with children?" will be important to you. Most of the authorities consulted by CU say that there is not much difference among the breeds in their attitudes toward children; that the personality of the individual dog, regardless of breed, is the really important consideration.

At the same time, some experts were willing to offer a few generalizations. One such is that small dogs are more likely than big dogs to be snappish with children, the reasons being two: First, while a big dog simply can move away from, or brush aside, a child who is annoying him, a small dog's only defense often is to snap; second, big dogs, because of their size and strength, usually are less fearful than small dogs, hence more placid and slower to anger.

One of CU's consultants said that although, generally speaking, he would prefer a large dog if he had small children, he had found that some large breeds ordinarily are less suitable for children than others. For example, he said, Boxers and Dalmatians have such powerful, muscular bodies and are so animated that often they will unintentionally knock down a small child who is playing with them. A Dalmatian can do this simply with a wag of his strong, heavy tail, and a Boxer may do it by wagging his body—which, since he has almost no tail, is *his* way of expressing pleasure.

On the other hand, older children, especially boys, will like such good-size, rough-and-tumble breeds as the Boxer, Dalmatian, or Airedale. For younger children, the larger herding dogs —Collies and Sheepdogs, for example—are recommended. The toy breeds may appeal to smaller and less active children, but the experts warn that toy dogs often are delicate and high-strung and, because of their small size, are more readily handled and hurt. Once hurt or dropped or roughly handled, they may resent later advances.

Incidentally, price and breed popularity do not go hand in hand. Far from it. The explanation, according to trade sources: the less popular breeds generally are in shorter supply and, consequently, the buyer who wants one of these rarer specimens usually pays a higher price for it.

WHERE TO BUY HIM

Once you have decided, if only tentatively, the questions of size and hair length—and, possibly, suitability for children, you would do well, in the opinion of CU's consultants, to visit some nearby kennels, or go to a dog show or two to observe, in the flesh, good specimens of various breeds.

If you have decided on a mixed-breed pup, the sources likely to be available to you include local SPCA, Humane Society, and Animal Rescue League shelters; individual dog owners with pups to dispose of (you probably can locate plenty of these through classified ads in your newspaper and through inquiries among friends and neighbors); and pet shops.

Purebred dogs can be bought directly from breeders or from dealers, pet shops, or such mail-order houses as Sears and Wards. A letter or postal card sent to the American Kennel Club, 221 Fourth Ave., New York 3, N.Y., will bring you a list of reputable breeders in your area who concentrate on the breed you are interested in.

Although many pet shops are just as reliable as a good breeder, the weight of expert opinion seems to be in favor of buying from a local kennel, where you can examine not only the puppy but his parents as well.

A local source, whether breeder or pet shop, usually will sell a dog on approval and subject to an examination by the buyer's veterinarian. You probably would be wise to avoid complicated sales agreements such as those which bar showing of the puppy or which reserve future puppies for the seller.

Whoever the seller, if you have any doubt about him, it would be wise to check with the Better Business Bureau in the area where he operates.

STATE OF HEALTH

Before you commit yourself to a purchase, check the dog's health. A healthy puppy looks well-fed—almost roly-poly—lively, and bright-eyed. He should, of course, have no obvious deformities. His eyes should be clear, without discharge or redness, his ears and nose free of discharge, and his nose moist. His coat should be clean and shiny, without bare spots, and if he is long-haired, it should be good and thick. He should be free of fleas, ticks, and lice.

Some dogs, particularly white-haired ones, seem prone to hearing defects. Check the hearing of the pup you're considering by whistling to him or snapping your fingers at him when he is not looking at you. Look for a distended abdomen (an indication of digestive trouble) and for signs of diarrhea and navel hernia. See if his teeth look white and his gums firm and pink.

His legs should be straight, and he should move about easily and lightly (albeit with normal puppy awkwardness). He should have a hearty appetite. Find out which injections he has had, which ones he will need, and if he has been thoroughly wormed.

Finally, note the general condition of the seller's premises and person; if they are clean and neat, chances are better than otherwise that the pup has been well cared for.

REGISTERING THE PUREBRED PUPPY

To the owner of a household pet, a recognized registration may be only a point of pride, but to a breeder of purebred dogs, it is virtually a necessity; without it, he could not get nearly so good a price for his pups.

Although the American Kennel Club is the leading registrar of dogs in this country, there are others, principally devoted to particular breeds or types of dog. Sporting dogs, for example, can be registered in the Field Dog Stud Book, published in Chicago; Foxhounds, with the Foxhound Association; and so on. Registrations with such groups frequently are recognized by the American Kennel Club; check with the A.K.C. first.

Although many people regard an A.K.C. registration certificate as certifying to the quality of the individual dog, the A.K.C. makes no such claim for its certificates. Their primary purpose, according to an A.K.C. spokesman, is simply to satisfy the buyer of a dog that the dog is purebred and that its parentage has been honestly represented by the breeder or dealer.

When a litter of puppies eligible for registration is born, the breeder may register each pup in the litter, but to do so, he must give each a name; and once a dog's name is registered with the A.K.C., it cannot, at least on the record, be changed. So, since most dog buyers want to do the naming themselves, the breeder usually enrolls the litter as a group. He sends the A.K.C. filled-in forms giving the names and registration numbers of the pups' parents and grandparents, a certification signed by the owner of the sire that on a stated day his dog was bred to the female named as the dam, the date of birth of the litter, and the number of pups born.

The A.K.C. then sends the breeder a registration certificate for the litter as a whole and, for each puppy in the litter, an individual-dog registration application form. The form has spaces on the back which the breeder uses when he sells the pup to record the date of sale and a description of the dog (sex, coloring, and markings) and to endorse the paper over to the buyer, who should be named.

If the breeder sells a pup directly to the person who is going to keep him, the new owner simply sends the filled-in application form along, with the $2 registration fee, to the A.K.C., which will then issue a registration certificate for the pup.

If the breeder sells the whole litter or any of the pups to a wholesaler or dealer, he should fill in the wholesaler's or dealer's name on each application form. After that, each time a pup changes hands, a "supplemental transfer form" should be filled in for it and stapled to its application form. The purpose of all this paperwork is to assure the final buyer that the dog he is buying is in fact the dog it is represented to be and to provide him and the A.K.C. with a complete record of the dog's chain of ownership.

No end of confusion, with a consequent flood of complaints to the A.K.C., has resulted from the failure of some breeders, wholesalers, and dealers to follow the procedures just outlined.

In response to the growing demand for purebred dogs, a number of small breeders have sprung up, especially in rural sections of some midwestern states. They sell largely to dealers who scour the countryside buying up puppies for city dealers, pet shops, and the mail-order houses. Often the puppies, though purebred, are turned over to the dealer without marking or other identification. The registration applications often are signed in blank (without insertion of the dealer's name) and contain no description of the puppy. Such an application form is pretty much like a blank check. If a pup covered by such a form happens to die or gets lost somewhere along the line, an unscrupulous dealer could use the form for any other pup who appeared to be of the same breed and about the same age.

The A.K.C. reports that it is trying hard to eliminate this problem, that its representatives carefully investigate complaints and make continuing independent checks in the field. (A.K.C. regulations permit inspection by club representatives of kennel and shop premises and records, under penalty of cancellation of registrations.)

The buyer of a new puppy can help, they say, by insisting on a properly executed registration certificate or application form at the time he buys his dog.

NANCY HALE

A FICTION WRITER FACES FACTS

Nancy Hale (1908-   ), born in Boston, is novelist, short-story writer, playwright, journalist, lecturer, and artist. She was educated at The Winsor School, in Boston, and studied art at the school of the Boston Museum of Fine Arts and at her father's studio. She has published seven novels; four books of short stories; an autobiography, A New-England Girlhood *(1958); a book of criticism,* The Realities of Fiction *(1962); and an anthology,* New England Discovery *(1963), the subject of "A Fiction Writer Faces Facts." She has also produced two plays, been an assistant editor of* Vogue *and* Vanity Fair *and a reporter (the first woman) for the New York* Times, *and lectured at the Bread Loaf Writers' Conference.*

IN LATE AUTUMN of 1959, I had just returned from England. I was full of memories of emerald-green fields, stone villages glimpsed in wooded valleys, and the wonderful Norman churches of which there are so many in England that sometimes I feel I'd like to spend the rest of my life just hunting up Norman churches. My new novel, *Dear Beast,* had just come out. I was in a rosy frame of mind, and in a state of considerable confidence, when I got a letter from my agent, telling me that the publishing firm of Coward-McCann wanted me to edit an anthology of New England writing. It would be third in a series called American Vistas. A volume on Midwestern writing had already been signed for, and one on Southern writing had already appeared.

"I know you don't like to work on commission," my agent said in his letter, "and the new novel you are starting must, of course, come first. But I think you might enjoy doing this particular job—it oughtn't to be hard for you, with your knowledge of New England. You could do the preparatory work as your pick-up bedside reading."

It could only have been my roseate state of mind that made

»»» *Saturday Review,* XLVIII (June 12, 1965), 23-25, 80-81. Reprinted by permission of the *Saturday Review* and Nancy Hale.

me feel so genial about taking on the job of editing an anthology of New England writing covering the three and a half centuries of New England's existence. I must repeat I was in a mood where things sounded easy. My husband—who, as a distinguished textual critic, ought to know something about the difficulties of editing—said he thought, just as my agent did, I could toss the job off between sessions of writing my new novel. I accepted the offer with a letter in which, I remember, I said, "I am, of course, no scholar. But I hope the deep feeling for New England that I do have will be a substitute for scholarly learning."

Famous last words. I want to tell about the three years I spent working on the New England anthology, shedding blood, sweat, and tears—the tears, at least, literally. My struggles lay bare a fundamental difference between two kinds of knowing. One of them is a kind of cognition women are often reproached for using. It is always intriguing, in a horrible way, to hear about the sufferings of others.

My first intimation it was not going to be the kind of pleasant, literary, reading-to-go-to-sleep enterprise my agent and my husband seemed to visualize was when I met Jack Geoghegan, the Coward-McCann editor, with Von Auw, my agent. We met to discuss the contract. We talked about the length of time to be allowed for the editing—two years. We talked about the allowance to be made me, to pay for a researcher and for permissions on material outside the public domain. We talked about scope —the entire span of New England history from its beginnings up to the present—and about the book's intention—to tell that history in terms of the native literature. We talked about length—the idea was that the volume should conform to the Midwestern and Southern volumes.

As we talked, I could feel my heart sinking lower and lower. It was as though I physically felt, rather than visualized, mountains of books—all unread by me—looming across the path. "There's going to be an awful *lot* of material," I said. "In a popular anthology you need only hit the high spots," Mr. Geoghegan replied cheerily.

"I don't see how I'm ever going to be able to do it in two years," I said.

He appeared to think I was fishing for compliments. "I have the greatest confidence in your taste and competence," he said. My remarks must have got progressively gloomier, for I remember that toward the end of the meeting he said, "Look, you don't have to sign this contract if you really don't want to."

That night at my club I slept badly. That sounds like Somerset Maugham, but the thing was, I felt licked before I had even started. My own profession is that of a so-called creative writer —that is to say, one who sparks his own work and invents what goes into it. The world of the creative writer is a vast one, for it is the world of imagination, the territory of fiction. But it is not the real world and it does not deal, except as it chooses to, with facts. Before my sleepless eyes the vision of all those unread books, that mountain of New England literature, grew higher and darker. I tried to remind myself what my various advisers had said to me—those sanguine men: "Oh, you have so much real knowledge of New England. It shows in everything you write." They didn't realize what I was having to realize in the watches of the night—that in terms of facts, information, dates, which are the hard cash of scholarly learning, I knew nothing; or as close to nothing as, at two in the morning, makes no difference.

Somewhere around dawn I slept, and when I woke up I had a bright idea. It felt so bright that I telephoned Mr. Geoghegan as soon as publishers get to their offices, which is at about ten. "I think I see how to do it," I said. "I don't really know anything about New England, but I have a lot of feeling for her, and I've heard a lot of New England stories all my life. I might go at the job by checking these feelings and stories against whatever the facts are. Which I would have to find out." Geoghegan sounded relieved, for I had stopped making noises like a silly woman. "Swell," he said. "I told you you could do a fine job." I said, "We might call it *New England Discovery*." "Say, that's all right!" he said. I said, "It'll be *my* discovery."

I, too, was pleased and relieved at my solution to the problem —so pleased and relieved that I did not work on the project for months, while I wrote on my new novel.

I was thinking in the back of my head about my problem, and I was doing a certain amount of reading about it—such as the wonderful books by the late Perry Miller about the early New Englanders, *Errand into the Wilderness* and *The New England Mind*. But as for getting down to work and selecting the pieces I was going to use in my anthology, as for determining how I was going to organize and execute my anthology, I did little or nothing at all that first year.

Now, doing nothing at all means something different to a writer of imaginative fiction from what it does to a scholar. If you are a scholar, you have got to be about your scholarship. If you are an imaginative writer, you learn, over the years, that what looks like doing nothing, and moreover feels like doing nothing, is the most important part. It is during those hours of looking out of the window or walking along Madison Avenue, or sitting on the sofa staring in front of you, that the important part of your novel or your short story gets done. I had been used to that kind of tempo in writing a book. What I was embarked on this time, however, was not a work of fiction. If it was not a work of scholarship either, but rather that *New England Discovery* that had solved my initial problem for me, it still needed something done about it, if my deadline was going to be met.

Two episodes stand out in my memory as occurring in this year 1960, both of them agonized and full of foreboding. One memory is of having lunch with my agent in what I remember as a dark and gloomy cavern. With an effort of memory, I can reconstruct it as the grillroom of the Sheraton East, which used to be called, and still is called by me, the Ambassador. We were both of us beset by trials. He, poor soul, had shingles, and I had the anthology. "I don't want to do it!" I said passionately. "I suppose you could back out," he said morosely. Instantly my New England conscience, reliable as a chronometer, sprang to the fore. "I couldn't do that now," I said. "They've got it scheduled to follow the Southern volume at the same interval as it followed the Midwestern one." There was a pause, while we both felt sorry for ourselves. "And I can't possibly make the New England volume conform to the other two," I burst out. "There's about fifty times the material to go into it. There was almost no writing in the Middle West, for heaven's sake, and hardly any in the South, compared to New England. You have no idea!" I said. "They've got to give me more space. And more time. All I've done is the necessary reading about the subject, and I'm going to need at least another year to read what I'll need to select from."

Von Auw said he would speak to Geoghegan about a time extension, and about a longer word-length for the book. Then I said, "I don't see how I'm ever going to read all I'll have to read, to make a really good anthology. There's mountains of material. . . ." Von Auw looked at me wearily. I must have been a trial to him, on top of his shingles. "There's plenty of other anthologies to work from," he said. "What the boys do is re-anthologize what's already been anthologized."

The one creditable thing I can say about myself at this point is that at this perfectly reasonable solution I jibbed. "I won't re-anthologize," I said. "It's got to be a completely fresh piece of collecting."

I suppose this may have been the fiction writer coming out. For when you write a novel or a short story your intention is to create a work of art. You do not help yourself to bits from other novels and short stories. You do not cobble together what may be a passable tale for reading purposes. Your intention is to compose a thing for which your modest ambition is that it should be perfect.

My other memory of this stage of the game is related to this one. It comes after Von Auw had written to me, when I got home, saying that Geoghegan had agreed to a year's extension and to a much increased number of pages. Now there was nothing for it; I had to march upon those mountains of books and wrestle with them. My memory is of having my husband find me in the kitchen—I was in tears. I was crying because I didn't see how I was going to read all of Mather's *Magnalia* and all of the Adams papers and all of William Dean Howells and all of Hawthorne and of Emerson and Thoreau and Channing and Oliver Wendell Holmes and all of Edward Taylor and William Cullen Bryant and Theodore Parker and Henry James and Edwin Arlington Robinson and Celia Thaxter and Henry Adams and Lydia Maria Child and Herman Melville, in order to take excerpts from them.

"But darling," my husband said, in his reasonable voice. "One doesn't do that." "You mean scholars don't do that?" I wailed. "I thought they did." "Heavens, no," he said. "You just have an idea of what you need, and then look for it. You don't have to read every word of a book to find what you want." "Really?" I said. It was a wonderful moment.

About then it was borne in upon me that in this work upon which I had embarked, it was not the content I had to invent, as in a work of fiction. It was the means by which I was going to collect the content. I had to invent, create if you like, a technique by which I could accomplish the finished book. For, as I much later wrote in my introduction to the anthology:

An anthology of any literature is, properly, a collection of valuable items selected from the wide reading of an authority in that field. The present anthology is something quite other. It is, in fact, an almost direct opposite, for instead of being culled from accrued knowledge, it has been, for its editor, a search and a discovery.

And yet that is not quite an accurate description of what I had to do in compiling this anthology, either. The knowledge that I did have, of New England, was accrued, all right. The trouble was that it was accrued in a part of my mind that made it almost inaccessible—in my memory. That is to say, my knowledge of and feeling for New England were the net products of a childhood spent listening to long, involved, eventful, and interminable legends of New England. To quote my introduction again:

I was brought up near Boston in a family much given to telling stories of the past. My father had an uncanny memory for tales, both historical and family, and I grew up with a strong, definite myth of New England. It was a myth that included such archetypes as the Puritan, exemplified for me by my ancestor John Hale of Beverly, persecutor of witches until his own wife was cried out upon. The Revolution seemed to me almost a family affair. When I was six, we were asked one day at school to tell what our ancestors had done in the American Revolution, and I reported with pride, "I had a great-uncle who was hanged."

And so on. About what another agent of mine, Elizabeth Nowell, used to call the stud book, I wrote:

Such so-to-speak dinner-table education is the veriest myth, for, like the ancient myths, it is gained from word of mouth, from hearing the praises of famous men sung, and from the personal connection that exists between the listener and the heroes of the lays. A sort of false confidence informs the possessor of a myth. He thinks he knows; but he doesn't. He only feels. It can be tempting, if one was brought up in New England, to feel that one knows something about, say, Emerson, when really the source of one's feeling is no more than a familiar photograph of Emerson seated on a sofa with one's grand-father. It is easy to feel one knows about the Plymouth Plantations just because one was taken to see the Rock as a child, and, at school, sang on so many mornings, "The break-ing waves—dashed high!" Brook Farm, not five miles down the road, seemed almost as familiar a place as home. But to be familiar with is not the same thing as knowing.

Or rather, I might add now, feeling *is* a kind of knowing, but it is a different kind of knowing from the kind that professional compilers of anthologies must call upon. Feeling is the kind of knowing that writers of fiction call upon—that, I suppose, is why my agent, my editor, and my husband all supposed that, judg-ing from my published work, I was equipped to do an anthology of New England writing. Perhaps I was, but it now devolved upon me to find the ways in which all that unconscious memory, legend, myth, which was the stuff of my kind of knowledge, could be brought up to the surface and translated into corrobora-tive excerpts from actual New England writing.

As a matter of fact, this finding myself up to the neck in something that I had to invent the means to cope with—like learning to swim after you are already in the deep water—was a very salutary experience. It was conducive to humility. For the truth is, fiction writers are afflicted with considerable hubris. "The artist," wrote Jung, "has a sense of God-almightiness." The reason for this is that the fiction writer, the artist, originates; which is a God-almighty thing to feel yourself doing. This is why you will find the artist looking down, ever so slightly, on the critic, who, let it never be forgotten, has to depend on the work of other people for his material. The artist tends to think anybody can be a factual writer, can be, for instance, an anthologist. I can tell you that I acquired a very real respect for people who can compile anthologies out of their conscious, negotiable knowledge, during those months when I was scared to death, working like a demon, and animated by absolutely no confidence in what I was doing. The fact that I was also writing a novel, a book about writing, and building and moving into a new house during this time made it no easier.

The only thing I had any faith in was the validity of that spark of an idea that had come to me after that sleepless night in New York—that it was possible to check my memories of New England, her literature and her myth, against whatever the facts were. I have described what I finally did, again in the introduction:

I began to try to substantiate the myth I carried about with me. The greater part of my task proved to be just that: substantiation of what I already believed. But where the myth turned out to be untrue I found I could lop it off. Where it was cloudy I could clarify it. Where it was in part, I could fill in legend with history.

The technique my brilliant researcher, Ruthe Smith, and I worked out was this: I made notes, dozens of notes, hundreds of notes, on things in New England literature I remembered, things I had read perhaps forty years before, things I had read about somebody else reading, things I had heard praises of, things I hadn't read but thought might possibly exist somewhere, things that I figured must exist somewhere. These notes were not what the scholars would call orderly. They were, many of them, on the backs of matchbooks picked up at the restaurants where the ideas struck me, or on the backs of envelopes snatched up to scribble on before I could forget an idea, or simply on the blue paper which I generally use for making notes. (The reason why it is blue paper is that its being blue makes it show up between the piles of white or yellow paper, so that I am less apt to lose my notes.) The idea was to get all that I knew about New England writing up out of my memory, up out of the unconscious, where it had been in residence, never having been called on before except to serve as an emotional background for fiction.

These masses of untidy scraps of paper Mrs. Smith and I would then discuss. I would perhaps need to explain what I meant by a line that read, "Where Portland sunk? . . . any literary account? . . . Lantern on porch of The Thickets," or a line that read, "One pretty girl almost lost her eyesight." In the former case, I would explain that I meant the famous wreck of the steamer Portland in the nineteenth century, and wanted to know whether anybody had ever written anything notable about it; the lantern was merely a reminder to myself of a porch light at the house where I spent my childhood summers, which had washed ashore off that wreck. In the case of the pretty girl who almost lost her eyesight, I would apologize and withdraw the note for my own use. It was a reminder of an ancient ballad, "Uncle Tracy's Thanksgiving," which I used to hear sung, that dates from the end of the seventeenth century.

Or I might pass across to Mrs. Smith notes that read, "What Bryant?" or "Longfellow necessary on Revere?" or else notes written out of sheer ignorance "What about King Philip's War? I want his death." Or "What relation were the Mathers to each other?" or "The first Thanksgiving—who gives it?" or "Something on the Deerfield Massacre" or "Where is a good description of Margaret Fuller?" Sometimes I was able to tell Mrs. Smith in these notes something *she* didn't know about, for a change.

"I want *The Ballad of the French Fleet,* with the bit about 'Lord, we would not advise,'" I put on one note, or else, "I want a recipe for Marlborough pie—no modern cookbook has one," or "Something about Rhode Island jonny-cake—journey-cake."

The next step was for Mrs. Smith to find me what I asked for, and in almost every case she could and did. To carry on with the examples I have already raised, and to show how the system worked, she turned up a hair-raising newspaper account of the sinking of the steamer Portland from the Boston *Daily Advertiser* of that date. I myself found the text for *Uncle Tracy's Thanksgiving* in Edward Everett Hale's *New England History in Ballads,* and this, too, we used.

For our example of William Cullen Bryant we settled, as might have been expected, on his *Thanatopsis.* But Mrs. Smith unearthed a letter from Paul Revere to Dr. Jeremy Belknap, which gives a full account of his famous ride in his own, not Longfellow's words. To represent Longfellow we used, instead, *The Ballad of the French Fleet,* which tells the story of the armada sent in 1746 by Louis XV to avenge the loss of Louisburg to the New Englanders. The Boston minister who got up to pray at this moment of peril said, according to Longfellow, "Lord, we would not advise, but if in thy Providence a tempest *should* arise. . . ." My father used to say that the Almighty must have been much obliged for the divine's kind suggestion.

For the death of King Philip, a sad event I wanted particularly to include, Mrs. Smith found an account in *Entertaining Passages Relating to King Philip's War,* by Thomas Church, son of a soldier in that war. I managed by myself to get the Mathers straightened out and suitably represented, by using an excerpt from Richard Mather's *Bay Psalm Book,* by using Increase Mather's *Essay for the Recording of Illustrious Providences,* (about some horrible fates that overtook those who didn't do what God wanted them to), and by using a bit from Cotton Mather's *Diary* (where he put down lists and lists of ways he could improve himself), and also a bit from the *Magnalia Christie Americana.* We never used any account of the first

Thanksgiving at Plymouth Plantations out of consideration for the Virginians. For an account of an Indian massacre, we used Mary Rowlandson's extraordinary *Story of Her Captivity Sufferings, and Restoration,* which gives, as few accounts have, the terrible sense of being a woman and looking out of one's window and seeing and hearing that the Indians have come. Mrs. Smith steered me to Thomas Wentworth Higginson's description of Margaret Fuller's conversations in his biography of the great Boston bluestocking. One recipe for Boston and one for Deerfield Marlborough Pie I got by the simple device of writing to Clementine Paddleford of the New York *Herald Tribune.* For Rhode Island jonny-cake, Mrs. Smith, who had never heard of it, produced Thomas Robinson Hazard's *Jonny Cake Papers,* which gives a fascinating account of the mystique of its making.

In writing commentary on the nearly 200 items I collected, I tried always to relate the item to my own experience. This required research on two levels—ascertaining the facts about the item to be included, and checking on the reliability of my own memory—which, while extensive, is far from accurate. This writing of commentary was the real hard work of the book in any ordinary sense, for it required extensive and attentive study of books of reference, and in a far from relaxed frame of mind, since at my back I always heard Time's winged chariot. By this time—the time I began writing commentary—I had less than three months left before the deadline.

The difference between knowing and being familiar with is nowhere better illustrated than by the requirements of this commentary. Let me give an example of what the difference between knowing and being familiar with is: most people are familiar with the painting of *Washington Crossing the Delaware.* They know which figure is that of Washington and what war the scene took place in. But suppose they had to supply all of the following information: What year did it take place? Where was Washington crossing from? To? What for? What was the name of his opposite number for the British side? Who else was in the boat? Who painted the picture? When? Where does it hang?

The answers to those questions constitute knowledge of this picture, and were the type of answers I required in writing the hundreds of pieces of commentary on New England text and pictures, both the used and the unused.

Looking back now on the three years that it took me to put together the anthology, I realize it was not this hard-working part that caused me the anguish I was caused. For one thing, this kind of work is journalism, and I have served my term at magazine and newspaper writing and know how to go about it when I know what I am supposed to go about. What scared me so about the whole proposition appears at this distance in time to have been something else than hard work. It appears to have been doubt of, instead of confidence in, the kind of knowing I had to draw upon. Yet it was this kind of knowing— knowing, I might say, by heart—that was the only original contribution I had to make to this work.

The day after Christmas, 1962, I packed up a huge carton to send off to Coward-McCann, so that it would arrive on the day before the deadline, which was January 1, 1963. The inventory of that carton reads:

2 cardboard files containing pictures in folders with caption material. 15 folders containing text, with two copies of commentary attached to each item. 1 pack file-cards of permissions granted for use of text, for Coward-McCann to make up according to their own style. 1 folder containing statements of Acknowledgment, plus list of complimentary copies requested by the sources of some of the pictures. Copy of Introduction. Copy of Table of Contents. 28 folders containing correspondence covering the granting of permissions, plus requests from publishers for complimentary copies. Folder containing reference list of all pictures.

Soon after the publishers' receipt of this carton of material for the New England anthology, I got a letter from the copy editor there, saying that she and Mr. Geoghegan liked the book so much that they were going to take it outside of the series for which it had been intended. The volume was published in a different format from the others and at a different price, with better-quality paper and a better reproductive process for the pictures.

All this was very gratifying and encouraging to the ego. I began getting more and more letters from other publishers, asking me to do other books on New England—one on Boston, I remember, one about New England villages, one about the state of Massachusetts, one about Vermont, one about Mrs. Jack Gardiner. Of course it was very flattering to be asked, but I think my feelings were summed up by something I heard myself say in New York about this time, at a publishers' cocktail party. A publisher asked me if I didn't have a lot of discards left over from the anthology, now that it had been put to bed. I thought of all those folders full of unused material, and said I certainly did have discards. "Well, you're going to make another book out of them, aren't you?" he asked. "Good Lord, no," I said before I thought. "But every professional anthologist uses his discards for another anthology!" he said.

But I am not a professional anthologist. However, I am very glad I undertook *New England Discovery*, if only because it may have taught me to have confidence in my ability to do something I felt I couldn't do. This is not to say that I think *New England Discovery* is an unqualified success.

There are several things I know to be wrong about the book. There is, for example, a great big fat mistake in one of the commentaries, even after all Ruthe Smith's and my researches. I don't know whether anybody else has spotted it or not, but I should think they would have. I know why I made the mistake, too. It was the unregenerate fiction writer in me coming out, putting down as fact what I only imagined the names of the three hills of Boston to be. One afternoon last summer, reading the Gloucester, Massachusetts, *Times*, of all journals, I found their names were quite other.

This, I suppose, would be the ideal moment to divulge what the right names are. But I don't think I will. I think that instead, I will tell a story I heard long ago from Arthur Sulzberger of the

New York Times, about a man who went to the dentist. "Ah, I got such a toothache!" he moaned. "You got no idea!" "Is this the tooth?" the dentist said, and he pulled out one of the man's teeth. "Ha-ha-ha—No it ain't!" the man said. "Oh, how my tooth aches!" The dentist pulled out another tooth, and said, "Is that the tooth?" "Ha-ha, no it ain't," the man said. The dentist, becoming more cautious, merely poked at another tooth, and said, "Is this the one?" The man with the toothache said, "*I* should pay you my good money to tell *you* which tooth it is that hurts."

ARGUMENTATION AND PERSUASION

ARGUMENT is that mode of discourse by which a writer presents his opinion on some question, whether it be the defects of a certain automobile or the merits of a political philosophy, and tries to convince his readers of the rightness of that opinion. Argumentation is the reasoned part of the discourse; persuasion, the non-reasoned part. More fully, argumentation is the logical chain of reasoning presented to show the basis for the opinion; whereas persuasion is any emotional appeal that the writer cares to use to force readers to adopt his opinion. This distinction is somewhat artificial, because the logical reasoning will have a persuasive force of its own upon logical readers. Currently, emotional appeals to the readers' sense of economy or of patriotism or love of home and mother are held to be the persuasive element of argument, apart from the persuasive force of logic. Most thoughtfully constructed arguments will contain both logical and emotional appeal.

Arguments arise whenever a person convinced of the truth of his own opinion tries to persuade others to accept it as true. He may address like-minded persons or persons with no opinion on the subject or those with differing opinions or all three types. The initial argument is likely to bring forth an answering argument, with a consequent train of rebuttals and replies and later arguments representing many shades of opinion. The existence of differing opinions is recognized in the debate, in which two opposing opinions are presented on the same occasion in a lecture hall or in the same book or the same issue of a periodical. Presentation of more than two opinions on a subject results in the panel discussion or the symposium.

The following arguments arose from a variety of circumstances. Warren's argument is essentially a reply to previous arguments;

consequently, his argument contains quoted opinions from the initial arguments and rebuttal of them. His argument begins with an analogy between the literature of Elizabethan England and the literature of the United States in the 20th century. The logical and persuasive force of this analogy depends upon whether the reader agrees that he is like an Elizabethan and whether he wants to be. Inspection of the strengths and weaknesses of the analogy exemplifies the strengths and weaknesses of analogy as a device of argumentation and persuasion. Warren argues his point that our literature gives a good, not a bad, impression abroad by analyzing 20th-century fiction to show its good themes ("redemption" in Faulkner, for instance), by making general statements about the value of a "critical" literature, and by relating his narrative example of the effect of American fiction on a young Italian soldier. By the way in this reasoned part of the argument, he pauses to persuade us in the name of "humility" and "democracy" to accept his logic. More thorough analysis shows that the emotional and logical appeals are inextricably mingled; the "good" theme of "redemption," for instance, is both an argument that Warren's opponent has misread Faulkner and is factually wrong and a persuasive appeal to find something generally recognized as good in Faulkner's work. Likewise, the other pieces in this section depend in varying degrees on both logic and emotion.

Rachel Carson's analysis of the choice between saving elms and saving robins is an excerpt from an argument of the kind that initiates discussion. Distressed by her observation of unfortunate side effects from the use of pesticides, Miss Carson wrote Silent Spring to open the question of what she considered thoughtless pollution of our natural environment. Her logical argument depends upon analysis of many examples of such pollution, which support her proposition that pollution must be stopped. Furthermore, by setting forth positive propositions favoring control of Dutch elm disease by means other than pesticides, she argues against choosing between trees and birds. But her argument is emotionally as well as logically appealing; she appeals to our love of birds and spring in such sentences as, "To millions of Americans, the season's first robin means that the grip of winter is broken." Indeed, in the storm of controversy aroused by the book, its critics damned it because of such emotional appeal and criticized less often her logical interpretations of scientific fact. Those who agreed with Miss Carson responded to her appeal to our sense of beauty as well as to the logic of her argument. The effectiveness of her rhetoric is best demonstrated by the despairing admission of her critics that she wrote well, so persuasively, albeit wrongheadedly, as to be difficult to answer.

The other arguments exemplify other occasions for or other kinds of discussion. Carter and King each gives his view of the progress made in racial integration. Each writer is responding to a public question currently much mooted; though neither is answering the other, they do have different opinions. The two views of grammar presented by Follett and Evans, on the other hand, exemplify expostulation and reply. Follett takes issue with views expressed elsewhere by Evans; then Evans answers Follett. An even more direct confrontation of opinions is that of Rice and Kitzhaber, whose opposing views of freshman English are presented in the same issue of a magazine.

ROBERT PENN WARREN

A LESSON READ
IN AMERICAN BOOKS

Robert Penn Warren (1905-   ) is a distinguished teacher, critic, novelist, and poet. He was educated at Vanderbilt, the University of California, Yale, and Oxford, where he was a Rhodes Scholar. He has taught at many universities, including Louisiana State, Minnesota, and Yale. His textbooks with Cleanth Brooks, especially Understanding Poetry *(1938), have extended his teaching far beyond his own classrooms and are perhaps his most important contribution to literary criticism. His best-known and probably best novel is* All the King's Men *(1946), which won a Pulitzer Prize and, as a movie (1949), was named the best of the year by the Academy of Motion Picture Arts and Sciences. Many of his best poems are in* Selected Poems, 1923-1943 *(1944). Like Allen Tate, he contributed to* The Fugitive, *was associated with the southern agrarians, has been an editor (of* The Southern Review *and* The Kenyon Review*), and is now associated with the New Criticism.*

ONCE UPON A TIME there was a nation, which we shall call X. At the time of which we write this nation stood at a moment of great power and great promise. A few generations earlier it had concluded a long and bloody civil war to achieve unity. More recently, in that unity, it had won a crashing victory over foreign foes. It had undergone, and was undergoing, a social revolution; there was unparalleled prosperity, a relaxing of old sanctions and prejudices, a widening of opportunity for all classes, great rewards for energy and intelligence. Its flag was on strange seas; its power was felt in the world. It was, even, producing a famous literature.

But—and here is the strange thing in that moment of energy and optimism—a large part, the most famous part, of that literature exhibited violence, degradation and despair as part of the human condition: tales of the old time of the civil war, tales

»»» *The New York Times Book Review*, December 11, 1955, pp. 1, 33. Reprinted by permission of the New York *Times* and Robert Penn Warren.

of lust and horror, brother pimping for sister, father lusting for daughter, a head of the state doting on a fair youth, an old man's eyes plucked out, another old man killed in his sleep, friendship betrayed, obligations foregone, good men cursing the gods, and the whole scene drenched in blood. Foreigners encountering this literature might well conclude that the Land of X was peopled by degenerates sadly lacking in taste, manners and principle.

This is England, Elizabethan England, that we are talking about, and not the United States in this year of Our Lord and the Great Prosperity. But *mutatis mutandis,* and with proper recognition of the fact that we can scarcely claim a William Shakespeare, only John Fords and John Websters, we can talk about the United States in this connection, and join in conversation with Father Bruckberger, who has lately appeared in these pages, and with the editorial writer of Life magazine for Sept. 12.

These writers are concerned, as we must all be concerned, with America's image in the eyes of the world. "Is it right," asks Father Bruckberger, a sympathetic Frenchman visiting our shores, "that the great *flowering* of the American novel should hamper * * * America's leadership of the free world?" And the editorial writer in Life: "Europeans are already prejudiced against America by savage animadversions in their own classics against our 'vulgar' democracy * * *. Small wonder that our own self-depreciation helps them enlarge the evil image * * *."

These two quotations raise a question, vexed and vexing, a question already old, no doubt, when the Greeks worried about it: how should esthetic value be related to prudential considerations? Presumably some of our literature has esthetic value (Father Bruckberger handsomely calls it a "flowering"), but it confirms some Europeans in their inherited low opinion of America, the country of "the almighty dollar," and of "respect to ordinary artisans," as Stendhal puts it, and the "land of money and selfishness, where souls are cold," as Balzac puts it. What do we do, then, when esthetic value is in conflict, or in apparent conflict, with political values?

Father Bruckberger does not undertake to answer this for us. On the one hand, he says that the "honor" of a literature is that it creates and sustains "a great quarrel within the national consciousness." But on the other hand, he bewails the effect abroad of this very quarrel within our national consciousness. Certainly, he is too informed to attempt to resolve the difficulty along the lines laid down by the editorial writer in Life, who, with certain ritualistic reservations, says that because America is now enjoying a boom, our literature should be optimistic, and applauds the current success of "The Man in the Gray Flannel Suit" because, though "flimsy art," it is "at least affirmative."

In fact, the editorial writer of Life takes as his golden text a quotation from Sloan Wilson, the author of "The Man in the Gray Flannel Suit": "The world's treated me awfully well, and I guess it's crept into my work * * *. These are, we forget, pretty good times. Yet too many novelists are still writing as if we were back in the Depression years."

Though I have not yet read "The Man in the Gray Flannel Suit," I should venture to doubt that the world is going to treat its author quite as well as it has treated Ernest Hemingway, William Faulkner, Theodore Dreiser, Sinclair Lewis, T. S. Eliot, Robert Frost, and quite a few other American writers who never found such a ready equation between bank balance and philosophy. What is really at stake in this is a question of freedom. If the creative act is of any value it is, in its special way, an act of freedom. It is, of course, conditioned by a thousand factors, but study of its conditions—economic, biologic, or whatever— has yet to reveal the secret of how that new intuition, the truly created object whose *newness* is the mark of freedom, comes to be. But Mr. Wilson, and presumably the approving editorial writer in Life, would deny this freedom, would, in fact, go even farther than Karl Marx in asserting the economic determinism of literature. If you are not making dough, you will not be a booster. Literature is a reflex of the stock market.

The philosophers of the Age of Conformism grant, however, that criticism was once all right, long back. As the Life editorial puts it: " 'The Great Gatsby' still speaks eloquently of Prohibition's frauds and deceits, 'Main Street' of the high tide of provincial self-satisfaction, 'The Grapes of Wrath' with a just anger for the unnecessary humiliations of Depression * * *." But criticism isn't all right in this day and time, for there is nothing really wrong now to be criticized, and anybody who is critical, who isn't "affirmative," is a fool or knave, a traitor or a sexual deviant, or a failure. May we not, however, in some chill hour between dark and dawn, have the thought that our own age may—just possibly—have its own frauds and deceits, deeper and more ambiguous than those anatomized in "The Great Gatsby," that though this is not the age of provincial self-satisfaction, it may be the age of national self-righteousness and require a sharper scalpel than even "Main Street," and that Divine Providence has given no written guarantee that It will not rebuke the smuggery of the Great Boom?

I do not think that the novel has yet been written to anatomize adequately this moment of our history, and I share the distaste of the editorial writer in Life for some of the works he alludes to, but the "American novel" which we should call for would not be less, but more, critical than those now current. At the same time I should hope that the literature to come will be more "affirmative," to use the word of the editorial. But the paradox here is that the literature that is most truly and profoundly critical is always the most profoundly affirmative.

In so far as a literature struggles to engage the deep, inner issues of life, the more will that literature be critical—the more, that is, will it engender impatience with the compromises, the ennui, the materialism, the self-deception, the complacency, and the secret, unnamable despairs that mark so much of ordinary life. Such a critical literature is at the same time affirmative because it affirms the will and courage to engage life at fundamental levels: the rock, if struck hard enough, will give forth the living waters.

The editorial writer in Life would not, I suppose, find these kinds of affirmation significant. He is concerned with doctrine, more or less explicitly put. But sometimes, even when doctrine is explicitly put, he has not, cannot, or does not, read it. Faulkner, he says, "for all his enormous gifts, can be searched in vain for that quality of redemption, through love and brotherhood, which always shines amid Dostoevsky's horrors." That very redemption, and its cost, is a recurrent theme of Faulkner's work. There is, for example, "The Bear," with old Ike's vision of man's place in creation: God created man to hold suzerainty over the earth in His name, "not to hold for himself and his descendants' inviolable title forever, generation after generation, to the oblongs and squares of the earth, but to hold the earth mutual and intact in the communal anonymity of brotherhood, and all the fee He asked was pity and humility and sufferance and endurance and the sweat of his face for bread."

But let us go back where we started: the bad political impression which some of our literature presumably gives abroad. What are we to do? If we can't get writers to write the kind of literature we think useful for foreign consumption—if there really isn't such a thing as literature to specification—what then?

The answer is, I think, simple—and appalling. We must trust in our humility, and in our strength.

We must trust in our humility, because only by humility, the recognition that we have not fulfilled our best possibilities, can we hope to fulfill those possibilities. Some day, far-called, our navies may melt away, and on that day we may need the wisdom of ultimate humility. Meanwhile, in our moment of strength we hope that our strength is more than a historical accident, an index of the weakness of others. We hope that it has a moral grounding. But if that hope is to be more than a hope, it must be subjected to the test of conscience, and literature is one of the voices of our national conscience, however faltering and defective that voice may sometimes be. We must rebuke our *hubris*, not out of fear, but from love of a truth that we hope is within us.

We must trust in our strength, because only the strong can afford the luxury of radical self-criticism. Only if we believe in our strength can we take the risks of our full political and cultural development, with all the disintegrative and paradoxical possibilities in that dialectic. We should trust our strength, because America has a secret weapon, if we choose to use it: the weapon of not having a secret. It is the weapon of radical self-criticism—*radical* in the non-political and literal sense of the word. There was an old name for this, a name not often now used in this connection. That name was *democracy*.

So much for ourselves. But what of those poor foreigners who are so really deceived by our literature? Are they, in the long run, quite so trapped in their prejudice, quite so incapable of the imaginative act, as Father Bruckberger seems to think? If so, why do they find our literature so fascinating, and why do they honor it? Can it be that, in a measure, they find in it a vital image of man, and some comment on his condition? Do they find in it, in the very fact of its existence, some mark of freedom?

I shall tell a story. A little while after the war in Europe I became acquainted with a young Italian who, in the first year of the war, as an officer in the Fascist Army, had deserted and taken to the mountains, to fight on our side. I once asked him what led him to this drastic step. He replied that American novelists had converted him. How, I asked. "Well," he said, "the Fascists used to let us read American fiction because it gave, they thought, a picture of a decadent America. They thought it was good propaganda for fascism to let us read Dreiser, Faulkner, Sinclair Lewis. But you know, it suddenly occurred to me that if democracy could allow that kind of criticism of itself, it must be very strong and good. So I took to the mountains."

RACHEL CARSON

from AND NO BIRDS SING

Rachel Carson (1907-1964), biologist and science writer, was educated at Pennsylvania College for Women and Johns Hopkins University. She joined the Bureau of Fisheries as a biologist in 1936 and from 1949 to 1952 was editor-in-chief of publications of the Fish and Wildlife Service. Her book The Sea Around Us *(1951) won the National Book Award. Her bestseller* Silent Spring *(1962) won the Schweitzer Medal of the Animal Welfare Institute, the Constance Lindsay Skinner Achievement Award of the Women's National Book Association, and a half dozen other awards from conservation and women's groups. The book created much controversy among agriculturalists, conservationists, and chemical makers and resulted in some reversal of government policy in the use of pesticides. In the following selection, the notes appear at the end as, in the book, they appear at the end in a "List of Principal Sources"—a placement of documentation increasingly prevalent in publishing.*

OVER INCREASINGLY large areas of the United States, spring now comes unheralded by the return of the birds, and the early mornings are strangely silent where once they were filled with the beauty of bird song. This sudden silencing of the song of birds, this obliteration of the color and beauty and interest they lend to our world have come about swiftly, insidiously, and unnoticed by those whose communities are as yet unaffected.

From the town of Hinsdale, Illinois, a housewife wrote in despair to one of the world's leading ornithologists, Robert Cushman Murphy, Curator Emeritus of Birds at the American Museum of Natural History.

Here in our village the elm trees have been sprayed for several years [she wrote in 1958]. When we moved here six years ago, there was a wealth of bird life; I put up a feeder and had a steady stream of cardinals, chickadees, downies and nuthatches all winter, and the cardinals and chickadees brought their young ones in the summer.

After several years of DDT spray, the town is almost devoid of robins and starlings; chickadees have not been on my shelf for two years, and this year the cardinals are gone too; the nesting population in the neighborhood seems to consist of one dove pair and perhaps one catbird family.

It is hard to explain to the children that the birds have been killed off, when they have learned in school that a Federal law protects the birds from killing or capture. "Will they ever come back?" they ask, and I do not have the answer. The elms are still dying, and so are the birds. *Is* anything being done? *Can* anything be done? Can *I* do anything?

A year after the federal government had launched a massive spraying program against the fire ant, an Alabama woman wrote: "Our place has been a veritable bird sanctuary for over half a century. Last July we all remarked, 'There are more birds than ever.' Then, suddenly, in the second week of August, they all disappeared. I was accustomed to rising early to care for my favorite mare that had a young filly. There was not a sound of the song of a bird. It was eerie, terrifying. What was man doing to our perfect and beautiful world? Finally, five months later a blue jay appeared and a wren."

The autumn months to which she referred brought other somber reports from the deep South, where in Mississippi, Louisiana, and Alabama the *Field Notes* published quarterly by the National Audubon Society and the United States Fish and Wildlife Service noted the striking phenomenon of "blank spots weirdly empty of virtually *all* bird life." The *Field Notes* are a compilation of the reports of seasoned observers who have spent many years afield in their particular areas and have unparalleled knowledge of the normal bird life of the region. One such observer reported that in driving about southern Mississippi that fall she saw "no land birds at all for long distances." Another in Baton Rouge reported that the contents of her feeders had lain untouched "for weeks on end," while fruiting shrubs in her yard, that ordinarily would be stripped clean by that time, still were laden with berries. Still another reported that his picture window, "which often used to frame a scene splashed with the red of 40 or 50 cardinals and crowded with other species, seldom permitted a view of as many as a bird or two at a time." Professor Maurice Brooks of the University of West Virginia, an authority on the birds of the Appalachian region, reported that the West Virginia bird population had undergone "an incredible reduction."

One story might serve as the tragic symbol of the fate of the birds—a fate that has already overtaken some species, and that threatens all. It is the story of the robin, the bird known to everyone. To millions of Americans, the season's first robin means that the grip of winter is broken. Its coming is an event reported in newspapers and told eagerly at the breakfast table. And as the number of migrants grows and the first mists of green appear in the woodlands, thousands of people listen for the first dawn chorus of the robins throbbing in the early morning light. But now all is changed, and not even the return of the birds may be taken for granted.

The survival of the robin, and indeed of many other species as well, seems fatefully linked with the American elm, a tree that is part of the history of thousands of towns from the Atlantic to the Rockies, gracing their streets and their village squares and college campuses with majestic archways of green. Now the elms are stricken with a disease that afflicts them throughout their range, a disease so serious that many experts believe all efforts to save the elms will in the end be futile. It would be tragic to lose the elms, but it would be doubly tragic if, in vain efforts to save them, we plunge vast segments of our bird populations into the night of extinction. Yet this is precisely what is threatened.

The so-called Dutch elm disease entered the United States from Europe about 1930 in elm burl logs imported for the veneer industry. It is a fungus disease; the organism invades the water-conducting vessels of the tree, spreads by spores carried in the flow of sap, and by its poisonous secretions as well as by mechanical clogging causes the branches to wilt and the tree to die. The disease is spread from diseased to healthy trees by elm bark beetles. The galleries which the insects have tunneled out under the bark of dead trees become contaminated with spores of the invading fungus, and the spores adhere to the insect body and are carried wherever the beetle flies. Efforts to control the fungus disease of the elms have been directed largely toward control of the carrier insect. In community after community, especially throughout the strongholds of the American elm, the Midwest and New England, intensive spraying has become a routine procedure.

What this spraying could mean to bird life, and especially to the robin, was first made clear by the work of two ornithologists at Michigan State University, Professor George Wallace and one of his graduate students, John Mehner. When Mr. Mehner began work for the doctorate in 1954, he chose a research project that had to do with robin populations. This was quite by chance, for at that time no one suspected that the robins were in danger. But even as he undertook the work, events occurred that were to change its character and indeed to deprive him of his material.

Spraying for Dutch elm disease began in a small way on the university campus in 1954. The following year the city of East Lansing (where the university is located) joined in, spraying on the campus was expanded, and, with local programs for gypsy moth and mosquito control also under way, the rain of chemicals increased to a downpour.

During 1954, the year of the first light spraying, all seemed well. The following spring the migrating robins began to return to the campus as usual. Like the bluebells in Tomlinson's haunting essay "The Lost Wood," they were "expecting no evil" as they reoccupied their familiar territories. But soon it became evident that something was wrong. Dead and dying robins began to appear on the campus. Few birds were seen in their normal foraging activities or assembling in their usual roosts. Few nests were built; few young appeared. The pattern was repeated with monotonous regularity in succeeding springs. The sprayed area had become a lethal trap in which each wave of migrating robins would be eliminated in about a week. Then new arrivals would come in, only to add to the numbers of doomed birds seen on the campus in the agonized tremors that precede death.

"The campus is serving as a graveyard for most of the robins that attempt to take up residence in the spring," said Dr. Wallace. But why? At first he suspected some disease of the nervous system, but soon it became evident that " in spite of the assurances of the insecticide people that their sprays were 'harmless to birds' the robins were really dying of insecticidal poisoning; they exhibited the well-known symptoms of loss of balance, followed by tremors, convulsions, and death."

Several facts suggested that the robins were being poisoned, not so much by direct contact with the insecticides as indirectly, by eating earthworms. Campus earthworms had been fed inadvertently to crayfish in a research project and all the crayfish had promptly died. A snake kept in a laboratory cage had gone into violent tremors after being fed such worms. And earthworms are the principal food of robins in the spring.

A key piece in the jigsaw puzzle of the doomed robins was soon to be supplied by Dr. Roy Barker of the Illinois Natural History Survey at Urbana. Dr. Barker's work, published in 1958, traced the intricate cycle of events by which the robins' fate is linked to the elm trees by way of the earthworms. The trees are sprayed in the spring (usually at the rate of 2 to 5 pounds of DDT per 50-foot tree, which may be the equivalent of as much as 23 *pounds per acre* where elms are numerous) and often again in July, at about half this concentration. Powerful sprayers direct a stream of poison to all parts of the tallest trees, killing directly not only the target organism, the bark beetle, but other insects, including pollinating species and predatory spiders and beetles. The poison forms a tenacious film over the leaves and bark. Rains do not wash it away. In the autumn the leaves fall to the ground, accumulate in sodden layers, and begin the slow process of becoming one with the soil. In this they are aided by the toil of the earthworms, who feed in the leaf litter, for elm leaves are among their favorite foods. In feeding on the leaves the worms also swallow the insecticide, accumulating and concentrating it in their bodies. Dr. Barker found deposits of DDT throughout the digestive tracts of the worms, their blood vessels, nerves, and body wall. Undoubtedly some of the earthworms themselves succumb, but others survive to become "biological magnifiers" of the poison. In the spring the robins return to provide another link in the cycle. As few as 11 large earthworms can transfer a lethal dose of DDT to a robin. And 11 worms form a small part of a day's rations to a bird that eats 10 to 12 earthworms in as many minutes.

Not all robins receive a lethal dose, but another consequence may lead to the extinction of their kind as surely as fatal poisoning. The shadow of sterility lies over all the bird studies and indeed lengthens to include all living things within its potential range. There are now only two or three dozen robins to be found each spring on the entire 185-acre campus of Michigan State University, compared with a conservatively estimated 370 adults in this area before spraying. In 1954 every robin nest under observation by Mehner produced young. Toward the end of June, 1957, when at least 370 young birds (the normal replacement of the adult population) would have been foraging over the campus in the years before spraying began, Mehner could find *only one young robin.* A year later Dr. Wallace was to report: "At no time during the spring or summer [of 1958] did I see a fledgling robin anywhere on the main campus, and so far I have failed to find anyone else who has seen one there."

Part of this failure to produce young is due, of course, to the fact that one or more of a pair of robins dies before the nesting cycle is completed. But Wallace has significant records which point to something more sinister—the actual destruction of the birds' capacity to reproduce. He has, for example, "records of robins and other birds building nests but laying no eggs, and others laying eggs and incubating them but not hatching them. We have one record of a robin that sat on its eggs faithfully for 21 days and they did not hatch. The normal incubation period is 13 days . . . Our analyses are showing high concentrations of DDT in the testes and ovaries of breeding birds," he told a congressional committee in 1960. "Ten males had amounts ranging from 30 to 109 parts per million in the testes, and two females had 151 and 211 parts per million respectively in the egg follicles in their ovaries."

Soon studies in other areas began to develop findings equally dismal. Professor Joseph Hickey and his students at the University of Wisconsin, after careful comparative studies of sprayed and unsprayed areas, reported the robin mortality to be at least 86 to 88 per cent. The Cranbrook Institute of Science at Bloomfield Hills, Michigan, in an effort to assess the extent of bird loss caused by the spraying of the elms, asked in 1956 that all birds thought to be victims of DDT poisoning be turned in to the institute for examination. The request had a response beyond all expectations. Within a few weeks the deep-freeze facilities of the institute were taxed to capacity, so that other specimens had to be refused. By 1959 a thousand poisoned birds from this single community had been turned in or reported. Although the robin was the chief victim (one woman calling the institute reported 12 robins lying dead on her lawn as she spoke), 63 different species were included among the specimens examined at the institute.

The robins, then, are only one part of the chain of devastation linked to the spraying of the elms, even as the elm program is only one of the multitudinous spray programs that cover our land with poisons. Heavy mortality has occurred among about 90 species of birds, including those most familiar to suburbanites and amateur naturalists. The populations of nesting birds in general have declined as much as 90 per cent in some of the sprayed towns. As we shall see, all the various types of birds are affected —ground feeders, treetop feeders, bark feeders, predators.

It is only reasonable to suppose that all birds and mammals heavily dependent on earthworms or other soil organisms for food are theatened by the robins' fate. Some 45 species of birds include earthworms in their diet. Among them is the woodcock, a species that winters in southern areas recently heavily sprayed with heptachlor. Two significant discoveries have now been made about the woodcock. Production of young birds on the New Brunswick breeding grounds is definitely reduced, and adult birds that have been analyzed contain large residues of DDT and heptachlor.

Already there are disturbing records of heavy mortality among more than 20 other species of ground-feeding birds whose food—worms, ants, grubs, or other soil organisms—has been poisoned. These include three of the thrushes whose songs are among the most exquisite of bird voices, the olive-backed, the wood, and the hermit. And the sparrows that flit through the shrubby under-story of the woodlands and forage with rustling sounds amid the fallen leaves—the song sparrow and the white-throat—these, too, have been found among the victims of the elm sprays.

Mammals, also, may easily be involved in the cycle, directly or indirectly. Earthworms are important among the various foods of the raccoon, and are eaten in the spring and fall by opossums. Such subterranean tunnelers as shrews and moles capture them in some numbers, and then perhaps pass on the poison to predators such as screech owls and barn owls. Several dying screech owls were picked up in Wisconsin following heavy rains in spring, perhaps poisoned by feeding on earth-worms. Hawks and owls have been found in convulsions—great horned owls, screech owls, red-shouldered hawks, sparrow hawks, marsh hawks. These may be cases of secondary poisoning, caused by eating birds or mice that have accumulated insecti-cides in their livers or other organs.

Nor is it only the creatures that forage on the ground or those who prey on them that are endangered by the foliar spraying of the elms. All of the treetop feeders, the birds that glean their insect food from the leaves, have disappeared from heavily sprayed areas, among them those woodland sprites the kinglets, both ruby-crowned and golden-crowned, the tiny gnatcatchers, and many of the warblers, whose migrating hordes flow through the trees in spring in a multicolored tide of life. In 1956, a late spring delayed spraying so that it coincided with the arrival of an exceptionally heavy wave of warbler migration. Nearly all species of warblers present in the area were represented in the heavy kill that followed. In Whitefish Bay, Wisconsin, at least a thousand myrtle warblers could be seen in migration during former years; in 1958, after the spraying of the elms, observers could find only two. So, with additions from other communities, the list grows, and the warblers killed by the spray include those that most charm and fascinate all who are aware of them: the black-and-white, the yellow, the magnolia, and the Cape May; the ovenbird, whose call throbs in the Maytime woods; the Blackburnian, whose wings are touched with flame; the chestnut-sided, the Canadian, and the black-throated green. These treetop feeders are affected either directly by eating poisoned insects or indirectly by a shortage of food.

The loss of food has also struck hard at the swallows that cruise the skies, straining out the aerial insects as herring strain the plankton of the sea. A Wisconsin naturalist reported: "Swallows have been hard hit. Everyone complains of how few they have compared to four or five years ago. Our sky overhead was full of them only four years ago. Now we seldom see any . . . This could be both lack of insects because of spray, or poisoned insects."

Of other birds this same observer wrote: "Another striking loss is the phoebe. Flycatchers are scarce everywhere but the early hardy common phoebe is no more. I've seen one this spring and only one last spring. Other birders in Wisconsin make the same complaint. I have had five or six pair of cardinals in the past, none now. Wrens, robins, catbirds and screech owls have nested each year in our garden. There are none now. Summer mornings are without bird song. Only pest birds, pigeons, starlings and English sparrows remain. It is tragic and I can't bear it."

The dormant sprays applied to the elms in the fall, sending the poison into every little crevice in the bark, are probably responsible for the severe reduction observed in the number of chickadees, nuthatches, titmice, woodpeckers, and brown creepers. During the winter of 1957–58, Dr. Wallace saw no chickadees or nuthatches at his home feeding station for the first time in many years. Three nuthatches he found later provided a sorry little step-by-step lesson in cause and effect: one was feeding on an elm, another was found dying of typical DDT symptoms, the third was dead. The dying nuthatch was later found to have 226 parts per million of DDT in its tissues.

The feeding habits of all these birds not only make them especially vulnerable to insect sprays but also make their loss a deplorable one for economic as well as less tangible reasons. The summer food of the white-breasted nuthatch and the brown creeper, for example, includes the eggs, larvae, and adults of a very large number of insects injurious to trees. About three quarters of the food of the chickadee is animal, including all stages of the life cycle of many insects. The chickadee's method of feeding is described in Bent's monumental *Life Histories* of North American birds: "As the flock moves along each bird examines minutely bark, twigs, and branches, searching for tiny bits of food (spiders' eggs, cocoons, or other dormant insect life)."

Various scientific studies have established the critical role of birds in insect control in various situations. Thus, woodpeckers are the primary control of the Engelmann spruce beetle, reducing its populations from 45 to 98 per cent and are important in the control of the codling moth in apple orchards. Chickadees and other winter-resident birds can protect orchards against the cankerworm.

But what happens in nature is not allowed to happen in the modern, chemical-drenched world, where spraying destroys not only the insects but their principal enemy, the birds. When later there is a resurgence of the insect population, as almost always happens, the birds are not there to keep their numbers in check. As the Curator of Birds at the Milwaukee Public Museum, Owen J. Gromme, wrote to the Milwaukee *Journal:* "The greatest enemy of insect life is other predatory insects, birds, and some small mammals, but DDT kills indiscriminately,

including nature's own safeguards or policemen . . . In the name
of progress are we to become victims of our own diabolical
means of insect control to provide temporary comfort, only to
lose out to destroying insects later on? By what means will we
control new pests, which will attack remaining tree species after
the elms are gone, when nature's safeguards (the birds) have
been wiped out by poison?"

Mr. Gromme reported that calls and letters about dead and
dying birds had been increasing steadily during the years since
spraying began in Wisconsin. Questioning always revealed that
spraying or fogging had been done in the area where the birds
were dying.

Mr. Gromme's experience has been shared by ornithologists
and conservationists at most of the research centers of the Midwest such as the Cranbrook Institute in Michigan, the Illinois
Natural History Survey, and the University of Wisconsin. A
glance at the Letters-from-Readers column of newspapers almost anywhere that spraying is being done makes clear the fact
that citizens are not only becoming aroused and indignant but
that often they show a keener understanding of the dangers and
inconsistencies of spraying than do the officials who order it
done. "I am dreading the days to come soon now when many
beautiful birds will be dying in our back yard," wrote a Milwaukee woman. "This is a pitiful, heartbreaking experience . . .
It is, moreover, frustrating and exasperating, for it evidently
does not serve the purpose this slaughter was intended to serve
. . . Taking a long look, can you save trees without also saving
birds? Do they not, in the economy of nature, save each other?
Isn't it possible to help the balance of nature without destroying
it?"

The idea that the elms, majestic shade trees though they are,
are not "sacred cows" and do not justify an "open end" campaign of destruction against all other forms of life is expressed
in other letters. "I have always loved our elm trees which
seemed like trademarks on our landscape," wrote another Wisconsin woman. "But there are many kinds of trees . . . We must

save our birds, too. Can anyone imagine anything so cheerless and dreary as a springtime without a robin's song?"

To the public the choice may easily appear to be one of stark black-or-white simplicity: Shall we have birds or shall we have elms? But it is not as simple as that, and by one of the ironies that abound throughout the field of chemical control we may very well end by having neither if we continue on our present, well-traveled road. Spraying is killing the birds but it is not saving the elms. The illusion that salvation of the elms lies at the end of a spray nozzle is a dangerous will-o'-the-wisp that is leading one community after another into a morass of heavy expenditures, without producing lasting results. Greenwich, Connecticut, sprayed regularly for ten years. Then a drought year brought conditions especially favorable to the beetle and the mortality of elms went up 1000 per cent. In Urbana, Illinois, where the University of Illinois is located, Dutch elm disease first appeared in 1951. Spraying was undertaken in 1953. By 1959, in spite of six years' spraying, the university campus had lost 86 per cent of its elms, half of them victims of Dutch elm disease.

In Toledo, Ohio, a similar experience caused the Superintendent of Forestry, Joseph A. Sweeney, to take a realistic look at the results of spraying. Spraying was begun there in 1953 and continued through 1959. Meanwhile, however, Mr. Sweeney had noticed that a city-wide infestation of the cottony maple scale was worse after the spraying recommended by "the books and the authorities" than it had been before. He decided to review the results of spraying for Dutch elm disease for himself. His findings shocked him. In the city of Toledo, he found, "the only areas under any control were the areas where we used some promptness in removing the diseased or brood trees. Where we depended on spraying the disease was out of control. In the country where nothing has been done the disease has not spread as fast as it has in the city. This indicates that spraying destroys any natural enemies.

"We are abandoning spraying for the Dutch elm disease.

This has brought me into conflict with the people who back any recommendations by the United States Department of Agriculture but I have the facts and will stick with them."

It is difficult to understand why these midwestern towns, to which the elm disease spread only rather recently, have so unquestionably embarked on ambitious and expensive spraying programs, apparently without waiting to inquire into the experience of other areas that have had longer acquaintance with the problem. New York State, for example, has certainly had the longest history of continuous experience with Dutch elm disease, for it was via the Port of New York that diseased elm wood is thought to have entered the United States about 1930. And New York State today has a most impressive record of containing and suppressing the disease. Yet it has not relied upon spraying. In fact, its agricultural extension service does not recommend spraying as a community method of control.

How, then, has New York achieved its fine record? From the early years of the battle for the elms to the present time, it has relied upon rigorous sanitation, or the prompt removal and destruction of all diseased or infected wood. In the beginning some of the results were disappointing, but this was because it was not at first understood that not only diseased trees but all elm wood in which the beetles might breed must be destroyed. Infected elm wood, after being cut and stored for firewood, will release a crop of fungus-carrying beetles unless burned before spring. It is the adult beetles, emerging from hibernation to feed in late April and May, that transmit Dutch elm disease. New York entomologists have learned by experience what kinds of beetle-breeding material have real importance in the spread of the disease. By concentrating on this dangerous material, it has been possible not only to get good results, but to keep the cost of the sanitation program within reasonable limits. By 1950 the incidence of Dutch elm disease in New York City had been reduced to $\frac{2}{10}$ of 1 per cent of the city's 55,000 elms. A sanitation program was launched in Westchester County in 1942. During the next 14 years the average annual loss of elms was only $2/10$ of 1 per cent a year. Buffalo, with 185,000 elms, has an excellent record of containing the disease by sanitation, with recent annual losses amounting to only $3/10$ of 1 per cent. In other words, at this rate of loss it would take about 300 years to eliminate Buffalo's elms.

What has happened in Syracuse is especially impressive. There no effective program was in operation before 1957. Between 1951 and 1956 Syracuse lost nearly 3000 elms. Then, under the direction of Howard C. Miller of the New York State University College of Forestry, an intensive drive was made to remove all diseased elm trees and all possible sources of beetle-breeding elm wood. The rate of loss is now well below 1 per cent a year.

The economy of the sanitation method is stressed by New York experts in Dutch elm disease control. "In most cases the actual expense is small compared with the probable saving," says J. G. Matthysse of the New York State College of Agriculture. "If it is a case of a dead or broken limb, the limb would have to be removed eventually, as a precaution against possible property damage or personal injury. If it is a fuel-wood pile, the wood can be used before spring, the bark can be peeled from the wood, or the wood can be stored in a dry place. In the case of dying or dead elm trees, the expense of prompt removal to prevent Dutch elm disease spread is usually no greater than would be necessary later, for most dead trees in urban regions must be removed eventually."

The situation with regard to Dutch elm disease is therefore not entirely hopeless provided informed and intelligent measures are taken. While it cannot be eradicated by any means now known, once it has become established in a community, it can be suppressed and contained within reasonable bounds by sanitation, and without the use of methods that are not only futile but involve tragic destruction of bird life. Other possibilities lie within the field of forest genetics, where experiments offer hope of developing a hybrid elm resistant to Dutch elm disease. The European elm is highly resistant, and many of them have been planted in Washington, D.C. Even during a period when a high percentage of the city's elms were affected, no cases of Dutch elm disease were found among these trees.

Replanting through an immediate tree nursery and forestry program is being urged in communities that are losing large numbers of elms. This is important, and although such programs might well include the resistant European elms, they should aim at a variety of species so that no future epidemic could deprive a community of its trees. The key to a healthy plant or animal community lies in what the British ecologist Charles Elton calls "the conservation of variety." What is happening now is in large part a result of the biological unsophistication of past generations. Even a generation ago no one knew that to fill large areas with a single species of tree was to invite disaster. And so whole towns lined their streets and dotted their parks with elms, and today the elms die and so do the birds.

LIST OF PRINCIPAL SOURCES

Page 104 [here, pp. 333–334]
  Audubon Field Notes. "Fall Migration—Aug. 16 to Nov. 30, 1958." Vol. 13 (1959), No. 1, pp. 1–68.
Page 105 [pp. 334–335]
  Swingle, R. U., et al., "Dutch Elm Disease," *Yearbook of Agric.*, U.S. Dept. of Agric., 1949, pp. 451–52.
Page 106 [p. 335]
  Mehner, John F., and George J. Wallace, "Robin Populations and Insecticides," *Atlantic Naturalist,* Vol. 14 (1959), No. 1, pp. 4–10.
Page 107 [p. 336]
  Wallace, George J., "Insecticides and Birds," *Audubon Mag.,* Jan.–Feb. 1959.
Page 107 [pp. 336–337]
  Barker, Roy J., "Notes on Some Ecological Effects of DDT Sprayed on Elms," *Jour. Wildlife Management,* Vol. 22 (1958), No. 3, pp. 269–74.
Page 107 [pp. 336–337]
  Hickey, Joseph J., and L. Barrie Hunt, "Songbird Mortality Following Annual Programs to Control Dutch Elm Disease," *Atlantic Naturalist,* Vol. 15 (1960), No. 2, pp. 87–92.
Page 108 [p. 337]
  Wallace, "Insecticides and Birds."

Page 108 [p. 337]
Wallace, George J., "Another Year of Robin Losses on a University Campus," *Audubon Mag.*, March–April 1960.

Pages 108–9 [pp. 337–338]
"Coordination of Pesticides Programs," *Hearings*, H.R. 11502, 86th Congress, Com. on Merchant Marine and Fisheries, May 1960, pp. 10, 12.

Page 109 [p. 338]
Hickey, Joseph J., and L. Barrie Hunt, "Initial Songbird Mortality Following a Dutch Elm Disease Control Program," *Jour. Wildlife Management*, Vol. 24 (1960), No. 3, pp. 259–65.

Page 109 [p. 338]
Wallace, George J., et al., *Bird Mortality in the Dutch Elm Disease Program in Michigan*. Cranbrook Inst. of Science Bulletin 41 (1961).

Page 109 [p. 338]
Hickey, Joseph J., "Some Effects of Insecticides on Terrestrial Birdlife," *Report* of Subcom. on Relation of Chemicals to Forestry and Wildlife, State of Wisconsin, Jan. 1961, pp. 2–43.

Page 110 [p. 338]
Walton, W. R., *Earthworms As Pests and Otherwise*. U.S. Dept. of Agric. Farmers' Bulletin No. 1569 (1928).

Page 110 [pp. 338–339]
Wright, Bruce S., "Woodcock Reproduction in DDT-Sprayed Areas of New Brunswick," *Jour. Wildlife Management*, Vol. 24 (1960), No. 4, pp. 419–20.

Page 110 [p. 339]
Dexter, R. W., "Earthworms in the Winter Diet of the Opossum and the Raccoon," *Jour. Mammal.*, Vol. 32 (1951), p. 464.

Page 110 [p. 339]
Wallace et al., *Bird Mortality in the Dutch Elm Disease Program*.

Pages 110–11 [pp. 339–340]
"Coordination of Pesticides Programs." Testimony of George J. Wallace, p. 10.

Pages 111–12 [pp. 340–341]
Wallace, "Insecticides and Birds."

Page 112 [p. 341]
Bent, Arthur C., *Life Histories of North American Jays, Crows, and Titmice*. Smithsonian Inst., U.S. Natl. Museum Bulletin 191 (1946).

Page 112 [p. 341]
MacLellan, C. R., "Woodpecker Control of the Codling Moth in Nova Scotia Orchards," *Atlantic Naturalist*, Vol. 16 (1961), No. 1, pp. 17–25.

Page 113 [p. 341]
Knight, F. B., "The Effects of Woodpeckers on Populations of the Engelmann Spruce Beetle," *Jour. Econ. Entomol.*, Vol. 51 (1958), pp. 603–7.

Page 114 [pp. 342–343]
Carter, J. C., To author, June 16, 1960.

Page 115 [pp. 343–344]
Sweeney, Joseph A., To author, March 7, 1960.

Page 115 [p. 344]

   Welch, D. S., and J. G. Matthysse, *Control of the Dutch Elm Disease in New York State.* New York State College of Agric., Cornell Ext. Bulletin No. 932 (June 1960), pp. 3–16.

Page 116 [pp. 344–345]

   Matthysse, J. G., *An Evaluation of Mist Blowing and Sanitation in Dutch Elm Disease Control Programs.* New York State College of Agric., Cornell Ext. Bulletin No. 30 (July 1959), pp. 2–16.

Page 116 [p. 345]

   Miller, Howard, To author, Jan. 17, 1962.

Pages 116–17 [pp. 345–346]

   Matthysse, *An Evaluation of Mist Blowing and Sanitation.*

Page 117 [p. 346]

   Elton, Charles S., *The Ecology of Invasions by Animals and Plants.* New York: Wiley, 1958.

TWO VIEWS OF INTEGRATION

HODDING CARTER

OUR TOWN IS CONSERVATIVE

Hodding Carter (1907-   ) is the distinguished editor and publisher of the Greenville (Mississippi) Delta Democrat-Times; *in 1946 he won the Pulitzer Prize for editorial writing. Educated at Bowdoin College, he later was a Nieman Fellow in journalism at Harvard. Entering journalism as a reporter for the New Orleans* Item-Tribune, *he was a bureau manager for United Press in New Orleans and for Associated Press in Jackson, Mississippi, before starting his own newspapers, the Hammond (Louisiana)* Daily Courier *and the Greenville (Mississippi)* Delta Star. *Among his books are* The Lower Mississippi *(1942) in the* Rivers of America *series,* Southern Legacy *(1950),* Where Main Street Meets the River *(1953),* Robert E. Lee and the Road of Honor *(1954), and* The Doomed Road of Empire *(1962).*

ON THE NIGHT of January 21, 1965, four men and a woman made in Greenville, Mississippi, my home town for twenty-nine years, a happier contribution to regional history than has been our state's wont in many a year. The woman is the wife of an able ophthalmologist. The men are, respectively, a certified public accountant, an automobile dealer, a dentist, and a lawyer. Four are Mississippi born, one a transplanted Louisianan.

They are the five members of the Greenville Separate School District Board. And what they did that night was to vote to desegregate the public school system voluntarily under a plan acceptable to the federal government and to themselves. No other school board in the Deep South has taken similar action without compulsion. The vote was unanimous. The next day the Mayor and the six members of the City Council endorsed the school board's epochal decision, not because such endorsement

»»» *The Virginia Quarterly Review,* XLI (Spring, 1965), 202-206. Reprinted by permission of *The Virginia Quarterly Review* and Hodding Carter.

was necessary, but as an indication of community approval. So did our state senator and two of our three representatives. That afternoon our newspaper carried comments from a variety of community leaders of both races. All save one approved.

There was no breast-beating, no smug self-adulation, no phony pretense to liberalism as such. The members of the board and the council simply said that our school children should not be deprived of needed federal funds that would be cut off if we failed to act by March 1, and that since compliance with the civil-rights dictates of Congress and the Supreme Court was inevitable anyway, what was the sense of futile defiance?

The Governor of Mississippi, the right Honorable Paul Johnson, Jr., didn't agree then. Neither do most Mississippi politicians. Since then, several other Mississippi school boards have followed Greenville's suit. But the almost universal reaction among the white people of Mississippi is that those damn people in Greenville just have to be different. I don't know if we have to be or not. I do know that we are. Let's look back a little.

Item: Qualified Negroes—and the qualifications are honestly imposed—have been voting in Greenville for twenty years.

Item: Almost as long ago, Greenville added Negroes to its police force.

Item: Our airport and small railroad depot were integrated without incident when Negroes in Jackson, our state capital, were being beaten and arrested for challenging the old taboos.

Item: The voters of Greenville have never given a majority to present Governor Paul Johnson, Jr., or to his father, the late Governor Paul Johnson, to former Governor Ross Barnett or to the late Senator Theodore Bilbo. It gave top-heavy majorities to former Congressman Frank Smith, who, until he was gerrymandered out of his seat when Mississippi lost a Congressman in 1962, was the only member of the state's House delegation who could be listed as an intelligent moderate.

Item: Within the past year Greenville has quietly desegregated its public library and public golf course.

Item: During the "long hot summer" of COFO's student invasion of Mississippi, Greenville was the only major city (47,000) not to have a home bombing, a church burning, a beating or a single harassment arrest.

Item: On the few occasions when the COFO workers formed picket lines, the police turned out in unneeded strength to guarantee their safety. This protection was also afforded when white and Negro students held a mixed dance, probably the most extreme non-violent provocation that can be offered in the Deep South.

Item: Ours was the first daily newspaper in Mississippi which gave the appellation Mrs. to a Negro married woman.

Item: As far as is known, there is no Black Muslim organization in town.

Item: An unofficial steering committe of business and professional men which greatly influences the City Council is prepared to recommend appointment of a Negro to the City Planning Commission and the Council itself is expected to name a Negro to the Park Commission. Except for the school board, these are the most important appointive bodies in our city's government.

These indices are incomplete, but they should suffice to show that Greenville is not Mississippi save geographically.

Most non-Southerners generally observe that it must be very pleasant to live in a liberal Southern community. They are generally surprised when I tell them that our community is not liberal but conservative and that our leaders want to keep it that way. For Greenville is conservative in the best sense of the word. We have traditionally eschewed radicals of the left and of the right. The back of the Ku Klux Klan of the twenties was broken in Greenville and Greenville was the only community in Mississippi in which Klansmen were arrested in 1964 when they sought to burn crosses as part of a statewide demonstration of strength. The Citizens' Council never really got off the ground in Greenville, despite its support by a number of good citizens. I don't believe that we can boast a John Birch society. We did give Barry Goldwater a majority, though not by the statewide tally of eight to one.

How does this add up to conservatism? Here's how: We are trying to conserve for the present generation and the future ones something that was given to us by some uncommonly gentle people, a landed aristocracy whose leaders took seriously—as many of their nearby fellow planters and townsmen did not—an old patriarchal concept of *noblesse oblige,* which at its best can almost make tolerable the intolerable by tincturing a hapless feudal relationship of master and man with a common respect and, on the master's part, a sense of duty toward the chattel and the chattel's considerably freer son. *Noblesse oblige* in the lower Mississippi Valley, as elsewhere where it may persist, also entails a sense of personal responsibility for keeping alive the best that has been handed down, including commitment to a goal of civic decency and responsibility and an unashamedly sentimental pride not so much for the past as for the men who left certain legacies that have nothing to do with money. And since it is at least as difficult to live up to a good past as to live down a bad one, many of us in Greenville are kept right busy.

Enough of generalization. It may be useful now to reflect on what it takes specifically to keep a conservative town conservative minded and so keep alive the sense of civic decency and responsibility which I am certain Greenville has to a far greater extent than any other Deep Southern town of comparable or greater population.

Obviously, the answer is the people themselves, the actions of the city fathers whom they elect, the public servants whom these city fathers appoint, the attention given to these public figures by the community newspaper, and the kind of spiritual leadership to be found in the churches.

What I write now is not Chamber of Commerce braggadocio nor is it written in foolish optimism. But for the nearly thirty years we have published our newspaper in Greenville a majority of the voters have shown an almost uncanny talent for electing most of the time the best candidates for the City Council. I am certain the Negro voter has helped here. Not in all these years has any evidence of corruption been uncovered. On the positive side, the appointed municipal judges and police chiefs have been incorrupt and have proven that justice can be evenhanded and color blind. Of the two judges who have sat during these years one is an Irish-American Catholic, the other a Jew, which in an overwhelmingly Protestant community also may be an indication of a conservatism which seeks to rule out religious bias in public affairs. The three police chiefs who have served during the past three decades have been career police officers and each is a graduate of the FBI police academy. They have permitted neither non-racial nor racial sadism in the police force they have led.

As for other Council-appointed groups or individuals, the caliber of the school board is reflected not only in its decision to submit a desegregation plan, but by the unusual fact, indicative of public confidence, that not a single proposal for new school buildings for the children of either race has failed to receive more than a majority of the votes in the required bond elections. Consequently, we have no sub-standard school buildings, which is more than New York can say.

Since the Greenville newspaper is ours, I will say no more than that it has supported every proposal, decision, or performance by public officials, civic groups, and individuals which we thought to be for the civic good.

This leaves the ministers. I wish I could say that they were in the active forefront in facing the problems of racial readjustments. Only the Roman Catholic church and the Episcopal church have admitted Negro worshipers, the one since its establishment in Greenville, the other in recent months. In Greenville the clergy are largely silent in the face of the most difficult domestic issue of our time, an issue that will never be solved until its spiritual aspects have been made known from the pulpit.

I have already said that we are not possessed of foolish optimism. We are a long way from doing all that we should and must do. The Negro knows this and today he is saying so loudly. And while the outcry is understandable, it adds to the difficulty of maintaining conservative leadership in each race. Whether we can remain a conservative community I don't know. The new-comers attracted to Greenville by our needed industrial development are mostly not in the tradition of *noblesse oblige*. A contest may come sooner than I think. And as the unmollified Mississippi Negroes press for more, the going will be tough. And unless more Mississippi towns stand beside us, the going will be tougher still.

MARTIN LUTHER KING, JR.

"LET JUSTICE ROLL DOWN"

Martin Luther King, Jr. (1929-   ), American clergyman, was born in Atlanta and educated at Morehouse College, Crozer Theological Seminary, and Boston University. He is president of the Southern Christian Leadership Conference and won the Nobel Prize for Peace in 1964 for his work in the civil rights movement among Negroes in the South. In his books Stride Toward Freedom *(1958) and* Why We Can't Wait *(1964) and in the following article, his fifth annual report on civil rights in* The Nation, *he discusses the progress and problems of the civil rights movement.*

WHEN 1963 CAME to a close, more than a few skeptical voices asked what substantial progress had been achieved through the demonstrations that had drawn more than a million Negroes into the streets. By the close of 1964, the pessimistic clamor was stilled by the music of major victories. Taken together, the two years marked a historic turning point for the civil rights movement; in the previous century no comparable change for the Negro had occurred. Now, even the most cynical acknowledged that at Birmingham, as at Concord, a shot had been fired that was heard around the world.

Before examining 1964 in greater depth, some comment is necessary on the events currently unfolding in Alabama. After the passage of the Civil Rights Act, and with the defeat of Barry Goldwater, there was widespread expectation that barriers would disintegrate with swift inevitability. This easy optimism could not survive the first test. In the hard-core states of the South, while some few were disposed to accommodate, the walls remained erect and reinforced. That was to be expected, for the basic institutions of government, commerce, industry and social patterns in the South all rest upon the embedded institution of segregation. Change is not accomplished by peeling off super-

»»» *The Nation*, CC (March 15, 1965), 269-274. Reprinted by permission of *The Nation* and Martin Luther King, Jr.

ficial layers when the causes are rooted deeply in the heart of the organism.

Those who expected a cheap victory in a climate of complacency were shocked into reality by Selma and Marion, Ala. In Selma, the position was implacable resistance. At one point, ten times as many Negroes were in jail as were on the registration rolls. Out of 15,000 eligible to vote, less than 350 were registered.

Selma involves more than disenfranchisement. Its inner texture reveals overt and covert forms of terror and intimidation—that uniquely Southern form of existence for Negroes in which life is a constant state of acute defensiveness and deprivation. Yet if Selma outrages democratic sensibilities, neighboring Wilcox County offers something infinitely worse. Sheriff P. C. Jenkins has held office in Wilcox for twenty-six years. He is a local legend because when he wants a Negro for a crime, he merely sends out word and the Negro comes in to be arrested. This is intimidation and degradation reminiscent only of chattel slavery. This is white supremacist arrogance and Negro servility possible only in an atmosphere where the Negro feels himself so isolated, so hopeless, that he is stripped of all dignity. And as if they were in competition to obliterate the United States Constitution within Alabama's borders, state troopers only a few miles away clubbed and shot Negro demonstrators in Marion.

Are demonstrations of any use, some ask, when resistance is so unyielding? Would the slower processes of legislation and law enforcement ultimately accomplish greater results more painlessly? Demonstrations, experience has shown, are part of the process of stimulating legislation and law enforcement. The federal government reacts to events more quickly when a situation of conflict cries out for its intervention. Beyond this, demonstrations have a creative effect on the social and psychological climate that is not matched by the legislative process. Those who have lived under the corrosive humiliation of daily intimidation are imbued by demonstrations with a sense of courage and dignity that strengthens their personalities. Through demonstrations, Negroes learn that unity and militance have more force than bullets. They find that the bruises of clubs, electric cattle prods and fists hurt less than the scars of submission. And segregationists learn from demonstrations that Negroes who have been taught to fear can also be taught to be fearless. Finally, the millions of Americans on the side lines learn that inhumanity wears an official badge and wields the power of law in large areas of the democratic nation of their pride.

In addition to these ethical and psychological considerations, our work in the black-belt counties of Alabama has enabled us to develop further a tactical pattern whose roots extend back to Birmingham and Montgomery. Our movement has from the earliest days of SCLC adhered to a method which uses non-violence in a special fashion. We have consistently operated on the basis of total community involvement. It is manifestly easier to initiate actions with a handful of dedicated supporters, but we have sought to make activists of all our people, rather than draw some activists from the mass.

Our militant elements were used, not as small striking detachments, but to organize. Through them, and by patient effort, we have attempted to involve Negroes from industry, the land, the home, the professions; Negroes of advanced age, middle age, youth and the very young. In Birmingham, Montgomery, Selma, St. Augustine and elsewhere, when we marched it was as a community, not as a small and unimpressive, if symbolic, assemblage. The charge that we were outside agitators, devoid of support from contented local Negroes, could not be convincing when the procession of familiar local faces could be seen block after block in solid array.

The second element in our tactics after Montgomery was to formulate demands that covered varied aspects of Negro life. If voting campaigns or lunch-counter sit-ins appeared central in press reports, they were but a part of our broader aims. In Birmingham, employment opportunities was a demand pressed as forcefully as desegregation of public facilities. In Selma, our four points encompass voting rights, employment opportunities, improved interracial communication and paved streets in the

Negro neighborhoods. The last demand may appear to Northerners to lack some of the historic importance of voting rights. To the Southern Negro the fact that anyone can identify where the ghetto begins by noting where the pavement ends is one of the many offensive experiences in his life. The neighborhood is degraded to degrade the person in it.

We have found that when we make a package of our demands, our goals are clarified and victory becomes easier. This has not meant that we would refuse to recognize partial gains or to call a pause when we had made significant progress. Taking a leaf from the trade unions, we have accepted less than full victory, knowing that a degree of success is a foundation from which later struggles can be launched for additional gains.

We have come to believe that the combining of concrete demands, flexibly handled, with mass community involvement, all conducted with nonviolent direct action is the formula for accomplishment in the South. The widespread public interest and sympathy we receive are less a tribute to outstanding personalities than a response to the deeper attraction of a whole people on the move for realizable objectives.

Some may wonder whether the continued turmoil in 1965 implies that the gains of 1963-64 were illusory. Not so. We have already scored victories in the black belt which would have seemed foolish dreams a few years back. Violence has been controlled, though not eliminated.

What did we accomplish in 1963-64 specifically and where will it take us?

The Civil Rights Act of 1964 is important even beyond its far-reaching provisions. It is historic because its enactment was generated by a massive coalition of white and Negro forces. Congress was aroused by them from a century of slumber to a legislative achievement of rare quality. These multitudinous sponsors to its enactment explain why sections of the Act were complied with so hastily even in some hard-core centers of the South.

The Mississippi Summer Project of the combined civil rights organizations was accorded the traditional Mississippi welcome of murder, arson and terror, and persisted under fire until even the Klan recognized that its sanctuary had been overrun. The isolated Negroes of that state were drawn into the vibrant national struggle. To mark their new status they formed a political party whose voice was heard loudly and clearly at the Democratic National Convention and in the Congress.

But perhaps the most significant development of 1963 and 1964 was the emergence of a disciplined, perceptive Negro electorate, almost 100 per cent larger than that of the 1960 Presidential election. Mississippi, the Civil Rights Act, and the new massive Negro vote each represents a particular form of struggle; nevertheless, they are interrelated. Together, they signify the new ability of the movement to function simultaneously in varied arenas, and with varied methods.

Each accomplishment was the culmination of long years of ache and agony. The new Negro vote best illustrates this point. Quietly, without the blare of trumpets, without marching legions to excite the spirit, thousands of patient, persistent Negroes worked day in and day out, laboriously adding one name to another in the registration books. Finally on November 7, in an electoral confrontation vitally important to their existence, they displayed the power which had long been accumulating. On the following day every political expert knew that a mature and permanent Negro electorate had emerged. A powerful, unified political force had come into being.

Goldwater had sneered at the Negro and fawned on the segregationists, confident that thus he would establish a viable Republican Party throughout the South. When the votes were counted, Florida, Tennessee and Virginia, which had been Republican since 1948, shifted to the Democrats by the margin provided by the Negro vote. In other Southern states the Negro vote either won for Johnson or narrowed the Goldwater victory to razor-thin proportions. The inevitable growth merely of the Negro vote gives assurance that the victories of Goldwater's adherents, few as they are, have a short life expectancy.

Aside from its numerical triumph, the Negro electorate demonstrated a capacity for cool, intelligent selection. Aware that President Johnson had kept faith, they awarded him an astounding 95 per cent of their total in a manifestation of unity and discipline unique in political history. Even an absurd last-minute maneuver to split the vote by urging Negroes to write in my name for President proved a dismal failure.

Another proof of the Negro electorate's maturity was its response to the call of Negro leaders to turn away from other forms of action during the campaign. We asked the Negro voter to make his ballot the primary weapon of the hour. He not only responded with discipline but became a vigorous community mobilizer in electoral campaigns, North and South. In 1963, we found the Negro ready to take to the streets in the millions to demonstrate; in 1964, he was equally alert and energetic in ringing doorbells to swell the landslide that was destined to give reaction its most stunning rebuke since the days of Franklin Roosevelt.

While elsewhere electioneering was being conducted systematically, another detachment was assaulting the fortress walls of Mississippi, long immune to the discipline of justice. As the confrontation boiled and seethed even in remote rural counties, the revulsion of decent Americans mounted. The wanton burning of churches, the inexpressibly cruel murder of young civil rights workers, not only failed to paralyze the movement; they became a grisly and eloquent demonstration to the whole nation of the moral degeneracy upon which segregation rests.

The Civil Rights Act was expected by many to suffer the fate of the Supreme Court decisions on school desegregation. In particular, it was thought that the issue of public accommodations would encounter massive defiance. But this pessimism overlooked a factor of supreme importance. The legislation was not a product of charity of white America for a supine black America, nor was it the result of enlightened leadership by the judiciary. This legislation was first written in the streets. The epic thrust of the millions of Negroes who demonstrated in 1963 in hundreds of cities won strong white allies to the cause. Together, they created a "coalition of conscience" which awoke a hitherto somnolent Congress. The legislation was polished and refined in the marble halls of Congress, but the vivid marks of its origins in the turmoil of mass meetings and marches were on it, and the vigor and momentum of its turbulent birth carried past the voting and insured substantial compliance.

Apart from its own provisions, the new law stimulated and focused attention on economic needs. An assault on poverty was planned in 1964, and given preliminary and experimental shape.

The fusing of economic measures with civil rights needs; the boldness to penetrate every region of the Old South; the undergirding of the whole by the massive Negro vote, both North and South, all place the freedom struggle on a new elevated level.

The old tasks of awakening the Negro to motion while educating America to the miseries of Negro poverty and humiliation in their manifold forms have substantially been accomplished. Demonstrations may be limited in the future, but contrary to some belief, they will not be abandoned. Demonstrations educate the onlooker as well as the participant, and education requires repetition. That is one reason why they have not outlived their usefulness. Furthermore, it would be false optimism to expect ready compliance to the new law everywhere. The Negro's weapon of nonviolent direct action is his only serviceable tool against injustice. He may be willing to sheath that sword but he has learned the wisdom of keeping it sharp.

Yet new times call for new policies. Negro leadership, long attuned to agitation, must now perfect the art of organization. The movement needs stable and responsible institutions in the communities to utilize the new strength of Negroes in altering social customs. In their furious combat to level walls of segregation and discrimination, Negroes gave primary emphasis to their deprivation of dignity and personality. Having gained a measure of success they are now revealed to be clothed, by comparison with other Americans, in rags. They are housed in decaying ghettos and provided with a ghetto education to eke out a ghetto life. Thus, they are automatically enlisted in the war on poverty as the most eligible combatants. Only when they are in full possession of their civil rights everywhere, and afforded equal economic opportunity, will the haunting race question finally be laid to rest.

What are the key guides to the future? It would not be overoptimistic to eliminate one of the vain hopes of the segregationists—the white backlash. It had a certain reality in 1964, but far less than the segregationists needed. For the most part it was powered by petulance rather than principle. Therefore, when the American people saw before them a clear choice between a future of progress with racial justice or stagnation with ancient privilege, they voted in landslide proportions for justice. President Johnson made a creative contribution by declining to mute this issue in the campaign.

The election of President Johnson, whatever else it might have been, was also an alliance of Negro and white for common interests. Perceptive Negro leadership understands that each of the major accomplishments in 1964 was the product of Negro militancy *on a level that could mobilize and maintain white support.* Negroes acting alone and in a hostile posture toward all whites will do nothing more than demonstrate that their conditions of life are unendurable, and that they are unbearably angry. But this has already been widely dramatized. On the other hand, whites who insist upon exclusively determining the time schedule of change will also fail, however wise and generous they feel themselves to be. A genuine Negro-white unity is the tactical foundation upon which past and future progress depends.

The rapid acceleration of change in race relations in the nation is occurring within the larger transformation of our political and economic structure. The South is already a split region, fissured politically and economically as cleanly as the Mississippi River divides its banks. Negroes by themselves did not fragment the South; they facilitated a process that the changing economy of

the nation began. The old rural South, essentially poor and re-
tarded, had to industrialize as agricultural regions contracted
under the impact of heightened soil productivity. The exodus
from Southern farms coincided with the influx of industry seeking the natural resources and cheaper labor market of the area.

The new industry introduced modern methods of production
in order to compete with the North as well as with the flood of
imports, especially those from Germany and Japan. In the altering of job patterns, a new kind of white worker and manager
emerged, the more sophisticated skills requiring a cultural and
social milieu entirely inconsistent with the tobacco-road society
of the past. A new South was born with powerful potentiality
for growth and influence.

Negroes were drawn off the farms into urban service and into
limited, semi-skilled occupations. Though many migrated North,
most remained in the South. Just as they had not been content
to erode with the old plantations, they were not disposed to take
a permanent place as industrial untouchables. The ferment of
revolutionary change by the backward and dispossessed peoples
of the whole world inspired them to struggle. In some areas, economic and social change enabled them to advance against an
opposition that was still formidable but of a different quality
than that of the past. The new South, with its local needs and
with an eye to its national image, could not adhere to the brutal,
terroristic overseer psychology of bygone days. For these reasons Atlanta, Savannah and some cities of Florida are markedly
different from the underdeveloped belts of Mississippi, Louisiana
and Alabama.

When the Negro devised the new weapon of nonviolent direct
action he was, paradoxically, building a bridge to the new South.
It gave him the capacity to impede development of the new
economy without using violence or acting with the motivation
of revenge. The new Southern power elite, already struggling
with the old plantation aristocracy, had to choose between some
alteration of social patterns or stagnation and dislocation.

Hence, in different places and with different approaches, the Negro Freedom Movement found some forces they could negotiate with, and who objectively became allies—usually reluctant, unstable and fearful, but allies, nevertheless—in forcing change.

In the next period, Negroes are likely to find new white Southern allies of even greater importance among the rural and urban poor. It is an irony of American history that Negroes have been oppressed and subjected to discrimination by many whose economic circumstances were scarcely better than their own. The social advantages which softened the economic disabilities of Southern poor whites are now beginning to lose some of their attractions as these whites realize what material benefits are escaping them. The section of the Civil Rights Act of 1964 which withholds federal aid when it is used discriminatorily in federally assisted programs has revolutionary implications. It ties the interests of whites who desperately need relief from their impoverishment to the Negro who has the same needs. The barriers of segregation are splintering under the strain of economic deprivation which cuts across caste lines. To climb the economic ladder, Negro and white will have to steady it together, or both will fall.

The intense yearning in contemporary society for material goods will inexorably act as pressure on the poor white to moderate his bias. The operation of these interacting forces is at an early stage, but it is real. Many poor whites who are still mired in prejudice voted for the same candidate as had the Negro. They could participate in a *de facto* alliance in the privacy of the polling booth. However, when the votes were counted, the reality of this alliance became evident, and before long the open secret will have to be frankly acknowledged.

This is already occurring among many who have run for office in different areas of the South. Many old-line political leaders have been contending for office. The faces were the same as of old, but looking closely, one could see that some of the features had changed. Especially, the language had changed: "Negro," not "darky"; "the law of the land," not "States' rights"; the "new prosperity and affluence," not the "old Southern traditions." These new phrases may be uttered with many private agonies, but their commitments are public.

Space does not permit a sufficient discussion of the President's program, nor is it yet adequately elaborated. But without wishing to diminish the high respect which the President earned from the civil rights movement, one aspect of his program should be studied, if only because of the emphasis he has given it. The President's concept of consensus must be subject to thoughtful and critical examination. *The New York Times* in a perceptive editorial on December 20 asked if Mr. Johnson really means to be a "consensus President." It pointed out that such were Coolidge and Eisenhower, who "served the needs of the day but not of decades to come. They preside over periods of rest and consolidation. They lead no probes into the future and break no fresh ground." The *Times* then added, "A President who wants to get things done has to be a fighter, has to spend the valuable coin of his own popularity, has to jar the existing consensus. . . . No major program gets going unless someone is willing to wage an active and often fierce struggle in its behalf."

The *Times* is undeniably correct. The fluidity and instability of American public opinion on questions of social change is very marked. There would have been no civil rights progress, nor a nuclear test-ban treaty, without resolute Presidential leadership. The issues which must be decided are momentous. The contest is not tranquil and relaxed. The search for a consensus will tend to become a quest for the least common denominator of change. In an atmosphere devoid of urgency the American people can easily be stupefied into accepting slow reform, which in practice would be inadequate reform. "Let Justice roll down like waters in a mighty stream," said the Prophet Amos. He was seeking not consensus but the cleansing action of revolutionary change. America has made progress toward freedom, but measured against the goal the road ahead is still long and hard. This could be the worst possible moment for slowing down.

A consensus orientation is understandably attractive to a political leader. His task is measurably easier if he is merely to give shape to widely accepted programs. He becomes a technician rather than an innovator. Past Presidents have often sought such a function. President Kennedy promised in his campaign an executive order banning discrimination in housing. This substantial progressive step, he declared, required only "a stroke of the pen." Nevertheless, he delayed execution of the order long after his election on the ground that he awaited a "national consensus." President Roosevelt, facing the holocaust of an economic crisis in the early thirties, attempted to base himself on a consensus with the N.R.A.; and generations earlier, Abraham Lincoln temporized and hesitated through years of civil war, seeking a consensus before issuing the Emancipation Proclamation.

In the end, however, none of these Presidents fashioned the program which was to mark him as historically great by patiently awaiting a consensus. Instead, each was propelled into action by a mass movement which did not necessarily reflect an overwhelming majority. What the movement lacked in support was less significant than the fact that it had championed the key issue of the hour. President Kennedy was forced by Birmingham and the tumultuous actions it stimulated to offer to Congress the Civil Rights Bill. Roosevelt was impelled by labor, farmers and small businessmen to commit the government in revolutionary depth to social welfare as a constituent stimulus to the economy. Lincoln signed the Emancipation Proclamation under the pressure of war needs. *The overwhelming national consensus followed their acts; it did not precede them.*

The contemporary civil rights movement must serve President Johnson in the same fashion. It must select from the multitude of issues those principal creative reforms which will have broad transforming power to affect the whole movement of society. Behind these goals it must then tirelessly organize widespread struggle. The specific selection of the correct and appropriate programs requires considerable discussion and is beyond the purview of this study. A few guidelines are, however, immediately evident.

One point of central importance for this period is that the distribution of Negroes geographically makes a single national tactical program impractical. During the Civil War, Frederick Douglass perceived the difference in problems of Negroes in the North and in the South. He championed emancipation, aside from its moral imperatives, because its impact would transform the South. For the North, his principal demand was integration of Negroes into the Union Army.

Similarly today, the Negro of the South requires in the first place the opportunity to exercise elementary rights and to be shielded from terror and oppression by reliable, alert government protection. He should not have to stake his life, his home or his security merely to enjoy the right to vote. On the other hand, in the North, he already has many basic rights and a fair measure of state protection. There, his quest is toward a more significant participation in government, and the restructuring of his economic life to end ghetto existence.

Very different tactics will be required to achieve these disparate goals. Many of the mistakes made by Northern movements may be traced to the application of tactics that work in Birmingham but produce no results in Northern ghettos. Demonstrations in the streets of the South reveal the cruel fascism underlacing the social order there. No such result attends a similar effort in the North. However, rent strikes, school boycotts, electoral alliances summon substantial support from Negroes, and dramatize the specific grievances peculiar to those communities.

With the maturation of the civil rights movement, growing out of the struggles of 1963 and 1964, new tactical devices will emerge. The most important single imperative is that we continue moving forward with the indomitable spirit of those two turbulent years. It is worth recalling the admonition of Napoleon (he was thinking of conquest, but what he said was true also of constructive movements): "In order to have good soldiers, a nation must always be at war."

TWO VIEWS OF GRAMMAR

WILSON FOLLETT

BARGAIN BASEMENT ENGLISH

Wilson Follett (1887-1963), a native of Massachusetts, was educated at Harvard. He was for many years a publishers' reader, and he wrote books on Joseph Conrad and other novelists and edited The Work of Stephen Crane *(12 volumes, 1925–1927). His work as reader and editor left him, he once said, with "an acute distaste for slovenly writing." This distaste provoked him to write essays like "Bargain Basement English" that plead—not for what is permissible or endurable usage, not for what will "do at a pinch"—but for good usage.*

LINGUISTIC SCHOLARSHIP, once an encouragement to the most exacting definitions and standards of workmanship, has for some time been dedicating itself to the abolition of standards; and the new rhetoric evolved under its auspices is an organized assumption that language good enough for anybody is good enough for everybody. We have come into a time when the ideals preached and, sometimes, practiced by exalted authority can only take shape in uses of English that are at best tolerable and at worst revolting. Such official pressure as is now put on the young learner is no longer in the direction of forcing him to ask himself whether his way of saying something could have been made better at a bearable cost—as, in a language so rich and various as ours, it generally could have. Everything now taught him concentrates on the lowly question, Will it do at a pinch?

For the handiest possible conspectus of what the new ideal is, one can do no better than to glance at a recent comprehensive manual of rhetorical practice. *A Dictionary of Contemporary*

»»» *Atlantic Monthly,* CCV (February, 1960), 73-76. Reprinted by permission of Wilson Follett. (Originally published in the *Atlantic Monthly* under the title "Grammar Is Obsolete.")

American Usage, by Bergen Evans and Cornelia Evans, comes from authors of prestige and influence, one of them a university professor of English and conductor of a radio and television program devoted to questions of spoken and written usage, the other a writing consultant in the Department of Health, Education, and Welfare and a prize-winning novelist. The reason for turning to this 570-page, 600,000-word volume is not that its publisher proclaims it to be "up-to-date, complete, authoritative" —an assertion of three attributes inherently unattainable by any such work compiled by mortals—but rather that it is declared with strict accuracy to be "based on modern linguistic scholarship." It is essentially a popularization of findings about modern English arrived at and promulgated by contemporary philologists, semanticists, virtuosos of historical and descriptive (as opposed to prescriptive) grammar and morphophonetics, and learnedly implacable assailants of the discarded idea that to speak or write well means hard work, the taking of sometimes painful thought, the constant rejection of labor- and thought-saving alternatives, and the practice of canons that are mastered only by arduous self-cultivation and discipline.

The Evanses manage to convey, along with many shrewd discriminations and salutary warnings often very engagingly phrased, an overall impression that acceptable usages are arrived at by a process about as automatic as breathing; that to torment oneself with questions of better and not so good is to be a seeker after gratuitous trouble and, what is worse, a purist; and that the way to attain effective expression is to keep our ears open, bank on our natural and inescapable linguistic inheritance, and cultivate an English that will make us indistinguishable from the ostensibly educated surrounding majority. Let us see where anyone will come out if he accepts and applies the combination of what these authors recommend, what they defend or condone, and what they do themselves. He will come out speaking and writing an American English faithfully represented by the scattering that follows:

"Ask whoever you see." "He had as much or more trouble than I did." "He works faster than me"; "he is taller than me." "More unique." "Different than." "The reason is because. . . ." "I can't imagine it being him." "Let's you and I"; "let's you and me." "Bob as well as Frank were there." "Neither D. nor A. are at home"; "neither he nor I are timid"; "either of them are enough to drive a man to distraction"; "neither of them had their tickets"; "I do not think either of them are at home"; "each carried their own pack"; "each of the men were willing to contribute." "Every member brings their own lunch"; "either the boy or the girl left their book." "I cannot help but think." "Nobody was killed, were they?" "Less than three." "If one loses his temper." "We did not find a one." "The sheriff with all his men were at the door." "Not one of them were listening." "Some grammarians claim that this is not permissible." "He allowed that we were right." "Refer back to." "Back of" (behind). "Between each house"; "between every pause." "He blamed it on me." "I haven't but a minute to spare." "I don't doubt but that you are surprised." "Who did you see?" "Who are you looking for?" "Children whom we know are hungry." "Everyplace"; "anyplace"; "someplace"; "someway"; "noplace"; "I have looked everyplace." "It is not I who is angry." "These kind of men are dangerous." "You don't know Nellie like I do." "It is you who will be blamed for it, not them." "That's her at the door now." "A minimum of sufficiency." "We most always go shopping on Saturday." "Very amused." "Overly cautious." "Datas"; "phenomenas"; "much data"; "very little data"; "the data is now in." "I asked him what was he doing." "The rationale for his attack on the President." "As regards." "Somebody left their umbrella." "I will get one someway." "There will only be him left." "Subsequent to his release from the Air Force he got a job with a commercial air line." "A continuous use [of a word in a specified way] is vulgar." "He went no further than Philadelphia." "Neither of these reasons justify the use of the present tense." "He failed, due to carelessness."

This little anthology could be several times multiplied from the same source; thus much will do to imply a general pattern. Some of the specimens are patently better, or less bad, than others. Say of the whole, if you wish: "Some of it might be worse." There is no point in using a microscope on the gradations or on the merits of the arguments used to defend this locution or that. It is enough if we perceive—as we cannot very well escape doing—that collectively they define a stratum of diction that invites defense and seems to require it, one that it is now fashionable to defend with all the resources of specialized learning. No one could possibly contemplate any such handful and then declare its components above challenge and in no need of condoning; no one could associate them with an unremitting effort to discover and to utilize the best that our common language is capable of. A collection of the same size could hardly vary much from this one if it deliberately set out to specialize in the marginal, the dubious, the suspect. What it seems to represent is the pattern of habits deliberately adopted by the educated when they set out to show that they are no better than anyone else, if as good. It goes to show the lengths to which we can carry conformism and the terror of being noticeable in a society that is (as Bierce said of the republic long before H. L. Mencken was heard of) daft with democracy and sick with sin.

If anyone wanted to execute a piece of writing that would be from beginning to end the densest possible concentration of what the elder rhetoricians classified as solecisms, he could hardly do better than to attune his prose to the dicta laid down in *A Dictionary of Contemporary American Usage*. The book is an astute, artful, and tireless harvesting of whatever in American speech is barely tolerable to those who do not make a virtue of pushing either tolerance or intolerance to pathological extremes. And it is a translation into practical advice of what the most erudite philologists and lexicographers have for some time been telling us about the sources of health and vitality in our language. The great nuclear principle seems to be that we should speak and write not as well as we can learn how, but ignobly enough to escape notice.

Now, a resort to this kind of first aid may result in some tactical advantage to the purveyor of insurance or real estate, the chairman of a fund-raising campaign, the soapbox orator, the candidate for minor office. Even that advantage can be doubted: there seems to be a fairly powerful undertow of envious popular respect for the man who uses language with easy distinction, provided that he does it in quiet assurance with no air of showing off or of spitting on his hearers to see if they can swim, as the rude old Yankee folk saying has it. An instance is the standing that ex-Governor Adlai Stevenson seems to have with all classes of his fellow countrymen, whether they applaud his political opinions or not. But whatever the practical momentary advantages of slovenly diction, what is its long-range bearing on education, on the language itself, on its literature? Will, say, two or three consecutive generations of calculated effort to speak and write without excellence enhance the prospect of our producing an Irving, a Hawthorne, a Melville, a Henry James, a Howells, a Sarah Orne Jewett, a Willa Cather? Or will it tend to blight that prospect? Did the virtue of English prose, from Sir Thomas Browne and the King James translators to Bernard Shaw, come out of the acceptance of language on the permissive or lowest-common-denominator basis—out of a preoccupation with what was tolerable, what could barely be endured in default of better?

Is it not one of the shames of modern scholarship that it has so little to say for what is really good, what is best, and so much to say for what is merely allowable or defensible? Scholarship is trying, of course, to discount the factor of taste as nonscientific; but is it scientific to discount it? Taste is the faculty of criticism, the faculty of intelligent choice; and to it belongs the last word about any given use of language. After all, the argument from usage carries only a permissive force, not a mandatory one. Even if it were possible to prove an overwhelming preponderance for "He failed, due to carelessness" and "You don't know Nellie like I do," the proof could mean only that one may use these expressions without being condemned. There would be nothing to say that anyone has to use them, and all of us would still have the freedom of "His failure was due to carelessness" or "Carelessness caused him to fail" and "You don't know Nellie as I do" or "the way I do," which will never raise any problems or any eyebrows.

Nobody is under compulsion to like a construction just because it exists or to use it if he does not like it. This is a principle that applies equally to present and to past usages. We have the whole range of linguistic resources at our disposal; and there is no virtue in flirting with ways of expression that we think dubious or inferior when there are alternative ways—as there always are—to which no exception can be taken. The formation of any style, even a bad one, is an affair of constant acceptances and rejections; and everyone has to lean on his own taste for acceptance of the better and rejection of the worse.

The discussion of usage was probably never shrouded in more fog than it is now. Those who want to fling wide the gates to all manner of laxity maintain firmly that change is the great inescapable law, that the only criterion is what people are doing with language *now,* and they can find no words severe enough for resistance to change, especially when resistance takes the form of quoting classic sources; but if they can unearth in Chaucer or Wycliffe or Donne or Hazlitt some parallel to whatever change is being resisted, they cite it as if it settled the matter forever. Whether the use cited was typical or exceptional in that author is a question not raised; it is enough that the passage exists. The Evanses give us a list of twenty authors, Shakespeare to Maugham—a list as easily extended back to Chaucer—who use *like* as a conjunction, but there is no attempt to show that any one of them regularly or even frequently used it so. A dictionary that illustrates a secondary meaning with a quotation may, for all we can tell, be using the only known occurrence of the word in that sense.

The radical, the innovator, the grammatical iconoclast and libertine is ready to beat down all opposition as tradition-bound and ridiculously conservative, but he is equally ready to demonstrate that whatever is objected to has been English for four or five hundred years. Both forms of argument are supposed to be unanswerably crushing. If some locution now current defies a past consensus, so much the worse for the past; but at the same time any locution ever written by a good writer is *ipso facto* attack-proof, and if a precedent can be adduced for anything, however shabby, the case is closed.

Actually not everything ever written by a good writer, or even by quite a number of good writers, is good, any more than everything ever written by a bad writer is bad. Every good writer has committed himself at one time or another to practices without which he would have been a better writer. It is our privilege to pick and choose, alike from the superior and the inferior, alike from the past and the present. For the winnowing of the past we have the guidance of perspective in addition to taste; for the present, taste alone has to suffice. For taste there is no substitute, nor is there any excuse for not using as much of it as we have. The unexpressed excuse that underlies most refusals to use it is the delusive feeling that every demolition of a barrier, old or new, is a freeing of the language from needless restraints and a further emancipation of its users.

What is overlooked is that language and its users grow by restraints, too. Especially in a time when looseness of many kinds is a dominant fashion, it may be salutary to cultivate a tightness and exactitude not customarily demanded. Linguistic resources are expanded not only by the seizing of new liberties as fast as they become available but also by the rejection of liberties that may be only license. A writer is not alone what he writes; he is likewise everything that he will not write because he finds it not good enough, and his power may be as much a function of his renunciations as of his self-indulgences. The libertarians will pity him as self-deprived and call his austerity a crotchet, but he and we are the gainers by his discriminations, and the language may be the loser by the indiscrimination of the loose constructionist.

In no domain is there a clearer illustration of the power of negative choice than in the domain of diction. Good writing has always been marked, and is marked today, by selection of words for their central and not their peripheral meanings. A word, particularly an abstract word, has a core of meaning from which it gradually spreads over associated meanings, perhaps in several directions, until it overlaps words that have likewise spread out from entirely different, possibly remote centers.

The liberalistic view now regnant ranks all such extensions as improvements of language, all as equally good. But the fine writer or speaker is habitually aiming at bull's-eyes, not at general target areas, and he does not care for the idea of shelling the woods with language. His dictionary gives *apparent* as one synonym of *evident,* and vice versa, but he still finds an important kind of integrity in applying *apparent* to the thing that seems to be so whether it is or not and in saving *evident* for that which both seems to be and is so. *Infer* once meant exactly what *imply* means now—it is generally, perhaps always, so used in the seventeenth-century plays of John Ford—but the two words have developed a clear differentiation whereby *imply* goes with the transmitting end and *infer* with the receiving end of the same process of deduction; smoke *implies* fire, but when you smell smoke you *infer* fire. It is a clear loss, not a gain, when we ignore the differentiation in such sentences as these from the best-selling murder story of the decade: "The defense is trying to infer that the prosecution is trying to conceal something." "And surely you do not mean to infer that it would be an unjust verdict if X. were acquitted on the ground of temporary insanity?" *Infer* is being so chronically abused by many who should know better that lexicography no longer quite sees what to do with it, but a decent writer sees, and he is well aware that the widespread confusion makes the English vocabulary not richer, but poorer. True, "language grows," as Greenough and Kittredge said in 1901, "by the felicitous misapplication of words"; but there is no profit to be had out of misapplication per se, without the felicity —a reservation that brings us straight back to the necessity of taste.

The obvious and growing indifference of many publishing houses to hundreds or thousands of such distinctions as those illustrated cannot be called one of the more gladdening signs of the times. No practicing editor of any great competence ever sees a book manuscript for which he could not do appreciable favors if he had a free hand and time, and ninety-nine of any hundred published books could have profited by good offices that they never received. But these phenomena, depressing as they are, seem not quite so shocking as the latter-day hospitality of the very learned to every popular usage that volunteers to make the language more fuzzy, inarticulated, and fumbling.

What steadily preoccupies everyone fit to be called a writer is the possibility of improving everything in his work that is improvable. In no other way can he contribute his much or his little to the effectiveness of language as an instrument of precision combined with power. The linguistic scholarship that impedes and discourages where it might help him is operating beneath its privilege, not to say beneath its obligation. Let those who choose define usage as what a swarm of folk say or write by reason of laziness, shiftlessness, or ignorance; the tenable definition is still what the judicious do as a result of all that they can muster of conscious discrimination. It is time we had a philosophy of usage grounded in the steadfast conviction that the best, whether or not we have it in us to attain it, is not too good to be aspired to.

BERGEN EVANS

GRAMMAR FOR TODAY

*Bergen Evans (1904-   ), professor of English at Northwestern University,
is the author of* The Natural History of Nonsense *(1946) and* The Spoor of
Spooks *(1954), exposés of popular fallacies. Active in radio and television, in
1959 he won the George Foster Peabody award for excellence in radio and
television broadcasting. With his sister Cornelia Evans, he compiled* A
Dictionary of Contemporary American Usage *(1957) upon the principles of
grammar and usage explained in the following essay.*

IN 1747 SAMUEL JOHNSON issued a plan for a new dictionary of
the English language. It was supported by the most distinguished
printers of the day and was dedicated to the model of all correctness, Philip Dormer Stanhope, Fourth Earl of Chesterfield. Such
a book, it was felt, was urgently needed to "fix" the language,
to arrest its "corruption" and "decay," a degenerative process
which, then as now, was attributed to the influence of "the
vulgar" and which, then as now, it was a mark of superiority and
elegance to decry. And Mr. Johnson seemed the man to write it.
He had an enormous knowledge of Latin, deep piety, and
dogmatic convictions. He was also honest and intelligent, but the
effect of these lesser qualifications was not to show until later.

Oblig'd by hunger and request of friends, Mr. Johnson was
willing to assume the role of linguistic dictator. He was prepared
to "fix" the pronunciation of the language, "preserve the purity"
of its idiom, brand "impure" words with a "note of infamy," and
secure the whole "from being overrun by . . . low terms."

There were, however, a few reservations. Mr. Johnson felt it
necessary to warn the oversanguine that "Language is the work
of man, a being from whom permanence and stability cannot be
derived." English "was not formed from heaven . . . but was
produced by necessity and enlarged by accident." It had, indeed,

»»» *Atlantic Monthly,* CCV (March, 1960), 79-82. Reprinted by permission
of Bergen Evans.

been merely "thrown together by negligence" and was in such a state of confusion that its very syntax could no longer "be taught by general rules, but [only] by special precedents."

In 1755 the *Dictionary* appeared. The noble patron had been given a great deal more immortality than he had bargained for by the vigor of the kick Johnson had applied to his backside as he booted him overboard. And the *Plan* had been replaced by the *Preface,* a sadder but very much wiser document.

Eight years of "sluggishly treading the track of the alphabet" had taught Johnson that the hopes of "fixing" the language and preserving its "purity" were but "the dreams of a poet doomed at last to wake a lexicographer." In "the boundless chaos of living speech," so copious and energetic in its disorder, he had found no guides except "experience and analogy." Irregularities were "inherent in the tongue" and could not be "dismissed or reformed" but must be permitted "to remain untouched." "Uniformity must be sacrificed to custom . . . in compliance with a numberless majority" and "general agreement." One of the pet projects of the age had been the establishment of an academy to regulate and improve style. "I hope," Johnson wrote in the *Preface,* that if "it should be established . . . the spirit of English liberty will hinder or destroy [it.]"

At the outset of the work he had flattered himself, he confessed, that he would reform abuses and put a stop to alterations. But he had soon discovered that "sounds are too volatile and subtle for legal restraints" and that "to enchain syllables and to lash the wind are equally undertakings of pride unwilling to measure its desires by its strength." For "the causes of change in language are as much superior to human resistance as the revolutions of the sky or the intumescence of the tide."

There had been an even more profound discovery: that grammarians and lexicographers "do not form, but register the language; do not teach men how they should think, but relate how they have hitherto expressed their thoughts." And with this statement Johnson ushered in the rational study of linguistics. He had entered on his task a medieval pedant. He emerged from it a modern scientist.

Of course his discoveries were not strikingly original. Horace had observed that use was the sole arbiter and norm of speech and Montaigne had said that he who would fight custom with grammar was a fool. Doubtless thousands of other people had at one time or another perceived and said the same thing. But Johnson introduced a new principle. Finding that he could not lay down rules, he gave actual examples to show meaning and form. He offered as authority illustrative quotations, and in so doing established that language is what usage makes it and that custom, in the long run, is the ultimate and only court of appeal in linguistic matters.

This principle, axiomatic today in grammar and lexicography, seems to exasperate a great many laymen who, apparently, find two hundred and five years too short a period in which to grasp a basic idea. They insist that there are absolute standards of correctness in speech and that these standards may be set forth in a few simple rules. To a man, they believe, of course, that they speak and write "correctly" and they are loud in their insistence that others imitate them.

It is useless to argue with such people because they are not, really, interested in language at all. They are interested solely in demonstrating their own superiority. Point out to them—as has been done hundreds of times—that forms which they regard as "corrupt," "incorrect," and "vulgar" have been used by Shakespeare, Milton, and the Bible and are used daily by 180 million Americans and accepted by the best linguists and lexicographers, and they will coolly say, "Well, if they differ from me, they're wrong."

But if usage is not the final determinant of speech, what is? Do the inhabitants of Italy, for example, speak corrupt Latin or good Italian? Is Spanish superior to French? Would the Breton fisherman speak better if he spoke Parisian French? Can one be more fluent in Outer Mongolian than in Inner Mongolian? One has only to ask such questions in relation to languages other than one's own, languages within which our particular snobberies and struggles for prestige have no stake, to see the absurdity of them.

The language that we do speak, if we are to accept the idea of "corruption" and "decay" in language, is a horribly decayed Anglo-Saxon, grotesquely corrupted by Norman French. Furthermore, since Standard English is a development of the London dialect of the fourteenth century, our speech, by true aristocratic standards, is woefully middle-class, commercial, and vulgar. And American speech is lower middle-class, reeking of counter and till. Where else on earth, for instance, would one find crime condemned because it didn't *pay!*

In more innocent days a great deal of time was spent in wondering what was the "original" language of mankind, the one spoken in Eden, the language of which all modern tongues were merely degenerate remnants. Hector Boethius tells us that James I of Scotland was so interested in this problem that he had two children reared with a deaf and dumb nurse on an island in order to see what language they would "naturally" speak. James thought it would be Hebrew, and in time, to his great satisfaction, it was reported that the children were speaking Hebrew!

Despite this experiment, however, few people today regard English as a corruption of Hebrew. But many seem to think it is a corruption of Latin and labor mightily to make it conform to this illusion. It is they and their confused followers who tell us that we can't say "I am mistaken" because translated into Latin this would mean "I am misunderstood," and we can't say "I have enjoyed myself" unless we are egotistical or worse.

It is largely to this group—most of whom couldn't read a line of Latin at sight if their lives depended on it—that we owe our widespread bewilderment concerning *who* and *whom*. In Latin the accusative or dative form would always be used, regardless of the word's position in the sentence, when the pronoun was the object of a verb or a preposition. But in English, for at least four hundred years, this simply hasn't been so. When the pronoun occurs at the beginning of a question, people who speak natural, fluent, literary English use the nominative, regardless. They say "Who did you give it to?" not "Whom did you give it to?" But the semiliterate, intimidated and bewildered, are mouthing such ghastly utterances as a recent headline in a Chicago newspaper: WHOM'S HE KIDDING?

Another group seems to think that in its pure state English was a Laputan tongue, with logic as its guiding principle. Early members of this sect insisted that *unloose* could only mean "to tie up," and present members have compelled the gasoline industry to label its trucks *Flammable* under the disastrous insistence, apparently, that the old *Inflammable* could only mean "not burnable."

It is to them, in league with the Latinists, that we owe the bogy of the double negative. In all Teutonic languages a doubling of the negative merely emphasizes the negation. But we have been told for a century now that two negatives make a positive, though if they do and it's merely a matter of logic, then three negatives should make a negative again. So that if "it doesn't make no difference" is wrong merely because it includes two negatives, then "It doesn't never make no difference" ought to be right again.

Both of these groups, in their theories at least, ignore our idiom. Yet idiom—those expressions which defy all logic but are the very essence of a tongue—plays a large part in English. We go to school and college, but we go to *the* university. We buy two dozen eggs but a couple *of* dozen. *Good and* can mean *very* ("I am good and mad!") and "a hot cup of coffee" means that the coffee, not the cup, is to be hot. It makes a world of difference to a condemned man whether his reprieve is *upheld* or *held up*.

There are thousands of such expressions in English. They are the "irregularities" which Johnson found "inherent in the tongue" and which his wisdom perceived could not and should not be removed. Indeed, it is in the recognition and use of these idioms that skillful use of English lies.

Many words in the form that is now mandatory were originally just mistakes, and many of these mistakes were forced into the language by eager ignoramuses determined to make it conform to some notion of their own. The *s* was put in *island*, for instance, in sheer pedantic ignorance. The second *r* doesn't belong in *trousers*, nor the *g* in *arraign*, nor the *t* in *deviltry*, nor the *n* in *passenger* and *messenger*. Nor, so far as English is concerned, does that first *c* in *arctic* which so many people twist their mouths so strenuously to pronounce.

And grammar is as "corrupted" as spelling or pronounciation. "You are" is as gross a solecism as "me am." It's recent, too; you won't find it in the Authorized Version of the Bible. *Lesser, nearer,* and *more* are grammatically on a par with *gooder. Crowed* is the equivalent of *knowed* or *growed,* and *caught* and *dug* (for *catched* and *digged*) are as "corrupt" as *squoze* for *squeezed* or *snoze* for *sneezed.*

Fortunately for our peace of mind most people are quite content to let English conform to English, and they are supported in their sanity by modern grammarians and linguists.

Scholars agree with Puttenham (1589) that a language is simply speech "fashioned to the common understanding and accepted by consent." They believe that the only "rules" that can be stated for a language are codified observations. They hold, that is, that language is the basis of grammar, not the other way round. They do not believe that any language can become "corrupted" by the linguistic habits of those who speak it. They do not believe that anyone who is a native speaker of a standard language will get into any linguistic trouble unless he is misled by snobbishness or timidity or vanity.

He may, of course, if his native language is English, speak a form of English that marks him as coming from a rural or an unread group. But if he doesn't mind being so marked, there's no reason why he should change. Johnson retained a Staffordshire burr in his speech all his life. And surely no one will deny that Robert Burns's rustic dialect was just as good as a form of speech as, and in his mouth infinitely better as a means of expression than, the "correct" English spoken by ten million of his southern contemporaries.

The trouble is that people are no longer willing to be rustic or provincial. They all want to speak like educated people, though they don't want to go to the trouble of becoming truly educated. They want to believe that a special form of socially acceptable and financially valuable speech can be mastered by following a few simple rules. And there is no lack of little books that offer to supply the rules and promise "correctness" if the rules are adhered to. But, of course, these offers are specious because you don't speak like an educated person unless you are an educated person, and the little books, if taken seriously, will not only leave the lack of education showing but will expose the pitiful yearning and the basic vulgarity as well, in such sentences as "Whom are you talking about?"

As a matter of fact, the educated man uses at least three languages. With his family and his close friends, on the ordinary, unimportant occasions of daily life, he speaks, much of the time, a monosyllabic sort of shorthand. On more important occasions and when dealing with strangers in his official or business relations, he has a more formal speech, more complete, less allusive, politely qualified, wisely reserved. In addition he has some acquaintance with the literary speech of his language. He understands this when he reads it, and often enjoys it, but he hesitates to use it. In times of emotional stress hot fragments of it may come out of him like lava, and in times of feigned emotion, as when giving a commencement address, cold, greasy gobbets of it will ooze forth.

The linguist differs from the amateur grammarian in recognizing all of these variations and gradations in the language. And he differs from the snob in doubting that the speech of any one small group among the language's more than 300 million daily users constitutes a model for all the rest to imitate.

The methods of the modern linguist can be illustrated by the question of the grammatical number of *none*. Is it singular or plural? Should one say "None of them is ready" or "None of them are ready"?

The prescriptive grammarians are emphatic that it should be singular. The Latinists point out that *nemo*, the Latin equivalent, is singular. The logicians triumphantly point out that *none* can't be more than one and hence can't be plural.

The linguist knows that he hears "None of them are ready" every day, from people of all social positions, geographical areas, and degrees of education. He also hears "None is." Furthermore, literature informs him that both forms were used in the past. From Malory (1450) to Milton (1650) he finds that *none* was treated as a singular three times for every once that it was treated as a plural. That is, up to three hundred years ago men usually said *None is*. From Milton to 1917, *none* was used as a plural seven times for every four times it was used as a singular. That is, in the past three hundred years men often said *None is*, but they said *None are* almost twice as often. Since 1917, however, there has been a noticeable increase in the use of the plural, so much so that today *None are* is the preferred form.

The descriptive grammarian, therefore, says that while *None is* may still be used, it is becoming increasingly peculiar. This, of course, will not be as useful to one who wants to be cultured in a hurry as a short, emphatic permission or prohibition. But it has the advantage of describing English as it is spoken and written here and now and not as it ought to be spoken in some Cloud-Cuckoo-Land.

The descriptive grammarian believes that a child should be taught English, but he would like to see the child taught the English actually used by his educated contemporaries, not some pedantic, theoretical English designed chiefly to mark the imagined superiority of the designer.

He believes that a child should be taught the parts of speech, for example. But the child should be told the truth—that these are functions of use, not some quality immutably inherent in this or that word. Anyone, for instance, who tells a child—or anyone else—that *like* is used in English only as a preposition has grossly misinformed him. And anyone who complains that its use as a conjunction is a corruption introduced by Winston cigarettes ought, in all fairness, to explain how Shakespeare, Keats, and the translators of the Authorized Version of the Bible came to be in the employ of the R. J. Reynolds Tobacco Company.

Whether formal grammar can be taught to advantage before the senior year of high school is doubtful; most studies—and many have been made—indicate that it can't. But when it is taught, it should be the grammar of today's English, not the obsolete grammar of yesterday's prescriptive grammarians. By that grammar, for instance, *please* in the sentence "Please reply" is the verb and *reply* its object. But by modern meaning *reply* is the verb, in the imperative, and *please* is merely a qualifying word meaning "no discourtesy intended," a mollifying or de-imperatival adverb, or whatever you will, but not the verb.

This is a long way from saying "Anything goes," which is the charge that, with all the idiot repetition of a needle stuck in a groove, the uninformed ceaselessly chant against modern grammarians. But to assert that usage is the sole determinant in grammar, pronunciation, and meaning is *not* to say that anything goes. Custom is illogical and unreasonable, but it is also tyrannical. The least deviation from its dictates is usually punished with severity. And because this is so, children should be taught what the current and local customs in English are. They should not be taught that we speak a bastard Latin or a vocalized logic. And they should certainly be disabused of the stultifying illusion that after God had given Moses the Commandments He called him back and pressed on him a copy of Woolley's *Handbook of English Grammar.*

The grammarian does not see it as his function to "raise the standards" set by Franklin, Lincoln, Melville, Mark Twain, and hundreds of millions of other Americans. He is content to record what they said and say.

Insofar as he serves as a teacher, it is his business to point out the limits of the permissible, to indicate the confines within which the writer may exercise his choice, to report that which custom and practice have made acceptable. It is certainly not the business of the grammarian to impose his personal taste as the only norm of good English, to set forth his prejudices as the ideal standard which everyone should copy. That would be fatal. No one person's standards are broad enough for that.

TWO VIEWS OF FRESHMAN ENGLISH

WARNER G. RICE

A PROPOSAL
FOR THE ABOLITION
OF FRESHMAN ENGLISH

Warner G. Rice (1899-   ), born in Aurora, Illinois, was educated at the University of Illinois and at Harvard. After teaching at Illinois, Harvard, and Radcliffe College, in 1929 he went to the University of Michigan, where he has served as chairman of the Department of English since 1948. His literary interest is the English Renaissance and the works of Milton; as an administrator, he has studied new ways of preparing college teachers. His article below is based on an address given at the 1959 convention of the National Council of Teachers of English.

IT MAY APPEAR that any proposal for the removal of Freshman English, as it is now commonly taught, from the curricula of colleges and universities should begin with some definition or descriptions of the subject under discussion. But a simple, exact description is difficult to provide, since more than fifty-seven varieties of Freshman English are currently being offered; and perhaps in a College Section meeting of the National Council [of Teachers of English] it is necessary to say no more than that Freshman English is the course that the CCCC [Conference on College Composition and Communication] is principally concerned about, the course for which scores of handbooks, workbooks, and anthologies have been compiled. It is the course in composition or communication arts regularly required of practically all students during the first college year. It may include

»»» *College English*, XXI (April, 1960), 361-367. Reprinted by permission of the National Council of Teachers of English.

some literature, it may make an attempt to provide general education, but its primary purposes are usually stated to be the improvement of the thinking processes of the freshman as concomitant to his improvement in the skills of listening, speaking, and—more especially—reading and writing.

There are, of course, already some colleges and universities in which no such course is now being taught. Most teachers know about General Education A at Harvard, about Freshman courses in other ivy-league colleges which do not fit the usual pattern, and about experimental courses elsewhere. But Freshman English of the kind to which I have referred grows and expands much more rapidly than it diminishes. It is my belief that this growth is undesirable for many reasons—some academic, some economic; that Freshman English, as commonly taught, is not essential to the wholesome life of institutions of higher learning in this country. Accordingly I recommend that it be eliminated from the college curriculum.

Some of the reasons for abolishing Freshman English are these:

(1) Since acceptable work of college grade should require a reasonably good command of communication skills, students who enter institutions of higher learning without this competence waste their time and the time of their teachers.

(2) If good habits of reading, writing, and speaking have not been inculcated before the student is of college age, it is unlikely that he will be greatly benefited by two semesters of Freshman English. Something can be accomplished, of course; but no miracle will be wrought, since it is late for elementary instruction. If the elements have been mastered, the improvement of skill will depend partly on the student's maturation, partly upon practice in expression in situations not artificially contrived but stimulating to the writer or speaker because he is eager to communicate information and ideas about which he feels a special concern.

(3) Many of the students in the present Freshman English courses are ill-motivated. The subject is required, not an elective.

They are often aware that they are not under the instruction of the most experienced and capable of the Department's teachers. They fail to discover the connection between the purposes and the materials of the course, feel that it has too indeterminate a subject-matter, that they are writing in a vacuum, or that they are repeating high school exercises. When such circumstances exist, their time can be put in to better advantage elsewhere.

(4) Freshman English, though it is relatively inexpensive on a cost-per-credit-hour basis, is, in the aggregate, a major item in the English Department's budget. If it can be eliminated (not simply replaced), the savings will be considerable. And as the pressure of numbers increases, as economic barriers grow higher, colleges and universities must plan to use their staffs and facilities more and more efficiently for higher education, not for elementary instruction. The elimination of Freshman English will encourage the current movement to fix responsibility for instruction in elementary subjects—language courses, mathematics up to the calculus, etc., upon the high schools; and here the responsibility must increasingly reside.

(5) The elimination of Freshman English will improve the situation in which college teachers find themselves. Since Freshman courses now account (in sum) for at least half the man-hours devoted to students in departments of English, their abolition will result in the diversion of teaching energies into different, and more attractive, channels. Though there are thousands of expert, devoted, and effective teachers of the present Freshman English course, few wish to make this activity their principal concern. And since a large part of the teaching is done by beginners whose interests lie elsewhere (in the completion of graduate studies, in developing "courses of their own"), and who are neither psychologically nor professionally prepared for the task which they have undertaken, the removal of the course will reduce supervisory problems and improve morale.

Some observations are certainly called for on all these points. It may reasonably be objected that it is one thing to maintain that competence in reading and composition should be gained in the high school, but quite another to insure that it be done. Here, in answer, it is sufficient to remark that there need be no doubt that the job can be done (under the right conditions), and that the temper of the public, which pays the taxes necessary to support secondary education, is inclining toward an insistence that the high school accomplish such tasks. There is, to be sure, the difficulty that some states require that tax-supported universities admit all high school graduates who apply, whatever their degree of preparation. As long as this situation continues, it is claimed, there will be a need for Freshman English and sub-Freshman English. The appropriate comments here seem to be (a) that this arrangement is educationally unsound, too expensive to be continued, and vulnerable to determined attack, and (b) that English departments should in any case cease to perform the function of admissions offices (as they now do by their passing and failing of Freshmen), and insist that the setting of standards of competence be made a college matter. The abolition of sub-Freshman English can logically be followed by the abolition of Freshman English.

It may be argued, of course, that if Freshman English courses are not now as valuable as they should be, they can be improved. Probably this is true; but in fact they will not be improved along the lines now followed without an enormous effort to train college teachers for Freshman work, the employment of many more experienced (and more expensive) instructors, and the provision of attractive academic careers in the field—all developments long sought, but not probable on a large scale. That Freshman English should not be abandoned simply because it is not popular must certainly be acknowledged—but only if it is agreed that its purposes cannot be achieved in other ways. That they can be better achieved in other ways it is the purpose of the argument which follows to show.

First, however, it is necessary to deal with a matter of undeniable importance to departments of English. Freshman English courses, being required, bring large enrollments—and numbers mean power. Small, expensive graduate seminars or honors classes are often more easily financed if they can be balanced against large inexpensive courses than they could be if no such courses existed; and this is only one of the advantages of size. Moreover, in many universities, the instruction of Freshmen provides a principal means of subsidizing scores of graduate students, whose numbers justify a large graduate program. To close out the Freshman course might mean the cutting down of graduate enrollments; and in this day of teacher shortages, such an action cannot seriously be contemplated. These considerations cannot simply be brushed aside; but it may be supposed that since many other departments manage very well without a required Freshman course, the department of English, having made some uncomfortable but not really difficult adjustments, could follow their example. If Freshman English were abolished, somewhat fewer teachers would be needed; but it ought still to be possible to use many graduate students to assist with instructional tasks more congenial to them than composition, and for which their preparation would be more appropriate.

Other difficulties must still be confronted, however. College faculties will not welcome the abolition of Freshman English, because with it must go the comfortable assumption that the English department is solely responsible for good writing. This assumption is certainly false; but it has been encouraged by the incautious willingness of English departments to sponsor and direct the required course. A change in attitude may be hard to effect, but there is evidence that this change can be managed. It must be managed, as later paragraphs will attempt to show, if good standards in reading and writing are to be maintained.

Opposition to the abandonment of Freshman English by the colleges may be expected from many administrators and teachers in the secondary schools. Their position is understandable. For a generation they have been engaged in a large, and generally successful, social service enterprise, and have transferred many of their traditional teaching duties to other agencies—especially the college. In a time of increasing technological unemployment, growing juvenile delinquency, and intensified needs for counseling, psychiatric care, and similar services, the community will probably demand that the school continue to concern itself with recreation, health, guidance, vocational courses, home and family living, and like matters. But there is a growing sense that the school must do more on the academic side, too. Many curricula are being reshaped. Advanced Placement courses are growing in popularity. The two- or three-track systems now being tried, though they may not be perfect, likewise give evidence that the college-bound student is likely to be helped and encouraged to achieve more than has lately been expected of him.

What will be expected of him by the college which has eliminated the kind of Freshman English course which is now being taught? Obviously such a college will expect a level of proficiency in reading which will insure that he can understand and analyze prose of moderate difficulty, as well as poetry of at least the simpler sort; and that his writing in expository and argumentative essays exhibits no gross errors. This proficiency will be tested by examination—preferably by an examination developed and administered over a wide area by the CEEB [College Entrance Examination Board] or some similar agency. If, as an applicant for admission to an institution of higher learning, he falls below the standard which that institution sets in English, he will be refused, though of course not prohibited from trying again to qualify.

Reading and writing skills of an adequate kind are not now so unusual among college freshman as to discourage the expectation that they can be widely achieved. Such skills are certainly mastered by pupils in the secondary schools of Europe. They will not be attained in the United States, however, without a powerful effort on the part of secondary schools and colleges alike. They will not be taught, that is, as long as a large proportion of high school teachers of English come to their tasks insufficiently prepared, and as long as most high school teachers are heavily overburdened, with too many classes, each containing too many pupils, and with taxing extra-curricular assignments to boot. It is the professional obligation of the NCTE and of other teachers' organizations to make the representation required to bring home to school administrators, PTA groups, citizens' committees, and so on, the importance of improving the qualifications of teachers of English and of making their loads tolerable.

In this effort colleges and universities must play an active part. This they can do only if members of their English departments interest themselves actively in the preparation and professional welfare of teachers. That they, like their colleagues in other fields, have been backward in this matter is obvious enough; but the time has certainly come for improvement. The serious attention given to the Master of Arts in Teaching programs in a number of universities is a good sign, while the TEPS [Teacher Education and Professional Standards] conferences sponsored by the NEA [National Education Association] have had good effects in bringing together representatives of schools of education with those from subject-matter areas—for, like the current debates over certification, these meetings have focused attention upon the importance of high standards of preparation in the subjects which a teacher professes to be able to teach. What is needed now is a widespread endeavor to exploit these gains, largely through the general introduction of improved teacher training programs.

It is, indeed, in the education and training of secondary school teachers, rather than through the enlargement of Freshman English programs, that the hope for an improvement in communication skills lies. In discharging this obligation, departments of English must persuade men and women of first-rate ability to undertake the task. They must forge alliances with schools of Education, in order to avail themselves of the talents and opportunities which exist there, must participate in the offering of courses in methods, and must aid in the supervision of practice teaching. Members of English departments must go into the high schools, acquaint themselves with the conditions under which teachers are working, and give practical advice toward the solution of real classroom problems. And they must reach agreements, through direct contact with secondary educators and by constant consultation with their colleagues in the schools, as to the standards which college-bound students can reasonably be expected to meet.

There is much beyond this to be attempted; among many possibilities, these at least can be mentioned:

(1) Summer programs for the upgrading of insufficiently prepared teachers of English. These teachers must, in order to carry out their assignments adequately, not only take more courses of the conventional kind, but also receive special instruction in the effective techniques of teaching composition and literature in special workshops and seminars.

(2) Summer programs designed especially for teachers of Advanced Placement programs.

(3) Interneships for high school teachers in the Freshman English programs now being taught, so that they may, by working alongside college teachers, come in contact with the best methods currently in use.

(4) Seminars and workshops offered in the field, with demonstration lessons in high school classrooms followed by meetings of teachers to discuss methods and materials, to improve existing course plans and syllabi, and to familiarize all concerned with the levels of proficiency expected.

(5) The strengthening of undergraduate English programs now prescribed for prospective teachers, and the improvement of their professional preparation through cooperation with schools of Education.

All these activities, and others of a similar character, are now actually being carried on; but they are not yet well supported, and far too few members of English staffs have become really expert in them. Some of the talent which has been expended in the development of Freshman English courses can, however, profitably be directed to such work. It does not, admittedly, promise more professional advancement or prestige than Freshman English now provides, but it offers the best means of employing the energies of college teachers who are really concerned about the improvement of communication skills.

The task of convincing college faculties that English departments cannot properly accept the entire, or even the principal, responsibility for developing an expert command of what is generally called English is a large one. The complaint is often heard that Freshman Composition must be incapably taught because students who have received satisfactory grades in the course fail, as seniors or graduates, to write accurately and effectively. It is certainly true, however, that the proficiency desired can be gained only by constant and disciplined practise; and if this condition is not met in a majority of courses (not in one or two only), no great success is to be expected. It follows that if there is a general desire for improvement, there must be an effort, in many quarters, to insure it. Teachers of every subject from anthropology to zoology must assist.

That they can assist, if their professions of concern are heartfelt, is obvious. And perhaps only a sentence or two need be devoted to the possibility that they may not be in earnest—or, to put the case more charitably, that new forms of communication—the graph, the picture on the page or on the screen, the voice, "live" or recorded, and other media (e.g., the coded tape), are now equal to, or of greater importance than, the written word. It is not necessary to go as far as Professor Marshall McLuhan to acknowledge that to some degree this is true; and the speculation that expert writers will become a special class, skilled in translating the ideas of technologists into a *lingua franca,* is not absurd. But for the present, at least, the familiar communication arts are necessary, and all educated persons must cultivate them.

And as the teacher of science should not say to his pupil, "Your astronomy is good, but your mathematics bad," the two being intimately related, so the teacher of philosophy or history should not say, "Your argument is good, but ill-expressed," for the expression is intimately bound up with the argument. And certainly the majority of college teachers are competent to help undergraduates improve their expression. That the task is arduous, and that many recoil from it, is unfortunately true. This reluctance must be overcome.

It may be met in several ways. The conversion of senior professors to the view that they are responsible for correcting the English of their students may be impossible; but at least junior teachers, assistants, and paper-graders—who perform a considerable part of the work of essay reading—can be assigned the task, and, if their powers are not sufficient, can be trained by English departments to make the proper annotations and comments. That incidental benefits would accrue from such a practise is obvious—young social scientists, historians, and philosophers would learn to write better English, since the best way to learn is to teach; and they would develop habits of dealing with the English of their students which would, as the years went by, improve the whole academic program. It is too much to expect that a complete reform can be speedily effected in this way; but progress toward implementing it would be in the right direction. For the goal must be acceptance of responsibility for better English by the whole college community. Nothing less will prove genuinely efficacious in the end.

It will be asked what will replace the Freshman English now taught if, by various expedients, it proves possible to get along without it. The answer must be firm and emphatic: Nothing. College requirements should simply be reduced by whatever number of hours Freshman English now absorbs. And perhaps it is not vain to hope that if similar policies are applied in other fields, if admissions standards generally are raised, so that the college student's first year is not devoted almost exclusively to such studies as composition, elementary French, and algebra, the curriculum leading to the bachelor's degree can be shortened to three years without loss, and present college facilities thus be made accessible to a larger number of students.

There need be no question, of course, as to the propriety of offering some English course to first-year students. But the English course designed for Freshmen should be (as some now are) a course in the subjects which the English Department is best prepared to teach—language and literature. It should be elective, or should have an acknowledged place in a program of general studies. Like other courses, it should make considerable demands upon the student's skill in reading and writing. Its purposes, like its subject matter, should be clearly defined, and clearly within the competence of those assigned to teach it. Such courses can be designed so as to employ the energies of many of those graduate students now holding appointments as teaching assistants. That they would apply themselves under such circumstances more willingly and more capably than they apply themselves to the tasks now assigned them is sure—and it is even probable that they would prove, under these conditions, more effective in teaching writing than they now are.

If a serious shortage of teachers occurs, as the experts predict it will, there will be other tasks which teaching assistants can usefully perform—in connection with large lecture courses, or in conjunction with mechanical aids. In free-reading programs they might give tutorial or preceptorial direction to groups of students. There need be no fear lest, with the abandonment of the present Freshman English course, there will be too few places for beginners to get interneship training—and there may even be a good chance that more attention will be given to their guidance and supervision, with a consequent gain to students, if they are working with senior staff members in fields of special interest to the latter.

By way of summary, the proposals outlined above will require, for their effective implementation, the following:

(1) Improvements in the professional environment of the high school English teacher which will permit and encourage

superior classroom performance and increased attention to college-bound students.

(2) The improvement, through better teacher-training programs and more intelligent certification procedures, of the qualifications of high school English teachers.

(3) Cooperative efforts by college and university departments of English, school administrators, Schools of Education, and teachers themselves, directed toward (a) the further training of those now insufficiently prepared, (b) a general increase in competence, and (c) the development of better methods and curricula.

(4) The widespread use of proficiency tests in English as a means of determining which applicants are, and which are not, ready for college work.

(5) The substitution of substantial writing requirements in many freshman and sophomore college courses for the present Freshman Composition requirement.

(6) The use of proficiency tests for college juniors to insure that all those concerned will emphasize the importance of communication skills during the first two college years, and that students proceeding to concentration or "major" programs will have a reasonable competence in these techniques.

(7) The relegation of necessary corrective disciplines in English to noncredit, extra-fee courses.

(8) The delegation of responsibility for maintaining satisfactory standards in English to a college committee or other college agency.

(9) The development of Freshman English courses which have as their subject matter language and literature.

It is obvious that in these proposals there is little that is new. The chief reason for bringing together many familiar recommendations on this occasion is that the moment is propitious for a concerted effort to bring about an improvement in the English program. The public is aroused, there is a demand for greater effectiveness in education at all levels, money is available for experimentation, the pressures of a growing population and of economic stringency force a reconsideration of current practises. Impatience with lax and wasteful programs makes possible reforms which could not have been introduced ten or twenty years ago.

If a change is to be made, however, it must be attempted on a wide, not a narrow, front. The fate of good innovations which are introduced sporadically and at widely scattered institutions has shown how great an effort must be expended if academic inertia is to be overcome. The decision of a strong regional group of colleges and universities to insist on higher standards of achievement in English would be sufficient, however, to modify the pattern of teaching in a large group of secondary schools; and when this was accomplished, there would be a good chance that improvement would become general. The situation is sufficiently critical so that if reforms in the teaching of English are not made within the structure of secondary and higher education, there may occur a collapse which will invite action from outside authorities.

ALBERT R. KITZHABER

DEATH—OR TRANSFIGURATION?

Albert R. Kitzhaber (1915-   ), professor of English at the University of Oregon, was educated at Coe College, Washington State College, and the University of Washington. He has been director of freshman English at the University of Kansas, of the Portland High School Curriculum Study, and of the Dartmouth Study of Student Writing, and is the author of Themes, Theories, and Therapy: The Teaching of Writing in College *(1963). His article below is based on an address given at the 1959 convention of the National Council of Teachers of English.*

I THINK THAT probably no one would want to make an unqualified defense of the present Freshman English course in all its infinite varieties—of its aims, its methods, its content, and its accomplishments. I need not go into detail regarding all its shortcomings, but I will mention a few of the most obvious simply to make it clear that I am aware of them and that I recognize them as defects.

For example: The aims of the course, when we stop to think of them, are surely over-ambitious—to eradicate, in three hours a week for 30 or 35 weeks, habits of thought and expression that have been forming for at least 15 years and to which the student is as closely wedded as he is to his skin; and to fix indelibly a different set of habits from which the student will never afterwards deviate. It is little wonder that we generally fall short of achieving these aims.

Another weakness is the lack of general agreement about course content, so that depending on the prejudices of the teacher, departmental policy (or lack of it), or current fads, the course may center on literature or semantics or logic or "communication skills" or several varieties of grammar or mental stimulation or life adjustment. One result of this uncertainty

»»» *College English*, XXI (April, 1960), 367-373. Reprinted by permission of the National Council of Teachers of English.

over proper content is that the course becomes a receptacle for odds and ends of instruction (use of the library, Freshman orientation, research methods) that belong to English no more than they do to other subjects; and these additions dilute the course.

Most of the textbooks and most of the work of the course, as it is usually constituted, cannot be said even by the most charitably disposed critic to be on the same level of intellectual rigor and maturity as textbooks and classwork in other freshman courses such as chemistry or economics. I am thinking of such stultifying activities as diagramming sentences or doing workbook exercises on the apostrophe or distinguishing between a topic outline and a sentence outline.

Finally, we must generally admit that the course too seldom succeeds in teaching students to write as we want them to. Often we find that students who thought and wrote well when the course began still write and think well when it ends; we have neither helped them nor (presumably) hurt them. Students who were confused thinkers and writers at the first of the course may think and write better at the end; but if they do, it is difficult for us to prove that our instruction has been solely responsible —and in any case, there is too seldom a comforting relationship between the degree of improvement and the quantity of labor expended.

In the face of all this, and exasperated by administrators, by colleagues in other departments, and by the general public, all of whom subject us to a running fire of largely uninformed criticism, we can be forgiven if we are lured by the temptation to solve the difficulty, as far as we are concerned, in a simple and dramatic way: abolish Freshman English—declare that we have no more responsibility for teaching writing than any other teacher does, and let someone else worry about it.

But before we decide to dynamite Freshman English and end its 75 years of troubled life, I think we should remember that a few things can be said in favor of the course, that it has been and is by no means a totally unsuccessful and profitless operation. For example, we are all aware of the role of Freshman English in subsidizing graduate study in our field. This circumstance is really not germane to an evaluation of the course itself, and I would oppose using it as an argument for preserving the course. At the same time, the function is necessary and will remain so; though I have no way of arriving at exact figures, I would be surprised if at least 75 per cent of those who hold doctorates in English have not at some time accepted employment in the Freshman course to help them on their way to an advanced degree.

Equally important, though again peripheral to an assessment of the course, is the indispensable opportunity that Freshman English continues to offer for letting young teachers gain actual classroom experience. Administrators, students, and parents of students sometimes talk as if they want colleges and universities to employ only experienced teachers, apparently forgetting that there is no way for an inexperienced teacher to become an experienced teacher unless someone, sometime, gives him a class of his own and lets him begin to teach.

There is a tendency also to assume rather glibly that *because* a great many classes in Freshman English are taught by graduate students, *therefore* those classes are poorly taught. Sometimes they are, it is true; there is no substitute for mature wisdom. But neither is there any substitute for the youthful vigor and enthusiasm and idealism that, when applied to students not far separated in years from their teacher, can often achieve startlingly good results, even when mastery of subject matter is less than complete.

And not only is some of the teaching in Freshman English good, I am sure that some of the courses are solid and worthwhile. When we talk of "Freshman English as it now exists" we are dealing with a very large abstraction. Freshman English now exists in many, many forms; it is not reasonable to assume that all of them are completely reprehensible. I do not mean to say that we cannot come to an understanding about Freshman English in its general or typical form; I merely suggest that we should recognize the qualitative range that must exist in this course as surely as it does in others.

Finally, I think there must be some value in requiring all Freshmen to take at least one course that has writing as its focus—a course that talks about writing a good part of the time, that makes students do a lot of writing, and that expects teachers to read and correct the writing carefully. Results will be partial at best; but there is a fair likelihood that they ought to be at least a little better than in a course that does not focus on writing to the same extent.

So much for the two sides of the coin. Now let us suppose that Freshman English were generally abolished in the near future. What would be some of the results? Again, I will mention only a few of the most obvious.

In the first place, I'm sure you are all aware of the specter of technological unemployment that hovers over this discussion. I mention this, but I would not want to base on it an argument for retaining the Freshman course. We have enough troubles without inviting the charge of featherbedding.

It might be argued that abolishing Freshman English would save money for the colleges at a time when educational costs are rising sharply. It would—but only if nothing were put in its place and students were allowed to graduate with that many fewer credits. I doubt that this would happen; any college or university is full of ambitious departments convinced that unless students can be made to take more of their courses, the future of the nation has been imperiled. I think the vacuum would be filled almost at once, and with something that would almost certainly cost more to teach than Freshman English. One administrative advantage of Freshman English, though not one that I view with much satisfaction, is that it is relatively inexpensive: it needs no equipment except a classroom and a blackboard, and it employs teachers who, even if they have professorial rank, usually are paid at a lower rate than their counterparts in many other departments.

Another result, or at least a theoretical one, of abolishing

Freshman English would be to distribute the responsibility for teaching writing among the entire faculty. Now, if the rest of the faculty would really accept this responsibility and discharge it adequately, I would cheer at least as loud as anyone else in our profession, for the imperfect success of the present Freshman course is due in considerable part to the failure of other teachers (both school and college) to insist that their students use reasonably correct and precise English.

I am thoroughly in favor of doing everything possible to make other teachers recognize the stake that they themselves, as well as their students, have in fostering a ready control of good written English. But I would not be optimistic enough to expect the job to be so well done by these other teachers that the English department need not concern itself with student English any more than another department would. Even with the best will in the world, teachers of foreign language, of mathematics, and to some extent, of laboratory science courses ordinarily have rather limited opportunities to police the written English of their students. The best opportunities, outside the English department itself, would probably be found in history and social science courses and in some courses in Education.

Now if by good written English we mean no more than written English free, or relatively free, from mechanical errors—grammar, spelling, punctuation—any educated person ought to be competent to do the necessary checking. (Whether college faculties consist wholly of educated persons, in this sense, is perhaps another question.) This is precisely the view of good English held by most of our lay critics. But I would hope that when English teachers, at least, talk about good written English they have a less impoverished concept in mind, one that takes into account not just mechanical correctness, which is surely a minimum objective at best, but logical consistency and rhetorical effectiveness also. It may be that teachers of sociology or home economics or engineering drawing are fully as well equipped as English teachers are to check on and to foster logical consistency in writing. I hope they are. But I am not convinced that they are equally well prepared to pass judgment on and to teach rhetorical effectiveness. English teachers, as well as teachers of speech, work in the main stream of the rhetorical tradition. The rhetoric of written English is a legitimate part of English subject-matter which we should be able to teach with an expertness that other teachers could not equal and would not expect to equal. To the extent that I may be mistaken in this belief, I suggest that some inquiry is called for into undergraduate and graduate curricula for prospective college English teachers.

If Freshman English is abolished, obviously the job that it is trying to do, even though imperfectly, must be done somewhere. The logical place is the high school. I think myself that the high school is where much of the present work of Freshman English ought to be taken care of. I suspect that most high school English teachers would agree, if for no other reason than to get the college people off their backs. But I'm sure we all know that it won't be enough for us merely to say "It's not our job, let the high schools do it," and then proceed on the assumption that the high schools *can* and *will* do it. We in the colleges have several distinct advantages over our high school colleagues: smaller classes, lower total work loads, more thorough professional preparation (on the average), and more mature students—yet our results in the Freshman course usually have pleased neither ourselves nor our critics. We would be whimsical to assume that high school teachers, laboring under much less favorable conditions—indeed, conditions that we would think intolerable—could do a job well that we have done indifferently at best. They will need help, especially from us.

What kind of help? What can and should we in the colleges do to help? Not very long ago I would have answered these questions with the usual benevolent generalities: we should promote better relations between high school and college English teachers, we should encourage the high schools to raise their standards and to require more themes, we should urge that teacher preparation be improved by requiring more hours of

English—and so on. Such pronouncements have the advantage of showing that you are on the side of right and progress, without requiring you to become personally involved in tiresome details.

But I think that now I can offer considerably more specific answers to these questions. For a little more than a year I have been working with a project that involves the eleven public high schools of Portland, Oregon—one of the best school systems in the United States, incidentally—and nine Oregon colleges and universities, this number including virtually all the important collegiate institutions of the state, with the exception of the three colleges of Education. We call this project, which has been financed by the Fund for the Advancement of Education, the Portland High School Curriculum Study. Last spring the Study engaged over fifty college professors from the chief subject-matter fields to evaluate the college-preparatory curriculum in the Portland high schools with a view to recommending ways of upgrading both it and college curricula and correlating the two in ways and to a degree that have heretofore been impossible.

The thirteen volumes containing the findings and recommendations of the Study have now been presented to the School Board. Several of the volumes bear on our discussion, but especially the one on the curriculum in English language and composition. It was prepared by two well-known members of NCTE, Professor Robert M. Gorrell of the University of Nevada and Professor Paul Roberts of San Jose State College. By drawing on the substance of their report, as well as on the other reports and the general recommendations of the Study, I want to describe for you a systematic effort by college English teachers to help their high school colleagues teach more successfully than they have been able to do the principles and practice of good writing, and in this way to take the first step toward enabling the high schools to do much of what Freshman English now attempts. The pattern that has been worked out in Portland is not the only one possible, but it is the most ambitious effort of this sort that I have heard of and it is close to the action stage.

To begin with, Professor Roberts and Professor Gorrell spent a good deal of time visiting English classes in the Portland high schools, talking with teachers and administrators, and reading textbooks and syllabuses. They kept in close touch with a larger committee that was studying the literature curriculum and with another professor who was examining the work in speech; language and writing, literature, and speech are all part of the English curriculum in Portland as they are generally in high schools, and they are taught, almost entirely, by the same teachers. After informing themselves thoroughly of what the existing English curriculum is, in both theory and practice, all the consultants agreed to recommend that the high school English curriculum be restricted to two basic purposes: teaching the student to read with understanding and appreciation, and acquainting him with significant works of literature; and giving him some understanding of what language is and how it works, and helping him use his own language well in thinking, writing, and speaking. These purposes represent a considerable pruning of other concerns now attached to the English curriculum. The consultants agreed also on a very tentative allotment of time through the four years of courses: two-fifths to literature, two-fifths to practice in writing and speaking, and one-fifth to language.

The study of language, as recommended by Professor Gorrell and Professor Roberts, would be a major innovation in the high schools. They argue that in addition to the application of language study to writing, a knowledge of the nature, development, and working of language, particularly English, is an essential ingredient of a liberal education and that this study should be pursued for its humanistic value through all four years of the English curriculum.

The report on English language and composition contains many other specific suggestions and recommendations for the high school curriculum for students with college potential but I will not have time to mention them here. I will say only that all of them comprise a systematic attempt to improve high school instruction in writing to the point where many of the present aims of Freshman English in college could be accomplished before students graduate from high school.

To bring the new English curriculum into being, the consultants for literature, language and composition, and speech have recommended the appointment of four committees, one for each course; each committee will be composed of two college professors of English and two high school teachers, all of them relieved of one-fourth of their teaching duties for at least the 1960-1961 school year and all working full-time for six weeks next summer. It is planned to enlist the aid of specialist consultants from college English departments for at least the next three years initially, and perhaps permanently. Funds will be provided to bring these people in from time to time during the year as they are needed for help with curricular problems.

Because few high school teachers—in Portland or elsewhere —are adequately prepared to teach the revised English curriculum that has been proposed, we are planning to set up special six-week institutes in the summers of 1960 and 1961 for a selected group of teachers representing each high school. In the two summers they will take a total of four courses from a list of eight in literature, language, and speech. The consultants recommend also that a small group of especially outstanding teachers be selected each year (eventually one from each English department) for a year of graduate study in English at full salary. These teachers and the ones who attend the institutes can serve as specialist consultants in their own departments. They can help appreciably to orient their colleagues toward the new courses and to set a standard of achievement in teaching.

Since the only realistic long-term solution to the problem of teacher preparation is to revise teacher education programs in the colleges, all the reports, including the report on language and composition, are making detailed suggestions to guide such revision, and the participating colleges and universities have agreed to consider these thoroughly at the appropriate time.

The reports urge us college teachers not to rest content with pious lamentations about the high school teacher's thirty-hour class schedule and 160 or 180 students; instead, we should lend our own prestige, influence, and powers of persuasion to a campaign for a reduced work load. High school teachers and administrators by themselves have been virtually powerless to bring about the needed reforms, and even with our help the job will not be easy. But it should not prove impossible. We might heighten our zeal by reflecting that in helping the high school teachers in this way we are also helping ourselves; that unless substantial improvements can be made in these and other working conditions for high school English teachers, our hope of getting the high schools to accomplish successfully the aims now assigned to Freshman English is merely wistful.

This is what we are doing in Portland and what we plan to do. You will notice that our project calls for a degree and kind of cooperation between teachers at the two levels that probably is unprecedented, a systematic and continuing endeavor by the college English teachers to concern themselves actively with the high school curriculum and the professional welfare of their high school colleagues. It seems to me that this is the only realistic way to improve high school instruction, and it depends on our clear recognition of the stake that we as college teachers have in a sound high school curriculum, and our consequent responsibility toward our colleagues in the lower schools.

Now, let's assume that by means of the procedures I have outlined, or something like them, the high schools will begin to graduate substantially larger numbers of young people who usually can write clear, accurate sentences and organize them into logical paragraphs, and who can use standard English with some confidence and spell and punctuate it correctly. I don't suggest that all high school graduates will have this ability, but rather I would hope that the majority of those who are of college caliber would. (I define students of college caliber as approximately the top 40 or 45 per cent in ability and academic achievement.)[1] It seems to me that under such happy conditions—but *only* under them—we could safely eliminate the typical Freshman English course as it is now constituted.

But I would still recommend a required Freshman course in English. Let me explain.

I think that a lot of the trouble we are having with the present Freshman course comes from the widespread failure of college English departments to recognize sufficiently that the teaching of language and writing is one of their inescapable responsibilities, and to include among requirements for future English teachers a selection of courses pertinent to the teaching of these. This deficiency puts a great many teachers of Freshman English (and high school English) at a serious disadvantage, and goes far to explain such phenomena as the introduction of other kinds of content from outside the field of English (witness the usual Freshman anthology), the continued survival of a set of desiccated rhetorical principles devised by second-rate theorists in the nineteenth century, and the fantastic state of innocence in some English teachers regarding language research in the last half or three-quarters of a century. The last of these is at least partly responsible for the astonishing variety of grading standards that nearly any English staff exhibits, and perhaps wholly responsible for the curious " 'tis so " " 'tain't so" arguments in English faculty meetings over such things as the use of "due to" and "the reason is because."

Perhaps this failure of college English departments to take sufficient account of language and rhetoric as legitimate subject matter will explain the widespread notion that all we need aim at in teaching students to write is a minimum level of competence. We tend to ask, "Do they write well enough to get by?" and if we think they do we usually exempt them from part

[1] I base this figure on a study made of the 1958 graduating class in the Portland high schools, which showed that 41 per cent of these students had an I.Q. of 110 or above. It is not unreasonable to expect, assuming desire and diligence, that students within this range of ability could profitably complete a four-year course of study in many curricula at many accredited colleges and universities.

or all of the Freshman course. A more proper question, I think, would be, "How much better can they be taught to write?"—for writing is a skill with no top limit. The policy of exempting the better students puts us in the curious position of appearing to say that we have things to teach the poor and the average student but nothing to offer the good one. I cannot bring myself to believe that properly qualified college English teachers should be unable to help even the best students improve their command of written English.

What I am suggesting, in short, is the creation of a new course in Freshman English, *after* the necessity for the existing one has been removed. Its exact outlines would need to be worked out by wiser heads than mine, but I would suggest that it be a course in which the student does a great deal of writing and the teacher criticizes that writing with care, concentrating on the development of a firm and mature style. It need not be writing done in a vacuum, for it should be based on the legitimate subject matter of the course. This subject matter should be literature, language, and rhetoric—all at a more advanced level than in the high school courses; earlier study will certainly not have exhausted any of these bodies of material. And I would suggest in passing that since we already have a New Criticism and a New Grammar, we begin thinking about the desirability of working out a New Rhetoric, surely long overdue.

Anticipating a revised English curriculum in high school and a new and upgraded freshman course in college, I would propose an early revision of the pattern of courses taken by students intending to teach English at either level. The program of these students should certainly include, besides sufficient courses in literature, substantial work in language, rhetorical theory, and advanced expository writing. In this I follow the recommendations of Professor Gorrell and Professor Roberts.

I can sum up very briefly my position with regard to the question we are discussing. I am dissatisfied with the present Freshman English course in its typical form; but I am convinced that any radical amelioration must wait on, not precede, changes in the English curriculum in high school. Attempted coercion of high school English teachers would get us nowhere. They would like to do a better job of teaching writing quite as much as we would like to have them do it; but we must help them, working with them as equals on a problem neither they nor we have so far been able to solve properly. If our combined efforts lead to the results we want, the need for the present Freshman course would disappear—but not the need for a new Freshman course that would take advantage of and build upon the revised high school courses. I would argue that such a course ought to be of at least as much value to the freshman as any other course he might take in that year—valuable because it would concentrate on trying to raise the level of his writing skill from competence to distinction, and valuable also because it would contribute significantly to his liberal education through the continued study of literature and language. Both of these are rightful concerns of an English department. Indeed, I think they are obligations.

ANALOGY, COMPARISON,

EVALUATION

A COMPARISON is a statement that two or more things are in some respects either alike or different or that they are in some respects alike but in others different. If, for example, someone says that his two sisters are alike in being shy but different in their interests —one being crazy about boys, the other about metaphysics—then his statement is a comparison. A comparison may serve one or more of the following purposes: (1) an informative purpose (to give information about all the things compared), (2) a rhetorical purpose (to clarify the unfamiliar by comparing it with the familiar), (3) a pseudological purpose (to reason that, if two or more things are alike in some respects, then they are alike in others), and (4) an evaluative purpose (to show that, by reference to some criteria or standards of evaluation, two or more things have a certain order of merit). If a comparison serves (2) or (3), it is usually called an analogy; if (4), an evaluation, though not every evaluation is a comparison.

Each of five of the following pieces serves one or more of these four purposes. Only Crowther serves an informative purpose (1) primarily (to give information about both English and American education), though he cannot, of course, for either an English or an American reader, help serving a rhetorical purpose (2) as well. Lyell and Huxley serve (2) primarily (to clarify the concept of geology and that of the laws of nature, respectively) but with a hint of a pseudological purpose (3). Trollope and Krutch serve an evaluative purpose (4) primarily (to show the relative merits of certain sorts of hotel and of certain sorts of place to live, respectively).

The three pieces remaining are evaluations but only implicitly comparisons. Johnson's unfavorable evaluation of "Lycidas" and Bush's favorable one do not (except for Johnson's fleeting reference to Abraham Cowley's elegy on the death of James Hervey and Bush's afterthought comparing "Lycidas" to the Epitaphium Damonis) compare Milton's poem with other poems. And Louis' unfavorable evaluation of the Encyclopædia Britannica does not compare that encyclopedia with others.

There is a good deal of evaluation elsewhere in this book—notably, in "Argumentation and Persuasion" and in "Reviews."

SIR CHARLES LYELL

GEOLOGY AND ASTRONOMY

Sir Charles Lyell (1797-1875) was a Scots geologist who was the father of modern geology. His chief work, Principles of Geology *(3 vols.; 1830-1833), was written to refute the dominant geological theory of his time—namely, that great geological changes are caused by catastrophic destructions (like the biblical flood) and repeated creations, and not by natural processes operating gradually and uniformly. This work, a classic of geology, prepared the public for Charles Darwin's theory of evolution.*

WHEN WE COMPARE the result of observations in the last thirty years with those of the three preceding centuries, we cannot but look forward with the most sanguine expectations to the degree of excellence to which geology may be carried, even by the labours of the present generation. Never, perhaps, did any science, with the exception of astronomy, unfold, in an equally brief period, so many novel and unexpected truths, and overturn so many preconceived opinions. The senses had for ages declared the earth to be at rest, until the astronomer taught that it was carried through space with inconceivable rapidity. In like manner was the surface of this planet regarded as having remained unaltered since its creation, until the geologist proved that it had been the theatre of reiterated change, and was still the subject of slow but never-ending fluctuations. The discovery of other systems in the boundless regions of space was the triumph of astronomy: to trace the same system through various transformations—to behold it at successive eras adorned with different hills and valleys, lakes and seas, and peopled with new inhabitants, was the delightful meed of geological research. By the geometer were measured the regions of space, and the relative distances of the heavenly bodies;—by the geologist myriads

»»» From *Principles of Geology*. London, 1830-33.

of ages were reckoned, not by arithmetical computation, but by a train of physical events—a succession of phenomena in the animate and inanimate worlds—signs which convey to our minds more definite ideas than figures can do of the immensity of time.

THOMAS HENRY HUXLEY

LIFE AND CHESS

*Thomas Henry Huxley (1825-1895), English biologist, is best remembered
as the champion and popularizer of Darwin's theory of evolution, but he
was a scientist in his own right as well as a doctor, an educator, and a
stylist of the essay. After studying medicine at Charing Cross Hospital, at the
age of twenty he took his M.B. degree from London University. Like Darwin,
he began his scientific career on a voyage with the Royal Navy; from 1846
to 1850 he was assistant surgeon of the Rattlesnake with a roving commission to investigate marine biology. Papers he published as a result of
the Rattlesnake surveying expedition established his scientific reputation; he
then entered upon a long career as a teacher insisting upon the importance
of science to a redefined liberal education.*

SUPPOSE it were perfectly certain that the life and fortune of
every one of us would, one day or other, depend upon his winning or losing a game of chess. Don't you think that we should
all consider it to be a primary duty to learn at least the names
and the moves of the pieces; to have a notion of a gambit, and
a keen eye for all the means of giving and getting out of check?
Do you not think that we should look with a disapprobation
amounting to scorn, upon the father who allowed his son, or
the state which allowed its members, to grow up without knowing a pawn from a knight?

Yet, it is a very plain and elementary truth that the life, the
fortune, and the happiness of every one of us, and, more or less,
of those who are connected with us, do depend upon our knowing something of the rules of a game infinitely more difficult
and complicated than chess. It is a game which has been played
for untold ages, every man and woman of us being one of the
two players in a game of his or her own. The chess-board is the
world, the pieces are the phenomena of the universe, the rules
of the game are what we call the laws of nature. The player

»»» From "A Liberal Education; and Where to Find It." *Macmillan's
Magazine,* XVII (March, 1868), 367-378.

on the other side is hidden from us. We know that his play is always fair, just, and patient. But also we know, to our cost, that he never overlooks a mistake, or makes the smallest allowance for ignorance. To the man who plays well the highest stakes are paid with that sort of overflowing generosity with which the strong shows delight in strength. And one who plays ill is checkmated—without haste, but without remorse.

My metaphor will remind some of you of the famous picture in which Retzsch has depicted Satan playing at chess with man for his soul. Substitute for the mocking fiend in that picture a calm, strong angel who is playing for love, as we say, and would rather lose than win—and I should accept it as an image of human life.

Well, what I mean by Education is learning the rules of this mighty game. In other words, education is the instruction of the intellect in the laws of nature, under which name I include not merely things and their forces, but men and their ways; and the fashioning of the affections and of the will into an earnest and loving desire to move in harmony with those laws. For me, education means neither more nor less than this. Anything which professes to call itself education must be tried by this standard, and if it fails to stand the test, I will not call it education, whatever may be the force of authority or of numbers upon the other side.

SIR GEOFFREY CROWTHER

ENGLISH AND AMERICAN EDUCATION

*Sir Geoffrey Crowther (1907-   ), British economist, was educated at
Cambridge and later studied in this country at Yale and Columbia. He thus
observed both British and American education firsthand. Associated since
1932 with* The Economist, *an influential London journal of economics and
world affairs, he edited the magazine from 1938 to 1950. The author of
several books on finance, he has lately served as chairman of Britain's
Central Advisory Council for Education. His survey of education in England
and his trips to the United States led him to the comparisons set forth in
the following essay, based on his address at the Conference of High School
Principals and Supervisors in Baltimore in 1959.*

FOR THE past three years I have been engaged, with my colleagues of the Central Advisory Council on Education in England, in a comprehensive study of the English educational system.
I had some of my own education in the United States, and I
have been a frequent visitor to America ever since. This double
experience has bred in me a growing sense of astonishment that
two countries which share the same language, so many of the
same cultural traditions and ways of life, whose political, religious, and social aspirations are so largely identical, should have
educational systems so utterly different as to provide almost no
basis for a comparison between them.

That is a strong statement, and my present purpose is to try
to justify it. Let me first say, however, that I have no intention
whatever of trying to show that one national system is, on balance, better than the other; only that they are much more different than is usually realized.

The American and the English educational systems are different in purpose, structure, and method. Let us start with purpose. The two systems grew up in response to very different
pressures and needs. In America, you have always been very

»»» *Atlantic Monthly,* CCV (April, 1960), 37-42. An address given in Baltimore in 1959. Reprinted by permission of Sir Geoffrey Crowther.

conscious of the need to build up a new society. You have wanted to construct something bigger, richer, better than you have. This is said to arise from something in the American national character, but that seems to me to turn the logic upside down; it is the American national character that has arisen from the circumstances in which the American people have found themselves. From the start it was necessary to create a supply of ministers of religion, of lawyers, and of skilled artisans—I place them in the order of importance in which they were regarded at the time. Later on there came the obvious necessity of incorporating the great waves of immigrants into your society. Still later came the great task, in which you are still engaged, of knitting your varied economic, social, and racial groups into the harmonious and balanced society in which the principles of democratic government can work properly.

Consciously or unconsciously, American education has at all times been designed to serve these social purposes. It has been regarded as an instrument by which society can build its own future. From its nature, it has inescapably been concerned with the rank and file of the people. Its chief concern for many generations has been to do something to the masses—and I think the word is *to*, not *for*—in the interests of the American dream.

All this, of course, is platitude in America. What may not be quite so familiar is the contrast in the historical situation in England. We have never been very conscious of the necessity to build a new society. At all relevant times we have had a fully developed society already in being. And at all relevant times we have also, I am sorry to say, been on the whole pretty satisfied with the society we have. For most of the last two hundred years, American education has been designed to do a job of construction; English education has been designed primarily for maintenance, with improvement coming second. In the very latest period, perhaps, those attitudes have started to change. As with so many aspects of education, there seem to be the first signs of a tendency to change sides. Your education is becoming socially more conservative just when ours is becoming more consciously radical.

But that is a speculation for the future, on which I will not enlarge. I am talking of the influences of the past, which have shaped the structures of today. American education has always had to concern itself with the common man in his multitudes. The concern of English education has until very recently been with the maintenance of society, in the words of the old prayer which you will often hear in school and college chapels, "that there may never be wanting a succession of persons duly qualified to serve God in church and state." This is a conception which does not necessarily embrace the education of the great mass. There is a fine, rich, broad educational tradition in England. But it is not a tradition of education, above the minimum level, for the multitude. Post-primary education has always been thought of as a privilege in England; it was not until 1944 that the principle of secondary education for all was established, and it is hardly yet fully effective.

Let me pursue this contrast a little further. Let me give you two of the consequences, of which I would guess that one will shock you, while the other may perhaps surprise you more favorably.

I will start with the shocker. The consequence of our different attitude is that the sheer size, the volume or quantity, of English education is very much smaller than American. The age at which the legal compulsion to attend school expires is still only fifteen. Moreover, that is an effective leaving age, and more than four children out of five in fact leave school before they are sixteen. Of the sixteen-year-old age group—those between their sixteenth and seventeenth birthdays—only 22 per cent are still in full-time education. In the seventeen-year-olds, the figure falls to 13 per cent of the boys and 11 per cent of the girls. Among eighteen-year-olds, it is 8 per cent of the boys and 5.5 per cent of the girls.

What strikes Americans, I find, as even odder than these figures is the fact that we are not, as a nation, greatly disturbed by them, although many of us think they ought to be larger. But we cannot assume that public opinion is on our side. I am very doubtful whether there would be any support in public opinion for a policy of keeping the majority of children in school after sixteen, and I am certain that you would find hardly anyone in England who believes, as you do, in keeping all children at school until eighteen. Our college students represent about 3 per cent of each age group, and there is an expansion program in hand that will raise it to about 5 per cent. Anybody who suggested that we needed any more than that would meet with the strongest resistance, and not least from the universities themselves.

This attitude does not arise from any lack of love for our children. It is not because we think we can't afford it. The proportion of our national income that we spend on general welfare services—social security, health, and the like—is about the highest in the world. It is not from lack of generosity or lack of means that we confine education after the middle teens to a minority. It is because we sincerely believe that it is the right thing to do, in the interests of the children themselves. After all, there can be no absolute rules about education. Nobody believes that any child should be allowed to leave school at twelve. I do not suppose a time will ever come when, even in America, it will become legal or compulsory for everyone to stay in full-time education until twenty-five. Where you fix the age between those limits is surely a matter of judgment. And why should it be the same age for all children? Our belief in England is that, balancing what can be got out of school against what can be got out of life, the average boy or girl has probably had the optimum dose after eleven years of schooling—and do not forget that we begin, by legal compulsion, at the age of five. Eleven years, after all, is one year out of every six or seven of the average lifetime.

Now let me give you the other side of the medal. Because education after fifteen or sixteen is confined to a minority, that minority gets every assistance that the state can provide. It is nowadays, to an overwhelming extent, a minority chosen for intelligence and attainment. There are, of course, still the independent schools, where very substantial fees have to be paid. But the pressure of numbers upon them is such that a stupid boy or girl will have great difficulty getting in. And in the state schools, selection is by merit only. But once selected, a boy finds himself with his foot not so much on a ladder as an escalator. He will have the best resources of the best schools concentrated on him. If he can secure a place in a university, and that also is a matter of selection by merit, the state will pay his tuition fees and his living expenses, not only during the session but during the vacation as well. There is no such thing as working your way through college in England. We do not need a National Merit Scholarship scheme because we have one already. Nor is this a recent thing. It has been expanded in recent years, but it has always existed.

Let me move on to structure. The outstanding difference here lies in the fact that we have a very much smaller degree of local control than you do. There are about 50,000 school boards in the United States, each of them, I suppose, more or less free to run the schools as it thinks best. That gives a total population in the average school board area of about 3500 persons. In England there are about 130 local education authorities, which gives an average population per area of about 300,000. Moreover, there are two other differences, apart from this sharp difference in size. Your school boards consist, I believe, in most states, of persons specially elected for the purpose, with no other duties. In England the schools are run by the county council, or the borough council, which is the general-purpose government of the area.

Second, your school boards raise their own money by direct taxes, or at least the greater part of it. In England about 70 per cent of the expenditure of the local education authorities is met out of grants from the central government in London. There are advantages and disadvantages in this. It means that we do not have the enormous range in standards between rich areas and poor areas that you do. It means a much greater degree of standardization of conditions of employment among the teachers, and therefore of interchangeability between school and school and between area and area. But it also inevitably means a greater degree of uniformity imposed from the center. We think our system is decentralized, because it allows much more local freedom and variety than exist in the school systems of most Continental European countries. But there is no doubt that it is much more highly centralized than the American system.

The other great difference under the heading of structure is the principle of selection upon which our system is based. All children, except the minority in fee-paying schools, go to undifferentiated schools from the age of five to the age of eleven. At eleven or thereabouts, a proportion of them, varying from area to area but averaging between 20 and 25 per cent, is selected for what we call grammar schools, which include children to the age of eighteen, though not all the pupils stay that long. The remainder go to what are called secondary modern schools, which include children to age fifteen and increasingly to sixteen, but no older.

You will see from this description that the crucial time for an English child is at the age of eleven or a little more. The selection test then applied—the famous or infamous eleven-plus examination—is supposed to be a classification purely by ability and aptitude, without any suspicion of being derogatory to those who are not selected. But, of course, everybody wants to be selected, and with the growing pressure of numbers as a result of the post-war bulge of population, the selection has been getting steadily more competitive. As the result of agitation, the Labor Party has adopted the policy of abolishing the eleven-plus examination by sending all children at that age to the same schools, the so-called comprehensive secondary schools. The Labor Party has moved toward this system in several of the areas where it controls the local council, and even in Conservative areas there is a distinct movement to experiment with systems that do not involve sending children to different schools at the age of eleven.

I have several times seen this movement quoted in America

as evidence that English education is turning away from selection. I think this is a grave misunderstanding. The public objection to selection at eleven is social and political, not educational. It is an objection on the part of parents to having their children sent to different schools, not to their having different educations. And the remedies that are being applied are wholly in terms of institutions, not in terms of the education they provide. I know, for example, one large new comprehensive school built by a Labor council. Every child entering that school is tested and placed in one of fifteen "streams," differentiated by the children's intelligence and aptitude. This selection is done by the teachers; the parents have nothing to do with it; and the children are not even supposed to know which stream is which in intelligence grading. A child placed in one of the top streams will have an almost wholly different education from a child placed even in one of the middle streams. If this is not selection, I do not know the meaning of the term. But this is what we mean by a comprehensive school. Many people in England will tell you that the comprehensive school has been copied from the American comprehensive high school, some meaning it as a compliment, some as the reverse. I have often told them that they could hardly be more mistaken.

Nonselection—if that is the opposite of selection—as it is practiced in America is totally unknown in England. By nonselection I mean the principle of treating all children alike, allowing them to sort themselves out by their choice of courses, by what they find easy and difficult, or by their varying ambitions—with counseling assistance, no doubt, but without any compulsory segregations. I am sure that your system seems as odd to us as ours does to you. There is no retreat from selection in England; the only change is that a growing number of people—but still a minority —think that the selection should be within a common school, not between schools.

The differences between the two countries in educational method make an enormous subject, and I must restrict myself to four points out of many that it would be possible to make.

The first of these differences in method lies in the position of the teacher, in the relative positions of the teacher and the textbook. One of the things about American education that most strikes the English visitor is the importance you attach to textbooks. We have no parallel to that. To begin with, I do not think there are more than two or three, at most, of the local education authorities in England that tell their schools what textbooks to use. That is left to the teacher, occasionally the principal, or the head of department in a large school. And in the higher grades, more often than not, there is not a textbook at all. A teacher will often recommend a book as covering the subject pretty well and as being useful for reference but will not make any attempt to go through it chapter by chapter.

This system places a much greater responsibility on the individual teacher, and I have often been asked in America whether we do not have a lot of trouble with it. So far as the political and social responsibility of the teacher is concerned, I cannot recall having heard of a single case arising through a teacher's being accused of using a book which seems offensive or objectionable to somebody in authority. That is partly, perhaps mainly, because our system of large authorities and rather remote and indirect public control puts the individual teacher largely out of the reach of vigilance committees, whether of parents or of the local chamber of commerce. There is also a strong tradition against anything that smacks of political interference with the schools.

Educational responsibility, however, is another matter. Quite clearly, a system like ours, which places so much responsibility on the individual teacher, cannot work well unless the average standard of intelligence, knowledge, and teaching competence is high. Up to the present, we have been able to maintain that standard. It is partly, of course, a matter of numbers. In the whole of England last year there were only some 260,000 schoolteachers. We were a little short, but 300,000 would have given us all we need. And this is in a country about one quarter the size of the United States. I do not know how many schoolteachers there are in the United States, but I am very sure it is many more than four times 300,000. I do not see how you could possibly have coped with the enormous increase in the American school population in the past forty years without being willing to take thousands of young men and women who needed close support from a textbook before they could teach. Indeed, under the pressure of rising numbers in the schools, I fear we shall find before long that we shall have to give the teacher more assistance, and that implies more external control on his teaching. This particular contrast is not, however, entirely a matter of numbers. It is partly also the result of a different tradition of teacher training, which, in England, has always laid a much greater emphasis on the content of what is to be taught than in America and much less on questions of pedagogic method.

The second difference in method is the absence in England of the course system which is so universal in your schools and colleges. Indeed, the word "course" has a wholly different meaning in the two countries. If you asked an English school child what courses he was taking, he wouldn't know what you meant. If you asked him what subjects he was taking, he would answer English, Latin, mathematics, history, and so forth. But that would not mean, as it would in America, that those were the subjects he had chosen to take. They would be the subjects that his form, or class, was taking, and therefore that he was taking with the rest of the class. Until the boy is about fifteen or sixteen, it is unlikely that he or his parents have had any say in the choice of form in which he is placed. And at no age does he have any say in deciding the curriculum of that form. At the higher ages, there is a choice between three or four different curriculums, but each curriculum has to be taken, within narrow limits, as it stands.

Here, indeed, is a contrast with the American system. Perhaps it is not quite so sharp a contrast in practice as it is in principle, as I observe that, more and more, those American boys and girls who have ambition to gain admittance to a good college find their choice of courses in high school made for them by the college entrance requirements. But there is one important consequence for teaching that is worth bringing out. In an English school, in any year but one (and that one is what we call the fifth form year, about the age of fourteen or fifteen), you can assume that the pupils who are taking a subject in one year will be taking the same subject next year. The study of a subject can therefore be planned as a continuous process over a period of years. That is what we mean when we use the word "course." We mean a whole balanced curriculum of six or seven or eight subjects, planned to continue over three or four or five years. Once a boy or girl enters on such a course, he or she will normally pursue it to the end. And all the boys and girls in a course will take substantially the same subjects, with perhaps slight options, as between a second classical or a second modern language. You will therefore understand how bewildered we are when we contemplate one of your neat, packaged, self-contained, nine-month courses, such as high school physics. It is no good asking an English schoolboy when he enters college how many years of French he has had at school. Two boys might both truthfully answer nine years. But they might mean totally different things, and neither one would mean what you thought he meant.

How, then, do we measure what a student has accomplished, if we cannot count up the number of courses he has satisfactorily taken? The answer is that we rely, to an extent wholly unknown to you, on general examinations. Every year—sometimes every term—the pupil has to take a written examination in all the subjects of the curriculum, and his further progress depends, sometimes entirely, on his performance in that examination. Most of these examinations are set and assessed within the school itself, by his own teachers. But at three crucial points in his career the examination is set and assessed by an external body. The first of these is the eleven-plus examination, which determines to which sort of secondary school the child should go. The second comes at fifteen or sixteen and is called the Ordinary Level of the General Certificate of Education, set and assessed by one of nine examining boards closely associated with the universities. This examination can be taken in any number of subjects from one upwards, but the most usual practice is to take it in from five to nine subjects. Third, there is the Advanced Level of the General Certificate of Education, which is taken at eighteen or thereabouts and which plays a large part in university entrance.

I have been describing the practice of the grammar schools; that is, the schools for the brightest 20 to 25 per cent of the children. Examinations, especially written examinations, play a much smaller part in the life of the less intelligent children. Even in this case, however, they play a much larger part than they do in America; and there is a rising demand for public examinations, at lower standards of intelligence than those of the General Certificate of Education, for these less gifted children. I cannot honestly say that the children themselves clamor for examinations, but employers do, and therefore so do the parents. All the questions that Americans ask and answer in terms of the number and variety of courses a student has taken we ask and answer in terms of the examinations he has passed.

I have left to the last what is the sharpest difference of all between our two systems. This is our system of specialization, in which England is, I think, unique in the world. A student will take the examination for the Ordinary Level of the General Certificate of Education at the age of fifteen or sixteen in a wide range of subjects drawn both from the humanities and from the natural sciences. But once he has passed that examination, he will specialize. That is to say, he will devote two thirds, or perhaps even more, of his time in school to a narrow range of subjects. In one boy's case it may be physics, chemistry, and mathematics; in another's it may be chemistry and biology, or it may be history or modern languages and literature, or classical languages and philosophy. But, whatever the choice, the greater part of the pupil's attention, in the classroom and in his private study time, is given to his specialty, and he will take the advanced level examination at eighteen in his special subjects only. When he gets to the university, the specialization is even more intense. The range of subjects does not usually get any narrower, but the student gives 100 per cent of his time to it.

I have found that to Americans, and indeed to educationalists from every country in the world except England, this seems a very strange system indeed. Perhaps you will have difficulty in believing that I really mean what I say. So let me cite my own case, though it is now more than thirty years old. I was a modern languages specialist. For my last three years at school, from the ages of fifteen to eighteen, I studied mostly French and German language and literature, perhaps three or four hours a week of history, and one hour of Scripture on Sundays. For another two years at Cambridge, even the history and the Scripture were cut out, and I studied French and German exclusively. Five years of my life were given to those languages. My experience was perhaps a little extreme; I think the admixture of general and contrasting subjects would nowadays, in a good school, be a little bigger. But the difference would not be great. The English boy or girl is a specialist from the age of fifteen or sixteen.

The advisory council of which I am chairman was specifically requested by the Minister of Education to review this system of specialization. We examined it most carefully and discussed it at great length, both with witnesses and among ourselves. In the end we came to the conclusion that we wanted to see it continued. We found that it was being pushed too far, and we have made a number of suggestions for removing what we think are abuses. But we have reported in favor of this system of specialization. And that is a unanimous conclusion reached by a council made up of educators of all kinds. Perhaps you will find that fact as extraordinary as the system itself, and I must try to give you some of our reasons for thinking that, in this matter, we in England are in step and the whole of the rest of the world is out of step.

Let me begin by telling you of one argument that we reject. This is the argument that every intelligent citizen, or every educated man, ought to know something about each subject in a range so wide that it compels a balanced curriculum; that no one can afford to be ignorant of history, government, science, languages, and so forth. To this, we would give our answer in two parts. First, it is true that there are certain elementary skills and knowledges that everyone must have—reading, writing, arithmetic, and several more. But these essential elements can be, and should be, provided by the age of sixteen. If you go on with them after that age, you will be wasting your time, because the knowledge you instill will be forgotten unless it can be attached to the main intellectual interest of a boy's or girl's life, which begins to emerge at about that age.

The second part of the answer is that it is only when you have got these essential elementary skills and knowledges out of the way that you can confront the real task of education. The acquisition of factual knowledge is by itself a poor test of any education and a lamentably poor test of the education of boys and girls of seventeen and eighteen. It has been said that the process of education is not to be compared to that of filling up an empty pot, but rather to that of lighting a fire. The proper test of an education is whether it teaches the pupil to think and whether it awakens his interest in applying his brain to the various problems and opportunities that life presents. If these have once been done, then factual knowledge can easily be assimilated. If these have not been done, then no amount of nodding acquaintance with widely varying fields of human knowledge will equip a boy or girl with an educated mind. We in England argue the case for specialization not primarily on the score of the information it provides but because it awakens interest, teaches clear thinking, and induces self-discipline in study.

We believe that, if you can find which of the recognized intellectual disciplines most arouses a boy's interest—and we confine his choice to five or six recognized disciplines, chosen for their intellectual content, not for their vocational value—if you can let him spend his time on what interests him, but insist that he must work hard at it, go deep into it, follow it up in the library or the laboratory, get around behind the stage scenery that defines the formal academic subject, you will really be teaching him how to use the mind that God has given him. This sort of intensive study takes a great deal of time, and that is why it can only be applied, for any one student, to a restricted range of subjects. No doubt you will say that the boy must be very narrow as a result. That may be. Are you sure that being narrow is worse than being shallow?

I find that English education has a high reputation among Americans. I am often asked, for example, whether it is not true that the eighteen-year-old boy in England is a year or two ahead of his American contemporary. I always answer that question, or assertion, by asking some others. What boy? If an English boy is still at school at eighteen, he is necessarily in the upper quartile in intelligence. Are you comparing him with the average American high school graduate, who is of average intelligence? And ahead in what? In the subjects to which he has been giving nearly all his time and attention for two years? It would be strange if he were not a long way ahead in those. Or over the whole range of a broad curriculum? He has been taught different things, by different methods, with a different purpose in view, in a different sort of school. There is no fair basis for a comparative judgment.

ANTHONY TROLLOPE

AMERICAN HOTELS

Anthony Trollope (1815-1882), British postal official and novelist, turned to writing as a means to augment his income from the Post Office and became a successful author. The Warden (1855) and Barchester Towers (1857), his first successes after three unlucky novels, established him as a popular writer; he went on to write forty-seven novels in all, as well as short stories, essays, biographies, and books of travel. In his Autobiography (written, 1875-1876; published, 1883), he claimed to have written more than any other English author then living, adding that quantity was not a sign of quality but merely of his diligence. The Victorians, shocked by his admission that he had written for money instead of art, promptly forgot him. Lately the Trollope revival has brought new appreciation of his work.

I FIND IT IMPOSSIBLE to resist the subject of inns. As I have gone on with my journey, I have gone on with my book, and have spoken here and there of American hotels as I have encountered them. But in the States the hotels are so large an institution, having so much closer and wider a bearing on social life than they do in any other country, that I feel myself bound to treat them in a separate chapter as a great national feature in themselves. They are quite as much thought of in the nation as the legislature, or judicature, or literature of the country; and any falling off in them, or any improvement in the accommodation given, would strike the community as forcibly as a change in the constitution, or an alteration in the franchise.

Moreover I consider myself as qualified to write a chapter on hotels;—not only on the hotels of America but on hotels generally. I have myself been much too frequently a sojourner at hotels. I think I know what an hotel should be, and what it should not be; and am almost inclined to believe, in my pride, that I could myself fill the position of a landlord with some chance of social success, though probably with none of satisfactory pecuniary results.

»»» Ch. 29 of *North America*. London, 1862.

Of all hotels known to me, I am inclined to think that the Swiss are the best. The things wanted at an hotel are, I fancy, mainly as follows:—a clean bedroom with a good and clean bed, and with it also plenty of water. Good food, well dressed and served at convenient hours, which hours should on occasions be allowed to stretch themselves. Wines that shall be drinkable. Quick attendance. Bills that shall not be absolutely extortionate, smiling faces, and an absence of foul smells. There are many who desire more than this;—who expect exquisite cookery, choice wines, subservient domestics, distinguished consideration, and the strictest economy. But they are uneducated travellers who are going through the apprenticeship of their hotel lives;—who may probably never become free of the travellers' guild, or learn to distinguish that which they may fairly hope to attain from that which they can never accomplish.

Taking them as a whole I think that the Swiss hotels are the best. They are perhaps a little close in the matter of cold water, but even as to this, they generally give way to pressure. The pressure, however, must not be violent, but gentle rather, and well continued. Their bedrooms are excellent. Their cookery is good, and to the outward senses is cleanly. The people are civil. The whole work of the house is carried on upon fixed rules which tend to the comfort of the establishment. They are not cheap, and not always quite honest. But the exorbitance or dishonesty of their charges rarely exceeds a certain reasonable scale, and hardly ever demands the bitter misery of a remonstrance.

The inns of the Tyrol are, I think, the cheapest I have known, affording the traveller what he requires for half the price, or less than half, that demanded in Switzerland. But the other half is taken out in stench and nastiness. As tourists scatter themselves more profusely, the prices of the Tyrol will no doubt rise. Let us hope that increased prices will bring with them besoms, scrubbing-brushes, and other much needed articles of cleanliness.

The inns of the north of Italy are very good, and indeed, the Italian inns throughout, as far as I know them, are much better than the name they bear. The Italians are a civil, kindly people,

and do for you, at any rate, the best they can. Perhaps the un-
wary traveller may be cheated. Ignorant of the language, he may
be called on to pay more than the man who speaks it, and who
can bargain in the Italian fashion as to price. It has often been
my lot, I doubt not, to be so cheated. But then I have been
cheated with a grace that has been worth all the money. The
ordinary prices of Italian inns are by no means high.

I have seldom thoroughly liked the inns of Germany which I
have known. They are not clean, and water is very scarce. Smiles
too are generally wanting, and I have usually fancied myself to
be regarded as a piece of goods out of which so much profit was
to be made.

The dearest hotels I know are the French;—and certainly not
the best. In the provinces they are by no means so cleanly as
those of Italy. Their wines are generally abominable, and their
cookery often disgusting. In Paris grand dinners may no doubt
be had, and luxuries of every description,—except the luxury of
comfort. Cotton-velvet sofas and ormolu clocks stand in the
place of convenient furniture, and logs of wood at a franc a log
fail to impart to you the heat which the freezing cold of a Paris
winter demands. They used to make good coffee in Paris, but
even that is a thing of the past. I fancy that they import their
brandy from England, and manufacture their own cigars. French
wines you may get good at a Paris hotel; but you would drink
them as good and much cheaper if you bought them in London
and took them with you.

The worst hotels I know are in the Havana. Of course I do
not speak here of chance mountain huts, or small far-off roadside
hostels in which the traveller may find himself from time to time.
All such are to be counted apart, and must be judged on their
merits, by the circumstances which surround them. But with
reference to places of wide resort, nothing can beat the hotels
of the Havana in filth, discomfort, habits of abomination, and
absence of everything which the traveller desires. All the world
does not go to the Havana, and the subject is not, therefore,

one of general interest. But in speaking of hotels at large, so much I find myself bound to say.

In all the countries to which I have alluded the guests of the house are expected to sit down together at one table. Conversation is at any rate possible, and there is the show if not the reality of society.

And now one word as to English inns. I do not think that we Englishmen have any great right to be proud of them. The worst about them is that they deteriorate from year to year instead of becoming better. We used to hear much of the comfort of the old English wayside inn, but the old English wayside inn has gone. The railway hotel has taken its place, and the railway hotel is too frequently gloomy, desolate, comfortless, and almost suicidal. In England too, since the old days are gone, there are wanting the landlord's bow, and the kindly smile of his stout wife. Who now knows the landlord of an inn, or cares to inquire whether or no there be a landlady? The old welcome is wanting, and the cheery warm air which used to atone for the bad port and tough beef has passed away;—while the port is still bad and the beef too often tough.

In England, and only in England, as I believe, is maintained in hotel life the theory of solitary existence. The sojourner at an English inn,—unless he be a commercial traveller, and, as such, a member of a universal, peripatetic, tradesman's club,—lives alone. He has his breakfast alone, his dinner alone, his pint of wine alone, and his cup of tea alone. It is not considered practicable that two strangers should sit at the same table, or cut from the same dish. Consequently his dinner is cooked for him separately, and the hotel keeper can hardly afford to give him a good dinner. He has two modes of life from which to choose. He either lives in a public room,—called a coffee-room, and there occupies during his comfortless meal a separate small table too frequently removed from fire and light, though generally exposed to draughts; or else he indulges in the luxury of a private sitting-room, and endeavours to find solace on an old horse-hair sofa, at the cost of seven shillings a day. His bedroom is not so arranged that he can use it as a sitting-room. Under either phase of life he can rarely find himself comfortable, and therefore he lives as little at an hotel as the circumstances of his business or of his pleasure will allow. I do not think that any of the requisites of a good inn are habitually to be found in perfection at our Kings' Heads and White Horses, though the falling off is not so lamentably distressing as it sometimes is in other countries. The bedrooms are dingy rather than dirty. Extra payment to servants will generally produce a tub of cold water. The food is never good, but it is usually eatable, and you may have it when you please. The wines are almost always bad, but the traveller can fall back upon beer. The attendance is good, provided always that the payment for it is liberal. The cost is generally too high, and unfortunately grows larger and larger from year to year. Smiling faces are out of the question unless specially paid for; and as to that matter of foul smells there is often room for improvement. An English inn to a solitary traveller without employment is an embodiment of dreary desolation. The excuse to be made for this is that English men and women do not live much at inns in their own country.

The American inn differs from all those of which I have made mention, and is altogether an institution apart, and a thing of itself. Hotels in America are very much larger and more numerous than in other countries. They are to be found in all towns, and I may almost say in all villages. In England and on the Continent we find them on the recognized routes of travel and in towns of commercial or social importance. On unfrequented roads and in villages there is usually some small house of public entertainment in which the unexpected traveller may obtain food and shelter, and in which the expected boon companions of the neighbourhood smoke their nightly pipes, and drink their nightly tipple. But in the States of America the first sign of an incipient settlement is an hotel five stories high, with an office, a bar, a cloak-room, three gentlemen's parlours, two ladies' parlours, a ladies' entrance, and two hundred bedrooms.

These, of course, are all built with a view to profit, and it may be presumed that in each case the originators of the speculation enter into some calculation as to their expected guests. Whence are to come the sleepers in those two hundred bedrooms, and who is to pay for the gaudy sofas and numerous lounging chairs of the ladies' parlours? In all other countries the expectation would extend itself simply to travellers;—to travellers or to strangers sojourning in the land. But this is by no means the case as to these speculations in America. When the new hotel rises up in the wilderness, it is presumed that people will come there with the express object of inhabiting it. The hotel itself will create a population,—as the railways do. With us railways run to the towns; but in the States the towns run to the railways. It is the same thing with the hotels.

Housekeeping is not popular with young married people in America, and there are various reasons why this should be so. Men there are not fixed in their employment as they are with us. If a young Benedict cannot get along as a lawyer at Salem, perhaps he may thrive as a shoemaker at Thermopylæ. Jefferson B. Johnson fails in the lumber line at Eleutheria, but hearing of an opening for a Baptist preacher at Big Mud Creek moves himself off with his wife and three children at a week's notice. Aminadab Wiggs takes an engagement as a clerk at a steam-boat office on the Pongowonga river, but he goes to his employment with an inward conviction that six months will see him earning his bread elsewhere. Under such circumstances even a large wardrobe is a nuisance, and a collection of furniture would be as appropriate as a drove of elephants. Then, again, young men and women marry without any means already collected on which to commence their life. They are content to look forward and to hope that such means will come. In so doing they are guilty of no imprudence. It is the way of the country; and, if the man be useful for anything, employment will certainly come to him. But he must live on the fruits of that employment, and can only pay his way from week to week and from day to day. And as a third reason I think I may allege that the mode of life found in these hotels is liked by the people who frequent them. It is to their taste. They are happy, or at any rate contented at these hotels, and do not wish for household cares. As to the two first reasons which I have given I can agree as to the necessity of the case, and quite concur as to the expediency of marriage under such circumstances. But as to that matter of taste, I cannot concur at all. Anything more forlorn than a young married woman at an American hotel, it is impossible to conceive.

Such are the guests expected for those two hundred bedrooms. The chance travellers are but chance additions to these, and are not generally the main stay of the house. As a matter of course the accommodation for travellers which these hotels afford increases and creates travelling. Men come because they know they will be fed and bedded at a moderate cost, and in an easy way, suited to their tastes. With us, and throughout Europe, inquiry is made before an unaccustomed journey is commenced, on that serious question of wayside food and shelter. But in the States no such question is needed. A big hotel is a matter of course, and therefore men travel. Everybody travels in the States. The railways and the hotels have between them so churned up the people that an untravelled man or woman is a rare animal. We are apt to suppose that travellers make roads, and that guests create hotels; but the cause and effect run exactly in the other way. I am almost disposed to think that we should become cannibals if gentlemen's legs and ladies' arms were hung up for sale in purveyors' shops.

After this fashion and with these intentions hotels are built. Size and an imposing exterior are the first requisitions. Everything about them must be on a large scale. A commanding exterior, and a certain interior dignity of demeanour is more essential than comfort or civility. Whatever an hotel may be it must not be "mean." In the American vernacular the word "mean" is very significant. A mean white in the South is a man who owns no slaves. Men are often mean, but actions are seldom so called. A man feels mean when the bluster is taken out of him. A mean hotel, conducted in a quiet unostentatious manner, in which the only endeavour made had reference to the comfort of a few guests, would find no favour in the States. These hotels are not called by the name of any sign, as with us in our provinces. There are no "Presidents' Heads" or "General Scotts." Nor by the name of the landlord, or of some former landlord, as with us in London, and in many cities of the Continent. Nor are they called from some country or city which may have been presumed at some time to have had special patronage for the establishment. In the nomenclature of American hotels the speciality of American hero-worship is shown, as in the nomenclature of their children. Every inn is a house, and these houses are generally named after some hero, little known probably in the world at large, but highly estimated in that locality at the moment of the christening.

They are always built on a plan which to a European seems to be most unnecessarily extravagant in space. It is not unfrequently the case that the greater portion of the ground-floor is occupied by rooms and halls which make no return to the house whatever. The visitor enters a great hall by the front door, and almost invariably finds it full of men who are idling about, sitting round on stationary seats, talking in a listless manner, and getting through their time as though the place were a public lounging room. And so it is. The chances are that not half the crowd are guests at the hotel. I will now follow the visitor as he makes his way up to the office. Every hotel has an office. To call this place the bar, as I have done too frequently, is a lamentable error. The bar is held in a separate room appropriated solely to drinking. To the office, which is in fact a long open counter, the guest walks up, and there inscribes his name in a book. This inscription was to me a moment of misery which I could never go through with equanimity. As the name is written, and as the request for accommodation is made, half a dozen loungers look over your name and listen to what you say. They listen attentively, and spell your name carefully, but the great man behind the bar does not seem to listen or to heed you. Your destiny is never imparted to you on the instant. If your wife or any other woman be with you, (the word "lady" is made so absolutely distasteful in American hotels that I cannot bring myself to use it in writing

of them,) she has been carried off to a lady's waiting room, and
there remains in august wretchedness till the great man at the bar
shall have decided on her fate. I have never been quite able to
fathom the mystery of these delays. I think they must have
originated in the necessity of waiting to see what might be the
influx of travellers at the moment, and then have become exaggerated and brought to their present normal state by the gratified
feeling of almost divine power with which for the time it invests
that despotic arbiter. I have found it always the same, though
arriving with no crowd, by a conveyance of my own, when no
other expectant guests were following me. The great man has
listened to my request in silence, with an imperturbable face,
and has usually continued his conversation with some loafing
friend, who at the time is probably scrutinizing my name in the
book. I have often suffered in patience; but patience is not
specially the badge of my tribe, and I have sometimes spoken
out rather freely. If I may presume to give advice to my travelling countrymen how to act under such circumstances I should
recommend to them freedom of speech rather than patience.
The great man when freely addressed generally opens his eyes,
and selects the key of your room without further delay. I am
inclined to think that the selection will not be made in any way
to your detriment by reason of that freedom of speech. The lady
in the ballad who spoke out her own mind to Lord Bateman was
sent to her home honourably in a coach and three. Had she held
her tongue we are justified in presuming that she would have
been returned on a pillion behind a servant.

I have been greatly annoyed by that silence on the part of the
hotel clerk. I have repeatedly asked for room, and received no
syllable in return. I have persisted in my request, and the clerk
has nodded his head at me. Until a traveller is known, these
gentlemen are singularly sparing of speech,—especially in the
West. The same economy of words runs down from the great
man at the office all through the servants of the establishment. It
arises, I believe, entirely from that want of courtesy which
democratic institutions create. The man whom you address, has

to make a battle against the state of subservience, presumed to be indicated by his position, and he does so by declaring his indifference to the person on whose wants he is paid to attend. I have been honoured on one or two occasions by the subsequent intimacy of these great men at the hotel offices, and have then found them ready enough at conversation.

That necessity of making your request for rooms before a public audience, is not in itself agreeable, and sometimes entails a conversation which might be more comfortably made in private. "What do you mean by a dressing-room, and why do you want one?" Now that is a question which an Englishman feels awkward at answering before five-and-twenty Americans, with open mouths and eager eyes; but it has to be answered. When I left England, I was assured that I should not find any need for a separate sitting-room, seeing that drawing-rooms more or less sumptuous were prepared for the accommodation of "ladies." At first we attempted to follow the advice given to us, but we broke down. A man and his wife travelling from town to town, and making no sojourn on his way, may eat and sleep at an hotel without a private parlour. But an Englishwoman cannot live in comfort for a week, or even, in comfort, for a day, at any of these houses, without a sitting-room for herself. The ladies' drawing-room is a desolate wilderness. The American women themselves do not use it. It is generally empty, or occupied by some forlorn spinster, eliciting harsh sounds from the wretched piano which it contains.

The price at these hotels throughout the Union is nearly always the same, viz., two and a half dollars a day, for which a bedroom is given, and as many meals as the guest can contrive to eat. This is the price for chance guests. The cost to monthly boarders is, I believe, not more than the half of this. Ten shillings a day, therefore, covers everything that is absolutely necessary, servants included. And this must be said in praise to these inns: that the traveller can compute his expenses accurately, and can absolutely bring them within that daily sum of ten shillings. This includes a great deal of eating, a great deal of attendance, the use of reading-rooms and smoking-rooms—which, however, always seem to be open to the public as well as to the guests,—and a bedroom with accommodation which is at any rate as good as the average accommodation of hotels in Europe. In the large Eastern towns baths are attached to many of the rooms. I always carry my own, and have never failed in getting water. It must be acknowledged that the price is very low. It is so low that I believe it affords, as a rule, no profit whatsoever. The profit is made upon extra charges, and they are higher than in any other country that I have visited. They are so high that I consider travelling in America, for an Englishman with his wife or family, to be more expensive than travelling in any part of Europe. First in the list of extras comes that matter of the sitting-room, and by that for a man and his wife the whole first expense is at once doubled. The ordinary charge is five dollars, or one pound a day! A guest intending to stay for two or three weeks at an hotel, or perhaps for one week, may, by agreement, have this charge reduced. At one inn I stayed a fortnight, and having made no such agreement was charged the full sum. I felt myself stirred up to complain, and did in that case remonstrate. I was asked how much I wished to have returned,—for the bill had been paid,— and the sum I suggested was at once handed to me. But even with such reduction the price is very high, and at once makes the American hotel expensive. Wine also at these houses is very costly, and very bad. The usual price is two dollars, or eight shillings, a bottle. The people of the country rarely drink wine at dinner in the hotels. When they do so, they drink champagne; but their normal drinking is done separately, at the bar, chiefly before dinner, and at a cheap rate. "A drink," let it be what it may, invariably costs a dime, or fivepence. But if you must have a glass of sherry with your dinner, it costs two dollars; for sherry does not grow into pint bottles in the States. But the guest who remains for two days can have his wine kept for him. Washing also is an expensive luxury. The price of this is invariable, being always fourpence for everything washed. A cambric handker-chief or muslin dress all come out at the same price. For those who are cunning in the matter this may do very well; but for men and women whose cuffs and collars are numerous it becomes expensive. The craft of those who are cunning is shown, I think, in little internal washings, by which the cambric handkerchiefs are kept out of the list, while the muslin dresses are placed upon it. I am led to this surmise by the energetic measures taken by the hotel keepers to prevent such domestic washings, and by the denunciations which in every hotel are pasted up in every room against the practice. I could not at first understand why I was always warned against washing my own clothes in my own bed-room, and told that no foreign laundress could on any account be admitted into the house. The injunctions given on this head are almost frantic in their energy, and therefore I conceive that hotel keepers find themselves exposed to much suffering in the matter. At these hotels they wash with great rapidity, sending you back your clothes in four or five hours if you desire it.

Another very stringent order is placed before the face of all visitors at American hotels, desiring them on no account to leave valuable property in their rooms. I presume that there must have been some difficulty in this matter in bygone years, for in every State a law has been passed declaring that hotel keepers shall not be held responsible for money or jewels stolen out of rooms in their houses, provided that they are furnished with safes for keeping such money, and give due caution to their guests on the subject. The due caution is always given, but I have seldom myself taken any notice of it. I have always left my portmanteau open, and have kept my money usually in a trav-elling desk in my room. But I never to my knowledge lost any-thing. The world, I think, gives itself credit for more thieves than it possesses. As to the female servants at American inns, they are generally all that is disagreeable. They are uncivil, im-pudent, dirty, slow,—provoking to a degree. But I believe that they keep their hands from picking and stealing.

I never yet made a single comfortable meal at an American hotel, or rose from my breakfast or dinner with that feeling of satisfaction which should, I think, be felt at such moments in a civilized land in which cookery prevails as an art. I have had enough, and have been healthy and am thankful. But that thankfulness is altogether a matter apart, and does not bear upon the question. If need be I can eat food that is disagreeable to my palate, and make no complaint. But I hold it to be compatible with the principles of an advanced Christianity to prefer food that is palatable. I never could get any of that kind at an American hotel. All meal-times at such houses were to me periods of disagreeable duty; and at this moment, as I write these lines at the hotel in which I am still staying, I pine for an English leg of mutton. But I do not wish it to be supposed that the fault of which I complain,—for it is a grievous fault,—is incidental to America as a nation. I have stayed in private houses, and have daily sat down to dinners quite as good as any my own kitchen could afford me. Their dinner parties are generally well done, and as a people they are by no means indifferent to the nature of their comestibles. It is of the hotels that I speak, and of them I again say that eating in them is a disagreeable task,—a painful labour. It is as a schoolboy's lesson, or the six hours' confinement of a clerk at his desk.

The mode of eating is as follows. Certain feeding hours are named, which generally include nearly all the day. Breakfast from six till ten. Dinner from one till five. Tea from six till nine. Supper from nine till twelve. When the guest presents himself at any of these hours he is marshalled to a seat, and a bill is put into his hand containing the names of all the eatables then offered for his choice. The list is incredibly and most unnecessarily long. Then it is that you will see care written on the face of the American hotel liver, as he studies the programme of the coming performance. With men this passes off unnoticed, but with young girls the appearance of the thing is not attractive. The anxious study, the elaborate reading of the daily book, and then the choice proclaimed with clear articulation. "Boiled mutton and caper sauce, roast duck, hashed venison, mashed potatoes, poached eggs and spinach, stewed tomatoes. Yes; and waiter,—some squash." There is no false delicacy in the voice by which this order is given, no desire for a gentle whisper. The dinner is ordered with the firm determination of an American heroine, and in some five minutes' time all the little dishes appear at once, and the lady is surrounded by her banquet.

How I did learn to hate those little dishes and their greasy contents! At a London eating-house things are often not very nice, but your meat is put on a plate and comes before you in an edible shape. At these hotels it is brought to you in horrid little oval dishes, and swims in grease. Gravy is not an institution at American hotels, but grease has taken its place. It is palpable, undisguised grease, floating in rivers,—not grease caused by accidental bad cookery, but grease on purpose. A beef-steak is not a beef-steak unless a quarter of a pound of butter be added to it. Those horrid little dishes! If one thinks of it how could they have been made to contain Christian food? Every article in that long list is liable to the call of any number of guests for four hours. Under such circumstances how can food be made eatable? Your roast mutton is brought to you raw;—if you object to that you are supplied with meat that has been four times brought before the public. At hotels on the continent of Europe different dinners are cooked at different hours, but here the same dinner is kept always going. The house breakfast is maintained on a similar footing. Huge boilers of tea and coffee are stewed down and kept hot. To me those meals were odious. It is of course open to any one to have separate dinners and separate breakfasts in his own room; but by this little is gained and much is lost. He or she who is so exclusive pays twice over for such meals,—as they are charged as extras on the bill; and, after all, receives the advantage of no exclusive cooking. Particles from the public dinners are brought to the private room, and the same odious little dishes make their appearance.

But the most striking peculiarity of the American hotels is in their public rooms. Of the ladies' drawing-room I have spoken. There are two and sometimes three in one hotel, and they are generally furnished, at any rate expensively. It seems to me that the space and the furniture are almost thrown away. At watering places, and sea-side summer hotels they are, I presume, used; but at ordinary hotels they are empty deserts. The intention is good, for they are established with the view of giving to ladies at hotels the comforts of ordinary domestic life; but they fail in their effect. Ladies will not make themselves happy in any room, or with ever so much gilded furniture, unless some means of happiness be provided for them. Into these rooms no book is ever brought, no needlework is introduced; from them no clatter of many tongues is ever heard. On a marble table in the middle of the room always stands a large pitcher of iced water, and from this a cold, damp, uninviting air is spread through the atmosphere of the ladies' drawing-room.

Below, on the ground floor, there is, in the first place, the huge entrance hall, at the back of which, behind a bar, the great man of the place keeps the keys and holds his court. There are generally seats around it, in which smokers sit,—or men not smoking but ruminating. Opening off from this are reading rooms, smoking rooms, shaving rooms, drinking rooms, parlours for gentlemen in which smoking is prohibited, and which are generally as desolate as the ladies' sitting-rooms above. In those other more congenial chambers is always gathered together a crowd, apparently belonging in no way to the hotel. It would seem that a great portion of an American inn is as open to the public as an Exchange, or as the wayside of the street. In the West, during the months of this war, the traveller would always see many soldiers among the crowd,—not only officers, but privates. They sit in public seats, silent but apparently contented, sometimes for an hour together. All Americans are given to gatherings such as these. It is the much-loved institution to which the name of "loafing" has been given.

I do not like the mode of life which prevails in the American hotels. I have come across exceptions, and know one or two that are comfortable,—always excepting that matter of eating and drinking. But taking them as a whole I do not like their mode of life. I feel, however, bound to add that the hotels of Canada, which are kept, I think, always after the same fashion, are infinitely worse than those of the United States. I do not like the American hotels; but I must say in their favour that they afford an immense amount of accommodation. The traveller is rarely told that an hotel is full, so that travelling in America is without one of those great perils to which it is subject in Europe. It must also be acknowledged that for the ordinary purposes of a traveller they are very cheap.

JOSEPH WOOD KRUTCH

THE SLOBURBS

Joseph Wood Krutch (1893-   ), since his retirement from the New York literary scene, has written of his new home in Arizona in such books as The Voice of the Desert *(1955) and* Grand Canyon: Today and All Its Yesterdays *(1958). He continues to remark upon our changing culture in his column* "If You Don't Mind My Saying So. . ." *in* The American Scholar, *from which comes the following piece on sloburbs Arizona-style.*

AT LOS ANGELES we were told that the San Francisco Airport was fogged in, and given a choice. We could go to a hotel for the night and hope that the weather would clear or we could resign ourselves to a nine hour bus ride. I chose the bus while reflecting sourly on the paradoxes of today's travel, so neatly illustrated by the fact that not many months before I had come to San Francisco from Tokyo in exactly the same time it would take me to get there from Los Angeles. One compensation—if you can call it that—did develop. I got the most extensive view I have ever had of what is now commonly called the Sloburbs. Also, the fullest realization of their horror.

Nowhere are they worse than in the Los Angeles area and nowhere are they more extensive. For several hours the same dismal scenes change so little that it is hard to believe one is moving at all. Gas station, motel, car lot, bar, hamburger stand; then gas station, motel, car lot, bar and hamburger stand again, all bathed in the hellish glow of neon. Daylight would have made everything look shabbier but not less unattractive.

Los Angeles can, of course, be accused of no more than a bad eminence. Nearly all American towns, even quite small ones, present a more or less extensive version of the same picture. The newer and faster-growing the community the more it tends to

»»» Reprinted from *The American Scholar*, XXXIV, No. 2 (Spring, 1965), 162-164. Copyright © 1965 by the United Chapters of Phi Beta Kappa. By permission of the publishers.

be a sloburb and nothing else, and sloburbs are so much alike that if you were carried into one blindfolded you would often find it impossible to say not only where you were, but even whether you were north or south or east or west.

Tucson, where I now live, is no exception. In fact, it is rather worse than many agglomerations because so much of its explosive growth is recent and takes the form of rapidly spreading sloburbs. They have not yet reached the area where I live but they are creeping toward it, and as I drove home the other day through spreading ugliness I was amazed again that this sort of anti-city could be so characterless. Everything looks improvised, random, unrelated to everything else, as though it had no memory of yesterday and no expectation of tomorrow.

Nor is this true only of the motel-bar-hamburger stand complex. It is almost equally so of a new kind of "business district" which is less a district than a ribbon of commercial establishments growing longer and longer as "downtown" shrinks or stagnates. Here the repetitive succession is not unlike that of the only slightly frowzier parade of eateries, drinkeries and sleeperies. The supermarkets (one every few hundred yards) are the most imposing of the commercial establishments. Between them come drugstores which sell more toys, sporting equipment and sandwiches than they do drugs; dimestores; TV repair shops and auto supply emporia in a sort of procession which is repeated as soon as the repertory has completed itself.

Yet this is far from being a depressed area. It is actually a very prosperous one and real estate prices skyrocket in what is only a little better than a sort of shantytown. Poverty, I reminded myself, creates slums and slums can be even uglier. But I wondered if ever before in history a prosperous people had consented to live in communities so devoid of every grace and dignity, so slumlike in everything except the money they represent. They are something new and almost uniquely unattractive—neither country nor village nor town nor city—just an agglomeration without plan, without any sense of unity or direction, as though even offices and shops were thought of as (like nearly everything else in our civilization) disposable and therefore not worth considering from any standpoint except the make-do of the moment.

A real metropolis has a quasi-organic unity. There is a nerve center, more or less elaborate, which includes whatever public buildings, theaters, auditoriums and major commercial emporia the community can support. From the impressiveness of this nerve center one can judge pretty accurately just to what degree it is a metropolis rather than a town or a village. Its suburbs and even its slums are related to the whole. But a large sloburb like that which surrounds and all but engulfs Los Angeles differs from that of the village on the highway in nothing except area. You could cut a piece off it and set the piece down anywhere and you could not tell that it had grown up around Los Angeles rather than where you found it. A suburb implies a city to which it is attached, but what we are increasingly developing are huge agglomerations that cannot be called suburbs because there are no urbs to own them.

Why, then, have the sloburbs become the most characteristic aspect of modern America, the only real urban development new to our time? They are as much our special contribution to the look and feel of our environment as the skyscraper was the contribution of the first half of the century.

If you accept the now usual assumption that whatever we do or are is the necessary result of "evolving technology," then the answer is easy. Technological progress has made the population explosion supportable and necessitated rapid growth. The automobile has made us mobile, and prosperity has not only created the demand for the superfluities to which two thirds of the enterprises in the sloburbs cater but also encouraged the tendency to regard everything, including architecture, as disposable. Stores, office buildings and even churches will be "turned in" for new ones in a year or two. That is progress.

If, on the other hand, you believe that evolving technology is only half the story, that human beings are capable of resisting as well as of yielding to pressures, then the question why we have consented to the sloburbs remains, why we are to all appearances so contented with them. Remember that sloburbs are the product of wealth and abundance. The motel-cafe regions cater to those who have much leisure; the merchandising sloburbs depend at least as much upon what might be called luxury goods as they do upon necessities. Why is there so little that is luxurious, or even decently dignified, about the buildings that house them, the merchandising methods they employ? Why should an abundant society be content to accept communities so obviously the antithesis of that "gracious living" that the service magazines talk about and declare to be nowadays open to all?

Easy answers to that question are also available if you want to accept them. Americans have no taste, no sense of dignity, no ability to discriminate between the informality to which they are committed and the slovenliness of the sloburbs. Their civic pride does not extend beyond pride in increasing size and the prosperity that means that most of its citizens are making money building sloburbs or operating them. Given the primary fact of profit, nothing else is very important. Certainly aesthetic considerations are not. Arizona, for instance, tempts the tourists with the pretense that its proudest boast is its natural beauty. But it really prefers billboards, as is evidenced by the fact that it recently again rejected the offer of the national government to grant a bonus if it would keep the main highways clear of them.

These also are, of course, familiar charges and not without an element of truth. But they are not quite the whole story, not quite fair. The typical American is not indifferent to everything except profit. He is merely indifferent to *some* of the things that others consider important. He has, for example, an enormous faith in schooling—which he assumes to be the same thing as education. In Tucson, for instance, by far the most imposing buildings are the absurdly elaborate schools which the citizens who prefer billboards to scenic grandeur seem willing to support through very high taxes. The consensus seems to be essentially this: It is just that a citizen should be taxed heavily and also expected to contribute generously. But he should never, under any circumstances, be prevented from making a profit. Hospitals, also, seem to be among the nonprofit institutions to which a citizen points with pride. But he is unwilling to do anything to slow the spread of sloburbs. The zoning regulations are a farce. If an area is zoned for residents only, that usually means that no business can be established there until somebody wants to establish one—at which time the zoning is promptly changed. Order, dignity, grace and beauty are things that are simply not worth paying even a small price for. Schooling, recreation and health should be supported. But the other parts of, and provisions for, the good life are not the community's business. Or perhaps all that this tolerance of sloburbs comes down to in the end is that same kindly slovenliness in manners and morals to which we seem more and more inclined. But such tolerance is enough to permit the development of communities that it is impossible to imagine an earlier generation submitting to without protest.

Some years ago I decided that for me the city was paying diminishing returns and I moved away from it. This was a choice I have never regretted, but it was related to my time of life as well as to certain aspects of my temperament. It did not mean that I had no regard for cities and what they have contributed to civilization. But the sloburbs have none of the advantages of country, village or genuine city life. They do not, like real cities, provide a sufficiently large minority of citizens of intellectual and artistic taste to support cultural institutions proportionate to the size of their populations. Neither do they provide that "life of the streets" that is another of the chief attractions offered by a real city. Anywhere in a sloburb one may buy gasoline, cocktails, beer and hamburgers. But one cannot go window-shopping or indulge in any of the other activities that in New York or San Francisco draw strollers down the streets of the urban core. Neither, of course, can one breathe fresh air or enjoy the beauties of nature. One can only breathe gas fumes and revel in the glow of neon. Of all the places into which one's lot may be cast, few—not even those minimum security prisons called Garden Apartments of the sort I pass on my way once or twice a year from Manhattan to Kennedy Airport—strike me as more dismal.

Thinking of a real city as something analogous to a living creature where highly differentiated organs are all related to and coordinated by a central nervous system, I found myself wondering to just what sort of creature an individual sloburb might be compared. Most of even the so-called primitive organisms are wholes in the sense that the parts are related to one another and cannot exist except in connection with some center. You can't in most cases just break off a section and expect it to survive. Neither can most of such simple organisms grow indefinitely without any natural boundaries or shape.

Hence, if a sloburb is analogous to any living thing it must be, I think, to one of the myxomycetes or slime molds. These remarkable blobs, found especially in damp, rotting logs, have no shape, no characteristic size and no community center. They consist of an agglomeration of one-celled individuals without a trace of the differentiation characteristic of even the more primitive multicellular organisms. You may break one blob into a hundred pieces and each will prosper as satisfactorily as it did when it was part of a larger blob. Put the pieces into contact again and they will merge, much as the sloburbs spreading out from two communities merge when they meet. And given favorable conditions, the size of the blob grows and grows without there being any theoretical reason why it should not ultimately cover the earth. Such an eventuality might make a good horror movie. But no better than one that showed the whole face of America covered ultimately by one vast sloburb.

TWO EVALUATIONS OF "LYCIDAS"

SAMUEL JOHNSON

"LYCIDAS"

Samuel Johnson (1709-1784)—English poet, playwright, lexicographer, and literary critic—was the outstanding literary figure of eighteenth-century England. He was outstanding not just for what he wrote, excellent as that is, but for his remarkable character and personality as they are delineated in the greatest biography in English, James Boswell's Life of Samuel Johnson (1791). His best poem is The Vanity of Human Wishes (1749); his only play, Irene (1749). His best literary criticism is in the Preface to his critical edition of Shakespeare (1765) and in his Lives of the Poets (1779-1781), from which " 'Lycidas' " is taken. His dictionary (1755) is the first monument of English lexicography.

ONE OF THE POEMS on which much praise has been bestowed is *Lycidas;* of which the diction is harsh, the rhymes uncertain, and the numbers unpleasing. What beauty there is we must therefore seek in the sentiments and images. It is not to be considered as the effusion of real passion; for passion runs not after remote allusions and obscure opinions. Passion plucks no berries from the myrtle and ivy, nor calls upon Arethuse and Mincius, nor tells of "rough satyrs and fauns with cloven heel." "Where there is leisure for fiction there is little grief."

In this poem there is no nature, for there is no truth; there is no art, for there is nothing new. Its form is that of a pastoral, easy, vulgar, and therefore disgusting: whatever images it can supply are long ago exhausted; and its inherent improbability always forces dissatisfaction on the mind. When Cowley tells of Hervey that they studied together, it is easy to suppose how much he must miss the companion of his labours and the partner of his discoveries; but what image of tenderness can be excited by these lines!

»»» From "Milton." From *Prefaces Biographical and Critical to the Works of the English Poets.* London, 1779-81.

> We drove a field, and both together heard
> What time the grey fly winds her sultry horn,
> Battening our flocks with the fresh dews of night.

We know that they never drove a field, and that they had no flocks to batten; and though it be allowed that the representation may be allegorical, the true meaning is so uncertain and remote that it is never sought because it cannot be known when it is found.

Among the flocks and copses and flowers appear the heathen deities, Jove and Phoebus, Neptune and Aeolus, with a long train of mythological imagery, such as a college easily supplies. Nothing can less display knowledge or less exercise invention than to tell how a shepherd has lost his companion and must now feed his flocks alone, without any judge of his skill in piping; and how one god asks another god what is become of Lycidas, and how neither god can tell. He who thus grieves will excite no sympathy; he who thus praises will confer no honour.

This poem has yet a grosser fault. With these trifling fictions are mingled the most awful and sacred truths, such as ought never to be polluted with such irreverent combinations. The shepherd likewise is now a feeder of sheep, and afterwards an ecclesiastical pastor, a superintendent of a Christian flock. Such equivocations are always unskilful; but here they are indecent, and at least approach to impiety, of which, however, I believe the writer not to have been conscious.

Such is the power of reputation justly acquired that its blaze drives away the eye from nice examination. Surely no man could have fancied that he read *Lycidas* with pleasure had he not known its author.

DOUGLAS BUSH

from MILTON

Douglas Bush (1896-   ) was born in Morrisburg, Ontario, and educated at the University of Toronto. He has taught at the University of Minnesota and Harvard, where he is now Gurney Professor of English. He has published many articles in literary journals and many books—among them Mythology and the Renaissance Tradition in English Poetry *(1932),* Paradise Lost in Our Time *(1945), and* English Literature in the Earlier Seventeenth Century 1600-1660 *(1945).*

IN THIS SAME year 1637, however, we have the first testimony of genuine spiritual disturbance. In 'Lycidas' the conflict that Keats discerned in Milton, between the pleasures and the ardours of song, appears as a bitter reality; the poem might have been called 'A Faith on Trial.' It is not to be read primarily as an elegy, and the degree of the author's sorrow for Edward King is quite irrelevant. 'Lycidas' achieves its emotional power because the drowning of a virtuous young man at once crystallizes and releases all Milton's thoughts and feelings about his own past, present, and future and about the great Task-Master's will. And this inexplicable event adds its heavy weight to the ennui, the paralysing doubts, which may attack the most zealous student after five long years of hard and outwardly unprofitable toil. What is the value of the laborious and consecrated life of learning if it is to be cut off before fame is won? The answer, that true fame can be assessed only by God and enjoyed only in heaven, is to be Milton's final answer, yet what we have at this point is half-conventional faith, the will to believe rather than emotional conviction, and doubt remains. God allows a blameless young cleric to die and hireling shepherds to infest His church, the church Milton had refused to enter. The lovely passage on flowers is a temporary escape,

»»» From *English Literature in the Earlier Seventeenth Century 1600-1660,* by Douglas Bush. Reprinted by permission of the Clarendon Press, Oxford.

not a solution. The problem returns in the picture of the dead youth's body washed beyond the stormy Hebrides or toward Namancos and Bayona's hold; here the volume of sound heightens the idea—which, like many of Milton's chief ideas, is conveyed indirectly—of the littleness of man in a world of forces that God does not seem to control. But the answer returns, the definition of true achievement and true fame, and now Milton rises above Apollo and Jove to the imagery of Revelation. The vision of the virgin soul of Lycidas received into heaven banishes the last shadow of doubt. Thus beneath the smooth surface of a conventional elegy, ebbing and flowing with the motives of the pastoral pattern, the waves of regret, anger, despair, and resolution roll upon one another. The spiritual struggle goes on before our eyes, rising steadily in intensity, momentarily assuaged or aggravated by the irregularly sweet or thunderous music, until the last movement asserts the victory of faith in a triumphant glimpse of the sure glory of heaven. Life is vindicated and serenity is won.

There is no more miraculous example in poetry of the way in which a great theme, artistic power, and complete sincerity can transform a supposedly dead convention. The pastoral device had early proved its usefulness as a dramatic mask, and Milton found in it both a disguise for personal utterance and a form which imposed order upon his surging emotions. Even the very Miltonic attack on the clergy has pastoral precedents from Petrarch to Mantuan and Spenser. The poem is infinitely complex in the associations it awakens, but all things, landscape and sea, Cambridge and Paradise, British lore and classic myth, Christian and pagan symbols, are wrought into an harmonious whole, an almost epic whole. Through this complexity and objective solidity Milton's personal struggle becomes universal. The entirely simple last line is an example of potent ambiguity. Does it mean that Milton will soon be crossing the sea, or that he is done with minor poetry, or that he must turn his back upon death and face life with renewed faith and energy?

On his way home from abroad in 1639 Milton learned of

the death of Charles Diodati, his oldest friend. To express real sorrow he resorted not only to the pastoral convention but to Latin. In the *Epitaphium Damonis,* which was written and privately printed in 1640, some main themes of 'Lycidas' reappear, the questioning of Providence, the author's ambitions (here the British epic), and the reception of the virgin soul into the upper world 'where the festal orgies rage under the heavenly thyrsus.' There are touching moments, as when Milton recalls his friend's cultured wit and gaiety poured out on summer walks and by the winter fire, but as a whole the elegy moves, slowly, on a level of pastoral artifice and suggests a Renaissance poet falling back, in the apathy of grief and vague personal discontent, on literary habit.

ARTHUR M. LOUIS

THE FRIENDLY BRITANNICA

Arthur M. Louis (1938-   ) was born in Toledo, Ohio, and educated at Columbia College and Columbia Graduate School of Journalism, where he took his master's degree. He was formerly a newspaperman in Philadelphia and an associate editor of both Automobile International *and* Fleet International; *he is currently an associate editor of* Fortune.

SOMEONE WITH the initials "LBJ" wrote the selection on Sam Rayburn for the current edition of the *Encyclopædia Britannica,* and if you turn to the list of contributors, you will find that the LBJ in question is precisely whom you thought. LBJ writes that his mentor and fellow Texan, the late Speaker of the House, was "noted for his tart common sense, honesty and unflagging patriotism," and that he was "energetic, studious, ambitious and affable." For scholarly purposes, LBJ's article is about as useful as Damon's utterances on Pythias. If Rayburn had any faults— and if memory serves, he did—they do not emerge from this encomium. Still, the piece undoubtedly has historical value, and it also proves that even Presidents cannot always dodge dangling participles: "After winning the battle in 1961 to enlarge the house committee on rules—the hardest internal house struggle in 40 years—Rayburn's health failed quickly."

What troubles one about the *Britannica*—a reference set that every American adolescent is taught to revere—is that the choice of LBJ to write about Sam Rayburn is not an isolated curiosity but a common flaw. There is a parallel in the choice of Clement Attlee to write the piece on George Lansbury, his one-time superior in the British Labour Party, or of Sen. John W. Bricker, who retired some years ago at the request of the electorate, to write on his friend and fellow Ohio conservative, the late Robert

»»» *The Nation,* CC (March 1, 1965), 224-225. Reprinted by permission of *The Nation* and Arthur M. Louis.

A. Taft. Lord Attlee is properly reserved, although anything but hostile, in appraising Lansbury, but Bricker cannot suppress an occasional burst of hot adulation, as when he writes of Taft: "His honesty, integrity and patriotism were never responsibly questioned," or when he asserts, "He had no trace of demagoguery. His appeal was to logic, rarely to emotion"—rarely, mind you.

The relationship of LBJ to Rayburn, during their many years together on Capitol Hill, is said to have been almost filial. But the *Britannica*, in its wisdom, offers us some authentic examples of filial piety, as when it has Nathaniel Benchley write on his father Robert, or Henry Cabot Lodge on his grandfather of the same name, or Gen. Douglas MacArthur on his father, Gen. Arthur MacArthur. These wise men undoubtedly knew their own progenitors, and had many useful things to say about them, but in a reference book of the *Britannica's* reputation, the subject's mother-in-law should be given equal time.

Q. Who is the last man you would summon for a balanced account of the American Telephone and Telegraph Company?

A. The chairman of the board of directors, naturally.

Q. And whom did the *Britannica* summon?

A. The chairman of the board of directors, naturally—Mr. Frederick R. Kappel.

And is there anyone less likely to give an impartial summation of the New Deal than Raymond Moley? The *Britannica* could think of no one *more* likely, and so they gave Moley a chance to toot his own horn, although almost immediately he sounded a sour note. Moley writes that the term "New Deal" was first used by Franklin D. Roosevelt "in his speech accepting the Democratic nomination for President on July 2, 1932. It had been written into the speech by his adviser and collaborator, Raymond Moley, who was the chief of what came to be known as the 'brains trust'" [*sic*]. But Arthur Schlesinger Jr., in the first of his volumes on the Roosevelt years, says the words were inserted by Samuel Rosenman, who, "nervous and restless," had approached his task fortified with hot dogs and a pot of coffee. In a footnote,

Schlesinger remarks that Moley had used the phrase two months earlier, in a memorandum to Roosevelt, but that the term "New Deal" also appears well back in literature, and that "New Deal for America" had been the title of an article appearing in *The New Republic* just before the convention.

If Moley toots a horn, then J. Edgar Hoover sounds a church organ. For it is he who wrote the article on the Federal Bureau of Investigation. Hoover devotes exactly one sentence of his long dissertation to the pre-Hooverian FBI: "Established July 26, 1908, by Atty. Gen. Charles J. Bonaparte, the investigative agency originally was known as the Bureau of Investigation." The FBI archives must have received more care after "reorganization of the agency followed Atty. Gen. Harlan Fiske Stone's appointment in 1924 of J. Edgar Hoover as director." Mr. Hoover continues:

Political considerations were divorced from personnel appointments, and promotions were placed on a merit basis. Continuity of direction has been afforded by the fact that each succeeding attorney general has reappointed J. Edgar Hoover as head of the FBI.

After recounting how six well-known criminals were killed in action by FBI agents during the 1930's, Hoover goes on to relate that "more than 15,000 Axis operators and sympathizers in South America were expelled, interned or rendered harmless" [!] during the Second World War, with the help of his agency, that "1771 potentially dangerous enemy aliens" were arrested in the United States the day after the attack on Pearl Harbor, and that these and later arrests were made "in an orderly manner." He also reminds us of the many times his agency has averted a Communist revolution in the United States.

Regrettably, the critics of the FBI are not well represented in Mr. Hoover's article. Indeed, one would never suppose that any existed, or that the FBI, by its conduct through the years, had offended anyone's concept of civil liberties. Perhaps one of the

"potentially dangerous enemy aliens" should have been asked
to write an epilogue.

To discuss the Girl Guides, the British counterpart of the Girl
Scouts, the *Britannica* called upon Lady Olave Baden-Powell,
their leader. And while there may be nothing sinister about this
organization, surely there could have been a less biased chroni-
cler of its good deeds. The same would apply to the choice of
Avery Brundage, a man with a talent for becoming involved in
controversy, as co-author of the entry on the Olympic Games.
The late Col. Edward M. House, Woodrow Wilson's representative at the start of the Conference of Paris, is co-author of the
article on that conference. Adlai E. Stevenson, a devoted friend
of Eleanor Roosevelt, wrote her biography and, as you might
expect, his article does not encompass Westbrook Pegler's point
of view. E. B. White, a mainstay of *The New Yorker* during the
editorship of Harold Ross, was chosen to write the *Britannica*
piece on Ross. It is a spate of unmitigated praise for Ross, and
for the way *The New Yorker* took shape under his direction.
As such, it is an endorsement of White's brand of journalism.

But all is as nothing to the *Britannica's* treatment of its own
great leader, William Benton, former politician, educator and
advertising man (Benton and Bowles), and for twenty-two years
publisher of the *Britannica*. Robert Maynard Hutchins, who is
chairman of the *Britannica's* board of directors, has the honor
of introducing Benton to posterity. The Hon. Mr. Benton, as the
Britannica's promotional literature calls him, occupies 77 printed
lines (with 10 lines equal to about 105 words). Since his background was largely in politics, specifically in the Senate and the
United Nations, I found it worth while to determine how the
length of his article compared with that of his peers. The Hon.
Richard M. Nixon is covered in 50 lines; The Hon. Adlai E.
Stevenson gets 39 lines, which is also the amount he wrote about
Mrs. Roosevelt. LBJ's article on The Hon. Sam Rayburn takes
up 37 lines. The late Vice President Alben Barkley is close behind with 36. The Hon. Henry Cabot Lodge, 2d, gets only 33,

although he at least does a bit better than Mr. Hutchins himself, who occupies 32. The article on The Hon. Barry Goldwater, written before the national conventions, requires only 23 lines. There are no articles on Strom Thurmond, Estes Kefauver, Herbert Lehman or Joseph Martin, and there is no mention whatever, in the entire *Britannica,* of William Knowland, Everett Dirksen, Mike Mansfield or Hubert Humphrey (again, before the conventions). On the other hand, The Hon. Mr. Bricker's article on The Hon. Mr. Taft is 137 lines long. And all the recent Presidents of the United States get more space than The Hon. Mr. Benton.

But what does the *Britannica,* through Mr. Hutchins, have to say about its publisher? The article opens on a favorable note: "His imagination and boldness appeared in everything he did in advertising." There are also some kind words for the University of Chicago, with which Benton, Hutchins and the *Britannica* have been intimately associated:

At 35 Benton sold his interest in the agency and in 1937 went to the University of Chicago to become vice-president of the university, where Robert M. Hutchins, a Yale classmate, was president. There he took leadership in making The University of Chicago Round Table the most distinguished forum in the country. . . . He was one of the young administrative officers who gave the university unparalleled vitality at that epoch in its history. While an officer of the university in 1942, he helped organize, with Paul G. Hoffman, the committee for economic development. As founding vice-chairman of its board of trustees and of its research committee, he helped develop its program of scholarly research that made it one of the most influential groups of businessmen in the country.

In 1949, so the article continues, The Hon. Mr. Benton "accepted" an appointment to the Senate, and in 1950 he was elected to fill out the remaining two years of the unexpired term:

In the senate he became a champion of freedom and justice throughout the world, defending the United Nations and fighting for civil liberties and civil rights. At the height of Joseph R. McCarthy's power, Senator Benton led the attack on McCarthyism, with a courage unmatched by that of any other politician of the time. [McCarthy receives 36 lines in the Britannica.] He introduced a resolution calling for McCarthy's expulsion from the senate and McCarthy's conduct in relation to this resolution later led to his censure by the senate.

The abrupt termination of Benton's career in the Senate is written off with the phrase, "After leaving the senate . . ." In fact, Benton did not leave willingly; he was beaten in the 1952 election, evidently because of his opposition to McCarthy. This would make Benton's anti-McCarthyism seem all the more courageous, and would perhaps qualify him for a profile in the television series based on President Kennedy's famous book; but someone's courage stopped short of mentioning in the *Britannica* that anyone ever licked the boss.

PART III

Forms

THE DISTINCTION between rhetorical modes and rhetorical forms is made in the headnote to Part II, "Modes." There are, of course, nonfictional forms other than the five represented here. Some of the others are represented elsewhere in this book: history (Ralegh, for example), the news story (Friedlander and Grutzner), the philosophical essay (Mill, Lovejoy, and Aldrich), the journal (Darwin), literary criticism and theory (Santayana, Johnson, and Tate), and the popular scientific book (Schwartz and Thiel, and Bates).

AUTOBIOGRAPHY

AND BIOGRAPHY

AUTOBIOGRAPHY and biography are forms of narration. In the first, someone writes about his own life; in the second, about the life of another. Biographical writing is more than sheer recounting of events; it uses narration in combination with other modes of discourse, as previously described in the section note "Narration," and hence is expository as well as narrative. The writer of an autobiography often pauses in his story of his life to ponder the significance of the events, to analyze their effect upon him, to compare and evaluate experiences he has had or persons he has known, or to give his opinions about the questions of his times. In a similar way, the biographer may analyze the character of his subject, compare him with other men, and evaluate him in several ways.

In the sample of autobiography below, G. E. Moore gives an analytical account of experiences in childhood and youth that, he thinks, helped form his character. One notable rhetorical point about his account is the summarized character of the narration. Moore develops the story of his early years by describing others, the persons who influenced him—his parents and his teachers. Only one bit of action is at all fully developed, and this action—his "religious phase"—is developed not so much by a step-by-step account of physical actions as by a record of his changing mental state. Thus Moore's purpose clearly is to tell us how his mind and character and views were formed, not just what physically happened to him.

Morison's biographical essay on Prescott reviews the major events of Prescott's career and evaluates Prescott's accomplishments. He is thus concerned with events in a way somewhat different from Moore. Morison is concerned about Prescott's char-

469

acter too, as his praise of him for overcoming his physical disabilities shows; but by discussing Prescott's historical writings, he devotes most of the essay to making good the claim that Prescott is "the American Thucydides." Morison uses quotation and bits of scenic presentation to support his praise of Prescott the historian and to display Prescott the man.

Examples of autobiography and biography are to be found elsewhere in this book. The first three pieces in "Narration" are autobiographical, as are the two in "Character Sketches." The latter are also biographical in a small way, since they concern the writers' impressions of other persons. Johnson and Bush in "Analogy, Comparison, Evaluation" pass judgments on Milton as a poet. Hicks in "Reviews" covers much of Mailer's writing career while reviewing Mailer's latest novel.

G. E. MOORE

HOME AND SCHOOL. 1873-1892

*G. E. Moore (1873-1958), born in England and educated at Cambridge, was one of the most eminent philosophers of his time. Though Moore wrote only four books—*Principia Ethica *(1903),* Ethics *(1912),* Philosophical Studies *(1922), and* Some Main Problems of Philosophy *(1953)—he exerted a vast influence upon philosophy through his lectures at Cambridge, where he taught from 1911 to 1939, through his editorship of the philosophical quarterly* Mind *from 1921 to 1947, and through his many reviews and articles published there and elsewhere.*

I WAS BORN in 1873 in a suburb of London called Upper Norwood, situated in Surrey about eight miles from the centre of London and nearly due south of it. When I was born, I already had two elder sisters and two elder brothers; and, after I was born, two more sisters and one more brother were added to the family, so that I grew up as a member of a family of eight, half of whom were boys and half girls. There were enough of us to make plenty of company for one another.

My father and mother had moved from Hastings to Upper Norwood about two years before I was born. One of their principal reasons for making this move was, I have always understood, that they wished to be able to send their sons as day-boys to a large boys' school, called Dulwich College, which had been established, about twelve years previously, by order of the Charity Commissioners, out of funds provided by the immense increase in the value of the estates of a much older foundation, called by the same name. The founder of the original Dulwich College was an actor called Edward Alleyn, who lived in the reigns of Elizabeth and James I. The new Dulwich College, when

»»» Ch. 1 of "An Autobiography." From *The Philosophy of G. E. Moore.* Ed. Paul Arthur Schilpp. *The Library of Living Philosophers,* Vol. IV. 2nd ed. New York: Tudor Publishing Company, 1952, Pp. 3-12. Reprinted by permission of the Library of Living Philosophers.

I attended it, was a school of much the same type and much the same standing as the more famous St. Paul's School. Both were principally attended by day-boys who were the children of middle-class parents resident in London or its suburbs: the proportion of boarders at Dulwich was, I should say, never more than about ten per cent. My parents had heard good reports of the new school under its first head-master, and my three brothers and I all went there as day-boys in due course. The College, which lay in the valley at the bottom of Sydenham Hill, was only about one mile's walk from our house, which was on the western slope of the hill. The upper part of that slope was (and, I believe, still is) largely covered with oak-woods, so that the neighbourhood was rather unusually attractive for a suburb so near London. Our house was on a fairly steep road; and starting up that road you could, in less than ten minutes' walk, reach the Crystal Palace, which then crowned the top of the hill. As we grew up, we all for several years had Season-tickets for the Palace; and it was a great privilege for us as children to be able to play in its immense grounds on the eastern slope of the hill. Our house itself was a typical middle-class suburban house of that period. I believe that my father and mother were its first occupants, the immediate neighbourhood having been only very recently developed. It was a detached house, built of red bricks, and standing in a garden of about half an acre, in which were at least three good-sized oak trees—relics of the oak-wood which till recently had covered the whole slope of the hill and which, I suppose, formed part of the wood from which Norwood took its name. In our road and neighbouring roads there were ever so many houses of a similar type.

My father had the degree of M.D., and had been in general practice for some years at Hastings; but after his move to London he soon gave up practice altogether. His father, who came originally from Plymouth, was also a medical man of some distinction; but, in addition to practising medicine, my grandfather was an author, having written several semi-psychological or semi-philosophical works, some of which went into more than one edition.

The title of one was *The Power of the Soul over the Body;* that of another *The First Man and his Place in Creation.*

My mother came of a Quaker family, the Sturges, well known in Birmingham and Bristol and in various places in the region between those two towns. One of her paternal uncles, Joseph Sturge, was in his time a prominent philanthropist, and, among other things, toured parts of the United States, before the Civil War, in support of the abolition of slavery. More than one biography of him has been published. My mother's father and mother were both of them Sturges and were first cousins; and I think I have heard that they were ejected from the Society of Friends, because the marriage of first cousins was disapproved. At all events my mother, at the time of her marriage to my father, was not a member of the Society. She and my father were both regular attendants at Baptist services; and for many years all of us used to walk regularly twice every Sunday to a small Baptist chapel in Upper Norwood, where the minister, the Rev. S. A. Tipple, was, I think, unusually unorthodox, broad-minded, gentle and refined.

My father gave to all of us the first rudiments of education, teaching us to read (from *Reading without Tears*), to write, and some elementary arithmetic, geography and English history. He also, as soon as we were three years old, began to teach us the piano; but those of us who showed no taste or talent for piano-playing were allowed to drop this after a time. As soon, however, as I was eight years old, I was sent, like my two elder brothers before me, to Dulwich College; and, so long as we lived at Upper Norwood, I used to walk (or partly run) the mile there and the mile back twice every week-day, except Wednesdays and Saturdays which were half-holidays. I stayed at the College for no less than ten years and two terms in all. I showed some aptitude for learning Greek and Latin, and had no particular preference for anything else; and so I stayed on what was called the Classical Side. I went up the school quickly so that my last six years were all spent in the two top forms on that Side—the last four in the Classical Sixth, which was the top form, and the two before in what was called the Classical Remove. During these six years almost all my time was spent on Greek and Latin, very few hours per week being given to French and German and to some mathematics; and during the last four of these years, of the time given to Greek and Latin a very large part was spent in translating pieces of English prose into Greek and Latin prose, and pieces of English verse into Greek and Latin verse. We had, in fact, to do four "compositions," as they were called, every week —one piece of Greek Prose and one piece of Latin Prose, one piece of Greek Verse and one piece of Latin Verse. I do not, in fact, at all regret that so much of my time was spent in this way, although perhaps I ought to regret it. Possibly it would have been better for me if some of those hours had been spent upon some of the Natural Sciences, of which I learned absolutely nothing at school, and some of them on Mathematics, of which I learned very little and for which I showed very little aptitude. But I have no settled opinion as to whether much of the time spent in translating English into Greek and Latin could, in my case, have been better spent in other ways. I think I did get a good education, and I am not at all sure that I should have got a better one by a different distribution of my time. One definite benefit I think I can ascribe to my having had to translate so many pieces of English. I became very well acquainted with a large number of very excellent examples of English prose and verse writing; and I thus learned to appreciate some qualities in English prose and poetry, which I doubt if I should have appreciated so well, had I not been forced to pay so much attention to so many specimens which exhibited these qualities.

As regards my intellectual development while at school, I think I was probably extraordinarily lucky in that no less than four of the masters with whom I had most to do, were, each of them, though very different from one another, men of unusual originality and force of character, with wide intellectual interests.

The one among these four, with whom I came into contact earliest, was E. D. Rendall, the head of the musical department at the school. Rendall was an enthusiastic musician, a fertile composer, and a very energetic conductor of the school orchestra and school choir. I first came under his influence as a member of the school choir; but I came to know him better and to be more influenced by him, owing to the fact that he gave me some private lessons in singing solos and duets, while I was still a little boy with a treble voice. At this time he introduced me to some of the best of Schubert's songs. I admired him and looked up to him; and I have no doubt that occasional remarks and comments which he threw out, as well as his general spirit, did a great deal towards opening my mind. During my last year at school I came to know him still better, since I then took private lessons from him in organ-playing and in the elements of harmony.

The next, in order of time, with whom I came in contact, was C. Bryans, a scholar of Eton and of King's College, Cambridge, who was master of the Classical Remove during the whole of the two years I spent at it. Bryans was as enthusiastic about classical studies as Rendall was about music. He made everything interesting that he talked about, and what he talked about included not only classical subjects; he was continually making *obiter dicta* upon all sorts of different topics. He was a humorist, and we liked his jokes; he had established the most friendly and human relations between himself and his class. But, besides all this, there were two special debts which I owe to him. He was a great admirer of German commentators on the Classics, and used to bring in to class his German editions of Thucydides and Livy, and discuss their notes to us; and he suddenly got the idea of teaching us German himself, although it was quite outside the ordinary curriculum. He set us to work at once on Goethe's *Faust* and Schiller's *Dreissigjähriger Krieg*. To him, therefore, I owe my start in learning German. I continued having lessons in it after I left his Form; and I thus got a grounding in German, which was very useful when later I wanted to read German philosophers in the original. The other debt I owe to him was due to the fact that he was concerned about my English style. Upon some essay which I had to write for him he wrote the comment "child-like and bland"; and, in order to help me to be less child-like, he lent me, to read in the holidays, Saintsbury's book of selections from English prose-writers—a book which, whether it helped or not to improve my style of writing, certainly opened my eyes to a good many things to which they had been closed before. That my style of writing was still greatly in need of improvement several years later seems to be shown by the fact that, when I went up to Cambridge, the classical scholar, A. W. Verrall, who was my tutor, was also concerned about it. The remedy which he recommended was that I should read Macaulay's speeches. I obediently took that remedy also, but whether with any effect upon my style, I have not the least idea.

With the other two masters at Dulwich, whom I take to have had a great influence on my intellectual development, I came into close contact simultaneously, namely when I was moved into the Sixth Form just before I was fifteen years old. One of these was the Classical Sixth master, W. T. Lendrum (who later changed his name to "Vesey"), and the other was the Headmaster, A. H. Gilkes.

Lendrum was a first-rate classical scholar, both learned and accurate, and having, in addition, a very genuine literary taste. It must have been a rare thing for so fine a scholar to be teaching in a school (Lendrum used, with a smile, to refer to his position at Dulwich as that of a mere "usher"), and at the end of 1890 he was in fact elected to a Fellowship at Caius College, Cambridge—a position of a dignity more suitable to the fineness of his scholarship. He was an Irishman, though an Ulster Irishman from Antrim, and there was a pleasant Irish tang in his way of speaking. He was fastidious, and quick-tempered, and had very violent dislikes; and he could make himself very unpleasant to people whom he despised or disliked. Now and then he made himself unpleasant to one of us, when he thought we needed taking down a peg or two; but, in spite of these rare outbursts, we all loved him, and very deservedly. His occasional remarks on English writers impressed me more than anything of the kind I had so far heard: they were the remarks of a man who felt strongly, and who had completely assimilated a very fine cultural tradition. And I was also, no doubt, impressed by the pains he took to be accurate—to get everything *exactly* right. To mention a less important matter, it was undoubtedly mainly due to the very thorough training he gave me for a period of more than two years, that I was able subsequently to win, first, a Major Scholarship at Trinity, then to obtain the highest honours then possible in the First Part of the Classical Tripos, and finally to win the Craven University Scholarship.

But remarkable as Lendrum was, I think there is no doubt that by far the most remarkable man of the four was the Head-master, A. H. Gilkes. Whereas the other three were Cambridge men, Gilkes was from Oxford: he had been a Junior Student of Christ Church. He had also been a pupil, and subsequently an under-master, at Shrewsbury School, and was proud of the wonderful succession of classical scholars which that school pro-duced for many years in the nineteenth century. Merely as a scholar, however, he himself was not to be compared to Lendrum. I remember feeling at the time a great contempt for some rules about Greek conditional sentences, which I thought he was far too fond of repeating to us, and which to me, trained by Lendrum on the basis of Goodwin's *Greek Moods and Tenses,* seemed to be hopelessly antiquated and inaccurate and unequal to the subtlety of the facts. Gilkes' eminence lay in other directions. He was a great admirer of Socrates, as depicted by Plato; and some of us thought (I think with some justice) that he himself had some, by no means negligible, resemblances to Socrates. To begin with, I think he produced the impression of being, in a pre-eminent degree, a *good* man—both good *and* benevolent; although, as regards the latter quality, he was capable of extreme severity when he met with any action, which he thought to be thoroughly vicious or base: I have seen him angry, and am very glad that I, personally, never excited his anger. But, as was, I think, also the case with Socrates, his goodness was rendered more attractive by its combination with a delicious and a subtle sense of humour: he was always ready, when occasion offered, to make quiet fun of us (or of other things) with a charming delicacy. And even in purely intellectual qualities he had, I think, some resemblance, though farther off, to Socrates. He used to take the whole Sixth Form once a week for a lesson, which was, I think, called "Divinity," but in which, in fact, he talked about an astounding variety of different subjects. We had to write an essay for him every week on the subject on which he had talked; and he thus put before us an enormous number of different questions, on every one of which he had something interesting and enlightening to say. He had, I think, in a wide sense, a very philosophic mind, though I do not remember to have ever seen any sign that he was interested in the sort of technical philosophical questions, with which I have been chiefly occupied and worried for the greater part of my life. However that may be, I was in close contact with him for no less than four years, from just before I was fifteen to just before I was nineteen; and I think his influence on me (as it certainly was on others) must have been, in one way or another, enormous.

I have singled out these four masters, because I think they had much the most to do with my intellectual development; but there were, of course, other masters at Dulwich, whom I remember with gratitude. There were besides clever boys, both in the Remove and in the Sixth, whose conversation and outlook certainly made a difference to me. But I never became very intimate with any of these. I was indeed rather lonely at school; but this never made me, to any serious degree, unhappy or discontented: I was always on very good terms with the vast majority of my class-mates. Nor was I at all inclined to criticise or condemn the masters. Certainly I liked some better than others; but I think that I actively disliked none at all, and was always inclined to think that each was doing the best possible under the circumstances. I remember that, very early, this attitude of mine seemed to surprise some of the boys, who had violent antipathies to some of the masters and thought very ill of them. I, on my side, was equally surprised that they could see any reason to take up such an attitude. On the whole, I enjoyed

my life at school, and was very well satisfied with it; and I left
Dulwich with a strong affection both for the school as a whole,
and for very many people in it.

One incident, which occurred during my school life, ought, I
think, to be recorded. When I was eleven or twelve years old,
I was led to adopt the religious views of a group of young men
who conducted what was called a "Children's Special Service
Mission" on the beach at a sea-side place where my family had
gone for the summer holidays. These views were of a type which
I think can be called "ultra-evangelical," and which can perhaps
be better described as very similar to the type characteristic of
the Salvation Army. They were views in which much stress was
laid "on the love of Jesus"—both the love which we ought to feel
towards him, and the love which he feels towards us. And it
seemed to me (and I still think this reasoning correct) that if
all that was said in the New Testament was true, and if Jesus
was really the Son of God and was still alive, (things which, at
that time, I did not think of questioning), then we ought far
more often to be thinking of him, and ought to love him far
more intensely, than most people who professed to be Christians
(including my own parents) seemed to me to do. Accordingly
I tried to think very constantly of Jesus, and to feel a great love
for him, and also to follow a rule of conduct which the young
men who converted me had recommended—namely, in all cases
of doubt as to what I ought to do, to ask the question "What
would Jesus do?" But this was not all. It seemed to me also to
follow that it was my duty to try to persuade other people to
do the same—in short, to try to convert other people, as these
young men had converted me. And my conviction that this was
my duty led to one of the most painful continued mental con-
flicts I have ever experienced. I did make efforts to do what
I conceived to be my duty in this respect, but I had to fight
against a very strong feeling of reluctance. There seemed to be
something utterly inappropriate and out of place in trying to
persuade my school-fellows, for instance, to love Jesus. I did
drive myself to distribute tracts along the promenade at the

sea-side (and this was not the hardest thing I actually drove myself to do), though I positively hated doing it, all the more because there happened to be at the same place the family of two other boys from Dulwich, whom I greatly admired, and I was desperately unwilling that they should see me distributing tracts. But I constantly felt that I was not doing nearly as much as I ought to do. I discovered that I was very deficient in moral courage.

This intense religious phase, with its conflict, cannot, I think, have lasted more than about two years, though I still continued for several more years to read daily by myself passages from the Bible, in addition to what my father read with us at family prayers every morning before breakfast. But my religious beliefs gradually fell away, and so quickly that, long before I left school, I was, to use a word then popular, a complete Agnostic. How in detail this change was brought about, I do not remember. But I think it must have been largely due to the influence of a fifth person, whom I have not yet mentioned, but who, I think, had probably as much to do with the course of my mental development as the four Dulwich masters I have named. This fifth person was my eldest brother, Thomas Sturge Moore, who has since become known as a poet, as a critic, and for his wood-cuts. My brother, who was at that time an art-student, was more than three years older than I was, and was consequently much more intellectually mature during the latter part of my period at school. Moreover he was (and is) a far readier talker than I, and far more fertile of ideas. I think there is no doubt that his conversation, including discussions which he sometimes had with my father at meal-times, had a great deal of influence on the formation of my opinions.

SAMUEL ELIOT MORISON

PRESCOTT,

THE AMERICAN THUCYDIDES

Samuel Eliot Morison (1887-   ), noted American historian, was born in Boston, was educated at Harvard, and later took an M.A. at Oxford. A member of the history faculty at Harvard from 1915 to 1955, he is the author of many books, notably a history of Harvard College and biographies of Columbus, John Paul Jones, and the founders of the Massachusetts Bay Colony. His most extensive work is his officially commissioned History of United States Naval Operations in World War II *(15 volumes, 1947–1962), much of it written from his firsthand observations while on active duty on eleven ships during the war.*

IN 1774 HORACE WALPOLE wrote to Sir Horace Mann, "The next Augustan age will dawn on the other side of the Atlantic. There will perhaps be a Thucydides at Boston."

There was; and three quarters of a century later Walpole's friend Miss Berry, then a venerable vestal of eighty-seven, had the satisfaction of meeting him in London. His name was William Hickling Prescott, and he was being received by political, social, and literary England in a manner that no American writer has experienced before or since. Macaulay gave him a breakfast party at the Albany; the Lyells took him to Royal Ascot; Oxford conferred on him an honorary D.C.L.; and the Earl of Carlisle entertained him and Queen Victoria at Castle Howard. Prescott sat next but one to her at dinner, and described her in a letter to his wife as "very plain, with fine eyes and teeth, but short and dumpy, with a skin that reddens easily with the heat of the room. I observed that the Queen did great justice to the bread and cheese."

This "American Thucydides," as people were beginning to call him, was then at the height of his fame. His three greatest

»»» *Atlantic Monthly*, CC (November, 1957), 165-168, 170, 172. Reprinted by permission of Samuel Eliot Morison.

works, *Ferdinand and Isabella, The Conquest of Mexico,* and
The Conquest of Peru, had appeared, greeted with enthusiasm
by the critics of both continents including even the snooty Scots
reviewers, and they had been eagerly bought by the public.
Prescott was then a tall, well-built gentleman of fifty-four, with
an infectious smile and hearty laugh that charmed everyone. A
pair of well-trimmed sideburns, in the fashion of the day, framed
a strong, handsome countenance with a fine Roman nose, brown
eyes, and a ruddy complexion. He was lively, agile, an excellent
horseman, and a fast walker; few except his intimate friends
suspected that for long intervals he was racked by rheumatism
and that one of his eyes was artificial.

This was in 1850, when Prescott was reaping the fruits of
thirty-five years of courageous struggle to overcome a grave
physical disability. It is a curious coincidence that the only other
American historian, Francis Parkman, to be mentioned in the
same breath with Prescott, had to undergo a similar experience.

Let us take a look at him at almost the start of the struggle.
It is the year 1817. Son of a Federalist lawyer and judge, grand-
son of Colonel William Prescott of Bunker Hill fame, young
William had gone through Harvard College gaily and easily, but
lost an eye as a result of a brawl in college commons. The infec-
tion had spread to the other eye and acute rheumatism set in.
After the local physicians had almost killed him with "copious
bleedings and other depletions," he had been sent to Europe in
search of better medical aid than could be had in America. First
he spent a winter with his maternal grandfather, Thomas Hickling, the United States consul at St. Michael's in the Azores, and
there he became sensible of the beauty and mystery of the Old
World. He then made an attenuated grand tour of Europe, consulted the best eye specialists in Paris, and returned to live in
his parents' house, a big square mansion with a garden on Pearl
Street, Boston. There the old malady returned. We may picture
Prescott confined for days, sometimes weeks, to a dark room
on the top story, a devoted sister reading aloud to him by lying
on the floor where she could catch the light that came in over

the threshold, since any stronger light gave the young man excruciating pain.

Yet Prescott refused to admit defeat, and gave careful thought to what he should do for a profession. And he wooed and won a girl of his own social circle, Susan Amory. They were married on his twenty-fourth birthday, and for the next twenty-four years lived with the elder Prescotts. The Amorys were one of those American Loyalist families—more numerous than is generally supposed—who managed to retain their property and social position through the turmoil of the American Revolution. Susan was a beautiful girl with a somewhat bovine character. "She didn't go out much—as an Amory she didn't have to," as a grand-daughter remarked; she was content to rear a family and to watch tenderly over her husband's health and interests. He was completely and romantically devoted to her. She inherited the sword of her grandfather, who had served in the Royal Navy on board one of the British ships that supported the assault on Bunker Hill, and William inherited that of his grandfather, who commanded the provincial troops in that battle; so they had the two mounted and placed on the wall of the Prescott library. These were the famous "crossed swords" which Thackeray saw on his visit to Boston and which inspired *The Virginians,* as the opening paragraph of that novel relates.

Even before he married, Prescott decided to fit himself for what he called "the literary life," although as yet he had little inclination to any particular branch of that far-spreading tree. It was not really necessary that he do anything, considering his infirmity, his social position, and his father's generosity. But in Boston every young man was supposed to "make an effort," as the phrase went; Prescott himself later observed that an American who neither made money nor cultivated letters might "as well go hang himself; for as to a class of idle gentlemen, there is no such thing here." That was true in general; but even in Boston there were young men of means who did nothing in particular, and not too well at that, flitting about between New York, New-port, and London. Henry James has immortalized the type of American who rejected his native country as a hopeless Boeotia and moved to Paris or Rome to dabble in the arts or pursue some pallid branch of scholarship. Prescott was made of stouter stuff.

As a scholar he had to start from scratch, having carried away from Harvard little more than a good knowledge of Latin and Greek. After many false starts and physical relapses, and with the guidance and advice of his older friend George Ticknor, he settled at the age of twenty-nine on a history of the reigns of Ferdinand and Isabella of Spain.

There were two main reasons for this choice. He wished to show his compatriots that their history had a richer and more varied background than the Virginia Colony, the Pilgrim Fathers, and the Protestant Reformation. He wished to prove to the world that an American could produce a work at once scholarly and literary that would bear comparison with the best of England, France, Germany, and Spain. He was eager for the good opinion of European scholars. They might brush off anything he could write on United States history as inconsequential; but they would have to listen to a work which was the result of prolonged research, a nice weighing of conflicting authorities, and a thorough knowledge of classical and modern languages; especially if it were well presented.

When Prescott made the great decision for Ferdinand and Isabella in 1826, ten years of almost unremitting labor were ahead of him. The material difficulties that he surmounted were even greater than his physical handicap. The way to perform the task with the greatest economy would have been to have settled in Madrid, as his friend the American minister there advised him to do. He could have worked there, or in London or Paris, far more effectively than in Boston, and have been nearer to specialists who could have kept his one good eye working. But Prescott was determined not to be an expatriate, even temporarily. He felt that he owed it to the memory of Colonel Prescott, and to his family and friends, to prove that an American could produce a literary and scholarly work of the highest quality right in Boston.

Yet how could that be done in Boston? There were no collections of old Spanish books there or anywhere else in the United States. Ticknor, blessed with ample means, imported the essential books as rapidly as he could find them and gave Prescott the run of his library; but Prescott was not content to "make new books, as apothecaries make new mixtures, by pouring out of one vessel into another," as Tristram Shandy once remarked. He must have the original sources, and with few exceptions these were still in manuscript. In those days there was no multi-volumed set of *Documentos Inéditos;* the Las Casas *Historia General de las Indias* had never been printed, nor the better part of Oviedo, nor Andres Bernaldez's chronicle of the Catholic Kings. These and hundreds of other manuscripts had to be copied for him in long-hand. The cost was not excessive, since there were plenty of un-employed intellectuals in Europe who were glad to do such work for starvation wages; the trouble was to find responsible scholars to direct research in public and private archives and to supervise the copying. Therein the United States consuls and diplomatic officials gave indispensable aid, and Dr. Friedrich Lembke, a German who had written a history of Spain to the year 800, con-sented to carry on vicariously for Prescott in return for a modest retainer.

Eventually, books and copies of manuscripts began to pour in to the paternal mansion on Pearl Street, where they were placed on shelves in the son's attic study. And he managed to surmount his physical handicap by methodical living, by having most of the material read aloud to him by a secretary who learned to pronounce Spanish, and by a simple device called a noctograph, which had been invented in London to enable the blind to write. This was a sort of slate crossed by a grid of stout brass wires between which, with an ivory-pointed stylus, one could write on carbon paper, which made an indelible impression on another sheet of paper placed underneath.

When, after ten years of work, the manuscript of *Ferdinand and Isabella* was completed, it was set up in type at the author's expense and four copies printed for his close friends to criticize.

These privately printed copies were hawked about English and American publishing houses for months with slight success. Finally a short-lived firm called the American Stationers Company of Boston agreed, for a thousand dollars, to print 1250 copies of the three-volume set to be retailed at six dollars, if the author would foot the bills for the stereotype plates; and Richard Bentley agreed to publish a small edition in London.

Ferdinand and Isabella appeared in Boston on Christmas Day, 1837, and in London a month or two later. It was an immediate and astounding success on both sides of the water, partly because it came as a complete surprise. The author's name was unknown in Europe; and so well had Prescott kept his secret in Boston, where everyone was supposed to know everyone else's business, and so gay and unrestrained had been his social life, that not more than six persons outside the immediate family knew what he had been doing. It was commonly supposed that he was reading for his own amusement. Only a week before *Ferdinand and Isabella* came out, an elderly relative stopped Prescott on the street to upbraid him for frittering away his life, and to tell him it was high time he amounted to something!

Prescott could have boasted, like Lord Byron, "I awoke one morning and found myself famous." To a German who had called it folly to publish Spanish history in the United States, "where the taste was for nothing higher than a periodical," Prescott wrote that 3300 sets of *Ferdinand and Isabella* had been sold in the first sixteen months; "that is pretty well for 'Brother Jonathan,' is it not? . . . The publishers indeed are quite as much surprised as I am."

He gained the favor of the critics by his vivid and spirited narrative style, arresting as a historical novel, yet with each detail authenticated in a footnote. I shall not attempt to analyze his style, because it is to be enjoyed and admired, not plucked apart. Certain modern critics regard it as artificial (of course every style, even Hemingway's and Joyce's, is that); and certainly nobody would think of imitating it today. But he was a master of *narrative*, which history essentially is, a fact which too many modern historians have forgotten. And the quality which gave his works permanent value, and which appealed most to the more discriminating critics, was (as Roger B. Merriman wrote) "the scrupulous care and integrity with which he used his materials, and the pains that he took to find the exact truth. All his statements are supported by abundant references; if there is any possible doubt as to the interpretation of his authorities, it is fairly expressed in the footnotes; in short, one may be certain of the source for every fact which Prescott gives, though one may differ with him over the significance of it."

Before his first work appeared, Prescott had decided on the next two, *The Conquest of Mexico* and *The Conquest of Peru.* Washington Irving, who had planned to do a *Mexico* himself, magnanimously dropped it in favor of the younger historian. Prescott's *Conquest of Mexico,* completed in 1843, was an even greater success than his first book, and has remained his best seller. Over 20,000 sets of it were sold during his lifetime; and as he had paid for the plates himself he collected substantial royalties. But the profits from each book were plowed into preparations for the next; into copying, salaries to secretaries and researchers, purchase of books and manuscripts. Only his inherited and invested income of somewhat over twelve thousand dollars a year enabled him to carry on.

Almost everyone who reads his works assumes that Prescott visited the scenes he wrote about, so vivid and convincing are his descriptions of scenery, battlefields, and the like. But, owing to his infirmities, he never went nearer South America than Washington, D.C. His lack of physical contact with these countries was compensated by a historical imagination, well controlled by the facts as related by Bernal Diaz and the early Spanish chronicles, and developed by correspondence with people who knew these countries at first hand. The most useful to him in that respect was Madame Calderón de la Barca, whose *Life in Mexico* has become a classic. She was Fanny Inglis, a charming and witty Scotswoman who had a private school in Boston and became a close friend of the Prescotts. After her marriage to the Spanish minister to the United States, who was later transferred to Mexico City, she continued to interchange letters with Prescott; and it is probably owing to her devotion that he was able to write his accurate and striking descriptions of Mexico City and Teotihuacan under the Aztecs.

It was also a subject of astonished praise that a Boston Protestant like Prescott could write so understandingly of Catholics and Catholicism, even asserting that there was something to be said for the Inquisition. He was the first English-speaking historian of Spanish lands whom a loyal Spaniard could read without disgust. For, Unitarian though he might be by conviction, Prescott judged historical characters by the standards of their day, not by those of nineteenth-century liberalism. He regarded the Catholic Church as one of the world's great religions, which was here to stay and not on the way out, as many liberals fondly imagined. And like other New Englanders who retained a "pious disbelief" after rejecting the Church, he found anticlericalism distasteful and the raillery of Voltaire disgusting.

Even more gratifying to Prescott than the acclaim of the critics was his popularity among all classes of American readers. When, shortly after the Mexican War, he visited Washington, he was delighted to hear from the Secretary of the Navy that the bluejackets of the *U.S.S. Delaware* had petitioned him to add *The Conquest of Mexico* to their ship's library; and that the secretary had not only done that, but ordered a set to be placed on board every ship of the United States Navy.

And there was one humble reader whom Precott obtained many years after his death, whose story would have gratified him immensely. That was Edward E. Ayer, a young Middle Westerner in the First California Cavalry, U.S. Army, who in 1862 was guarding the Cerro Colorado silver mine in Arizona against attacks by the Apache. Colonel Colt, of revolver fame, had given the mine a small library, and in it trooper Ayer discovered *The Conquest of Mexico*. He read it through twice, "and was astonished to find that history could be so interesting." After his discharge from the Army, Ayer was given by his father an interest in a country store in Illinois. On visiting Chicago to lay in a stock of goods he called at a bookshop and asked if they had a copy of this fascinating history. They had, and *The Conquest of Peru* as well, but the price was $17.50 for the set. Young Ayer— he was still only twenty-three years old—had only $3.50 to spare, but he offered to pay that for Volume I of the *Mexico,* and to buy a volume every month. The proprietor let him pay the $3.50 down and gave him the five volumes to take home. "My return was a triumphal procession," wrote Mr. Ayer almost fifty years later. "I was certainly the happiest boy in the world." And the world knows that Mr. Ayer became one of the greatest of American book collectors, to the ultimate benefit of the New-berry Library of Chicago. The place of honor in that library's Ayer Collection is given to these identical copies, which the owner eventually had sumptuously rebound in London at a cost over tenfold that of his original investment.

Prescott never wholly recovered from his physical disabilities, but he never let them get him down. Fortunately one of his secretaries recorded in detail his regimen, a Spartan one which would have crushed the life out of a less valiant and buoyant man. The scene of it is the house still numbered 55 Beacon Street, Boston, which the historian bought after the death of his father and where he wrote most of *The Conquest of Peru.* His atelier, as he called his study, was on the third floor, rear; one viewing the outside of it today from the little street that runs behind Beacon would suppose that a recent owner had installed a pic-ture window there, but the two large panes of plate glass were put in by Prescott in order to afford his weak eye maximum light.

The historian rose before seven, winter or summer, mounted one of his saddle horses and rode for an hour and a half, to Jamaica Plain or Cambridge. This he called "winding himself up." After breakfast he shaved, bathed, and changed, while Mrs. Prescott read aloud to him from a novel by Scott, Dickens, or Dumas. Prescott not only enjoyed a good novel; he learned from them how to make his histories tridimensional by including chapters on manners and morals—social history, as it is now called. At ten o'clock he went out for a half-hour walk and at ten thirty started work in his atelier. After glancing at the headlines of the morning paper, he had the secretary read aloud items that he thought would be interesting—but seldom found them so. Then came the correspondence. The secretary read letters that poured in from all parts of the world, and Prescott dictated the replies. Next came accounts. These were finished by noon, when the historian walked downtown to make purchases or talk to his friends; for all Boston, even the wharves, lay within twenty minutes walk of his house.

Returning at one, he began the real business of the day. The secretary read aloud from memoirs and other documents pertaining to the book then being written, Prescott interrupting frequently to dictate notes or to discuss the persons and events described. After all sources for the chapter at hand had been gone through, the secretary read aloud repeatedly the notes he had taken, and was often called upon to reread some of the sources. This process went on for days. Prescott was then ready to compose. He outlined the entire chapter in his mind, sometimes while sitting silent in his study, but more often when walking or riding. He wrote the first draft very rapidly, on his noctograph. The secretary numbered each sheet as it was finished and copied it in a large, round hand so that Prescott could read it himself. His memory was so remarkable that he could commit a chapter of forty or fifty printed pages to memory, mull it over on horseback, and decide on alterations and improvements. He would then dictate to his secretary the changes to be made in the manuscript and have the whole reread to him. Finally he dictated the footnotes.

This same secretary, Robert Carter, wrote after the historian's death, "Mr. Prescott's cheerfulness and amiability were truly admirable. He had a finely-wrought, sensitive organization; he was high-spirited, courageous, resolute, independent; was free from cant or affectation of any sort. . . . He was always gay, good-humored and manly; most gentle and affectionate to his family, most kind and gracious to all around him. . . . Though not at all diffident, he was singularly modest and unassuming. He had not a particle of arrogance or haughtiness. . . . Praise did not elate him, nor censure disturb him. . . . He was totally free from the jealousy and envy so common among authors, and was always eager, in conversation, as in print, to point out the merits of the great contemporary historians, whom many men in his position would look upon as rivals."

Prescott dined at home at two thirty or, if with friends, at three o'clock, the then fashionable hour. He enjoyed good food, well cooked, and limited himself to exactly two and a half glasses of sherry or Madeira. At dinner he relaxed, drew out his family and friends in conversation, and never talked shop. After dinner he smoked one of the Havana cigars with which he was kept supplied by his Cuban admirers, while Mrs. Prescott read aloud again. Another half-hour solitary walk followed, and at six o'clock the secretary returned for a two-hour evening session in the study. At eight the family had supper, and at ten thirty the historian retired.

The evening session of work was omitted if Prescott attended one of his club meetings or went to an evening party with his wife. The memory of one of these was preserved by President Charles W. Eliot of Harvard. "Prexy," in his old age, was asked by a young man whether he had ever heard Daniel Webster speak.

"Yes, once," said Dr. Eliot. "I was six or eight years old. My father was entertaining him at dinner, and I hid in a corner of the hall on Beacon Street to catch a sight of the great man. In the procession to the dining room Mr. Webster led in Mrs. Prescott, a remarkably handsome lady; and just behind them were Mr. Prescott with Mrs. Webster, who was exceedingly plain. As they passed me, Mr. Webster, who had been talking with great animation to Mrs. Prescott, turned half around and said in his booming voice, 'Prescott, what do you say to our swapping wives for this evening?' "

Besides the Beacon Street mansion, Prescott maintained two other homes—the ancestral farmhouse at Pepperell and a summer place at Nahant. At Pepperell he spent the spring and fall of each year, drawing strength from the soil that his ancestors had tilled for over a century; here the final chapter of *The Conquest of Peru* was composed. The house was rambling and unpretentious, but Prescott's friends and their children and his children's friends were often entertained there; life was free and easy, with riding, driving, and long walks, and charades and games in the evening. Prescott's favorite spot was a hill behind the house, with a superb view across the Nashua Valley to the rolling country of New Hampshire, dominated by the grand Monadnock. He had a seat built on the hill and used to sit there for hours, meditating and mentally composing; Monadnock had the same fascination for him as for Emerson and Thoreau. This mansion still stands.

The summer place was a flimsy wooden cottage, long since torn down, on the rocky peninsula of Nahant, north of Boston. In the eighteen-thirties and forties Nahant was a leading American summer resort, where many of Prescott's friends such as Longfellow, Sumner, Eliot, and Appleton passed the season, together with hundreds of visitors from New York, Philadelphia, and the South. Life at Nahant was no unmixed blessing for Prescott. He was pestered by visitors in working hours. The cottage, which he named "Fitful Head" after the dwelling of Norna in Scott's *Pirate,* lay on a cliff overhanging Swallows' Cave and so near the water that the piazza was sprinkled with spray in every gale. "It is a wild spot," he wrote to his friend Fanny, "and the winds at this moment whistle an accompaniment to the breakers that might fill a poet's cranium with the sublime. But I am no poet. I imagine myself however in some such place as the bold headland in the Algarve, on which Prince Henry of Portugal established his residence when he sent out his voyages of discovery."

The Conquest of Peru was completed by the end of 1846. The reviews were even more favorable than those of *Mexico*. But this historian was not one to rest on his laurels. He started promptly on *Philip the Second*. The work was interrupted by eye trouble and rheumatism, by tours to Albany, New York, and Washington, and by his visit to England in 1850. His English friends had long been urging him to come; but remembering the rigors of his early voyage to Europe in a sailing vessel, "bumping and thumping over the qualmish billows," he put it off until he could sail in a Cunarder, which made the voyage in only twelve days. One of his sons accompanied him, but Mrs. Prescott could not face an ocean voyage.

Prescott, like Irving and other American writers of his day, has been accused of being too deferential to the English by critics who mistake good manners for obsequiousness and regard a rude arrogance as the mark of sound Americanism. His letters are full of racy Americanisms like "OK," but for publication he tried to write the King's English, since he sought English-speaking readers all over the world. And to an English correspondent who sent him a long list of alleged Americanisms in *The Conquest of Peru* he replied, politely but firmly, that "realize" had become a verb, that "snarl" was a perfectly good noun for a tangle, and that "counterblast," to which his friend objected, had been taken from the famous tract of King James I against tobacco. Prescott was always sturdily American; if anyone doubts that, let him read in his collected *Miscellanies* his gently sarcastic remarks on Englishmen visiting America or his letters describing the scenery of England, which he thought "too tame." He longed to see "a ragged fence, or an old stump," as in his "own, dear, wild America."

In politics he was a steadfast liberal. His father had been a high Federalist, a member of the Hartford Convention; and the son, like almost everyone of his social standing in Boston, started as a Federalist and became a Whig. Boston society then took politics very hard and ostracized anyone who deviated from the accepted doctrine; George Bancroft, for example, was regarded as little better than a traitor after he joined the Democrats and accepted office under Polk, and Charles Sumner, until Brooks's assault made him a martyr, was generally looked upon as the most dangerous sort of radical. But Prescott always maintained an intimate friendship with both men. Instead of becoming a reactionary late in life, in 1856 he voted for the first Republican presidential candidate, John C. Frémont, and for Anson Burlingame for Congress, although his friend and neighbor Nathan Appleton was the Whig candidate. There is no doubt that he would have supported Lincoln in 1860 if he had lived.

The first two volumes of *Philip the Second*, published in 1855, met with the same favorable reception as did Prescott's earlier works. Work on the third volume was interrupted by a stroke, but it was finally published in 1858. He had started on the fourth and last when on January 27, 1859, he suffered a second stroke in his Beacon Street home and died within a few hours.

The entire community was moved by grief. Memorial meetings in Prescott's honor were held by the historical societies and academies of which he had been a member, as far West as Illinois and as far South as Maryland; all the noted orators, from Edward Everett down, held forth. He died "a man without an enemy; beloved by all and mourned by all," as Longfellow wrote in his diary. And Charles Sumner, writing from France, said, "There is a charm taken from Boston. Its east winds whistle more coldly around Park Street corner."

Yet in Boston, where Prescott had so splendidly fulfilled Horace Walpole's prophecy of an American Thucydides, there is not now, almost a century after his death, a statue, a tablet, or even an inscription to tell the visitor that here lived and worked the greatest of American historians.

CHARACTER SKETCHES

As THE PRECEDING section note, "Autobiography and Biography," observes, the character sketch is biographical in that one person tells anecdotes illustrating the character of another. Like the biographer, the writer of a character sketch utilizes incidents in the life of his subject that reveal personality. If protracted, the character sketch could become a full-scale biography; in fact, character sketches like the "profiles" in The New Yorker almost amount to that, so exhaustive is the treatment of the subject. But usually the character sketch concentrates in relatively few words the essence of the subject's character, perhaps only one trait. Again, like biography, the character sketch is not simply narrative; some analysis or evaluation usually accompanies the anecdotes, the incidents which reveal the characteristic traits of the subject by concentration upon them and repeated display of them.

In the following piece, Yeats presents in a few words his view of the character of his grandfather, giving the grandfather's essential austerity as shown in three or four incidents of his life. Yeats' memory of his fearful admiration of his grandfather also testifies to this austerity of character. Thus incident and remembered emotion mingle to sketch character.

Likewise, Edith Wharton recalls anecdotes about Henry James, but she sketches only one of James' traits, his difficulty in dealing with the practical world, as she saw it exhibited during motor jaunts in England. She develops James' character by recording his speech as well as his actions.

MY GRANDFATHER

William Butler Yeats (1865-1939), born in Ireland, was not only an essayist and a dramatist but also very probably the greatest modern poet writing in English. From 1885, with publication of some lyrics in the Dublin University Review, *until his death, he wrote and published verse without interruption. All his poems are collected in* The Variorum Edition of the Poems of W. B. Yeats *(1957), edited by Peter Allt and Russell K. Alspach; his plays, in* The Collected Plays of W. B. Yeats *(2nd ed.; 1952). Of his essays,* A Vision *(1925) is the most important. He founded the Irish Literary Theatre, which a few years later became the famous Abbey Theatre, directed plays there, and in these and many other ways, led the Irish literary revival. In 1923, he was awarded the Nobel Prize in Literature. His* Autobiography *(1953) reveals his splendid gift for personal narrative.*

SOME OF my misery was loneliness and some of it fear of old William Pollexfen my grandfather. He was never unkind, and I cannot remember that he ever spoke harshly to me, but it was the custom to fear and admire him. He had won the freedom of some Spanish city, for saving life perhaps, but was so silent that his wife never knew it till he was near eighty, and then from the chance visit of some old sailor. She asked him if it was true and he said it was true, but she knew him too well to question and his old shipmate had left the town. She too had the habit of fear. We knew that he had been in many parts of the world, for there was a great scar on his hand made by a whaling-hook, and in the dining-room was a cabinet with bits of coral in it and a jar of water from the Jordan for the baptizing of his children and Chinese pictures upon rice-paper and an ivory walking-stick from India that came to me after his death. He had great physical strength and had the reputation of never ordering a man to do anything he would not do himself. He owned many sailing ships and once, when a captain just come to anchor at Rosses Point reported something wrong with the rudder, had sent a messenger to say "Send a man down to find out what's wrong." "The crew all refuse" was the answer, and to that my grandfather answered, "Go down yourself," and not being obeyed, he dived from the main deck, all the neighbourhood lined along the pebbles of the shore. He came up with his skin torn but well informed about the rudder. He had a violent temper and kept a hatchet at his bedside for burglars and would knock a man down instead of going to law, and I once saw him hunt a party of men with a horsewhip. He had no relation for he was an only child and, being solitary and silent, he had few friends. He corresponded with Campbell of Islay who had befriended him and his crew after a shipwreck, and Captain Webb, the first man who had swum the Channel and who was drowned swimming the Niagara Rapids, had been a mate in his employ and a close friend. That is all the friends I can remember and yet he was so looked up to and admired that when he returned from taking the waters at Bath his men would light bonfires along the railway line for miles; while his partner William Middleton whose father after the great famine had attended the sick for weeks, and taken cholera from a man he carried in his arms into his own house and died of it, and was himself civil to everybody and a cleverer man than my grandfather, came and went without notice. I think I confused my grandfather with God, for I remember in one of my attacks of melancholy praying that he might punish me for my sins, and I was shocked and astonished when a daring little girl—a cousin I think—having waited under a group of trees in the avenue, where she knew he would pass near four o'clock on the way to his dinner, said to him, "If I were you and you were a little girl, I would give you a doll."

Yet for all my admiration and alarm, neither I nor any one else thought it wrong to outwit his violence or his rigour; and his lack of suspicion and something helpless about him made that easy while it stirred our affection. When I must have been still a very little boy, seven or eight years old perhaps, an uncle called me out of bed one night, to ride the five or six miles to Rosses Point to borrow a railway-pass from a cousin. My grandfather had one, but thought it dishonest to let another use it, but the cousin was not so particular. I was let out through a gate that opened upon a little lane beside the garden away from ear-shot of the house, and rode delighted through the moonlight, and awoke my cousin in the small hours by tapping on his window with a whip. I was home again by two or three in the morning and found the coach-man waiting in the little lane. My grandfather would not have thought such an adventure possible, for every night at eight he believed that the stable-yard was locked, and he knew that he was brought the key. Some servant had once got into trouble at night and so he had arranged that they should all be locked in. He never knew, what everybody else in the house knew, that for all the ceremonious bringing of the key the gate was never locked.

Even to-day when I read *King Lear* his image is always before me and I often wonder if the delight in passionate men in my plays and in my poetry is more than his memory. He must have been ignorant, though I could not judge him in my childhood, for he had run away to sea when a boy, "gone to sea through the hawse-hole" as he phrased it, and I can but remember him with two books—his Bible and Falconer's *Shipwreck*, a little green-covered book that lay always upon his table; he belonged to some younger branch of an old Cornish family. His father had been in the Army, had retired to become an owner of sailing ships, and an engraving of some old family place my grandfather thought should have been his hung next a painted coat of arms in the little back parlour. His mother had been a Wexford woman, and there was a tradition that his family had been linked with Ireland for generations and once had their share in the old Spanish trade with Galway. He had a good deal of pride and disliked his neighbours, whereas his wife, a Middleton, was

gentle and patient and did many charities in the little back parlour among frieze coats and shawled heads, and every night
when she saw him asleep went the round of the house alone with
a candle to make certain there was no burglar in danger of the
hatchet. She was a true lover of her garden, and before the care
of her house had grown upon her, would choose some favourite
among her flowers and copy it upon rice-paper. I saw some of
her handiwork the other day and I wondered at the delicacy of
form and colour and at a handling that may have needed a
magnifying glass it was so minute. I can remember no other
pictures but the Chinese paintings, and some coloured prints of
battles in the Crimea upon the wall of a passage, and the painting of a ship at the passage end darkened by time.

EDITH WHARTON

MOTORING WITH HENRY JAMES

Edith Wharton (1862-1937), a native of New York, began writing short stories in the 'Nineties. Her collections of stories, The Greater Inclination *(1899) and* Crucial Instances *(1901), were followed by her first long novel,* The Valley of Decision *(1902). Her later works include* The House of Mirth *(1905),* Ethan Frome *(1911), the Pulitzer Prize-winning* The Age of Innocence *(1920), and* Hudson River Bracketed *(1929). From her autobiography,* A Backward Glance *(1934), comes the following reminiscence of Henry James.*

NOT INFREQUENTLY, on my annual visit to Qu'acre [Queen's Acre], I "took off" from Lamb House, where I also went annually for a visit to Henry James. The motor run between Rye and Windsor being an easy one, I was often accompanied by Henry James, who generally arranged to have his visit to Qu'acre coincide with mine. James, who was a frequent companion on our English motor-trips, was firmly convinced that, because he lived in England, and our chauffeur (an American) did not, it was necessary that the latter should be guided by him through the intricacies of the English country-side. Signposts were rare in England in those days, and for many years afterward, and a truly British reserve seemed to make the local authorities reluctant to communicate with the invading stranger. Indeed, considerable difficulty existed as to the formulating of advice and instructions, and I remember in one village the agitated warning: "Motorists! Beware of the children!"—while in general there was a marked absence of indications as to the whereabouts of the next village.

It chanced, however, that Charles Cook, our faithful and skilful driver, was a born path-finder, while James's sense of direction was non-existent, or rather actively but always erroneously alert; and the consequences of his intervention were

»»» From *A Backward Glance* by Edith Wharton. Copyright, 1934, D. Appleton-Century Company, Inc. Reprinted by permission of the publisher Appleton-Century-Crofts, Inc.

always bewildering, and sometimes extremely fatiguing. The first time that my husband and I went to Lamb House by motor (coming from France) James, who had travelled to Folkestone by train to meet us, insisted on seating himself next to Cook, on the plea that the roads across Romney marsh formed such a tangle that only an old inhabitant could guide us to Rye. The suggestion resulted in our turning around and around in our tracks till long after dark, though Rye, conspicuous on its conical hill, was just ahead of us, and Cook could easily have landed us there in time for tea.

Another year we had been motoring in the west country, and on the way back were to spend a night at Malvern. As we approached (at the close of a dark rainy afternoon) I saw James growing restless, and was not surprised to hear him say: "My dear, I once spent a summer at Malvern, and know it very well; and as it is rather difficult to find the way to the hotel, it might be well if Edward were to change places with me, and let me sit beside Cook." My husband of course acceded (though with doubt in his heart), and James having taken his place, we awaited the result. Malvern, if I am not mistaken, is encircled by a sort of upper boulevard, of the kind called in Italy a *strada di circonvallazione,* and for an hour we circled about above the outspread city, while James vainly tried to remember which particular street led down most directly to our hotel. At each corner (literally) he stopped the motor, and we heard a muttering, first confident and then anguished. "This—this, my dear Cook, yes . . . this certainly is the right corner. But no; stay! A moment longer, please—in this light it's so difficult . . . appearances are so misleading . . . It may be . . . yes! I think it *is* the next turn . . . 'a little farther lend thy guiding hand' . . . that is, drive on; but slowly, please, my dear Cook; *very* slowly!" And at the next corner the same agitated monologue would be repeated; till at length Cook, the mildest of men, interrupted gently: "I guess any turn'll get us down into the town, Mr. James, and after that I can ask—" and late, hungry and exhausted we arrived at length at our destination, James still convinced that the next turn would have been the right one, if only we had been more patient.

The most absurd of these episodes occurred on another rainy evening, when James and I chanced to arrive at Windsor long after dark. We must have been driven by a strange chauffeur—perhaps Cook was on a holiday; at any rate, having fallen into the lazy habit of trusting to him to know the way, I found myself at a loss to direct his substitute to the King's Road. While I was hesitating, and peering out into the darkness, James spied an ancient doddering man who had stopped in the rain to gaze at us. "Wait a moment, my dear—I'll ask him where we are"; and leaning out he signalled to the spectator.

"My good man, if you'll be good enough to come here, please; a little nearer—so," and as the old man came up: "My friend, to put it to you in two words, this lady and I have just arrived here from *Slough;* that is to say, to be more strictly accurate, we have recently *passed through* Slough on our way here, having actually motored to Windsor from Rye, which was our point of departure; and the darkness having overtaken us, we should be much obliged if you would tell us where we now are in relation, say, to the High Street, which, as you of course know, leads to the Castle, after leaving on the left hand the turn down to the railway station."

I was not surprised to have this extraordinary appeal met by silence, and a dazed expression on the old wrinkled face at the window; nor to have James go on: "In short" (his invariable prelude to a fresh series of explanatory ramifications), "in short, my good man, what I want to put to you in a word is this: supposing we have already (as I have reason to think we have) driven past the turn down to the railway station (which, in that case, by the way, would probably not have been on our left hand, but on our right), where are we now in relation to . . ."

"Oh, please," I interrupted, feeling myself utterly unable to sit through another parenthesis, "do ask him where the King's Road is."

"Ah—? The King's Road? Just so! Quite right! Can you, as a matter of fact, my good man, tell us where, in relation to our present position, the King's Road exactly *is?*"

"Ye're in it," said the aged face at the window.

LETTERS

LETTERS are usually direct communications from one person to another; however, many find a wider audience, and others (letters to editors, for example) may not only find but also seek a wider audience. Letters always have a practical purpose: the writer wants to accomplish something. Usually, he wants his reader (or readers) to do something: to reform (Mark Twain's letter), to join an organization (James'), or to understand why something has been done, will be done, or will not be done (Wells' and Perkins'), for instance. Sometimes the letter writer's chief purpose is to let off steam (Twain's). Letters, therefore, tend to be advice-giving and argumentative and also to be witty, sometimes in a mean way. But their range of modes is wide. Perkins' letter, for example, is a kind of process explanation (about book publishing) and might have been included under that heading.

MARK TWAIN

LETTER TO FRANK A. NICHOLS, SECRETARY, CONCORD FREE TRADE CLUB

Samuel Langhorne Clemens (1835-1910), alias Mark Twain, in the following letter shows that his talent as a humorist extended to the writing of business correspondence. Inclusion of this letter meets a need unmet by manuals of business letterwriting, which unanimously omit discussion of the put-out letter, wherein a put-out writer tells off his correspondent.

Hartford, March, 1885.

DEAR SIR:

I am in receipt of your favor of the 24th inst., conveying the gratifying intelligence that I have been made an honorary member of the Free Trade Club of Concord, Massachusetts, and I desire to express to the Club, through you, my grateful sense of the high compliment thus paid me.

It does look as if Massachusetts were in a fair way to embarrass me with kindnesses this year. In the first place a Massachusetts Judge has just decided in open court that a Boston publisher may sell not only his own property in a free and unfettered way, but may also as freely sell property which does not belong to him but to me—property which he has not bought and which I have not sold. Under this ruling I am now advertising that judge's homestead for sale; and if I make as good a sum out of it as I expect I shall go on and sell the rest of his property.

In the next place, a committee of the public library of your town has condemned and excommunicated my last book [*Huckleberry Finn*], and doubled its sale. This generous action of theirs must necessarily benefit me in one or two additional ways. For instance, it will deter other libraries from buying the book and you are doubtless aware that one book in a public library prevents the sale of a sure ten and a possible hundred of its mates. And secondly it will cause the purchasers of the book to read it, out of curiosity, instead of merely intending to do so after the usual way of the world and library committees; and then they will discover, to my great advantage and their own indignant disappointment, that there is nothing objectionable in the book, after all.

And finally, the Free Trade Club of Concord comes forward and adds to the splendid burden of obligations already conferred upon me by the Commonwealth of Massachusetts, an honorary membership which is more worth than all the rest since it endorses me as worthy to associate with certain gentlemen whom even the moral icebergs of the Concord library committee are bound to respect.

May the great Commonwealth of Massachusetts endure forever, is the heartfelt prayer of one who, long a recipient of her mere general good will, is proud to realize that he is at last become her pet.

Thanking you again, dear sir and gentlemen, I remain

Your obliged servant

S. L. CLEMENS

(known to the Concord Winter School of Philosophy as "Mark Twain.")

HENRY JAMES

AND H. G. WELLS

LETTER OF INQUIRY

AND LETTER OF REPLY

Henry James (1843-1916), American novelist, spent much of his life abroad and became a British citizen in 1915. His many stories and novels, of which latter class The Ambassadors *(1903) is a pattern example, greatly influenced fiction writers of his own and later times. Likewise he continues as a literary force through his criticism, especially his prefaces to the New York edition (1907-1909) of his writings, prefaces since collected in* The Art of the Novel *(1934).*

H. G. Wells (1866-1946), English novelist and sociological and historical writer, was in his fiction the antithesis of Henry James, a fact that he made clear in Boon *(1915), his satire upon James and other writers. His better known novels are* Kipps *(1905) and* Tono-Bungay *(1909). Today he is equally remembered for his early science fiction such as* The Time Machine *(1895) and his historical and social commentary such as* The Outline of History *(1919; 5th revision, 1930) and* The Shape of Things to Come *(1933).*

In the following letters, James and Wells show their differing opinions about the Royal Society of Literature.

JAMES TO WELLS

The Reform Club,
March 20th, 1912.

MY DEAR WELLS.

It has been a great sorrow—verily a shock to me—to hear from Edmund Gosse that you are not disposed to avail yourself of our invitation to Membership of the Academic Committee [of the Royal Society of Literature]. Is it not possible to you to recon-

»»» Letters 54 (from James) and 55 (from Wells). *Henry James and H. G. Wells: A Record of Their Friendship, Their Debate on the Art of Fiction, and Their Quarrel.* Ed. Leon Edel and Gordon N. Ray. Urbana: University of Illinois Press, 1958. Pp. 157-160. Reprinted by permission of Paul R. Reynolds & Son, 599 Fifth Avenue, New York, New York, of H. G. Wells's Executors, and of the University of Illinois Press.

sider—under a fond and passionate appeal—that irresponsive and unsociable attitude? On hearing of your election I felt a greater pleasure than anything in my connection with the body had yet given me, and if you maintain your refusal I shall continue, in pain and privation, to yearn for you. So I am moved to try respectfully to contend with you to some good issue on the subject. Even if you have reasons more substantial than I imagine, or *can* imagine, have them, I mean, as the matter has hitherto struck you, I find it in me to promise you, as it were, in the light of my own experience (for I too have had an experience!) that they won't seem to you *after the fact*—that is if you only *would* come in!—half as valid as they do now. The thing is a *pleasant* and a plastic, elastic, aspiring thing, greatly appealing to our good-will—by which I especially mean to yours, that of your literary and creative generation; offering us no rigour, offering us opportunities for influence, for pressure in desirable directions and asking no sacrifice worth speaking of or grudging in return. It will be what the best of us shall make it, and it is open to the best of us to make it more interesting and more amusing (if you will—"in the highest sense of the term") to ourselves, and more suggestive to others. Above all it would be so fortified by your accession that a due consideration for the prestige of current English letters surely ought to move you. You would do something for us that we lack and don't want to lack—and we would do for *you*, I think, that you would find yourself *within* still more moved than without to that critical, that ironic, that even exasperated (if I may call it) play—or reaction!—which is the mark, or one of the marks, of your genius. Don't make too much of rigours and indifferences, of consistencies and vows; I have no greater affinity with associations and academies than you—*a priori;* and yet I find myself glad to have done the simple, civil, social *easiest* thing in accepting my election—touched by the amenity and geniality of the thought that we shall probably *make something* collectively—in addition to what we may make individually. Don't think I want to harass or overbear you if I say that if these words still leave you cold I frankly don't want to let the matter go without seeing you over it. I would come up

to Church Row—at any hour I might find you—after 3.30 p.m.—
for the purpose, or would earnestly await you here at your own
hour equally—with all the lively assurances of yours very faithfully

HENRY JAMES

WELLS TO JAMES

17, Church Row, Hampstead.
[*March 25, 1912*]

MY DEAR JAMES.

Your letter is most difficult to answer because I am not going
to do as you wish. It's most difficult because not only have I
a very deep affection for you but I have that snobbishness
towards you which is quite honourable. I do look up to, and
admire, and feel proud of my connexion with your beautiful
fine abundant mind—I like to be about with you and in the same
boat with you. If it was only you——. But I have an insurmount-
able objection to Literary or Artistic Academies as such, to any
hierarchies, any suggestion of controls or fixed standards in these
things. I feel it so strongly that indeed I would rather be outside
the Academic Committee with Hall Caine, than in it with you
and Gosse and Gilbert Murray and Shaw. This world of ours,
I mean the world of creative and representative work we do, is
I am convinced best anarchic. Better the wild rush of Boomster
and the Quack than the cold politeness of the established thing.
And if I don't join you at any rate you take something of my
heart into the Academic Committee. So far as that body does
have a use and exert a good influence it will do it the better
without my turbulent indiscretion. And if it was only a Friendship and not Academic and quasi-official and with a Royal
Charter, how gladly would I come!

Forgive this —— the only word to express my feelings is—
disobedience, and believe me

Always yours,
H. G. WELLS.

MAXWELL E. PERKINS

LETTER TO F. SCOTT FITZGERALD

Maxwell E. Perkins (1884-1947), a native New Yorker, was graduated from Harvard in 1907. For three years he worked as a reporter for the New York Times and then joined the publishing firm of Charles Scribner's Sons in 1910, where he remained as an editor and a director until his death. While he was editor, he worked with such authors as Ernest Hemingway, Thomas Wolfe, and Marjorie Kinnan Rawlings. An example of his advice is the following letter to F. Scott Fitzgerald, written before Fitzgerald's success.

In his letter of September 18 to Perkins, Fitzgerald had written: "Would it be utterly impossible for you to publish the book ["This Side of Paradise"] before Xmas or, say, by February?"

Sept. 23, 1919

DEAR MR. FITZGERALD:

I was very glad to get your letter of the 18th and to know that everything was ready with regard to "This Side of Paradise"; and we are now making an estimate upon the book preliminary to putting it in hand, which we shall do within a short time if the printers' strike does not make it impossible to put anything in hand.

It is this way about publishing before Christmas: there are two book seasons in the year and the preparations for each one are begun long before the season opens. The publishers' travelers go out in July and August over the country with trunks filled with dummies and samples of the Fall books, which are to have their greatest sale in the Christmas season. The Advertising Department and the Circularizing Department get up their material in

August and early September to make these books known considerably before publication and at the very time of publication. The advertising that is done from the first of September on is supposed to have its great effect in December, although the book may have appeared in August or September or October and may have sold considerably then. Now, if a book is accepted after all this preliminary work is done and comes out in November, as yours would have to do at the earliest, it must make its own way altogether: it will get no preliminary advertising; it will not be presented to the trade by salesmen on the basis of a dummy; and it will come to the bookseller, who is already nearly mad with the number of new books and has already invested all the money he can in them, as a most unwelcome and troublesome thing and will suffer accordingly. Even if it is a book by an author who has been selling well for years, it will be very considerably injured by this.

The next book publishing season is the Spring season. The moment the Christmas rush is ended, the travelers go out once more and see all the booksellers, equipped with samples, etc. The bookseller has made his money out of the previous season and is ready to begin afresh and to stock up on new books. The Advertising and Circularizing departments have prepared their work on it, and their accounts of the author, etc., and have advertised it in the trade magazines to reinforce the salesmen's selling argument. Then, when the book does appear in February, March or April, the trade is ready for it and knows about it and it can be competently advertised because the publicity force of the house has become familiar with it.

These are the reasons why there is no question but it would damage your book exceedingly to try to rush it out before Christmas. Whether or not it can be printed in February we cannot yet say, but it certainly can be published in that month or March and we shall remember that you want it to be as early as possible.

About the story, I know that Mr. [Robert] Bridges [then editor of *Scribner's Magazine*] would want to read it. He has been much interested in you and what you have done already and I hope he may have a chance at this.

"The Demon Lover" [a novel Fitzgerald was at work on] sounds good. Everybody ought to read Samuel Butler's "Note Books."

Sincerely yours,

[MAXWELL E. PERKINS]

REVIEWS

REVIEWS are analyses and evaluations of books or other artistic creations. They are analyses because they divide one book, say, into its constituent parts; they tell us something about its thesis or theme, for example, or about its organization or plot or about its style. Reviews are evaluations because, by reference to some criteria or standards of evaluation, they evaluate or rank the book; they tell us whether it is a good, a bad, or an indifferent instance of its form or genre and, sometimes, whether reading it can do the reader or the world some good. Of the three reviews below, the two of works of nonfiction—Fallout and A Book of Cats—are favorable; the one of a novel—An American Dream—is unfavorable. Worth noticing is how these reviews not only refer their evaluations (implicitly, at least) to criteria, but also support them with examples. In this way, analysis and evaluation cooperate. A standard for reviews themselves appears in "Definition," where Krutch defines the term "good review."

Review of *FALLOUT*

Fallout, a Study of Superbombs, Strontium 90 and Survival,
edited by John M. Fowler. Basic Books, Inc., ($5.50). This is a
valuable and an important book that comes to grips with a peril
as glaringly evident as the flash of an H-bomb. The "soaring
sixties" have begun, everything is going up, and we have a good
chance of going up too, unless we are prepared to act upon the
facts here set forth. They are not new facts; they have been made
known in journals and reports, in the testimony of competent
specialists, in repeated warnings of sober men. But various
attempts have been made to conceal, to obscure, to qualify, so
that the average person does not know what or whom to believe.
Official fallout pronouncements have given the impression that
the quantity is negligible; and when this position was refuted
conclusively, that what has been falling upon us is not much
more dangerous than the gentle rain from heaven. Fowler's book
corrects this impression in language plain enough, as Adlai
Stevenson says in a foreword, for anyone to understand. There
is much here for your enlightenment, naught for your comfort.
The different kinds of bomb and their products are examined,
the global pattern of fallout, the vexed problem of hot-spots
(as to which the so-called averaging doctrine is as convincing as
the argument that there is little danger of lead-poisoning to the
average citizen from a gang war), the steadily rising level of
fallout, the biological and genetic effects of radiation, the history
of radiation accidents, protection and treatment, the detection of
bomb tests. Ralph E. Lapp presents a dispassionate summary of
the effects of a nuclear war, and there is a horrifying chapter
on national survival that makes another chapter on civil defense
sound completely fatuous. Appendices are included on radiation

»»» *Scientific American*, CCII (June, 1960), 192, 194. Reprinted by permission of the *Scientific American*.

physics, fission and fusion, as well as a helpful glossary. This is the most level-headed, honest and comprehensive treatment of the subject that has appeared. But for a book that can do as much good as this book can, and which has only 250 pages and four pages of (essentially superfluous) plates, the price is much too high. Salvation ought to fit more purses.

MARGARET WILLY

Review of A BOOK OF CATS

Margaret Willy (1919-   )—poet, critic, editor, and teacher—was born in England and educated at the University of London. She has published two volumes of verse and several critical studies; edits English; *and has lectured for the British Council and at Goldsmiths' College, University of London.*

A *Book of Cats*. By DOROTHY MARGARET STUART. Methuen. 15s.

IN A BOOK which will delight, as well as greatly enlighten, cat-lovers, Miss Stuart traces the story of the cat from its known origins, in the homes and temples of ancient Egypt (cats figure in several surviving tomb-paintings) to the twentieth century and the Church Cat of St. Mary Redcliffe, Bristol, whose burial in the churchyard is marked by a simply inscribed stone. In between there is a wealth of information, anecdote, and intriguing titbits—'legendary, literary and historical', as the sub-title says—about members of the cat tribe. We see the cat in Aesop and in Celtic legend, in Chaucer, in Shakespeare—evidently, here, not much beloved—and in Dickens. We see him as the witches' familiar, but also as the friend of poets (Herrick, Cowper, and Christopher Smart with his Jeffry, 'a mixture of gravity and waggery . . . an excellent clamberer', and 'servant of the living God'); as well as championed by poets—it was over the tormenting of a kitten that Keats had his famous fight with the butcher-boy. We meet again, with proper veneration, that prince of cats, Dr. Johnson's Hodge, fed on oysters selected personally by his master; and the one of Horace Walpole's many cats who provided Gray with the doleful material for his ode *On a Favourite Cat, Drowned in a Tub of Gold fishes*. The author treats her subject with urbanity and affection; and her

»»» *English*, XIII (Spring, 1960), 29. Reprinted by permission of *English*.

essay is embellished with some enchanting illustrations, ranging from a drawing of a bronze figurine in the British Museum of the Egyptian goddess Bast, with kittens, a painting of the Earl of Southampton in the Tower accompanied by a sturdy feline companion (black-and-white), or the 'catte' embroidered by Mary, Queen of Scots in captivity, to the cheerful grin of Tenniel's Cheshire Cat.

GRANVILLE HICKS

A LITERARY HOAX?

Granville Hicks (1901-   ) was educated at Harvard and later served as counselor in the American Civilization program there as well as taught at Smith College and Rensselaer Polytechnic Institute. A literary critic and editor of several magazines, he has written novels and books of social commentary and biography. His latest book is Part of the Truth *(1965), an autobiography. As contributing editor of the* Saturday Review, *he writes the column "Literary Horizons," in which the following review appeared.*

EVER SINCE the publication of his first novel, *The Naked and the Dead,* in 1948, Norman Mailer has been a figure of importance on the American literary scene. The novel had a strong impact when it was published and has lasted well; in spite of its indebtedness to Dos Passos and Hemingway and in spite of some clumsiness, it stands as the best American novel about World War II and as the most remarkable exhibition in recent times of the naturalistic technique. Since its appearance, however, Mailer's work has received rather more condemnation than approval. *The Barbary Shore* was generally regarded as an interesting and—because Mailer was not content to repeat himself—an honorable failure, but a failure. Parts of *The Deer Park* were greatly admired, but as a whole it was not a success. And since that novel was published, nearly ten years ago, we have had only collections of odds and ends, of which *Advertisements for Myself (SR,* Nov. 7, 1959) was the most notable.

However, spotty as his career has been, Mailer's name is almost always mentioned when there is talk about American literature since the war. Some people will say that this is because of his gift for getting his name before the public in nonliterary as well as literary contexts, and it is true that he has made more

»»» *Saturday Review,* XLVIII (March 20, 1965), 23-24. Reprinted by permission of the *Saturday Review* and Granville Hicks.

headlines than most of his contemporaries. But, on the other hand, he continues to be taken seriously by persons whose judgments have to be respected—for instance, Diana Trilling, who wrote an essay about him in *The Living Present*. Mailer's new novel—*An American Dream* (Dial, $4.95)—has stirred up talk during its appearance as a serial in *Esquire*, and one can predict that quantities of words are going to be spent on it in the weeks to come.

This, it should be pointed out, is not the big novel that, in *Advertisements for Myself*, Mailer announced he was writing. It seems, on the contrary, to be a book that he conceived and executed on the spur of the moment. At the end he dates it, "September 1963-October 1964." The jacket indicates that serial publication had begun in *Esquire* before the book was finished: "Mailer undertook to write *An American Dream* under the same conditions of serial deadline that Conrad, Dickens and Dostoevsky met in their day." (That, I think, is the extent of the resemblance between this work and the work of the aforementioned authors.)

The only way to suggest the quality of the novel is to summarize it at some length. This is how it begins: "I met Jack Kennedy in November, 1946. We were both war heroes, and both of us had just been elected to Congress. We went out one night on a double date and it turned out to be a fair evening for me. I seduced a girl who would have been bored by a diamond as big as the Ritz." The narrator is named Stephen Richard Rojack, and the girl is called Deborah Caughlin Mangaravidi Kelly. President Kennedy does not play much of a part in the novel, though he is mentioned later, but the girl does, and so does the business of being a war hero. Rojack quickly goes on to tell how he killed four Germans in Italy, an occurrence that left an enduring mark on his psyche.

Rojack, we learn, was graduated from Harvard *summa cum laude*, became a hero, went to Congress. Deciding he was not made for politics, he committed political suicide by supporting Henry Wallace in 1948. After that he became "a professor of existential psychology" at a university in New York City, wrote a book, and achieved success on a television program. He married Deborah seven years after he seduced her, but, at the time the novel begins, they are separated.

The novel, according to the jacket, covers a period of thirty-two hours. At the outset Rojack, suffering from what is no doubt existential nausea, contemplates suicide, but instead of killing himself, he goes to see his wife, whom he strangles. (This is the cliff-hanging climax of the first installment.) After making love, in a rather eccentric fashion, described in detail, to his wife's maid, he throws his wife's body out the window onto the East River Drive. He makes love to the maid again, though rather hurriedly this time, and descends to the street, where he is taken in charge by the police. His story, of course, is that his wife jumped.

Released by the police because of some mysterious influence, Rojack immediately goes to a joint to see a singer named Cherry, who, along with some gangsters, was involved in the traffic jam that took place when Deborah's body hit the pavement. After defying her former lover, a prizefighter, he takes her to her apartment on the East Side and, one may be sure, makes love to her.

The next day, after losing both his television job and his teaching job, he keeps an appointment with the police. Although the evidence against him seems strong, he is again released. He returns to Cherry's bed, and in due season he hears her story. She was at one time the mistress of a mysterious millionaire with underground connections, who turns out to be none other than Barney Kelly, father of Rojack's late wife. More recently she has been the mistress of a Negro singer, Shago Martin, who comes to pay a call and is thrown downstairs by Rojack.

Rojack has one more appointment, with his father-in-law, Kelly. He sees Deirdre, Deborah's daughter, presumably by her first husband, a child of whom he is fond. While he is talking with Kelly, the phone rings. "It was Jack," Kelly says. "He said to send you his regards and commiserations." After a conversation in which it appears that the situation may have international implications, Kelly reveals that Deirdre is in fact his daughter. (The novel would obviously be incomplete without a touch of incest.) There is another business of near-suicide, after which we have a report of the murder of Shago Martin, and then Rojack arrives at Cherry's apartment just in time to hear her dying words.

I hope it is clear that not for a moment can the novel be taken seriously as a portrayal of life in America—or anywhere else. This is the make-believe world of Ian Fleming and Mickey Spillane. However, Mailer has a streak of pretentiousness that keeps the book from being the good dirty fun that Fleming's books, if not Spillane's, often are.

I should like to believe that the novel is a hoax, and perhaps to some extent it is. Look at the title. What do Americans dream about? Sex and violence—as television producers and magazine publishers well know. So here, it may be argued, we have sex and violence reduced *ad absurdum* if not *ad nauseam*. In other words, the book may be a satire, an expression of moral indignation.

What I see as the great obstacle to the acceptance of this theory is the fact that in other works Mailer has spoken in favor of sex, in all forms and in as great a quantity as possible. He also has sometimes seemed to regard violence as quite a good thing. Mrs. Trilling quotes him as having said that a murder might redeem the murderer: ". . . in the act of killing, in this terribly private moment, the brute feels a moment of tenderness, for the first time perhaps in all his experience. What has happened is that the killer is becoming a little more possible, a little bit more ready to love someone." I cannot see that the assorted murders in *An American Dream* have this redemptive quality, although perhaps that is what Mailer meant to convey.

But if one rejects the theory that the novel is a hoax, one faces a distressing alternative. If one believes that Mailer intended *An American Dream* to be taken seriously, one has to conclude that he has gone to pieces as a writer. The least one can say for the earlier novels is that he tried hard, and in *Advertisements for*

Myself he expressed the highest ambitions for his future work. *An American Dream,* however, seems to be something that he dashed off in spare moments. He accepted the challenge of *Esquire* and produced his monthly installments, ending each in the tradition of *The Perils of Pauline.* If the book is not a joke, a bad joke, it is something worse.

The absurdity of the book is not limited to the plot. Stephen Richard Rojack is a kind of superman, not only a high-powered intellectual but also a handy man in a fight. Mailer identifies himself with Rojack so closely that the poor professor is allowed to have no reality. We don't believe in him as a Congressman or as a professor or even as a lover; he exists simply as a projection of Norman Mailer's fantasies about himself. He is Mailer, as Mailer would like to be. The other characters are but dummies for Mailer-Rojack to manipulate.

The writing is the sloppiest Mailer has ever done. Here is a passage to suggest a tense moment: "I didn't realize until I reached the street that I had been holding my breath. My uneasiness was almost tangible now; I could feel some sullen air of calm, exactly that torporous calm which comes before a hurricane. It was nearly dark outside. I would be late, but I had to walk to the precinct, I had the conviction that if I entered a taxi there would be an accident." (Rojack is given to premonitions of this sort.) Here is a tender passage: "Once, in a rainstorm, I witnessed the creation of a rivulet. The water had come down, the stream had begun in a hollow of earth the size of a leaf. Then it filled and began to flow. The rivulet rolled down the hill between some stalks of grass and weed, it moved in spurts, down the fall of a ledge, down to a brook. It did not know it was not a river. That was how the tears went down Cherry's face." There are also some fancy passages about smell, Mailer having, it appears, a remarkable nose.

In the essay to which I have alluded, Mrs. Trilling wrote: "Where do we, where shall we, where can we derive our moral sanctions: from a failing tradition or from the wild, free impulses of our racial infancy, from the ego or the id? This is the ultimate pressing question of our time, separating our historical period from any that came before it. And because Mailer not only knows the full force of the question but passionately devotes himself to its answer, he transcends the follies and excesses which attend Hipsterism and claims his place in the forefront of modern writers." She also wrote: "Intense as his literary dedication unquestionably is, his religious mission is now infinitely more compelling. Just as he writes in order to preach the word of God, he acts in order to attain to God, by whatever thorny path. And when he invites us to follow his example he literally means us to join a religious crusade."

I wonder what Mrs. Trilling makes of *An American Dream.* It is possible, I suppose, to regard it as a momentary lapse and to believe that Mailer will go on to do work that will justify and even enhance his reputation. But it seems to me to represent such a failure of critical judgment that I cannot lightly dismiss it. It makes me wonder how much longer Mailer will hold "his place in the forefront of modern writers."

DOCUMENTED RESEARCH

ARTICLE

MANY of the pieces in this book are based upon printed materials; insofar as that is so, they could be called research articles of a sort. But in most of those cases, the documentation is informal in the texts of the pieces themselves, though H. L. Mencken, for instance, does footnote his discussion of euphemisms. The documented research article, then, is not just an article based on research in printed and manuscript sources; it is the article in which such research is formally attributed to sources by a method of systematic documentation.

Several purposes are served by such documentation. One is the honest purpose of clearly and painstakingly attributing to the sources not only the passages quoted from them but also the facts and the ideas taken from them which appear in the article writer's paraphrase. Another is the establishment of authority for the article itself: to show by careful documentation that the article writer has done the research requisite to coverage of the subject enhances the authority of his treatment of it. A third purpose served by documentation is the courtesy it accords to other scholars: they can find the original sources and check further into the subject, if they desire. Thus documentation is a potential enlargement of the scope of the article, because it helps others to approach the subject and treat it themselves, perhaps in more detail or perhaps from another view. Yet another purpose served grows from the establishment, by documentation, of what comes from the sources and what from the author of the article. A reader can see readily how much original thought has gone into an article, and can credit properly its author for his ability to organize disparate materials into a coherent discussion of a topic scattered among dozens of other documents, letters, articles, and books. Documentation helps in its way to show what the article writer has made of his subject. It shows whether he has bundled together quotations and borrowed notions and shoved them at the reader in an untidy package, or whether he has seen the connections among his collection of research, has made the relationships of fact and opinion clear, and has thought about his subject sufficiently to have made an original contribution to the thought on it.

Systematic documentation is a convention peculiar to the form of the research article. That it is not merely a matter of form, the discussion of its purposes has shown; indeed, such documentation is the hallmark of the scholarly article. It consists of distinguishing clearly by quotation marks the words of others from the writer's own, and of showing by footnotes or other accepted methods the source of quoted passages and of paraphrased facts, opinions, and ideas borrowed from sources. Various systems of documentation are in vogue in various disciplines. Beardsley in his article follows the system specified in The MLA Style Sheet, issued by the Modern Language Association of America and generally used by writers of literary and humanistic studies. Social scientists and technical and scientific writers follow other systems of documentation.

As Beardsley's article demonstrates, the research article, even when its topic is seemingly as broad as his, focuses rather particularly on certain aspects of a topic. So Beardsley, writing "On the Creation of Art," asks what theories about the process of artistic creation exist, presents a few and evaluates them, concludes that the evidence shows that artists create their works in very different ways, and finally examines the question of the aesthetic relevance of knowledge of this process, concluding that "it is interesting in itself to know, if we can, how the artist's mind works, but I do not see that this has any bearing upon the value of what he produces." Most of the article is concerned with discovery of the process of artistic creation—if there is only one—and, if possible, formulation of a theory explaining the process. Such concentration on the process itself limits the broad possibilities suggested by his title.

In his research, Beardsley cites writings by other theorists on the creative process and statements by artists and poets about how they created or first thought of a painting or poem. The former are secondary sources; the latter, primary ones. Furthermore, the rough drafts of a poem, the first sketches of a picture, and the first scores of a musical composition are primary sources, not only for Beardsley, but for his secondary sources. It is worth noting that Beardsley quotes sparingly and paraphrases more often; he reserves quotation for vividly stated ideas (Collingwood's theory of expressionism or Valéry's memory of how he began to write a certain poem). Presentation of his research is only a prelude to Beardsley's main purpose of developing his own ideas on the creative process; the article, like all good research articles, makes an original contribution to the thought on the topic.

MONROE C. BEARDSLEY

ON THE CREATION OF ART

Monroe C. Beardsley (1915-   ), born in Bridgeport, Connecticut, was educated at Yale. He has taught at Yale, Mount Holyoke, and Swarthmore, where he is now professor of philosophy. He has published several books and many articles on logic and aesthetics—among them Practical Logic *(1950),* Aesthetics: Problems in the Philosophy of Criticism *(1958), and "On the Creation of Art."*

FROM THE TIMES of Homer and Hesiod, creative artists have wondered about the source of their power to summon into existence things hitherto unseen and even unthought. In our day, it has begun to seem feasible to solve this problem with something like conclusiveness. Yet much of its mystery remains.

A number of distinct questions are involved here, only one of which I shall take up. For example, I shall not inquire why the artist creates in the first place—what obscure impulses compel him to make shapes or melodies, to dance or tell stories. This question has been given two sorts of answer. The first is in terms of conscious motives (the artist wants fame, money, love, power, etc.)—and here it seems pretty evident that there must be a vast variety of true answers, depending on the artist, the work at hand, and even the time of day or night. The second is in terms of unconscious needs and drives—and this I am not competent to pursue. Again, I shall not inquire how the creative process begins—what evokes the first stroke of the brush, the first words of the poem. In the creation of every work, no doubt something does come first, perhaps a single little fragment, perhaps a rush of ideas. This initial element of what later becomes the work has been referred to by various metaphors, some of them misleading, as we shall see—*germ, cell, seed, nucleus;* I will call it

»»» *Journal of Aesthetics and Art Criticism,* XXIII (Spring, 1965), 291-304. Reprinted by permission of Monroe C. Beardsley and of the publishers, The American Society for Aesthetics.

the *inceptive element,* or, for short, *incept.* The incept of the work may simply pop into the artist's mind—like Mozart's melodies or Housman's verses—or it may come from external sources, accidentally, like the notes struck by a cat on the keyboard or the pattern made by mud in the gutter. When it does come from within, it no doubt has preconscious causal conditions, though to trace them would surely be a difficult undertaking.

What I mean by the creative process is that stretch of mental and physical activity between the incept and the final touch—between the thought "I may be on to something here" and the thought "It is finished." My problem is about what goes on in this interval—how the work of art itself comes into existence and takes on its character through the stages or phases of this process.

I

Many students of art have assumed, or expected to find, that there is such a thing as *the* process of art creation—that is, a pattern universally or characteristically discoverable whenever substantial works of art are produced. They would allow, of course, for many differences between one creative process and another, depending on the artist's habits and temperament, the medium in which he moves, and the demands of the particular work in progress. But they argue that beneath these differences there is what we might call the *normal creative pattern,* and that to understand this pattern would contribute much to our understanding of the finished product.

Nor is it unreasonable to suppose that there is such a creative pattern to be isolated and described. First, it might be said, the common character of works of art in all media—whatever it is that enables us to class them together—presents a prima-facie case for a creative pattern. For things that are alike may well have been produced in a similar way. Second, there is the analogy with aesthetic experience. For if there is a pattern of appreciation common to the arts, then why should there not be a pattern of creation, which would, in a sense, be its inverse?

Third, there is the analogy with other kinds of creative activity. Dewey's classic description of the process of inquiry, or problem-solving, remains the standard one, though it has been refined and extended since its first appearance in *How We Think*. Practical and scientific problems differ considerably among themselves, just as works of art do, and if there is a common pattern of thought provoked by the former, there may be a common pattern of activity required for the latter.

It is true that the theory of a common character of the arts and the theory of a special aesthetic experience have been questioned in recent years.[1] I appreciate the force of the objections, which I won't go into here, but, like many others, I am not ready to abandon either of the theories. In any case, of course, the three arguments I have mentioned above are not conclusive; they are but suggestive analogies. If there is a common creative pattern, then it can be discovered only by direct study of creative processes. And we might expect to find three main sources of evidence: the artist, the psychologist, and the philosopher.

Our first inclination, of course, is to turn to the creative artist himself, for he ought to know, if anyone does, what is going on in his mind during that mysterious interval between the first pin-fall or brick-fall of an idea and the final laying down of pen or brush. And it is true that much of our best and most useful information about creative processes does come from artists. The trouble is that, for reasons of their own, they are often inclined to the most whimsical and bizarre statements, and seem to enjoy being deliberately misleading. For example, Christian Zervos tells us that Picasso once said to him:

I take a walk in the forest of Fontainebleau. There I get an indigestion of greenness. I must empty this sensation into a picture. Green

---

[1] The former by Paul Ziff and Morris Weitz, whose views I have discussed in "Art and the Definitions of the Arts," *JAAC*, XX (1961), 175-187; the latter by George Dickie, in "Is Psychology Relevant to Aesthetics?" *Philosophical Review*, LXXI (1962), 285-302, and more fully in "The Phantom Aesthetic Experience," forthcoming.

dominates it. The painter paints as if in urgent need to discharge himself of his sensations and his visions.[2]

But this is a most curious description of the creative process. If the painter suffers from a surfeit of green, does he avoid looking at green any more for a while? No, he goes to his studio, squeezes out the green pigment, and proceeds to cover a canvas with it. This is like drinking grapefruit juice to cure an acid stomach. To make the indigestion theory of artistic creation plausible, the green-surfeited painter would surely go off to paint a *red* painting—red being the chromatic analogue of sodium bicarbonate.

We have had, by the way, many other metaphorical models of the creative process or the mind during creation—though perhaps none more colorful than Picasso's heartburn. The famous treatise of John Livingston Lowes, *The Road to Xanadu,* is full of them—the "hooked atoms" jumbled about, the "deep well" of the unconscious into which the poet dips, the imagination as "loom." Once we read of Shelley's "fading coal." Now it is the digital computer that furnishes the most tempting figure.

Or consider a famous statement by Henry James, in his preface to *The Spoils of Poynton.*[3] He begins by saying that the "germ" of his novel, as he called it, lay in a story told at a dinner party in London. James dilates upon "the sublime economy of art," which starts with such a "prick of inoculation," when the virus is communicated, and then goes on to build a work out of itself. The lady who told the story began by mentioning a woman at odds with her son over the furniture in an old house bequeathed to the son by his father. James remarks, "There had been but ten words, yet I had recognized in them, as in a flash, all the possibilities of the little drama of my *Spoils,* which glimmered then and there into life." James says he didn't want to hear any more of the story, because the germ was complete in

[2] Brewster Ghiselin, ed., *The Creative Process: A Symposium* (U. of California, 1952), p. 51.

[3] Henry James, *The Art of the Novel,* ed. R. P. Blackmur (N. Y., 1934), pp. 119-124.

itself; the seed had been "transplanted to richer soil." This claim has often been repeated and taken as a text. But if we look in his *Notebooks,* where he tells a good deal about the process of writing *The Spoils of Poynton,* we find that in fact, on the day after the party (December 24, 1893), James wrote down not only the germ but the whole story, as it was told him, and that in fact many other germs came into the picture before very long, as well.[4]

Probably the greatest contributions made by creative artists to the solution of our problem are not their own theories about what they do, but the records they leave us in the form of sketches and early drafts. We cherish, for example, the notebooks of Beethoven, the sketches and studies in which Picasso worked out his ideas for *Guernica,* and the rich materials contributed to the special collection at the University of Buffalo by living poets who are willing to allow scholars to study their methods of work, their ventures, erasures, substitutions, corrections, and revisions. I shall have occasion to make use of these materials later.

As for the psychologists, despite the considerable effort (or at least speculation) that has gone into the study of the artist's unconscious, not much is available by way of well-established conclusions about the way the poet's or painter's mind is actually working when he is on the job.[5] Some of the most interesting contributions have been made by gestalt psychologists, for example, Rudolf Arnheim, in his psychological study of some materials in the Buffalo collection, and in his recent study of *Guernica.*[6]

---

[4] *Notebooks,* ed. F. O. Matthiessen and Kenneth Murdock (N. Y., 1947), pp. 136-137. For further stages in the development of this novel (tentatively entitled *The House Beautiful*) see the references on p. 138. (This information was kindly given to me by Professor S. P. Rosenbaum of Indiana University.)

[5] Douglas Morgan, "Creativity Today," *JAAC,* XII (1953), 1-24; and Stuart E. Golann, "Psychological Study of Creativity," *Psychological Bulletin,* LX (1963), 548-565.

[6] *Poets at Work* (N. Y., 1948), by various authors, and *Picasso's Guernica: the Genesis of a Painting* (U. of California, 1962).

Among the most valuable of the psychological investigations are those undertaken nearly thirty years ago by Catharine Patrick.[7] She first secured a group of 55 poets (with 58 "non-poets" as a suitable control group), and, after putting them at ease, confronted them with a certain picture and made them write a poem about it. She asked them to talk aloud as they thought, and took down their words in shorthand. Then she went to the painters, and, tit for tat, presented them with a part of a poem by Milton, which they were to illustrate in some way—while again, she took down their vocal musings, and also kept note of what they were drawing, as time passed. Every encounter was carefully timed. And the results were supplemented by questionnaires.

These interviews resulted in a good deal of very interesting material. Professor Patrick set out to determine whether the typical process of artistic creation passes through the four stages classically distinguished by Graham Wallas in his book on *The Art of Thought*—the stages of preparation, incubation, inspiration, and elaboration. And she concluded that these stages can indeed be distinguished. But the most remarkable feature of her material, it seems to me, is precisely the opposite. All four of these activities are mixed together; they are constantly (or alternately) going on throughout the whole process.

When we turn to the philosophers, we find a few who have tried to bring together into something of a general theory the insights of artists and psychologists. They, too, of course, have their own occupational hazards, or professional vices, and are too readily drawn away from contact with actual works of art into theorizing about what might ideally be true. For one who has a metaphysical axe to grind, it is easy enough to find a congenial formula to describe the creative process. Depending on the angle of approach, the artist will be said to be converting sensations into intuitions, receiving divine inspiration, reshuffling the atoms of immediate experience, embodying the ideal in sensuous form, working out the consequences of an initial postulate, or

[7] *Creative Thought in Poets, Archives of Psychology*, No. 178 (1935); "Creative Thought in Artists," *J. of Psychology*, IV (1937), 35-73.

affirming the authenticity of existence. But I am looking for less ambitious theories than these.

II

Philosophic reflection on the available empirical data has given us two widely-held accounts of the creative process. When we consider any artistic work of major proportions, whose creation we know something about, we are often struck by the gap between the final achievement and its humble incept. Clearly, the process between can be said to have moved in a desirable direction. Now in the usual case, although lucky accidents may make an important contribution, this process appears to be at least partly controlled. The problem for the aesthetician is, then: What is the nature of this control?

The earliest people who raised this question—Homer, Hesiod, and Pindar—were inclined to give it a supernatural answer, attributing their own feats to the intervention of the Muses. And the theory of divine inspiration, often in a pantheistic version, remains with us. But if we insist upon a naturalistic theory of artistic creation, we find two main ones. And these are distinguished in a way familiar to other branches of philosophy.

According to what I shall call the Propulsive Theory, the controlling agent is something that exists prior to the creative process, and presides over it throughout. According to the Finalistic Theory, the controlling agent is the final goal toward which the process aims. No doubt the two theories run into each other in the minds of some philosophers, and perhaps we need not strain to keep them wholly distinct. But even if there are not two theories, there are at least two errors—and this is what I am most concerned to note.

The theory of art as expression is probably the most popular form of the Propulsive Theory of the creative process. And I shall take R. G. Collingwood as representative of expressionism at its best.

When a man is said to express emotion, what is being said about him comes to this. At first, he is conscious of having an emotion, but not conscious of what this emotion is. All he is conscious of is a per-turbation or excitement, which he feels going on within him, but of whose nature he is ignorant.[8]

Before the emotion is expressed, the artist is oppressed by it; he works so his mind will become "lightened and eased" (p. 110). His aim is to make his emotion clear to himself (pp. 111, 114)—indeed, to discover what the emotion is (p. 111). Thus Collingwood postulates a single emotion that preserves its iden-tity throughout the process of creation—if the work is to be genuine—and determines the main course of that process.

The first difficulty with this theory is that no principle of identity can be provided for this emotion.

If artists only find out what their emotions are in the course of find-ing out how to express them, they cannot begin the work of expres-sion by deciding what emotion to express (p. 117).

Well said. But, on the other hand, after the artist has expressed his emotion, and come to experience it clearly, how does he know it is the same emotion he started with? He cannot compare them, since the other was unknown to him. How does he know that the emotion he feels now is not a new and different emotion—an emotion that is perhaps felt as the *effect* of the finished work, rather than as its cause? As far as I can see, Collingwood has no answer to this. And, moreover, in order to preserve his theory he has to say some rather surprising things. For example,

No artist, therefore, so far as he is an artist proper, can set out to write a comedy, a tragedy, an elegy, or the like. So far as he is an artist proper, he is just as likely to write any one of these as any other (p. 116).

I am sure that statement would have startled Sophocles or Shakespeare—not to mention Racine and Molière. According to Collingwood, the genuine artist says, "I feel an emotion coming on; no telling what it is until I write something (or paint it, or compose it); how will I know what I've felt until I see what

[8] R. G. Collingwood, *The Principles of Art* (Oxford, 1938), p. 109. See also Alan Donagan, *The Later Philosophy of R. G. Collingwood* (Oxford, 1962), ch. 5, §3.

I've done?" If he insists from the start on writing a tragedy, he will be forcing his emotion into some channel, and the result cannot be art.

The whole concept of *clarifying* an emotion is itself very obscure. I have a suspicion that when Bruckner finished one of his enormous symphonies, his emotions were no more clear to him than they were at the start. At least, they are no more clear to me. They are big emotions; anyone can see that. But clarity is hardly the word for them. On the other hand, nothing could be more clear than the special quality of the opening of Mozart's *G Minor Symphony;* but what reason do we have for thinking that Mozart's composition of this symphony began with some obscure or indescribable emotion, rather than with the subject of the first four bars? And what about artists who have spent years on a single work—are we to say that the very same emotion was there throughout, striving to clarify itself?

An interesting and well-worked-out version of the Finalistic or goal-directed theory of art creation has recently been presented by David Ecker.[9] He describes the creative process as "qualitative problem-solving," borrowing the concept from John Dewey. The stages of the process, he says, consist of a series of problems and solutions: if I use this cool green here I can get this plane to recede; "this jagged shape contrasts sharply with those open volumes" (p. 285), etc. Now he makes it clear that the problems posed are within the work itself: "Artistic problem solving takes place in the artist's medium" (p. 285). The problem need not be verbally formulated (p. 286), and various logical terms that might be applied to the process (such as "verification" and "hypothesis") are "grossly misleading" (p. 288). But the process is to be analyzed in terms of the categories of means and end; the choices involved, and the general direction, are controlled by the previsioned goal. (It is plain that Ecker's account would be strongly repudiated by Collingwood; according to Ecker, the poet *must* begin by intending to write a

[9] "The Artistic Process as Qualitative Problem Solving," *JAAC*, XXI (1963), 283–290.

tragedy, or comedy, or something—for otherwise he has no problem to solve.) Ecker quotes a very illuminating passage from the sculptor Henry Moore:

> . . . I sometimes begin a drawing with no preconceived problem to solve, with only the desire to use pencil on paper, and make lines, tones and shapes with no conscious aim; but as my mind takes in what is so produced a point arrives where some idea becomes conscious and crystallizes, and then a control and ordering begins to take place.
>
> Or sometimes I start with a set subject; or to solve, in a block of stone of known dimensions, a sculptural problem I've given myself, and then consciously attempt to build an ordered relationship of forms . . . [10]

The first part of this statement is very clear, and restricts one side of Ecker's theory. There may be, says Moore, no "preconceived problem to solve"—the only problem, if there is any, arises after the occurrence of the incept, the first lines of the drawing. The "control and ordering" begins with the elements of the work itself. The second part of the statement can be understood, it seems to me, in a similar way. Sometimes, says Moore, he starts with a subject—say, he is to make a reclining figure. Or a set of outside dimensions, within which to work. But basically this is the same sort of thing; the incept can be some lines randomly drawn on paper, or the subject, or the block of untouched marble, with its own particular size and shape.

The trouble appears when this is called a *problem*. What is the problem? It might be: "How can I make a good drawing using these lines I've already drawn?" Or "How can I make a good sculpture of a reclining figure?" Or "How can I make a good sculpture out of this block of marble?" But these are queer things to call *problems:* they are really *tasks*, the terms of which are voluntarily accepted by the artist. The main question involved in each of them is simply: "What do I do next?" A problem arises out of a conflict of some kind—a goad that the sculptor does not require. And it calls for a specific and determinate solution or set of solutions—which is not what the sculptor achieves.

[10] Ghiselin, *op. cit.*, p. 77.

Elsewhere I have stated my objections to the end-means terminology in art.[11] Actually, when Ecker gives his examples of
ends and means, it is clear that he is not really talking about
these at all, but about the relation between what I call regional
qualities and their perceptual conditions. The cool green is not a
means to the receding plane; it is one of the localized features
of the visual design that help to make the plane recede. The
recession of the plane, to put it another way, is a comparatively
large-scale property of the work, which depends (in part) upon
a comparatively small-scale property, the cool green. Now, if we
ask which the artist first intended and has as an "end-in-view,"
it is tempting to say, with Ecker, that the artist

arranges qualitative *means* such as lines, colors, planes, and textures, to achieve his qualitative *end,* which we might name "cubist,"
"impressionist," or "expressionist" (p. 287).

But Ecker has already conceded that the end-in-view may be
"some intended order" as well as a "pervasive quality" (p. 286).
It may often be the case that what the artist is consciously after
is a certain arrangement of lines, colors, planes, and textures,
and the resulting regional quality is unexpected. It is odd to
speak of the color as a "means" when it is chosen for no ulterior
motive.

The error here is a subtle one, but a very crucial one in
talking about art. It consists in jumping from the fact that
regional qualities depend upon their perceptual conditions to the
conclusion that the former are therefore always ends-in-view and
the latter means, in the process of creation. Perhaps no great
harm would usually be done, but this way of speaking leads to
an impasse, which is fully exhibited in a sentence quoted from
John Dewey by Ecker:

The doing or making is artistic when the perceived result is of such
a nature that *its* qualities *as perceived* have controlled the question
of production.[12]

[11] *Aesthetics: Problems in the Philosophy of Criticism* (N. Y., 1958), pp.
78–80.
[12] *Art as Experience* (N. Y., 1934), p. 48.

Take the finished painting; note its quality. Now suppose we have photographs of various stages of the work, taken at daily or hourly intervals, let us say, while the painter was working. None of these, of course, has the *specific* quality of the finished painting. But Dewey says this quality was all along controlling the artist's work. Since the quality did not exist until the painting was finished, it could only have been in the artist's mind. Does that mean that from the earliest stages of a painting, from the incept onward, the painter has definitely in mind some regional quality that he is trying to bring into existence on the canvas? It is conceivable that this is sometimes the case, but most of the experience of artists goes against it: it would be remarkable if the exact regional quality of the final painting were that plain to the painter from the start.

Now, Dewey's statement can be interpreted in a somewhat more plausible way, if we introduce the notion of degrees of intensity for these regional qualities. The final painting, let us say, is characterized by a firm semi-geometrical solidity and rigidity, with decisive lines and interlocking forms. We look at the first tentative strokes put down by the painter, in the earliest photograph, and we see that somehow, dimly but unmistakably, this final quality is foreshadowed in the early draft—a touch of it is already there, though nothing like the way it is there at the end. So the process of creation lying between these stages could be described, at least in part, as one in which a regional quality hit upon early in the game is gradually intensified with the complication of new lines and colors. So in this sense, it could be that the final quality has been at work throughout—not as a fore-seen goal to which the process is heading teleologically, but as a present quality whose immediately perceivable value suggests to the painter that it would be even more valuable if there were, so to speak, more of it.

There is no doubt that something like this does often happen. Sometimes, we can see in the earliest stages of a great work that the quality we value so highly in the finished product has begun to emerge. But this is not always the case, by any means. Sometimes the quality that appears most definitely at the start turns out not to be fruitful; the artist's attempt to intensify it leads to radical formal rearrangements that end by destroying the original quality and substituting a very different one. The melody that was first tried out as a quick rondo theme becomes the subject of a slow movement—almost unrecognizably altered. The poem that started out as a few ironic lines about a current political issue transforms itself, almost against the poet's will, into a moving meditation on the human condition. Nor is such a process—contrary to what Dewey implies—any the less artistic because not the same, but different, qualities have been active in generating the process at different stages.

Vincent Tomas has effectively criticized the finalistic view that artistic creation is "a paradigm of purposive activity."[13] There is a sense of "heading somewhere," though without a given goal in terms of which success or failure can be defined as it can when the torpedo is launched towards a target. Yet, paradoxically, "the artist *can* say that certain directions are not right." And Tomas' solution, sound so far as it goes, is to emphasize the critical ingredient in creation. His theory is that creation is a self-correcting process, in which the artist constantly redirects its aims. Tomas does not show in detail how the artist does this. But I believe he is right, and I will try to develop and defend this theory.

III

The real nature of the artist's control over the creative process will elude anyone who looks for a single guiding factor, whether a need or an end. It is internal to the process itself. I do not plan to argue for a single creative pattern, but to show how, in the absence of any such general pattern, each individual process that eventuates in a work of art *generates* its own direction and momentum. For the crucial controlling power at every point

---

[13] "Creativity in Art," *Philosophical Review*, LXVII (1958), 1–155; "A Note on Creation in Art," *Journal of Philosophy*, LIX (1962), 464–469. The former is reprinted in Tomas, ed., *Creativity in the Arts* (Englewood Cliffs, N. J., 1964).

is the particular stage or condition of the unfinished work itself, the possibilities it presents, and the developments it permits. There are three things to discuss here, and I will say something about each—the incept, the development, and the completion of the work.

The first control over the artistic process is set up by the incept itself. And I want to emphasize, as I have said before, that the incept may be any sort of thing: the first sentence of a story or the last, a simple plot situation, a character, theme, scene, figure of speech, or tone or style. Paul Valéry has told us, instructively:

My poem *Le Cimetière marin* began in me by a rhythm, that of a French line . . . of ten syllables, divided into four and six. I had as yet no idea with which to fill out this form. Gradually a few hovering words settled in it, little by little determining the subject, and my labor (a very long labor) was before me.[14]

Elsewhere, Valéry adds that his playing around with possibilities of this rhythm led to a certain kind of stanza, then—

Between the stanzas, contrasts or correspondences would be set up. This last condition soon required the potential poem to be a monologue of "self," in which the simplest and most enduring themes of my affective and intellectual life, as they had imposed themselves upon my adolescence, associated with the sea and the light of a particular spot on the Mediterranean coast, were called up, woven together, opposed . . . All this led to the theme of death and suggested the theme of pure thought.[15]

This is exactly opposite to the usual idea that the poet must begin with his theme, or thesis, and that he characteristically then devises a suitable subject or set of images, and finally settles on the appropriate stanzaic form and meter. Now, I'll have to confess at this point that I am wide open to one kind of skeptical criticism. Considering that this particular poem is one of the most obscure poems in the French language, it might be said, we

[14] "Poetry and Abstract Thought," *The Art of Poetry*, trans. Denise Folliot (N. Y., 1961), p. 80.
[15] "Concerning 'Le Cimetière marin,'" *ibid.*, p. 148.

can draw no general conclusions from Valéry's method of composing it—what can you expect from a poet who begins with
rhythms and ends with themes? Still, Valéry's account shows
there is no one, privileged, order in which a poem has to get
written. And even in the composition of more conventional
poems, many different items (including metrical patterns)
actually come first. Stephen Spender, for example, tells us in an
essay that one of his poems began with a vision of the sea, and
that another time, the words "A language of flesh and roses"
came into his head as the incept of a possible poem while he was
standing in the corridor of a train looking at a landscape of pits
and pitheads—though at the time he was writing his essay, the
words had not yet grown into an actual poem.[16] From a famous
essay by Allen Tate, we gather that two elements of his "Ode
to the Confederate Dead" were present from the start—the
idea he calls *solipsism* and the idea of the dead—though it took
ten years to fuse them together.[17] And according to Muriel
Rukeyser, her poem "Orpheus" began with a sudden terrifying
image of disintegration that came to her as she walked along
a crowded street in New York.[18]

One of the most important questions about the role of the
incept in the creative process is this: Does it exercise a pervasive
influence throughout? If the Propulsive Theory is correct, one
would expect to find the incept dominating the whole process, for
whatever appears first would presumably be closely related to
the original emotion. On second thought, I am not sure this really
follows: it is hard to say what can be predicted from Collingwood's unknown and unknowable emotion. Again, if the Finalist
Theory is correct, one would also expect the incept to dominate,
for it would presumably embody the original problem or goal
which directs the process to the end.

[16] "The Making of a Poem," *Partisan Review*, XIII (1946), 294–308 (also
in Tomas, *op. cit.*).

[17] "Narcissus as Narcissus," *On the Limits of Poetry* (N. Y., 1948).

[18] Frank Barron, *Creativity and Psychological Health* (Princeton, 1963),
p. 229n. For examples of fiction incepts see Malcolm Cowley, ed., *Writers
at Work* (N. Y., 1959), esp. pp. 7–8.

Now, one thing is evident: once an element is chosen, it sets up demands and suggestions as to what may come next, and also places limits upon it. Draw a single line on a piece of paper. If you do not think what you have there is worth much attention, the question is what you can do next to improve upon it. You can balance it, cross or oppose it by other lines, thicken and emphasize it, transform it into a more complex line or a shape, etc. Or, of course, you can erase it—but then you are rejecting it as an incept, and putting an end to that particular creative process. That every stage of the process powerfully affects the succeeding stage is plain; but our present question is whether the first stage is somehow dominant over all. Artists have spoken rather differently about this. For instance, Picasso once said that "Basically a picture doesn't change, that the first 'vision' remains almost intact, in spite of appearances."[19] But he also said that a picture cannot be thought out ahead of time, and "changes as one's thoughts change." The sketches for *Guernica* do have a notable continuity despite all the changes. The bull and the horse were there in the first sketch, and a woman appeared in one of the later sketches done the same day.

Another example is provided by Beethoven's long series of sketches for the spacious melody that he used for the variations in the slow movement of his string quartet in E flat, *Op. 127*. These have been studied by Victor Zuckerkandl.[20] When they are placed side by side, they illustrate the force of the incept very clearly. The first full bar of the final melody, with its step-wise motion upward from A flat to F, is there almost complete from the very first sketch, though with a slightly different rhythm; and the rest of the story is a struggle, resumed from time to time over a long period, to find an adequate continuation and completion of that incept. Beethoven tries various ways of carrying on the melody, and abandons them; he tries the initial bar in the key of C, in duple tempo, with turns and rhythmic alterations, to see if it can be made to move into the long flowing line that the incept seems to call for. The whole keeps changing its regional character as it grows, yet some of its outstanding final qualities can be described as intensifications of qualities that were there in the first sketch. But this is by no means true of all of Beethoven's work; Allen Forte, a careful student of the piano sonata, *Op. 109*, has remarked that "in many instances one can hardly recognize the final version from the initial sketches."[21]

Indeed, an incept that initiates a successful creative process may become almost lost in it. Of course there must be some continuity from incept to final work, otherwise we could not say that the incept was the start of that particular work. But there is a wide range of deviation from the straight line of development. An ingredient that has one quality as it first appears to the artist may later find a context that alters its quality completely. Dostoyevsky's novel *The Idiot* is an interesting case in point. We have a large collection of manuscript notes and drafts to tell us the agonizing story of Dostoyevsky's working out of that novel. In the very early stages, the Idiot (as he is called from the beginning) is

described as a powerful, proud, and passionate individual. There is something Byronic about him, and he resembles those criminal, self-willed creations Valkovski and Svidrigailov. He is sensual, performs extravagant actions, and perhaps his most marked trait is egoism.[22]

Could anything be farther from the Idiot of the final novel? For two months, through eight detailed plans for the novel, Dostoyevsky worked toward the deadline for the first installment (published January 1868). As the plans succeed each other, we see certain characters take on the Christlike characteristics of Prince

---

[21] *The Compositional Matrix* (Baldwin, N. Y., Music Teachers National Association Monographs, 1961), p. 4. Cf. Ernst Krenek's analysis of the sketches for the false entry of the subject in the *Eroica*: "The Problem of Creative Thinking in Music," in *The Nature of Creative Thinking*, a symposium published for the Industrial Research Institute, Inc. (New York U., 1952), pp. 54–57.

[22] Ernest J. Simmons, *Dostoyevsky* (Oxford U., 1950), p. 202. See his whole book for very illuminating accounts of Dostoyevsky's creative processes.

Myshkin as we now have him, and we see the Idiot developing a double nature that prepares the way, in the eighth plan, for his reversal of personality. Even so, the novel was still significantly changing between the first installment and the later ones.

Once the work is under way, with a tentative commitment to some incept, the creative process is kept going by tensions between what has been done and what might have been done. At each stage there must be a perception of deficiencies in what now exists, plus the sense of unrealized possibilities of improvement. The motivating force, as Tomas says, is a negative critical judgment. And this same point has been made by Valéry. To understand poetry, he remarks, we must study

> word combinations, not so much through the conformity of the meanings of these groups to an idea or thought that one thinks should be *expressed*, as, on the contrary through their effects once they are formed, from which one chooses.[23]

In other words, as the poet moves from stage to stage, it is not that he is looking to see whether he is saying what he already meant, but that he is looking to see whether he wants to mean what he is saying. Thus, according to Valéry, "Every true poet is necessarily a first rate critic"—not necessarily of others' work, but of his own.[24]

Each time the artist—whether poet, or painter, or composer—takes a step, he adds something to what is already there (A),

[23] "A Poet's Notebook," *op. cit.*, p. 178. Compare John Dryden's dedication of *The Rival Ladies* (in Ghiselin, *op. cit.*, p. 77): "When the fancy was yet in its first work, moving the sleeping images of things toward the light, there to be distinguished, and then either chosen or rejected by the judgment." The drafts of Yeats's "Sailing to Byzantium," written on looseleaf pages over several years, show how fertile he was in alternative possibilities for lines we now know so well, and that his problem was to select and combine; see Curtis Bradford, "Yeats's Byzantium Poems: A Study of Their Development," *PMLA*, LXXV (1960), 110–125 (I am indebted to Professor Robert Daniel, of Kenyon College, for this example). Cf. Martin K. Nurmi, "Blake's Revisions of *The Tyger*," *PMLA*, LXXI (1956), 669–685.

[24] "Poetry and Abstract Thought," *ibid.*, p. 76. This is echoed by Richard Wilbur in *The Nature of Creative Thinking*, p. 59, and by Ben Shahn, in *The Shape of Content* (see selection in Tomas, *op. cit.*, p. 20).

and makes another and different object (B). If he judges B worse than A, he must go back. If B is better than A, the question is whether it is good enough to stand alone as a work of art. If not, the question is whether B can be transformed into still another and better object, C. If this is impossible, if every attempt to improve it only makes it worse, then the whole project is left unfinished, for it is unfinishable.

One of the most puzzling questions about the creative process is how the artist knows when to stop. If the Propulsion Theory is correct, the answer is that he stops when his original impulse has exhausted itself. If the Finalistic Theory is correct, then the artist compares his work at every stage with the intact memory of his original vision of his goal, and when they match the work is done. But without these theories, it becomes more difficult to explain what it means to come to an end of a creative process.[25]

There are really two questions here: how the artist knows when *he* is finished, and how he knows when the *work* is finished. The first question is no doubt the easier. The artist comes to a point when he can no longer think of any way to improve his work. This becomes more and more difficult as the work progresses. In the early stages, lines and colors, stanzas and melodic fragments, can be added quite freely to see whether they can be assimilated. But in the later stages, as the work becomes more complex, the effect of every addition or alteration is more serious; a wrong line or color, a wrong word or melodic figure, can throw the whole thing badly off. Of course, the artist can never be certain he has done all he can. Happy is the painter, who can say, with Matisse,

Then a moment comes when every part has found its definite relationship and from then on it would be impossible for me to add a stroke to my picture without having to paint it all over again.[26]

Many a painter has been notorious for a never-say-die de-

[25] I. A. Richards, "How Does a Poem Know When It Is Finished?" in Daniel Lerner, ed., *Parts and Wholes* (N. Y., 1963).

[26] "Notes of a Painter," in Eliseo Vivas and Murray Krieger, eds., *The Problems of Aesthetics* (N. Y., 1953), p. 259.

termination to hang on to his paintings in the hope that he will think of a way of bettering them—unless extreme poverty or a wily dealer induces him to part with them. (Valéry, by the way, says he wouldn't have published "*Le Cimetière marin*" when he did, had it not been snatched from him. "Nothing is more decisive than the mind of an editor of a review," he remarks— though perhaps he could have put up more of a fight.)[27]

The artist generally knows, then, pretty well whether *he* is finished—but that is not the same as saying that the *work* is finished. For when the artist has done all he can, the question remains whether the work has enough to it, whether it is worthy of standing by itself, as an object of aesthetic enjoyment. If he judges so, the artist says it is done. If he judges not, the artist says it is unfinished. And of course the threshold of contentment varies enormously from artist to artist.

These points are illustrated by the famous puzzle of Schubert's unfinished symphony. Unlike most great unfinished works, it was not cut short by death (Schubert had six more years to live), but simply abandoned by the composer after he had completed two magnificent movements. Hans Gál has proposed an interesting solution.[28] Schubert began a scherzo in B minor, which would have been the third movement. In the manuscript, the parts are at first quite fully indicated, then they drop out, as the composer loses interest, and the movement trails off in the trio. The trouble is that the opening subject is one of startling emptiness and dullness—and yet it is a compulsive theme, hard to get away from once it is started, especially if the scherzo must be in the conventional key. "Those obstrusive four bars," as Gál calls them, get a grip on the composer; he cannot shake them off, or, apparently, find a way of starting anew so long as every time he picks up the manuscript they stare him in the face. If we agree with Gál's hypothesis, the scherzo is a formidable example of a composition that cannot be well finished—even by a master. It must have

[27] *Op. cit.*, p. 144.
[28] "The Riddle of Schubert's Unfinished Symphony," *The Music Review*, II (1941), 63–67.

required a powerful force indeed to make a composer leave off a symphony so excellently begun.[29]

In one respect, the foregoing account diverges from a remark by Rudolf Arnheim in his study of Picasso's *Guernica*. Arnheim speaks of the creative process as being "goal-directed throughout"[30]—a view I challenged earlier. And summing up the whole process, he says,

A germinal idea, precise in its general tenor but unsettled in its aspects, acquired its final character by being tested against a variety of possible visual realizations. When at the end, the artist was willing to rest his case on what his eyes and hands had arrived at, he had become able to see what he meant.[31]

I would not put such stress upon the words, if these two sentences had not been so exact and eloquent up to the final clause. But the words "become able to see what he meant" seem to imply that what Picasso ended with was an expression, an explication, an embodiment, a realization, or whatever, of what was already in his mind at the start. Better, I think, to say that he had become able to mean something much better than he was able to mean a few months before, and that what he now was able to mean—that is, to make—was enough.

To draw together these remarks and examples, perhaps we can decide how far to generalize. Though there are no universal *stages* of the creative process, there are two clearly marked *phases*, which constantly alternate throughout. They involve an interplay between conscious and preconscious activities. There is the *inventive* phase, traditionally called *inspiration*, in which new ideas are formed in the preconscious and appear in consciousness. And there is the *selective* phase, which is nothing more than criticism, in which the conscious chooses or rejects the

[29] It is harder to understand what distractions led Mozart to abandon the more than 100 unfinished compositions (not counting the *Requiem*) that his widow preserved for us. See Erich Hertzmann, "Mozart's Creative Process," *Musical Quarterly*, XLIII (1957), 187–200.

[30] *Op. cit.*, p. 134.

[31] *Op. cit.*, p. 135.

new idea after perceiving its relationships to what has already tentatively been adopted.

The problem of what goes on in the preconscious is apparently still unsolved. We would like to know how it is that a composer, having sung two bars to himself, suddenly thinks of a way to continue it—or that a painter, having outlined a figure, thinks of certain colors that might be added—or that a poet may look at a line he has just written and think of possible substitute words. To take a few examples from R. P. Blackmur,[32] suppose the poet has written "breathless tiptoeing," and it occurs to him that "flowering tiptoeing" might be better; or suppose he has written "chance deepening to choice" and substitutes "chance flowering to choice." Whether the new words are better than the old is the question to be decided by his conscious mind; but why one set of words rather than another comes to consciousness is the more mysterious question.

The psychological dispute seems to be formulable this way: to what extent are the preconscious processes associative; to what extent do they involve closure or strengthening of gestalts?[33] As far as I can make out both of these processes seem necessary to account for what the preconscious presents to the conscious. If, for example, "flowering" replaces "deepening" because of some meaningful connection of this figure with other images earlier in the poem, then we can say that the unconscious has found some degree of closure. On the other hand, the substitution may have only a very remote relationship to other words already set down, but it may serve to break down an existing gestalt, to introduce a more unstable cluster of meanings, which may lead to a more inclusive synthesis later. In this case, the word *flowering* would be described as due to free—or at least freer—association. It seems evident, in any case, that unless the preconscious can produce both kinds of ideas—those that

[32] *Poets at Work,* p. 48.

[33] This is the point at issue, for example, between Lawrence S. Kubie, *Neurotic Distortion of the Creative Process* (U. of Kansas, 1948), esp. pp. 53–61, and Arnheim, *Picasso's Guernica,* p. 70.

close a gestalt and those that break one—poems could not get composed, nor could paintings or musical works.

IV

It is no doubt high time to face up to the question that is bound to arise after all these reflections and speculations about the creative process: what is the point of them? Or, in other words: what difference does it make to our relationship with the arts that we understand the creative process in one way or another? And here my answer is brief and unequivocal. It makes no difference at all. I think it is interesting in itself to know, if we can, how the artist's mind works, but I do not see that this has any bearing upon the value of what he produces. For that value is independent of the manner of production, even of whether the work was produced by an animal or by a computer or by a volcano or by a falling slopbucket.[34]

This statement would be vigorously repudiated by some who have studied the creative process: they claim that their studies throw light on the "meaning" and "beauty" of poems, to use the words of Donald Stauffer, writing on "Genesis, or the Poet as Maker."[35] If we knew, says Stauffer, the genesis of a poem by Housman, it would "enable us to interpret this particular work with more precision." But his method puts the enterprise in none too favorable a light, it seems to me. Digging through the early stages of the composition of Marianne Moore's poem, "The Four Songs," he finds a typescript in which the poem is entitled "Poet to Lover (Admitting Limitations)." Moreover, he turns up other titles that the poet considered and rejected: "Poet to Plain-Reader," "Poet to Ordinary Man," and, oddly, "Asphodel." (This poem has as many titles as the White Knight's song "A-sitting on a Gate.") All these titles, says Mr. Stauffer, "should prove of value in interpreting the complete poem,"[36]

[34] For a decisive argument along this line, see John Hospers, "The Concept of Artistic Expression," *Proceedings of the Aristotelian Society*, LV (1955), 313–344.

[35] In *Poets at Work*, p. 43.

[36] *Ibid.*, p. 63.

and he proceeds to put them to use. But think of the implications. The poet discards the titles, and the genetic interpreter plucks them out of the wastebasket and uses them as though they had not been discarded. This is a pretty high-handed way to treat Marianne Moore. The logic of the situation is clear. Either the title of a poem makes a difference to the way it is read, or it does not. If not, then knowing the discarded titles has no effect on our interpretation. If so, then each title makes a slightly different poem, and Mr. Stauffer is simply refusing to read the poem that Miss Moore wanted us to read. Granted that her choice does not have to be final; some of the titles she threw away could conceivably be better than the one she kept. (After all, remember the time she was commissioned to suggest names for a brand-new car that the Ford Motor Company was planning to bring out. She came up with some lovely ones, but in the end they called it the Edsel.) But if you do not accept her title, then at least do not pretend that you are interpreting her final poem.

The informed observer will, of course, detect in these genetic maneuvers a particularly persuasive form of that vulgar error which William Wimsatt, Jr. and I stigmatized some years ago as the Intentional Fallacy. I do not know whether it is in good taste for me to rake over these old coals, but whenever a fallacy gets to be so old-fashioned and so familiar as this one, it is always heartening to find new instances of it, so that you know you are not beating a dead horse—even if he is not exactly the picture of health. What we attacked under a single name (intentionalism) were in fact two closely related forms of unsound argument: that which attributes a certain meaning to a work on the ground that the artist intended the work to have that meaning, and that which appraises the work at a certain value on the ground that it does or does not fulfill the artist's intention. If we took to interpreting poems in terms of what they were like before they were finished, we would be turning the whole creative process upside down, by refusing to consider the final product on its own terms. Let this method become popular, and you can expect poets, painters, and musicians to keep their wastebaskets emptied, by burning their early sketches just as soon as possible.

Is this our final conclusion, then—that questions about creativity are irrelevant to questions about actual works of art? Somehow it does not seem enough. From the beginning of thought about art, though in many different forms, the creativity of art has been noted and pondered. Associationists, intuitionists, romantics, and idealists have offered explanations. In the making of such works, something very special seems to be happening; something fresh is added to the world; something like a miracle occurs. All this is true. There is such a thing as creativity in art, and it is a very important thing. What I want to say is that the true locus of creativity is not the genetic process prior to the work but the work itself as it lives in the experience of the beholder. Let me explain—all too briefly and puzzlingly, no doubt—what I mean.

To begin with, what is a melody? It is, as we all know, a gestalt, something distinct from the notes that make it up, yet dependent upon them for its existence. And it has its own quality, which cannot be a quality of any particular note or little set of notes. Recall that melody from Beethoven's E flat Quartet—grave, serene, soaring, affirmative, yet in a way resigned. Now when we hear a melody, however simple, we hear two levels of things at once: the individual notes and the regionally qualified melody that emerges from them. We hear the melody being born out of the elements that sustain it; or we hear the elements, the tones and intervals, coming together in an order that calls into existence an entity distinct from them, and superior to them. In the experience of a melody, creation occurs before our very ears. And the more intense the created qualities, the more complex the sets of cooperating elements, the tighter their mutual relations, the more fully we can participate in that basic aesthetic experience.

I need not argue in detail that the same holds for works of fine art. The essential feature of such a work—I am tempted to say, but recognizing that I am likely to sound dogmatic—the essential feature is not merely that certain visual elements (lines, shapes, colors) are assembled together, but that as we concentrate on their natures and relations, we become aware, suddenly or gradually, of what they add up to as a whole. For what they add up to is not an addition at all, but the projection of a new pattern, a new quality of grace or power.

When we consider a poem in this perspective, we see again that the important creativity is in the operation of the work itself. The sound-qualities, such as meter and rhyme-patterns, are one sort of emergent; more importantly, the interactions and interanimations of words, in figurative or unusual language, create hitherto unmeant meanings; and more importantly, the objects and events of the poem mysteriously are made to accumulate symbolic reverberations, by which they seem to have a significance far beyond themselves. And this takes place in the act of reading; the excitement of seeing it happen is precisely the peculiar excitement of reading poetry.

The British literary critic, L. C. Knights, has made some comments that seem to me very similar to what I want to say, in a special issue of *The Times Literary Supplement,* on "The Critical Moment."[37] His example is from Wordsworth's famous sonnet,

> Dull would he be of soul, who could pass by
> A sight so touching in its majesty.

That is a strange combination of ideas—"touching" and "majesty." Knights says this:

The peculiar pleasure of that last line—though the pleasure is independent of conscious recognition of the source—comes from the movement of mind by which we bring together in one apprehension 'touching' and 'majesty': feelings and attitudes springing from our experience of what is young and vulnerable, that we should like to protect, fuse with our sense of things towards which we feel awe, in respect of which it is we who are young, inexperienced or powerless.

[37] July 26, 1963, p. 569.

The "movement of mind" of which he speaks, in bringing these two opposed feelings into a fusion, through the words of the poem, is an act of creation, for out of that fusion comes a new, complex, vital feeling that has elements of both and yet is reducible to neither. So, says Knights, the creative use of words "energizes" the mind—"new powers of vision and apprehension come into being."

It may seem that this way of looking at artistic creativity demeans the artist by making not him, but the work itself, the creative thing. But I do not think so. I do not forget that man is the maker—of nearly all the great works we have, or are likely to have. But the finest qualities of a work of art cannot be imposed on it directly and by fiat; the artist can, after all, only manipulate the elements of the medium so that *they* will make the quality emerge. He can only create a solemn melody by finding a sequence of notes that will have that quality. The powers he works with are, in the end, not his own but those of nature. And the miracle he makes is a miracle that celebrates the creative potentialities inherent in nature itself. But when in this way the artist makes plain to us over and over the marvellous richness of nature's potentialities, he also presents us with a model of man's hope for control over nature, and over himself. Artistic creation is nothing more than the production of a self-creative object. It is in our intelligent use of what we are given to work with, both in the laws of the universe and in the psychological propensities of man, that we show our mastery, and our worthiness to inhabit the earth. In this broad sense, we are all elected, or perhaps condemned, to be artists. And what keeps us going in the roughest times is the reminder that not all the forms and qualities and meanings that are to emerge in the fullness of time have already appeared under the sun—that we do not know the limits of what the universe can provide or of what can be accomplished with its materials.

INDEX OF AUTHORS AND TITLES

*INDEX OF RHETORICAL TERMS
AND EXAMPLES*

INDEX OF RHETORICAL TERMS AND EXAMPLES

In a broad sense of "rhetoric," this is an index of rhetorical terms and examples: it refers the reader both to discussion of rhetorical concepts (principles, modes, forms, devices, and the like) and to pieces or parts of pieces exemplifying them. In general, a given term ("lucidity," say) not only appears under a general entry ("Style," in this case) but has an entry of its own. This index does not try, however, to index all examples of such rhetorical concepts as coherence, description, and logical organization, exemplified throughout the book.